THE UNITED STATES OF SUBURBIA

HOW THE SUBURBS TOOK CONTROL OF AMERICA AND WHAT THEY PLAN TO DO WITH IT

G. SCOTT THOMAS

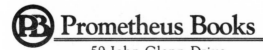 Prometheus Books

59 John Glenn Drive
Amherst, New York 14228-2197

Published 1998 by Prometheus Books

01 00 99 98   5 4 3 2 1

Library of Congress Cataloging-in-Publication Data

Thomas, G. Scott.
    The United States of Suburbia : how the suburbs took control of America and what they plan to do with it / G. Scott Thomas.
        p.   cm.
    Includes bibliographical references and index.
    ISBN 1–57392–243–9 (cloth : alk. paper)
    1. Suburbs—United States. 2. Suburban life—United States. I. Title.
HT352.U6T48   1998
307.76′0973—dc21   98–33521
                                                              CIP

Printed in the United States of America on acid-free paper.

For Laura and Lindsay

"When you can measure what you are speaking about, and express it in numbers, you know something about it; but when you cannot measure it, when you cannot express it in numbers, your knowledge is of a meager and unsatisfactory kind: it may be the beginning of knowledge, but you have scarcely, in your thoughts, advanced to the stage of science."

William Thomson, Lord Kelvin (1824–1907)

Also by G. Scott Thomas

The Pursuit of the White House

The Rating Guide to Life in America's Small Cities

Where to Make Money

The Rating Guide to Life in America's Fifty States

Contents

Preface

There was a time when cities were the dominant force in American politics. Franklin Roosevelt and Harry Truman could not have reached the White House without decisive help from urban bosses. John Kennedy might have wasted away in the Senate if not for thousands of mysterious, last-minute votes from Chicago. Even Ronald Reagan, surely no friend of big cities, believed so deeply in the traditional image of urban power and wealth that he pledged to turn all of America into "a shining city on a hill."

The 1996 presidential election confirmed a dramatic change in political geography, however. Bill Clinton virtually ignored the nation's cities as he single-mindedly pursued suburban voters, often steering to the right of the Democratic Party's historically urban-oriented positions. Bob Dole, his Republican challenger, was on the same trail behind him, both figuratively and literally.

"They never campaigned in the lower-income areas. It was malls. It was suburbs. It was Hilton Hotels," complained consumer activist Ralph Nader, himself a minor-party presidential candidate in 1996. Journalist Michael Lewis pointed out that Jack Kemp, the Republican vice-presidential nominee, had made a well-publicized trip to Harlem. "Exactly," replied Nader, "and he got so much attention because it was so exceptional."[1]

Nader was right. The 1996 campaign, if nothing else, proved that cities are no longer strong enough to dictate national policy or to command the attention of presidential candidates. Power has shifted to the smaller, quieter communities lying beyond the city limits. The United States has entered the Suburban Age.

The suburbanization of America is nothing new. Brooklyn was considered a suburb of New York City as early as 1815, long before the city swallowed it whole.* "There," wrote Walt Whitman, "men of moderate means may find homes at a moderate rent, whereas in New York City there is no median between a palatial mansion and a dilapidated hovel."[2] The same desire for affordable housing inspired the legendary exodus from urban America that followed World War II. Mil-

---

*In 1898 Brooklyn, the Bronx, Queens, Staten Island, and Manhattan were consolidated into New York City.

lions of veterans and their families streamed into subdivisions springing up outside of big cities from Boston to Los Angeles. The prototypical modern suburb, Levittown, rose from the potato fields of Long Island half a century ago.

What *is* new is suburbia's dominant position in American politics. Suburban voters, who once followed the lead of their big-city counterparts, now hold the reins of national power. They controlled enough electoral votes by 1996 to decide who became president and enough seats in Congress to determine who held the majority. It cannot be disputed that suburbanites will dictate America's course in the twenty-first century. Just ask Bill Clinton.

Journalists, for the most part, ignored this significant demographic shift in 1996, opting instead to blather on about an endless series of meaningless campaign events. Their deepest insights into the new suburban majority were contained in a few condescending stories about "soccer moms." Hence *The United States of Suburbia,* in which I seek to fill in the blanks.

- This book details the steady rise of suburbia. I begin the story in 1939, when big cities were at their zenith, and take it to the present day, when America has its first Speaker of the House from a suburban district (Newt Gingrich) and its first Democratic president to target suburban voters (Clinton).
- It forecasts demographic trends during the coming quarter-century. I use a computer model to predict the future populations and racial compositions of ninety-three major cities and their suburbs. Suffice it to say that big changes are on the way.
- It looks into the suburban mind. I discuss the five core beliefs that motivate suburbanites and then enumerate their ten key policy objectives, most of which are surprisingly moderate. The media's stereotype of the conservative suburban resident is sadly inaccurate, as we shall see.
- It foretells the nation's political future. I envision a major party gaining the upper hand during the twenty-first century by casting off its extreme wing and capturing the suburban center. Will it be the Democrats or the Republicans? That's the biggest question of all.

This forthcoming battle for political supremacy will engross millions of Americans. They will assess every candidate, dissect every platform, debate every controversy. It was exactly this kind of scrutiny—so typical of presidential campaigns—that exasperated Thomas Dewey, the former New York governor whose three tries for the White House ended in defeat, most notably in 1948. "I have learned from bitter experience," he once complained, "that Americans somehow regard a political campaign as a sporting event."[3]

The presidential election of 2000, in a sense, will be the next Super Bowl of American politics. The Democrats will be forced to choose between urban (Richard Gephardt) or suburban (Al Gore) strategies, while the Republicans will have to decide whether to endorse Gingrich-style conservatism or take a more moderate tack. The stakes will be high. The suburbs will decide who wins.

G. Scott Thomas
Tonawanda, New York
April 1998

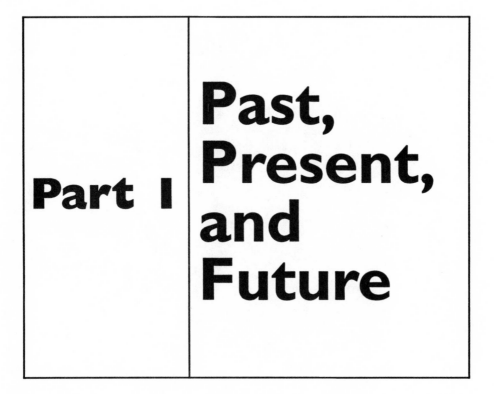

Part I | **Past, Present, and Future**

Blue Tide: Election Night 1996

The red light pops on. Tom Brokaw leans forward and nods briskly to the audience beyond NBC's cameras. "Good evening," he says, "and welcome to your future."[1]

Brokaw's words are typical anchorspeak, just another crisp phrase to start just another election night, but they will prove to be prophetic. The evening of November 5, 1996, for those who know where to look, will offer a preview of dramatic changes that will shape American politics deep into the twenty-first century.

But the future is not Brokaw's real concern—no matter what he might say—as he sets to work at 7 P.M. in his red, white, and blue studio, a gigantic American flag slowly flapping on a projection screen behind him.* The immediate business at hand is the election of the next president, a process destined to be *un*dramatic. National surveys are predicting that Bill Clinton will bury Bob Dole, and Brokaw now provides the first corroboration, declaring Clinton the winner in Florida, New Hampshire, and Vermont, thirty-two electoral votes in all. The three states are immediately shaded blue—Clinton's color—on a large map in the NBC studio.

The rout is on.

Celebration has already begun in Little Rock, where billboard-sized television screens transmit Brokaw's projections to the tens of thousands of people milling outside the Old State House. Clinton supporters eagerly cheer the impending landslide. Many wear T-shirts that boast "The Fat Lady Sings . . . Same Song, Different Verse."[2]

The president himself is high above the crowd in the Excelsior Hotel, savoring a triumph once thought impossible. Columnists wrote his political obituary two years ago, after voters repudiated him and swept Newt Gingrich's Republicans into power in the House of Representatives. Few believed then that the Comeback Kid could fashion one final political miracle. But it appears that he has.

The Republicans, of course, gave Clinton considerable help. Polls show that many voters are turning against the GOP today because they believe its congressional agenda is too harsh and too controversial. "Gingrich has done what no Democrat could do," liberal activist Robert Borosage gloated during the campaign. "He's like the aliens in

---

*All times in this chapter are expressed in Eastern Standard Time.

[the movie] *Independence Day.* He mobilized everybody and organized everybody against an alien threat."[3]

Also assisting the Democratic cause was Bob Dole, the career politician who was surprisingly inept on the campaign trail. "Once Clinton is perceived as a liberal," he told his aides in the spring, "the election's over."[4] It never happened. Dole failed miserably in his efforts to portray Clinton as a closet leftist. The challenger instead spent most of the autumn on the defensive, futilely insisting that he is neither too old nor too conservative to be trusted with the Oval Office.

But it is Clinton and his advisers who rightfully deserve most of the credit for tonight's victory. They targeted their campaign directly at moderate suburban voters, a stunningly innovative strategy for a Democratic Party that historically has relied on urban liberals. "Suburban voters are the balance of power in American presidential elections," explains Ann Lewis, deputy manager of the Clinton campaign. "It's a matter of arithmetic; it's where the votes are."[5] A computer analysis shows that suburban voters control twenty-three states with 320 electoral votes, fifty votes more than the threshold for victory. Big cities wield power in just two states, totaling thirty-six electoral votes.[6]

Both major parties are well aware of this political calculus. Clinton and Dole competed strenuously for the suburban vote, the president going so far as to sign a controversial welfare reform bill that is expected to cut financial assistance to millions of poor people, a large share of whom are city dwellers. "The presidential campaigns are nothing but one big infomercial for suburbs," snapped Dallas Mayor Ron Kirk a few days ago. His counterpart in Philadelphia, Edward Rendell, concluded sadly, "The political atmosphere for American cities is at its low ebb in this century."[7]

Rendell's point was dramatized a month ago, when Clinton and Dole met in Hartford, Connecticut, for their first presidential debate. Organizers promised a no-holds-barred confrontation that would clarify the candidates' positions on all issues of consequence. But David Rusk knew better.

The former mayor of Albuquerque, himself a noted urban theorist, predicted that Clinton and Dole would ignore one topic of mutual disinterest. "They will go to one of the nation's most depressed cities," Rusk said, "and they are likely to have a debate in front of the nation where they don't say a word about cities."[8]

He was nearly correct. The transcript of the Hartford debate, which totaled 16,890 words, showed the candidates' eagerness to discuss the topics dearest to suburbia: fifty-nine references to taxes, twenty-six to Medicare, fifteen to welfare, eight to tobacco. But Clinton

and Dole said "city," "cities," or "urban" only three times, all in paren-
thetical exchanges about drug use and New York.[9] Both men gingerly
avoided any discussion of urban policy, as if the great cities of America
simply had vanished in the night.

And that, in a way, was exactly what had happened.

7:30 P.M.

Clinton continues to roll. The networks declare him the winner in
West Virginia and Ohio. Both states turn blue on NBC's map. The
electoral vote count is Clinton 58, Dole 0.

The Ohio results devastate the Dole campaign. No Republican has
ever been elected president without carrying the home state of William
McKinley, William Howard Taft, and Warren Harding. Dole courted
Ohio voters assiduously, visiting them twelve times during the fall, end-
lessly asserting that Clinton has allowed the national economy to
become structurally weak. His message should have found a receptive
audience in a state where Republican-leaning suburbanites easily outnumber urban Democrats, but it fell flat. "People believe the economy
is rolling along pretty well," admits Mike Allen, Republican Party
chairman of Hamilton County. "It was a tough argument to sell."[10]

Exactly how tough is shown by the exit polls now starting to flow from
the Voter News Service (VNS), a consortium of the major networks. Ohio
voters surveyed today by VNS agree that the economy is more important
than any other issue awaiting the next president.* Good news for Dole?
Not at all. Fully 62 percent of those who listed the economy first also supported Clinton, while just 32 percent went for Dole and 6 percent for
Ross Perot of the Reform Party.[11] Ohioans—especially suburban Republican Ohioans—clearly are satisfied with the status quo.

The networks, reading these unmistakable signs, begin their post-
mortems even though voting continues across most of the nation. "I'm
still looking forward to a very good evening tonight," a relaxed and
smiling Christine Todd Whitman, New Jersey's Republican governor,
tells Brokaw. But she soon is drawn into a discussion of her party's post-
Dole future, citing the need to "appeal to people who are fiscally conservative and yet socially inclusive," an apt description of her constituents
in New Jersey, the most suburban state of all. "Our party is about inclusion," she says. "That's the definition of the Republican Party."[12]

---

*This poll—and all subsequent polls cited in this book—was conducted by a rep-
utable, independent survey firm. Sample sizes in every case were sufficiently large to yield
a margin of error of 4.5 percentage points or less. Most were in the range of 3 points.

An opposing viewpoint is volleyed back just minutes later by Pat Robertson, the Christian broadcaster who unsuccessfully sought the 1988 Republican presidential nomination. He amiably concedes to CBS's Dan Rather that Dole will lose tonight in a "blowout," but his expression turns grim as he complains that the Christian right was ignored throughout the campaign. The Republicans, Robertson insists, will never regain the White House unless they take boldly conservative stands on abortion and other social and moral issues. He declares: "They will lose every time that a national candidate does not address these things."[13]

The lines already are being drawn for the election of 2000.

8 P.M.

Dole finally gets on the map by winning his home state of Kansas and neighboring Oklahoma, forming a small red island in a sea of blue. But the networks also declare Clinton the victor in nine suburban-dominated states—Connecticut, Delaware, Illinois, Maryland, Massachusetts, Michigan, Missouri, New Jersey, and Pennsylvania. Their Republican roots are impeccable: Ronald Reagan carried eight of the nine states in 1980 and all of them in 1984; George Bush won eight in 1988. But all drop into the Democratic column tonight for the second election in a row. Clinton now has 198 electoral votes, just 72 short of victory.

Senate Majority Leader Trent Lott of Mississippi wearily watches the returns in his Capitol office. Lott was a key member of the Republican brain trust that struggled all year—and ultimately failed—to counter Clinton's conservative rhetoric. "It's awfully tough when you're running against an incumbent president, especially when you've got one that has taken our language, our agenda," he says. "I hope he's sincere about it."[14]

Lott turns his attention to Senate and House races, as do the networks. Will the Republicans retain their majorities in both houses, or will the president's coattails drag the Democrats back to power? The early signs seem to favor the latter. Democratic Senator John Kerry is reelected in Massachusetts, turning back a vigorous challenge from Republican Governor William Weld. And, in Illinois, Congressman Richard Durbin has won the Senate seat of retiring Paul Simon, a fellow Democrat.

What is truly interesting about these two races, however, is not the results themselves, but what they reveal about the mood and influence of the suburban electorate.

Massachusetts has been mythologized as an urban industrial state populated solely by liberal Democrats. It backed George McGovern in 1972, after all, while the rest of the nation overwhelmingly supported

Richard Nixon. But 72 percent of the state's residents now live in the suburbs, a shift that has moderated their opinions accordingly. VNS exit polls show that 47 percent of today's Massachusetts voters call themselves independents, compared to just 36 percent who identify with the Democrats. And a few of their stands are remarkably conservative: 56 percent in Massachusetts support the death penalty, while 48 percent say the federal government should be less intrusive in daily life.[15]

Kerry's victory, far from being an endorsement of his liberal policies, is being viewed by most analysts as a tribute to his charisma and campaign skills. "I got the message," jokes Weld in a surprisingly upbeat concession speech. "I'm not stupid. The message is I'm a real good governor, and I should stick to that."[16]

The Illinois race confirms that suburbanites, when given a choice, prefer the middle of the road, regardless of party. The Republican Party chairman in Lake County, directly north of Chicago, joked last year that Democrats should be housed with the other relics at the Lake County Museum. But Durbin is carrying Lake County tonight, even though it is the home of his Republican opponent, Al Salvi.[17]

The defining issue in this race was gun control. Durbin advocates it; Salvi opposes it vehemently. The Republican drew national attention to his campaign by making the absurd claim that gun-control activist Jim Brady, who was wounded in the 1981 assassination attempt on Ronald Reagan, once sold machine guns for a living. Suburban Chicago voters are weighing in with a comfortable 62,000-vote plurality for Durbin, propelling him to a lopsided victory statewide. "If you stand with the police and the families of Illinois for sensible gun control," the new senator tells reporters, "you'll be a winner."[18]

8:30 P.M.

"Headline of the hour," announces Dan Rather in typically quirky fashion. "The balloons and champagne are on standby at Clinton headquarters in Arkansas, fizzle on tap at Dole campaign central."[19] CBS's scoreboard shows Clinton with 204 electoral votes, Dole just sixty-seven.

Network computers are beginning to probe the dimensions of the president's triumph. Much of what they disgorge is unsurprising, such as the news that Clinton is winning the cities of the East and Midwest easily, in the tradition of every Democratic nominee from Al Smith to Michael Dukakis. Final returns from six selected cities will show Clinton nearly half a million votes ahead of Dukakis's 1988 margin in New York City, but in roughly the same ballpark everywhere else:

City	1988 Dem Margin	1996 Dem Margin	Clinton Gain
Baltimore	Won by 111,724	Won by 116,974	5,250
Detroit	Won by 217,197	Won by 261,430	44,233
New York City	Won by 675,388	Won by 1,172,711	497,323
Philadelphia	Won by 230,513	Won by 327,643	97,130
Saint Louis	Won by 69,170	Won by 69,112	−58
Washington	Won by 131,817	Won by 140,881	9,064

Source: Author's analysis of official election returns.

The real difference can be detected outside the city limits. Recent Democratic presidential candidates, saddled with liberal, urban-oriented platforms, have done terribly in the suburbs. The Detroit area offers a case in point. Jimmy Carter lost the Detroit suburbs by 190,000 votes in 1980, Walter Mondale by 449,000 in 1984, and Dukakis by 234,000 in 1988.

But Clinton's suburban strategy is paying rich dividends tonight. The president is adding 653,000 votes to Dukakis's margin within the six eastern and midwestern cities above, but he is bettering his predecessor by an amazing 2.37 million votes in the suburban regions that surround those same cities:

Area	1988 Dem Margin	1996 Dem Margin	Clinton Gain
Baltimore suburbs	Lost by 137,049	Lost by 11,751	125,298
Detroit suburbs	Lost by 234,343	Won by 218,129	452,472
New York City suburbs	Lost by 638,863	Won by 331,897	970,760
Philadelphia suburbs	Lost by 287,427	Won by 117,748	405,175
Saint Louis suburbs	Lost by 55,612	Won by 70,603	126,215
Washington suburbs	Lost by 105,797	Won by 190,250	296,047

Source: Author's analysis of official election returns.

Ann Lewis is right. It's a matter of arithmetic; the suburbs are where the votes are.

9 P.M.

The popular vote count still is surprisingly close, much closer than the pollsters had predicted. Clinton now has 6.3 million votes, Dole 5.9 million, Perot slightly more than 1 million. But those aren't the numbers that matter.

The networks start the hour by conceding Minnesota, New Mexico, New York, Rhode Island, and Wisconsin to the president in rapid succession, putting him over the top with 275 electoral votes. The crowd jamming the grounds of the Old State House lets loose with a tremendous roar. People are packed so tightly in front of the Excelsior Hotel that it takes them as long as half an hour just to cross the street.[20]

Leon Panetta, Clinton's chief of staff, wears a smile more of relief than of jubilation as he surveys the vast crowd from above. He tells ABC's Peter Jennings that the president won so easily because he targeted his message at middle-class voters, a group that had complained of Democratic neglect in prior elections. "I think his message on the economy, on jobs, on education, on crime, on health care—these were issues that affected American families," Panetta says, "and they recognized it."[21]

They did, indeed. Voter News Service exit polls are showing Clinton with a big edge in the cities, while Dole is narrowly ahead in rural areas. It is suburbia—the heartland of America's middle class—that is tipping the balance in this election. VNS's final figures will indicate that nearly half of the nation's votes were cast by suburbanites, a group that preferred Clinton over Dole by the comfortable margin of five percentage points:*

Section	Share of U.S. Vote (%)	Popular Vote within the Section (%)		
		Clinton	Dole	Perot
Urban	31	56	35	7
Suburban	49	47	42	9
Rural	21	44	46	10

Source: Voter News Service exit poll, November 5, 1996, as posted on CNN/Time AllPolitics website (http://allpolitics.com), November 12, 1996 [henceforth referred to as VNS exit poll 1996].

Clinton will go down in history as the first sitting Democratic president since Lyndon Johnson to win a new term in office. It is no coincidence that he also is the first Democratic president since Johnson to carry America's suburbs.

The revelry in Little Rock dominates the networks for almost a quarter-hour, obscuring one of the night's truly intriguing stories, the reelection of Senator Paul Wellstone in Minnesota. The Senate's most liberal Democrat seemingly would be out of step with a state where 47 percent of residents are suburbanites and just 15 percent live in big cities, but he actually is winning handily over Republican Rudy Boschwitz, himself a former senator.

Boschwitz made welfare his signature issue this fall, relentlessly attacking Wellstone for his vote against the welfare reform bill that Clinton later signed. The challenger's ads called the incumbent "Senator Welfare," blasted him for being "embarrassingly liberal," and equated him with hippies and gang members.

---

*Poll results in this book might not add precisely to 100 percent due to rounding (as in the column showing each section's share of the U.S. vote, which totals 101 percent) or because respondents who were undecided or supported minor candidates have not been listed (as in the popular vote columns).

Minnesotans actually agree with Boschwitz, according to today's exit polls. Forty-three percent say the federal legislation doesn't cut welfare benefits *enough,* while only 15 percent believe it is too harsh. But Wellstone is winning anyway, even drawing support from one-third of those who advocate stricter welfare reform.[22]

What's the moral of the Minnesota story? Voters in this heavily suburban state dislike government programs they consider to be wasteful and ineffective, but they dislike harsh political rhetoric even more. The Boschwitz campaign, contends Wellstone campaign manager Jeff Blodgett, "just collapsed under the weight of so many negative ads."[23]

9:30 P.M.

Singer Tony Bennett takes the stage in front of the Old State House. His unenviable task is to help keep the crowd entertained until the president arrives in a couple of hours. He starts, appropriately enough, by singing "The Best Is Yet to Come." Clinton now has 284 electoral votes, Dole 89.

Republican gloom about Dole's miserable performance dissipates briefly as the networks announce that the GOP is assured of fifty-one seats in the next Senate, enough to retain control. But all is not yet well: Republican diehards remain worried about the fate of Newt Gingrich and his band of conservatives in the House of Representatives. The Democrats are gaining seats in the House, especially in suburban districts. The question is whether they will pick up enough to push the Republicans back to the minority.

One fact is clear. The electorate is displeased with politicians from both parties. It might be said that the typical American voted today with one hand on the lever, the other on his nose.

Clinton has been reelected by an impressive margin, but his mandate is weak nonetheless. A majority of voters told VNS pollsters today that they want the federal government to do *less,* not more. They prefer a caretaker in the White House, not an activist. Dole and Perot supporters overwhelmingly advocate pulling the reins on government; one-third of Clinton voters agree:

	Opinion of Federal Government (%)	
	Should Do More	Should Do Less
All voters	41	52
Clinton voters	60	32
Dole voters	20	76
Perot voters	35	61

Source: VNS exit poll 1996.

The results are no better for Gingrich. It seems more likely than not that he will return as Speaker of the House, though with a reduced majority. Yet voters clearly are fed up with his politics of confrontation; 52 percent participating in today's VNS exit polls expressed disapproval of the Republican Congress's performance under his leadership:

	Opinion of GOP Congress (%)	
	Approve	Disapprove
All voters	42	52
Clinton voters	14	80
Dole voters	82	13
Perot voters	28	65

Source: VNS exit poll 1996.

Senate Minority Leader Thomas Daschle, a South Dakota Democrat, is among those trying to make sense of the reams of numbers spewing forth from VNS's computers. "If there is a mandate, it is to govern from the middle and to take things slowly," he tells a reporter. "They want us to work together and solve our nation's problems and cut out the partisanship."[24]

10 P.M.

The unthinkable has happened. A Democrat, Jeanne Shaheen, has been elected governor of New Hampshire. Democrats historically don't get elected *anything* in New Hampshire, where voters are renowned for their white-hot hatred of income taxes and their Pavlovian dedication to the Republican ticket.

Shaheen's campaign downplayed her Democratic connections and stressed unexciting, workaday issues such as electricity rates, economic development, and health care. The success of this strategy apparently is surprising even to the governor-elect, judging from her wide, almost disbelieving smile as she talks to Tom Brokaw. "I think that voters are interested in elected officials who are going to address what matters in their everyday lives," she says, sounding much like Daschle. "They're interested in ending the partisanship and in having elected officials who are going to get results."

The interview ends. Shaheen slips from the screen, and Brokaw turns toward his partner in NBC's studio, analyst Tim Russert, who seems to be laughing at a joke only he can hear.

"New Hampshire is starting to vote like a suburb of Massachusetts," Russert chuckles.

"Well," replies Brokaw briskly, "that is effectively what it has become, after all."[25]

True enough. New Hampshire's three southeastern counties—with 62 percent of the state's residents—now are part of what the federal government grandiloquently calls the Boston-Worcester-Lawrence-Lowell-Brockton New England County Metropolitan Statistical Area. New Hampshire, in other words, officially *is* a suburb of Massachusetts.

Exit polls clarify the political implications of this demographic shift. New Hampshire, once a bedrock of conservatism, has tilted markedly toward the middle. Fully 50 percent of today's New Hampshire voters told VNS that they are moderates, dwarfing the 31 percent who are conservatives. Equally surprising are their party affiliations: 40 percent call themselves independents, 35 percent are Republicans, 25 percent are Democrats.[26]

The Republicans paved the way for Shaheen's victory by ignoring the rise of suburbia, says GOP strategist Tom Rath. He contends that the party's candidates still behave as if they are facing a rural electorate. Their platforms are far too conservative, in his opinion, making it easy for a Democrat like Shaheen to capture the political center.

"We cannot allow the middle to be co-opted from us again because we're so preoccupied with our own primary," says Rath. "You're going to see continued movement to the middle."

Echoing this call for moderation is Fred Bramante, a Republican who ran as an independent candidate for governor. He suggests that the best way to appeal to New Hampshire's suburban majority is to combine the GOP's traditional fiscal conservatism with a middle-of-the-road social agenda.

"The Republican Party needs to change," says Bramante. "I'm a Republican. The most Republican state in the United States and this happens? They need to change."[27]

10:30 P.M.

The Democrats have renewed their lease on the White House; the Republicans have retained control of the Senate. America is guaranteed a divided, two-party government that will pursue a moderate, suburban-oriented agenda. Clinton, encouraged by the success of his campaign, surely will continue steering a centrist course. The Republicans, chastened by Dole's defeat and more than a year of negative publicity in general, almost certainly will tone down their fiery rhetoric.

But what about the House of Representatives?

House Republicans are trying to make history tonight. Not since 1928 have they secured majorities in consecutive elections. Network computers indicate that this prize is nearly within their grasp, but it is not coming easily. The final tally will show eighteen Republican congressmen—eleven from suburban districts—failing in their reelection bids.

The big issue in many of these losing races was not the economy or defense policy. It was Newt Gingrich, the blunt, cocky, often abrasive Speaker of the House, the first ever to hail from suburbia. "You know, the average person began to figure out, I think about three weeks ago, that their candidate was not named Newt," Gingrich complained this morning.[28]

That is fortunate indeed for the Republicans. Today's exit polls found that only 32 percent of Americans view Gingrich favorably, while 60 percent dislike him. The GOP's saving grace is the fact that most of its House members are reasonably popular in their own districts and ran well-funded campaigns. It also helps that voters remain leery of the opposition: 49 percent of the voters surveyed by VNS said that a Democratic-controlled House would be too liberal.[29]

ABC is the first to make the call. Its computer model confirms a Republican majority at 10:40. The task of reporting the news ironically falls to Cokie Roberts, whose mother and father both served in the House as Democrats. "Our model now shows that the Republicans will maintain control of the House of Representatives," she announces somewhat grimly, lips pursed.[30] The night's last big question is answered.

It is time for the speeches.

Ross Perot, running a weak third with 8 percent of the popular vote, is the first presidential candidate to make an appearance. Perot stunned political observers in 1992 by drawing an impressive 19 percent nationwide, 20 percent in suburban states. But this year's effort never got out of first gear. "It became too much a cult of personality and too little a movement," says pollster Frank Luntz, who was part of the Perot campaign four years ago.[31]

Perot acknowledges loud cheers from his supporters in Dallas. "You've worked night and day. You've done a tremendous job," he tells them in his familiar, grating drawl. "Take a little break, and then we'll climb back in the ring and keep the pressure on to see that everybody keeps those promises." More loud cheers. Perot breaks into a big grin. Visions of 2000 undoubtedly dance in his head.[32]

II P.M.

The polls close in California, the biggest prize of all with fifty-four electoral votes. NBC immediately shades the state blue, another Clinton win. Hawaii, Oregon, and Washington also flash blue, though it hardly matters. The nation, waiting to hear from Dole and Clinton, passes the time watching other Western contests.

Washington, a suburban-dominated state where 88 percent of voters are white, is deciding a governor's race between Gary Locke, a Democratic Asian-American, and Ellen Craswell, a Republican Christian rightist. Locke wins easily. Exit polls show that 49 percent of Washington voters consider themselves to be moderates; only 15 percent empathize with the Religious Right.[33] "If she was the Republican candidate and not a Christian conservative, I probably would vote for her," sixty-two-year-old Edwin Ray, a lifelong Republican, says of Craswell. He pulls the Democratic lever.[34]

Locke will be the first Asian-American governor of a mainland state. "It's kind of like taking 100 years to go two miles," he says in wonderment, referring to the distance between the governor's mansion and the residence where his grandfather worked as a houseboy.[35] But his state does not wholeheartedly share the governor-elect's immigrant dream. Washington voters told VNS pollsters today that America should not be quite so willing to accept newcomers from other lands: 49 percent want legal immigration reduced, while 41 percent say current levels should be maintained. Only 7 percent support an increase.[36]

Similarly mixed signals are coming from California. On the one hand, the Golden State is overwhelmingly approving the favorite cause of conservative Republicans, Proposition 209, a referendum to eliminate government-sponsored affirmative action programs. Voters in six of the state's major cities—Long Beach, Los Angeles, Oakland, Sacramento, San Diego, and San Francisco—are standing in defense of affirmative action, but they are unable to match the flood of yes votes from the suburbs:

	Yes (Repeal; %)	No (Maintain; %)	Margin
Statewide	54.6	45.4	Yes by 879,729
Components (share of state vote in percent)			
Six major cities (19.0)	42.1	57.9	No by 291,111
Suburbs of six cities (63.7)	55.9	44.1	Yes by 723,679
Smaller metro areas (13.4)	63.1	36.9	Yes by 340,277
Nonmetro counties (3.9)	64.2	35.8	Yes by 106,884

Source: Author's analysis of official election returns.

But Republicans are also receiving their share of bad news. Clinton's lopsided victory in California has been made possible by surprisingly high levels of support from GOP strongholds. The Los Angeles suburbs, famous for their conservatism, are giving the president a 185,000-vote margin. California voters also are tossing out three incumbent Republican congressmen, more than any other state. Among them is Orange County's Robert Dornan, known for his caustic attacks on liberals, gays, and abortion rights supporters. "The Republicans really took it in the shorts," says Republican consultant Allan Hoffenblum. "The hard-core right did very poorly in California."[37]

Dole emerges at 11:23 to give his concession speech in Washington, D.C. He is surprisingly alert, considering that he ended his campaign by traveling 10,534 miles to nineteen states in the final ninety-six hours. Images of the marathon persist: Dole exhorting Republicans in Las Vegas in the wee hours of Sunday morning, "Let me give you an inside tip. Bet on Bob Dole." Dole standing in front of a bronze statue of Harry Truman in Independence, Missouri, this very morning at three o'clock, with a sign on his lectern expressing the ultimate in wishful thoughts: "Upset of the Century."[38]

It was not to be. "I was thinking on the way down in the elevator that tomorrow will be the first time in my life I don't have anything to do," Dole begins, drawing loud, sustained cheers, almost as if he had claimed victory. He shifts gears abruptly: "We're going to keep the Senate; we're going to keep the House." His audience roars again, then begins to chant: "Thank you, Bob. Thank you, Bob."

Dole speaks for less than ten minutes. He jokes with the crowd for much of his speech—"You're not going to get that tax cut if you don't be quiet," he tells one shouting supporter who interrupts him—but his eyes are tearing toward the end. "We will meet again, and we will meet often," he promises. And then he is gone.[39]

11:30 P.M.

We live in an age of interactive computers and instantaneous communications, but vote counting remains a laborious, time-consuming process. Americans cast their ballots today in tens of thousands of locations—from isolated schoolhouses in Maine to inner-city church basements in Chicago, from tiny village halls in Wyoming to crowded community centers in the Los Angeles suburbs. It's a miracle that the networks are able to pull together the numbers as quickly as they do.

Slightly more than half of America's precincts have reported at this hour, yet the election, for all intents and purposes, is over. Clinton has been bouncing back and forth between 49 and 50 percent of the national vote for much of the evening. Dole has settled comfortably at 42 percent—somewhat better than the pollsters predicted—and Perot is hovering around 8 percent.

Precinct results will flow steadily into network computers throughout the early morning hours and long past sunrise. The final tally will show Clinton with 47.4 million votes, Dole with 39.2 million, and Perot with 8.1 million. The president's share will work out to 49.2 percent, making him the first chief executive since Woodrow Wilson to win two terms without once reaching a majority. But the electoral vote count—the only one of consequence—will be recorded as a landslide: Clinton 379, Dole 159.

Clinton has carried the urban electorate, to no one's surprise. The two states where city residents still hold the balance of power—New York and the District of Columbia—have combined to give the president thirty-six electoral votes and a margin of nearly 2 million popular votes over Dole.*

But the election obviously has been decided in suburbia, not in the big cities. Clinton has earned 237 electoral votes in the twenty-three states where suburbanites are in control, just thirty-three electoral votes less than the number needed for victory. The president's margin over Dole in these suburban states approaches 5.8 million popular votes, accounting for 70 percent of his total margin of 8.2 million:

	Popular Vote (%)				Electoral Votes	
	Clinton	Dole	Perot	Clinton's Margin	Clinton	Dole
Nationwide	49.2	40.7	8.4	8,203,716	379	159
Components (share of U.S. vote in percent)						
City states (6.8)	60.2	30.0	7.8	1,963,566	36	0
Suburban states (62.5)	49.6	40.1	8.4	5,761,008	237	83
All other states (30.7)	46.0	44.4	8.5	479,142	106	76

Source: Author's analysis of official election returns.

There can be no doubt that Clinton's suburban strategy has secured his reelection. Jimmy Carter, Walter Mondale, and Michael Dukakis pursued liberal agendas in the 1980s, losing suburbia and the White House in the process. Clinton's move toward the middle prevented a repeat performance. Dukakis was defeated in suburban-dominated states by more than 3.1 million votes in 1988; the president has reversed that deficit into a victory of nearly 5.8 million votes tonight—a turnaround of 8.9 million:

*The District of Columbia, of course, is not a state, but it has electoral votes, just as the fifty states do, so it is referred to as a state in this book.

| | Democratic Margin | | |
Area	1988	1996	Clinton Gain
City states	Won by 397,828	Won by 1,963,566	1,565,738
Suburban states	Lost by 3,158,045	Won by 5,761,008	8,919,053
All other states	Lost by 4,316,806	Won by 479,142	4,795,948

Source: Author's analysis of official election returns.

Tonight's victory, in a sense, can be traced back to 1985, when Clinton helped found the Democratic Leadership Council (DLC), a group dedicated to remaking the Democratic Party in a centrist image. The DLC has endorsed middle-class values from the beginning, urging the party not to tie its fate to traditional Democratic interest groups such as minorities and labor unions. Clinton was the group's chairman until 1991.

The DLC is predictably unpopular with urban liberals, especially urban minorities—Jesse Jackson sneers that DLC means Democrats for the Leisure Class—but its leaders are warmed tonight by the satisfaction of a job well done. DLC President Al From portrays Clinton's reelection as the debut of a new, improved Democratic Party. "This is clearly not our fathers' party," he will tell an interviewer a few months from now. "It is now the party of the new economy and suburban values."[40]

Midnight

It is after midnight in the East, slightly past eleven in Little Rock, when Clinton makes his long-awaited walk across the round, elevated platform that extends from the front steps of the Old State House. He pauses at the podium, framed by the brightly lighted building's imposing white pillars. Leaves fall steadily from the old trees arching above him. Thousands of flash bulbs pop in the vast crowd below.

No one could blame the president for savoring this moment. The 1992 election, after all, was as much a public repudiation of George Bush as a vote of confidence in Clinton. The economy went sour on Bush's watch, and he compounded his problems by pledging never to raise taxes—"read my lips"—and then raising them. His challenger rode the wave of public disgust into the White House.

The outcome this time is of Clinton's design, both an affirmation of his leadership and a ratification of his moderate course. It is a personal victory, and he has come home to Little Rock, where he learned the intricacies of politics, to claim it.

"Just four years from now, we will enter a new century of great challenge and unlimited possibilities," he begins, his voice high and slightly strained. "Now, we've got a bridge to build—and I'm ready if you are."[41] Thousands of supporters shout their assent.

The crowd is in a mood to celebrate; it reacts eagerly to any line that invites applause, cheering, sign pumping, flag waving. But the president aims for minds, not hearts. He seeks to explain his moderate philosophy, to justify his emphasis on the needs and desires of the suburban middle class. He talks about balancing the budget, guaranteeing access to a college education, shifting the focus from welfare to work, and taking a stand against drugs.

Clinton—campaign over, victory in hand—nevertheless is giving a campaign speech.

"Tonight, we proclaim that the vital American center is alive and well," he says. "It is the common ground on which we have made our progress. Today, our economy is stronger, our streets are safer, our environment is cleaner, the world is more secure, and, thank God, our nation is more united."

The president slowly, inevitably reaches the bottom of his laundry list of issues. His eyes moisten. He pauses to scan the tens of thousands of supporters gazing up at him on this late autumn night. They have become as quiet as such a large crowd possibly can be.

"Fifty years ago, when I was born in a summer storm to a widowed mother in a small town in the southwest part of our state, it was unimaginable that someone like me could have ever become president of the greatest country in human history," he says, his voice catching briefly. "It has been, for me, a remarkable journey."[42]

The same can be said of the nation itself.

America has undertaken its own remarkable journey during Bill Clinton's lifetime, evolving from a nation of cities in the 1940s to a nation of suburbs five decades later. Clinton, now bathed in reflected light from the fireworks streaming high above the Old State House, is among the first to understand this metamorphosis and to use it to his advantage. Its political impact will become crystal clear to the rest of us during the new century that lies ahead.

2 Inevitable as Sunrise: 1939–1990

The world teetered on the brink of war as the long, cold winter of 1939 melted into spring. The European democracies, once so optimistic about averting conflict with Adolf Hitler, now felt their first twinges of doubt. British Prime Minister Neville Chamberlain—he who had declared, "I believe it is peace for our time," upon ceding Czechoslovakian territory to Hitler in September 1938—was coming to realize that no diplomatic concession could divert the führer from his goal of European domination. World War II was beginning to seem inevitable; it would start before the summer was through.

But the sense of impending danger that gripped Europe in the spring of 1939 was not universal. It scarcely touched the United States, where a majority of citizens, believing that events on the opposite shore of the Atlantic were no concern of theirs, continued to endorse the nation's traditional policy of isolationism. The United States had intervened in World War I, heralded as the war to end all wars, and the results had been disappointing. Few Americans wanted to repeat the experience.

What was especially striking was the sense of optimism that pervaded America at the end of the 1930s. The economy finally was stirring from the long hibernation known as the Great Depression. The future, far from being dark and menacing, actually seemed bright and full of possibilities. This buoyant spirit reached its highest level of expression in New York City's glittering World's Fair, which debuted on April 30, 1939, and would run through the summer of 1940.

The fair's organizers envisioned a future undisturbed by war or economic dislocation. Their belief in the limitless potential of technology inspired their theme exhibit, Democracity, a multimedia depiction of the idealized city of 2039. Audiences watched in awe as twenty-four projectors rapidly flashed images on the interior dome of the exhibit's Perisphere, a giant ball 200 feet in diameter.

But Democracity was not the fair's most popular attraction. That distinction belonged to Futurama, a dazzling 35,000-square-foot diorama that cost $7 million to construct. Designer Norman Bel Geddes and his troops covered a seven-acre platform with 500,000 buildings, 10 million trees, and 50,000 cars, all in miniature. Ten thousand cars actually moved.

31

Futurama was a time machine that whisked visitors on a fifteen-minute journey to the distant year of 1960. The audience relaxed in upholstered armchairs as lights flashed in complicated patterns above and upon the diorama, creating the illusion of a flight across America from east to west. A highlight was a simulated pass over a large city, modeled on Saint Louis, with an imposing skyline. Spacious suburbs were linked to the urban core by superhighways designed for speeds as high as 100 miles an hour.[1]

Fairgoers were entranced by Futurama; many attended the show again and again. They were fascinated by its vision of America twenty years hence, with people living in comfortable, sprawling suburbs, shuttling quickly and easily to their jobs in downtown skyscrapers.

The America of 1940 was markedly different. Suburbs already existed—indeed, Boston, Philadelphia, and New York City had suburbs long before the American Revolution—but the white middle class still was concentrated in big cities, anchored there by family ties and employment opportunities. The 1940 census identified ninety-three cities with more than 100,000 residents; their combined population was 38.2 million. That meant nearly three of every ten Americans—28.9 percent, to be exact—were jammed into the ninety-three largest urban centers.[2]

These big cities dominated the nation. They not only had the most residents, they also had the best jobs and best stores, an inevitable result of local transportation patterns. Working-class and middle-class commuters in 1940 were just as likely to use public transit as their own autos. Streetcar routes radiated like spokes from downtown, with the busiest lines intersecting in the central business district, naturally making it the hub of employment and commerce.

Nowhere was urban power more evident than in America's four largest cities. Each had more residents than the vast suburban and rural territory that surrounded it. Chicago, for example, accounted for two-thirds of the population of its entire thirteen-county metropolitan region:

City	1940 City Population	City Share of Metro Population (%)
New York City	7,454,995	55.8
Chicago	3,396,808	66.9
Philadelphia	1,931,334	52.6
Detroit	1,623,452	55.5

Source: Author's analysis of U.S. Census Bureau data.

The typical big city of 1940 was overwhelmingly white, a characteristic that would seem unusual to future generations, but was then taken for granted. Most African-Americans still lived in the same rural South where their ancestors had been subjected to slavery. Philadelphia and Washington were the only major cities in the East or Midwest whose 1940 black populations exceeded 10 percent. White immigrants, in fact, were more common than blacks in urban settings. Foreign-born whites outnumbered American-born blacks in every large Eastern and Midwestern city except Washington.[3]

The fates of the white middle class and America's urban centers, in short, seemed intertwined. But appearances were deceiving.

The 1940 census indicated that eight of the nation's ten largest cities either had lost population since 1930 or had grown at a slower rate than America as a whole. Experts thought this alarming trend was likely to continue. A 1942 report from the Saint Louis City Plan Commission, for example, predicted that the Missouri city of 800,000 might be as small as 500,000 by 1980. "Unless prompt measures are taken," warned Boston Mayor Maurice Tobin in 1941, "the contagion will spread until virtual decay and destruction of the whole city has taken place." Higher levels of government demonstrated little concern. *Business Week* observed in July 1940 that federal agencies "seemed resigned to the internal decay of the cities."[4]

The problem was that the white middle class had begun to question its commitment to the big city. The suburbs were relatively small, but they were attracting an ever-larger number of city dwellers. Suburban population increased at twice the rate of central-city population in the 1920s—and at three times the city rate during the 1930s. Even the most ardent backers of city life had to admit that suburbia showed great potential.

All of this, in historian Alice Goldfarb Marquis's view, helped to explain the public's fascination with Futurama's superhighways and Democracity's tidy array of suburban apartment buildings and single-family homes. "Americans had always been ambivalent, if not downright suspicious, about cities, but all through the twentieth century they had been briskly immigrating into them," she wrote. "Was this bland, neat cosmopolis what they had been seeking?"[5]

The answer would come after the war.

Defining Terms

Several government agencies detected the first statistical blips foreshadowing the decline of big cities and the corresponding emergence of suburbia. Foremost among these social seismographs was the U.S.

Census Bureau, which in April 1940 dispatched a small army of enumerators to collect statistical information about every American citizen, a task repeated each decade. Also gathering valuable data were the U.S. Bureau of Labor Statistics, which tracked the nation's employment trends; the U.S. Bureau of Economic Analysis, which specialized in income studies; and a wide array of state and local government agencies.

This book uses the resulting storehouse of data to show how suburbia seized control of America from its big cities between 1940 and 1996—and to predict how this transfer of power will shape the nation in the twenty-first century.

The ninety-three cities mentioned earlier in this chapter—the places that had more than 100,000 residents in 1940—form the basis for this analysis. They are referred to in this book as *mother cities.** Mother cities were the nation's centers of demographic, economic, and political power prior to World War II. They, quite simply, dictated America's course in that long-ago era.

Most mother cities still have six- or seven-figure populations today, but thirteen have slipped. Wilmington, Delaware, plummeted from a 1940 population of 112,504 to a 1990 total of 71,529. Utica, New York, dropped from 100,518 to 68,637. It makes no difference. Wilmington, Utica, and their eleven fellows remain mother cities. The only fact of importance is that they were large and powerful during the golden age of cities.

Another 115 communities have climbed above the 100,000 threshold since 1940. Las Vegas, a sleepy village of 8,422 in 1940, blossomed into a boomtown of 258,295 by 1990. Phoenix soared from 65,414 to 983,403. No matter. Las Vegas, Phoenix, and others of their ilk are not mother cities. They carried little or no clout in 1940, and their subsequent development patterns have more in common with suburbs than with classic urban centers.

A second essential concept is that of the *metropolitan area,* which consists of a large city and its suburbs, or a combination of neighboring large cities and their suburbs, that are defined by the federal government as "socially and economically interrelated." The U.S. Office of Management and Budget (OMB) sets official metropolitan boundaries, using counties as its building blocks. The OMB can expand or contract metro areas to reflect population shifts, but this book applies the 1995 boundaries throughout the period of 1940–2020 to allow for uniform comparisons.

---

*See Appendix A for a list of all mother cities.

The next step is to use mother cities and metropolitan areas to subdivide the nation. *Inner America* is the collective name for the sixty-seven metro areas that encompass all ninety-three mother cities and their suburbs. Nine of these metros have two or more mother cities each. The Boston metro area, for example, includes Boston, Cambridge, Fall River, Lowell, New Bedford, Somerville, and Worcester, mother cities all, while the Chicago metro also has Gary, Indiana.*

Outer America consists of everything else—specifically, *fringe metros* and *nonmetro areas,* those places that historically have been outside the sphere of national power and influence. Fringe metros are metropolitan areas without mother cities. A few fringe metros—Las Vegas and Phoenix, for example—were sparsely settled in 1940, but are now sizable urban centers. Most remain relatively small today, such as Altoona, Pennsylvania, and Lincoln, Nebraska. Nonmetro areas are all counties that lie outside OMB's official metropolitan boundaries.

Setting the Stage

The atomic bombs that destroyed Hiroshima and Nagasaki in August 1945 brought World War II to an abrupt end. They also triggered the most explosive change ever in the American way of life.

The Pentagon's top brass, uncertain that the A-bomb would prove decisive, grimly and meticulously had been planning to invade Japan in 1946. Casualties were expected to be obscenely high, undoubtedly the worst of any battle in history. The sudden dawn of the atomic age, however, forced military planners to switch gears. Invasion no longer was their goal; demobilization was. Millions of soldiers and sailors eagerly awaited orders to head home.

But where would they go?

America was unprepared for its returning veterans. Relatively few homes had been constructed since 1929 because of the depression and the war. "In many ways," wrote urban historian Jon Teaford, "the 1930s and early 1940s were years of arrested urban development."[6] Housing was at a premium; there was tremendous pent-up demand.

Most vets could make do for a while by staying with their parents or by living in modified basements or garages that barely deserved to be called apartments. But the only long-term solution was construction. Contractors responded vigorously. Single-family housing starts (the

---

*See Appendix B for a list of all metro areas in Inner America and Appendix C for the components of those metros. This book defines *suburbs* as all parts of Inner America outside of mother cities.

number of new units built) rose from 114,000 in 1944 to 937,000 in 1946, then stayed above 1.2 million each year from 1947 through 1964.[7]

A similar construction boom had preceded the depression in the 1920s, adding greatly to the housing stock of America's major cities. But this time was different. Urban areas had run out of room. Mother cities might be scorned in the 1990s for their congestion, but they were actually twice as crowded half a century earlier, when their average density was more than 8,500 persons per square mile:

	Persons per Square Mile	
	1940	1990
All 93 mother cities	8,548	4,249
Selected mother cities		
New York City	24,933	23,705
Chicago	16,434	12,252
Philadelphia	15,183	11,736
Buffalo	14,617	8,082
Saint Louis	13,378	6,408
Pittsburgh	12,892	6,653
Detroit	11,773	7,411

Source: Author's analysis of U.S. Census Bureau data.

Most of the new postwar homes, logically enough, were built where there was available space—in the suburbs. Subdivisions sprang up on the outskirts of every American city. Many of these projects were ambitious, notably Levittown, New York, the largest private housing development in U.S. history. Abraham Levitt and his sons began acquiring 4,000 acres on Long Island in 1946; they eventually built 17,400 homes in their new community. Fourteen hundred Levittown houses were sold on a single day in 1949.[8]

Economists had been worried that the depression would resume once World War II was over, but their fears were unrealized. The middle class, buoyed by a rapidly growing economy, snapped up new homes as quickly as they came on the market. The boom seemed logical in retrospect. The United States, after all, was the only world power to enter the postwar era unscathed. Its traditional competitors —France, Great Britain, Germany, Japan—had been ravaged by war. Emerging rivals, such as China and the Soviet Union, were preoccupied with internal politics. America's share of world manufacturing consequently expanded from 32 percent in 1932 to 45 percent in 1950, and its share of world trade grew accordingly.[9] Consumer buying power reached an all-time high.

The federal government did its best to make new homes even more affordable. The Federal Housing Administration (FHA) and Vet-

erans Administration (VA) offered mortgage programs that required
tiny downpayments and featured low interest rates. At least 40 percent
of all homes sold each year from 1947 to 1957 were financed through
FHA and VA mortgages. The FHA further fueled the exodus to suburbia by redlining black and immigrant neighborhoods in major
cities, that is, by refusing to loan money to prospective homebuyers in
those heavily settled urban areas.[10]

Just one critical question remained. The suburbs were expanding
rapidly, but mother cities still boasted most of Inner America's jobs
and shops. How could residents of the new suburban frontier travel
conveniently and efficiently between their homes and the urban core?

Mass transit seemed a likely answer. Millions of American families
did not own cars as World War II ended; they relied heavily on buses
and streetcars. The nation's public transit systems carried 23 billion
riders in 1945, accounting for 35 percent of all passenger-miles traveled in urban areas.[11]

But prewar events in Southern California foreshadowed a different
solution. Los Angeles, from its earliest days, had deviated from traditional development patterns. Most mother cities were compact; Los
Angeles sprawled. It already had the highest ratio of cars to residents
of any city in the world by the mid-1920s.

The turning point came in 1926, when Los Angeles voters
approved a massive bond issue to expand their highway network. The
city's extensive light-rail transit system slipped into disuse as the automobile took charge. Los Angeles's decision would lead to the 1940
opening of the Arroyo Seco Parkway, later renamed the Pasadena
Freeway, the first strand of a web of expressways that would become
fabled worldwide for its intricacy.[12]

Consumers all across postwar America—many able to afford a car
for the first time—opted for the freedom of the Los Angeles model.
No longer would they travel only when streetcar schedules permitted;
no longer would they visit only those destinations that bus routes
served. Leaders of big cities, oddly enough, lent their support. Downtown department stores backed expansion of the Los Angeles expressway system, believing it would lure shoppers to the central city.
Detroit Mayor Albert Cobo predicted as late as 1949 that freeways
would "retard the decentralization of business into suburban areas
which pay no Detroit taxes."[13]

The national clamor for superhighways culminated in congressional approval of the 1956 Interstate Highway Act, which envisioned
a 41,000-mile national freeway system, including 5,300 miles of expressways in urban areas. Supporters hailed the proposed network as

an ideal mechanism to tie cities and suburbs together. Critics, what few there were, insisted that freeways would hasten the decentralization of metro areas and the decline of urban centers. "When the American people, through their Congress, voted a little while ago for a $26 billion highway program," wrote one of those critics, urban historian Lewis Mumford, "the most charitable thing to assume is that they hadn't the faintest notion of what they were doing."[14]

A Strange New Society

The Interstate Highway Act was the final ingredient required for the suburbanization of America. Everything was in place—millions upon millions of eager homebuyers, urban congestion forcing them toward the suburbs, a booming economy making it possible for them to buy new homes, a government willing to help them buy, and now, a freeway system helping them to commute easily to the central city from distant locations.

Americans embraced the freedom of movement encouraged by this new environment. The nation's population grew 35 percent during the first twenty years following World War II, but automobile registrations soared 180 percent in the same period—from 26 million in 1945 to 72 million in 1965. Mass transit was devastated. Ridership plummeted 64 percent in the postwar years, accounting for a mere 5 percent of all passenger-miles traveled in urban America by 1965.[15]

Frank Lloyd Wright was among the first to realize that this suburban wave was pushing America in a new direction. The noted architect fancied himself a social theorist of sorts and, in 1958, combined these interests in *The Living City*, a book that predicted the demise of the large city. "As it devours man," he wrote, "so now it must devour itself." Wright contended that cities were built to a scale better suited for the Middle Ages than the automotive age. The congested urban core, he believed, eventually would be eclipsed by a "new city"—essentially, what would come to be known as a suburban "edge city"—in which transportation would be easy and population density would be greatly reduced. "Decentralization is therefore innate necessity," he insisted. "A new city is inevitable as sunrise tomorrow morning though rain may fall."[16]

That new city, in fact, was already evolving. The postwar exodus to suburbia was of a proportion unprecedented in American history. Suburban population virtually doubled in two decades—growing 31 percent in the 1940s and then another 47 percent in the 1950s. The suburbs ballooned from a total of 31.1 million residents just before Pearl Harbor to 60.1 million in 1960.

Mother cities were also expanding, but at a much tamer pace—12 percent in the 1940s and just 5 percent in the 1950s. They added 7 million people during the same twenty years that the suburbs were growing by nearly 29 million:*

	Population			Share of U.S. Total (%)		
	1940	1950	1960	1940	1950	1960
Inner America						
Mother cities	38,167,315	42,910,650	45,157,927	28.9	28.4	25.2
Suburbs	31,133,540	40,890,639	60,082,442	23.6	27.0	33.5
Outer America						
Fringe metros	20,128,851	24,832,645	31,362,899	15.2	16.4	17.5
Nonmetro areas	42,734,863	42,691,864	42,719,907	32.3	28.2	23.8

Source: Author's analysis of U.S. Census Bureau data.

Suburbia had ranked third among the nation's four population sectors in 1940, trailing well behind nonmetro areas and mother cities. But the standings had turned upside down by 1960, the result of rapid expansion in the suburbs, sluggish growth in mother cities, and a slight population decline in nonmetros. Suburbia, home to 33.5 percent of all Americans, now was Number One.

Author Theodore White, crisscrossing the America of 1960 in pursuit of presidential candidates, wondered about the implications of this rapid change. He wasn't overly optimistic. "From the census, one had the impression of a strange new society being formed," he wrote in 1961, "a series of metropolitan centers growing and swelling in their suburban girdles until the girdles touched one another, border on border, stretching in giant population belts hundreds of miles long while wilderness rose again on the outside of the girdle (we now count more deer in the United States than when the settlers came) and rot blighted the inner urban cores."[17]

America's inner cities undeniably were in decline. Slums always had been part of the urban landscape—the 1940 census, for example, classified nearly 30 percent of all city dwellings as blighted—but poverty and decay spread rapidly in the wake of World War II. Mother cities, in effect, traded an economically stable group of residents for a poorer set. Well-to-do and middle-class whites streamed to suburbia, replaced in the city by blacks, Hispanics, and Appalachian whites who were searching for work. Approximately one-quarter of Mississippi's black population left the state during the 1940s alone, the largest share heading to Northern industrial cities. The African-American

*See Appendix G for population figures and projections for mother cities, suburbs, fringe metros, and nonmetro areas from 1940 through 2020.

influx to Washington, D.C., was so great that, in 1960, it became the first American city in which blacks outnumbered whites.[18]

Mother cities, it was true, were continuing to grow; their combined population increased 18 percent between 1940 and 1960. But the character of these cities was changing dramatically. Most urban newcomers were poor; many were nonwhite. The white middle class, once the foundation of life in the city, felt less and less at home there.

Suburban developers blatantly promoted an exclusive alternative, often setting a racial bar. The contract signed by every Levittown homeowner included a standard clause that said "no dwelling shall be used or occupied by members of other than the Caucasian race." William Levitt was unapologetic about these restrictive covenants. "We can solve a housing problem, or we can try to solve a racial problem," he said. "But we cannot combine the two."[19]

Urban Power

Politicians live a perilous existence. Their line of work is plagued by imprecision and doubt, compelling them to grasp tightly the rare cold, hard fact that comes their way. One of their few certitudes in 1940 was the knowledge that cities were the major force in American elections.

The White House virtually had been Republican property during the first three decades of the twentieth century, as the GOP won six of eight presidential elections between 1900 and 1928. The only Democrat to break the string—Woodrow Wilson in 1912 and 1916—received less than half of the popular vote each time. Republican hegemony lasted until the Great Depression, when angry voters repudiated the party's incumbent president, Herbert Hoover. Democrat Franklin Roosevelt won the 1932 election easily, then was reelected in 1936 with the largest popular majority in history.

The economy, of course, was the key factor motivating this sudden shift in political loyalties. But analyst Samuel Lubell argued persuasively that a second factor was of critical importance. He believed that two population currents had combined to create a large new urban electorate that was strong enough to influence national elections. "Between 1910 and 1930, for the first time, a majority of the American people came to live in cities," he wrote after World War II. "The second population shift might be described as the triumph of the (higher) birth rates of the poor and underprivileged (in cities) over those of the rich and wellborn."[20]

These urban voters, Lubell conceded, once had favored the Republicans. Warren Harding won the nation's twelve largest cities by an astounding margin of 1.64 million votes in 1920, and Calvin Coolidge carried those same cities by a lesser plurality in 1924. But 1928—a year *before* the onset of the Great Depression—brought a much different outcome. Hoover took the election, continuing the Republican streak, but he did not perform nearly as well in big cities as his predecessors. His opponent, Al Smith, a Catholic New Yorker who possessed an undeniable affinity for the poor and underprivileged, scored a breakthrough for the Democratic Party, carrying the nation's major cities by 38,000 votes. The Democratic margin in those twelve cities would soar under Roosevelt to 1.91 million votes in 1932 and 3.61 million in 1936.[21]

This book picks up the story in 1940, assessing the balance of power by putting states in four categories according to their population patterns: A *city state* is one in which mother cities have the most residents. A *suburban state* is one where the suburbs have the population edge. A *fringe state* is dominated by fringe metros, a *nonmetro state* by nonmetro areas. Each state's classification is determined by the type of community with the largest number of residents. A plurality—not a majority—is the sole requirement, exactly as the Electoral College requires a candidate to win merely a plurality of a state's popular votes to qualify for all of its electoral votes.*

The population breakdown for 1940 indicated that cities were still all-powerful. Only eight of America's forty-eight states were classified as city states, but they accounted for nearly 42 percent of the popular votes cast in the presidential election between Roosevelt and Republican Wendell Willkie:†

	States	Popular Votes (PV)	Share of PV (%)	Electoral Votes (EV)	EV per State
Inner America					
City states	8	20,784,474	41.7	162	20.3
Suburban states	6	9,416,332	18.9	85	14.2
Outer America					
Fringe states	3	735,509	1.5	18	6.0
Nonmetro states	31	18,964,103	38.0	266	8.6

Source: Author's analysis of U.S. Census Bureau data and official election returns.

---

*See Appendix I for the allocation of electoral votes in each presidential election from 1940 through 1996 (along with projections for 2000 through 2024).

†All votes in a particular state are allocated to its designated category, reflecting the power wielded by that state's dominant type of community. New York and Illinois, for example, were classified as city states in 1940. All of those states' popular votes—whether cast in cities, suburbs, or rural areas—consequently were included in the city states total. All votes cast in Georgia and South Dakota, likewise, were included in the nonmetro states total.

Two essential facts leap off this chart:

- City states had a clear edge in the popular vote count in 1940. Their only real competition was provided by nonmetro states, which fell 1.8 million votes behind. Suburbia most definitely was not a significant factor.
- Nonmetro states had the most electoral votes—266, exactly the number needed to win the presidency—but that total was dispersed among thirty-one states, equaling a mere 8.6 electoral votes per state. City states were considerably more appealing to presidential candidates, offering a juicy 20.3 electoral votes per state. They included most of America's political prizes: New York (forty-seven electoral votes), Illinois (twenty-nine), Ohio (twenty-six), California (twenty-two), and Michigan (nineteen).

Franklin Roosevelt was ideally suited for such an environment. Roosevelt, a patrician from New York's rural Hudson Valley, nonetheless had a rare ability to communicate with—and inspire loyalty from —the urban workingman, a power that secured him the governorship and then the presidency. FDR maintained strong ties with the labor movement and dealt with big-city party bosses without shame. He had a friendly relationship with New York City's Tammany Hall, and his links to Chicago's Democratic machine were so solid that it helped engineer his nomination for an unprecedented third term, even putting a party worker with a microphone in the bowels of Chicago Stadium. The worker's magnified voice, chanting, "We want Roosevelt," aided an otherwise tepid demonstration prior to the crucial roll call at the Democratic convention.[22]

FDR won a third term in 1940 and a fourth in 1944. City states backed him solidly in both elections—giving him a 143 to 19 electoral-vote lead over Willkie and a 113 to 25 edge over Thomas Dewey—but Roosevelt's margins were so large that urban support was hardly crucial in either case. Only one thing really mattered: There was a war going on, and America declined to turn its back on its commander-in-chief.

The Man from Independence

Harry Truman received the shock of his life on April 12, 1945. Eleanor Roosevelt summoned the vice president late that afternoon to the White House. She informed him upon his arrival that her husband was dead; Truman was the new president of the United States. "I felt like the moon, the stars, and all the planets had fallen on me," he told reporters the next day.[23]

World War II ended four months later, and with it went any semblance of bipartisanship. Republicans attacked the new president mercilessly. A restless nation, frustrated by spiraling inflation and a serious housing shortage, handed control of Congress back to the GOP in 1946. It generally was assumed that a Republican would win the presidential election two years hence.

Presidential adviser Clark Clifford was assigned the thankless task of plotting strategy for Truman's seemingly doomed campaign. He sat down in late 1947 to write a forty-three-page report to his candidate. It was blunt, provocative, and perhaps the most influential memo in the history of American politics.

Clifford believed that Truman could defy the odds and win a term of his own, but only if he targeted his campaign at urban voters in the East and Midwest, especially the *newest* urban voters in those regions. "Unless the Administration makes a determined campaign to help the Negro . . . on the problems of high prices and housing—and capitalizes politically on its efforts—the Negro vote is already lost," he wrote. "Unless there are new and real efforts . . . the Negro bloc, which, certainly in Illinois and probably in New York and Ohio, does hold the balance of power, will go Republican."[24]

Clifford was introducing an entirely new variable to the political equation. Franklin Roosevelt, after all, never had to worry about the black vote. About 70 percent of the nation's African-Americans lived in the eleven states of the old Confederacy as late as 1940; few had been allowed to vote. But World War II had triggered a massive northward migration of blacks. There soon were enough African-American voters to form influential blocs in several major cities; politicians from both parties were beginning to pay heed.

Truman was receptive to Clifford's argument. The president was a product of the infamous Pendergast political machine that controlled Kansas City and much of Missouri, an organization that author Irwin Ross labeled "one of the most corrupt political gangs in the country."[25] He respected the power of big-city bosses and the value of big-city votes. He ordered his staff to begin work on a comprehensive civil rights address, which he delivered on February 2, 1948. Fierce Southern opposition eventually forced Truman to drop some of his proposals and dilute others, but his basic message was received and understood by black voters. They rallied to his candidacy.*

---

*Clifford's memo, so prescient in so many ways, did not foresee the South's hostile response to Truman's civil rights program. "It is inconceivable that any politics ini-

The subsequent story is legendary. Truman, dismissed by the experts and derided by many leaders of his own party, took his campaign directly to the people, gave the Republicans hell, and defeated Thomas Dewey in the upset of the century. The president's final margin over Dewey was nearly 2.2 million popular votes, and he carried the Electoral College just as comfortably:*

| | Electoral Votes | | |
	Truman	Dewey	Other
Nationwide	303	189	39
Inner America			
City states	67	69	0
Suburban states	45	71	0
Outer America			
Fringe states	15	0	18
Nonmetro states	176	49	21

Source: Author's analysis of official election returns.

Truman obviously clinched the election in the Farm Belt. Dewey eked out margins of two electoral votes in city states and twenty-six in suburbia, but the president countered with an impressive surplus of 127 electoral votes in nonmetropolitan America. Much of the hell that Truman raised on his campaign trips had been directed against GOP farm policy. "This Republican Congress has already stuck a pitchfork in the farmer's back," he charged repeatedly, darkly hinting that farm states would suffer through another depression if Dewey won.[26] Rural voters believed him, setting aside their Republican loyalties. Only three Democratic candidates in the subsequent half-century would duplicate Truman's feat of winning the nonmetro bloc—Lyndon Johnson, Jimmy Carter, and Bill Clinton, the three Southerners nominated during that span.

But the enduring legend would say little about the farm vote, focusing instead on the president's success in heavily populated states. Truman carried Ohio by 7,000 popular votes, California by 18,000, and Illinois by 34,000.† A switch of just 29,500 votes in these three

---

tiated by the Truman Administration, no matter how 'liberal,' could so alienate the South in the next year that it would revolt," he wrote (cited in Allen Yarnell, *Democrats and Progressives* [Berkeley: University of California Press, 1974], p. 30).

*See Appendix J for a breakdown of presidential election results from 1940 through 1996 according to the four state classifications (city states, suburban states, fringe states, nonmetro states).

†Illinois (twenty-eight electoral votes) and Ohio (twenty-five) were classified as city states in 1948. The balance of power already had shifted in California (twenty-five), making it a suburban state.

states would have given their seventy-eight electoral votes—and the presidency—to Dewey.[27]

Political experts were quick to attribute Truman's nail-biting victories in Ohio, California, and Illinois to his successful cultivation of their sizable black electorates. Clifford's strategy, seemingly risky a year earlier, had been vindicated. The coming generation of Democratic contenders, raised on the mythology of 1948, would take it for granted that the best way to reach the White House—indeed, the *only* way—was to emphasize policies that favored cities and minorities. This belief had become ingrained by 1960, as Theodore White noted: "Since [1948], as the Negro migration from the South has quickened in pace and size, the importance of the Negro vote has grown to be almost obsessive with Northern political leaders."[28]

Power Shift

A second trend emerged in 1948, but was ignored by embarrassed pundits who were more concerned with salvaging their reputations. They had assured the nation that Thomas Dewey was a cinch to win the election; they now faced the task of explaining Harry Truman's improbable triumph. Their hand-wringing and blame-shifting obscured the first indications that cities and suburbs were becoming politically polarized.

Most candidates still focused on cities up to this time, dismissing suburbs as inconsequential satellites, usually with good reason. Nearly three-quarters of the votes in the New York City metropolitan area in 1940 had been cast in the mother city itself. The same imbalance was evident that year in other metros: 83 percent of all votes in the New Orleans area came from the city, as did 73 percent in Baltimore, 66 percent in Denver, and 60 percent in Philadelphia.[29]

It almost seemed ridiculous to make such distinctions, since cities and suburbs were nearly identical in makeup. The white middle class controlled *both*, guaranteeing competitive two-party elections in both. Future generations might find it inconceivable, but the Republican Party remained strong in major cities late into the 1940s. Baltimore, Buffalo, Cincinnati, Philadelphia, and Saint Louis had Republican mayors in 1946. All twenty-two of Philadelphia's city council seats went to the GOP in 1947. Suburbia, on the other hand, often backed Democrats. The San Francisco suburbs, for example, gave Roosevelt 53.4 percent support in 1940 and 55.4 percent in 1944, the latter higher than his nationwide percentage.[30]

But 1948 was different. The exodus of the white middle class from mother cities had been underway for three years. The suburbs were expanding rapidly and beginning to develop a distinct political personality, as reflected by election results from selected metro areas:*

Metro Area	Share of Metro Votes (%)		Winner's Margins	
	Mother City	Suburbs	Mother City	Suburbs
Baltimore	66.2	33.8	Truman by 23,736	Dewey by 16,440
Denver	65.2	34.8	Truman by 13,125	Dewey by 1,223
New York City	73.6	26.4	Truman by 488,257	Dewey by 343,605
Philadelphia	60.2	39.8	Truman by 6,737	Dewey by 124,216
Saint Louis	48.8	51.2	Truman by 99,998	Truman by 35,757
San Francisco	44.9	55.1	Truman by 7,591	Dewey by 20,848

Source: Author's analysis of official election returns.

If a beleaguered pundit had studied these returns closely—and there is no evidence that any did—he might have dazzled the political community by foreseeing three critical changes:

- Suburbia eventually would outvote mother cities, a development first glimpsed in Saint Louis and San Francisco. City residents cast a majority of ballots in both metros in 1940, but slipped below 50 percent by 1948. Urban power was eroding almost everywhere by the late 1940s. The city of Baltimore still accounted for 66 percent of the votes within its metro area, but its share had dropped more than six percentage points in just eight years.
- Suburban voters would vote differently than their urban counterparts, as shown in San Francisco. Its suburbs, once so enamored of Roosevelt, turned against Truman in 1948, even though the city remained Democratic. The GOP's influence also was growing steadily in suburban Baltimore, where Willkie lost by 6,100 votes in 1940. Dewey won there by 14,000 in 1944 and then increased his margin to 16,440 in 1948.
- The suburbs would gradually develop enough political muscle to control their metro areas, as politicians in the Philadelphia area were already noticing. The city of Philadelphia gave Roosevelt a 177,000-vote plurality in 1940, easily erasing Willkie's

*This chart—and several similar charts in the first three chapters—compares each candidate's performance in the listed mother city with his performance in its suburbs. Some metro areas (New York City and San Francisco, for example) encompass more than one mother city. This chart excludes votes from such secondary mother cities, as well as the counties in which they are located. It includes votes only from the listed central city and all surrounding counties that are purely suburban. Information was derived through the author's analysis of official election returns.

33,000-vote edge in the suburbs. But the balance of power had shifted by 1948, with Dewey's 124,000-vote suburban margin wiping out Truman's minuscule lead in the city.[31]

Population growth in suburbia accelerated during the years following Harry Truman's miraculous victory. The urban-suburban political gap widened with equal speed, as middle-class Republicans fled from cities, where they were replaced by blacks and Appalachian whites, two groups with strong Democratic inclinations. Most cities predictably fell under Democratic control. Chicago had seventeen Republican aldermen in 1947, but just three by 1959. Philadelphia's city council, totally Republican in 1947, had only two GOP members by the end of the 1950s.

Suburbia, meanwhile, became a Republican stronghold, much to the benefit of Dwight Eisenhower, who swept all 194 electoral votes from suburban states in 1952 and again four years later. His 1956 reelection campaign set new records for suburban support, rolling up victory margins of 37,000 votes in the communities outside Denver; 85,000 outside Baltimore; 108,000 outside San Francisco; 257,000 outside Philadelphia; and—topping them all—an astounding margin of 826,000 votes in the suburbs outside New York City.[32]

A Close Call

The Census Bureau conducts its national headcount once a decade, gathering a wealth of data about every city, town, and village. It not only tabulates the number of inhabitants in each place, but also how many languages they speak, how much money they earn, how long it takes them to commute to their jobs, and how many telephones they own, among thousands of other facts.

Most censuses detect incremental changes in the ways that Americans live and work; their findings are interesting, though unexceptional. But a select few are landmarks in population research, such as the 1890 census, the first to identify a generally continuous string of white settlements from one coast to the other, proof that the frontier had disappeared. Such, too, as the census of 1960, the first to show suburbia as a powerful new force in American life.*

The Census Bureau reported that the population of the United

---

*See Appendix H for state-by-state data from each census from 1940 through 1990, along with projections for 2000 through 2020.

States had grown by 28 million between 1950 and 1960. Two-thirds of that increase—19.2 million—occurred in the suburbs, which now had 60 million residents, compared to 45 million in mother cities. Suburbia had taken the upper hand in Inner America:

Share of Inner America Population (%)			
Components	1940	1950	1960
Mother cities	55.1	51.2	42.9
Suburbs	44.9	48.8	57.1

Source: Author's analysis of U.S. Census Bureau data.

This trend had broader implications. Stores already had begun following their customers out of the central city. The nation's first enclosed mall opened near Minneapolis in 1956—an omen for downtown retailers—and thousands of smaller strip plazas were springing up along suburban highways. A few pioneering corporations joined the parade, such as General Foods, which abandoned New York City for nearby White Plains in 1954. Big-city officials professed to be unworried, correctly pointing out that most large department stores, corporate headquarters, major banks, and law firms remained downtown. Mother cities, for the moment at least, were still economically dominant.[33]

But they were no longer politically dominant. The ranks of suburban states swelled to seventeen by 1960; their 240 electoral votes were just twenty-nine short of the total needed for victory. The once-proud list of city states had dwindled temporarily to two—New York (forty-five electoral votes) and Hawaii (three):

	States	Popular Votes (PV)	Share of PV (%)	Electoral Votes (EV)	EV per State
Inner America					
City states	2	7,475,784	10.9	48	24.0
Suburban states	17	37,428,612	54.4	240	14.1
Outer America					
Fringe states	8	7,494,378	10.9	84	10.5
Nonmetro states	23	16,439,445	23.9	165	7.2

Source: Author's analysis of U.S. Census Bureau data and official election returns.

The presidential nominees that year matched up well with the young, upwardly mobile suburban electorate. Republican Richard Nixon and Democrat John Kennedy, both in their forties, formed the youngest pair of major-party candidates in American history. Both were veterans of World War II, an experience they shared with millions of new suburbanites. And both had entered politics in 1946, the very year the suburban wave began to wash across America.

Nixon had something further in common with the voters, having launched his career as a congressman from the Los Angeles suburbs. Kennedy, for his part, initially represented Boston in the House of Representatives, but seemed uncomfortable with its brand of urban politics. His uneasiness was reciprocated. Chicago Mayor Richard Daley hurried to Kennedy's command post on the night of his nomination, as did party kingpins from Connecticut, Michigan, New York, Ohio, and Pennsylvania. But they didn't joke with the nominee as they had with Roosevelt. Nor did they flatter him as they did Truman. They stood silently about thirty feet from Kennedy, waiting to be summoned. Theodore White described them as "all shuffling restlessly in the same room, so strong yet so ill at ease."[34] The balance of power was shifting, and the urban bosses knew it.

That shift, however, was far from complete. Kennedy privately was caustic about the Democratic machines, yet he relied on them increasingly as election day neared. Nixon traveled far and wide to all fifty states, but Kennedy's schedulers focused on cities. The Democratic nominee, fully schooled in the Truman legend, appealed to African-American voters with growing fervor as October waned.

The election was one of the closest ever. Kennedy edged Nixon by fewer than 119,000 popular votes; his electoral-vote margin was 303 to 219, including a 135 to 105 margin in suburban states and a 48 to 0 sweep in city states. It was somehow fitting that a few thousand timely —and highly questionable—popular votes from Daley's Chicago clinched Kennedy's majority in the Electoral College.[35]

Every ballot was precious to Kennedy, but city voters clearly deserved the greatest credit for putting him over the top. They offset Nixon's suburban power in some metros, such as New York City and Philadelphia, and augmented Kennedy's small suburban majorities in others, like Detroit and Saint Louis:

| Metro Area | Share of Metro Votes (%) | | Winner's Margins | |
	Mother City	Suburbs	Mother City	Suburbs
Baltimore	51.1	48.9	Kennedy by 88,047	Nixon by 16,061
Detroit	37.4	62.6	Kennedy by 311,721	Kennedy by 39,820
New York City	59.0	41.0	Kennedy by 791,118	Nixon by 285,667
Philadelphia	46.9	53.1	Kennedy by 331,544	Nixon by 110,509
Saint Louis	31.9	68.1	Kennedy by 100,988	Kennedy by 47,269
San Francisco	28.1	71.9	Kennedy by 54,733	Nixon by 27,609

Source: Author's analysis of official election returns.

Kennedy, to be sure, could not have won the presidency without faring reasonably well in suburbia; almost 45 percent of his electoral votes came from suburban states. But a close inspection of the final numbers indicated that mother cities, not their suburbs, played the decisive role in his victory.

Pennsylvania was a prime example. It was classified as a suburban state because 40 percent of its residents lived in suburbs, compared to 26 percent in mother cities. But urban voters still had enough clout, under the right conditions, to determine its direction. Such was the case in 1960. Kennedy won Pennsylvania—and its thirty-two electoral votes— by the narrow margin of 116,000 popular votes. He would have lost it by 215,000 if not for his impressive majority in the city of Philadelphia.[36]

How could one city, badly outnumbered though it was, still wield so much power? The answer lay in the steady drain of white middle-class residents that was turning Philadelphia and other mother cities into Democratic monoliths. Sixty-eight percent of Philadelphia voters backed Kennedy, resulting in an enormous citywide margin of nearly 332,000 votes. The suburbs had a larger population base, but also were much more competitive politically, making it difficult for a Republican to match the Democratic tide from the city. Nixon drew 55 percent support in the Philadelphia suburbs, a respectable showing, but one that translated to a margin of just 110,000 votes.

The key to Kennedy's success, in other words, was not that he won the suburbs; Nixon actually carried most suburban regions. The key was that Kennedy did *well enough*—keeping Nixon's suburban margins small enough—to give city voters the opportunity to decide the outcome. That they did.

The new president never forgot his debt to the cities. Nor did Lyndon Johnson, who succeeded to the presidency upon Kennedy's assassination in 1963. They presided over eight years of unprecedented advances in minority rights—notably the Civil Rights Act of 1964 and the Voting Rights Act of 1965—and unprecedented generosity in urban aid. Kennedy inherited forty-four federal grant programs that annually allocated $3.9 billion to the nation's large cities. He and Johnson expanded the government's efforts to encompass more than 500 urban programs, allocating $14 billion a year by 1969.[37]

A Question of Color

Suburbanites generally approved of the federal government's first steps to secure civil rights for African-Americans. They supported Eisenhower when he sent troops to Little Rock to desegregate its public high school; they applauded Kennedy when he forced the integration of universities in the Deep South; and they agreed with Johnson when he declared that Americans of all races deserved the right to vote.

The simple fact is that civil rights was perceived to be a regional controversy in the 1950s and early 1960s—a case of North versus South. There were eighteen suburban states by 1964, but Virginia was the only one in the old Confederacy. Most suburbanites, feeling unthreatened by the racial issue, took a comfortably moral stand. Their optimism was reflected in a 1963 Gallup Poll in which 53 percent of all whites predicted that racial harmony eventually would be achieved.[38]

Watts changed all that.

Watts was a typical inner-city neighborhood of Los Angeles—typical in its poverty (roughly 30 percent of the adult males in Watts were unemployed in mid-1965) and typical in its blackness (the whites most commonly seen in Watts were policemen whose relations with neighborhood residents were usually strained and often hostile). Watts, in other words, was a slum, a place that meant nothing to the white suburbanites who controlled the Los Angeles metro area.

It suddenly became important to them on August 11, 1965, less than a week after President Johnson signed the Voting Rights Act into law. A riot began in Watts that day for reasons that remain obscure, and it continued for five days. The toll was shockingly heavy: thirty-four people were killed, 4,000 were arrested, and much of the neighborhood was burned to the ground.

The violence was not without precedent. Middle-aged and elderly Americans could remember race riots that had erupted in New York City and Detroit during World War II; younger people were familiar with the more recent clashes between whites and blacks in the South. Nor did Watts pose any particular threat to the white middle class. The riot had been confined to the neighborhood itself. Few whites, other than police and national guardsmen, were touched by it in any way.

The true significance of Watts was that it was the first outbreak of sustained, *televised* urban violence. Suburbanites, previously confident of their safety, now felt pangs of doubt. They grimly watched the nightly news as Watts dissolved into anarchy. Millions of whites instantly lost their faith in racial reconciliation. "Five days of violent, televised disorder opened the first major fissure in the consensus behind Democratic racial liberalism," journalist Thomas Byrne Edsall would recall nearly thirty years later. "Watts provided unmistakable evidence that the drive to achieve black equality would have tremendous costs as well as tremendous rewards."[39]

Watts was America's gateway to a series of long, hot summers. Perhaps the hottest was 1967, when Newark and Detroit exploded within ten days of each other. Twenty-five people were killed in the Newark riot, which apparently started after police beat a cabdriver. Detroit's numbers were worse: 43 dead, 7,000 arrested, 1,300 buildings destroyed, and total damage of a quarter of a billion dollars. These riots were, in one sense, expressions of frustration and despair by poor urban blacks. But violence did not bring them sympathy or aid; instead it alienated the suburban middle class.

The Democrats suffered the consequences. It was they who had marched in the vanguard of civil rights, they who had become heavily dependent on the black vote, they who had been so generous with urban aid. The 1968 presidential campaign was conducted in a political atmosphere superheated not only by urban unrest, but also by the Vietnam War—and white suburbanites placed the blame squarely on the Democratic Party. These disaffected voters did not lack for alternatives. Republican Richard Nixon, careful to avoid overtly racist appeals, made "law and order" a cornerstone of his campaign. Independent George Wallace struck a harshly populist tone, accusing Democratic leaders of losing touch with the working and middle classes.

The political chasm between cities and suburbs widened drastically in 1968, as seen in metropolitan Baltimore. Democratic nominee Hubert Humphrey drew 61.6 percent of the votes within the city of Baltimore, but just 34.6 percent in Baltimore's suburbs. Humphrey's urban–suburban gap of 27 percentage points was much larger than those for previous Democratic nominees. Franklin Roosevelt's disparity between Baltimore and suburban support had been only 10.8 points in 1940, Harry Truman's was 9.9 points in 1948, John Kennedy's was 16.5 points in 1960. Humphrey would have been satisfied with any of those performances, but instead slipped badly in the suburbs. The resulting gap was 10.5 points wider in the Baltimore area than Kennedy's had been just eight years before:

Gap between Dem Percent of the Vote in Mother Cities and Suburbs (in percentage points)			
Metro Area	1960	1964	1968	1960–68 Change
Baltimore	16.5	17.0	27.0	+10.5
Saint Louis	13.0	13.4	21.2	+ 8.2
Denver	7.7	7.1	13.4	+ 5.7
Detroit	19.3	13.0	23.1	+ 3.8
San Francisco	9.5	7.9	12.3	+ 2.8
New York City	19.3	12.5	21.3	+ 2.0
Philadelphia	23.5	13.7	21.9	− 1.6

Source: Author's analysis of official election returns.

Suburbia had turned its back on the Republicans in 1964. The party's conservative nominee, Barry Goldwater, did not win a single electoral vote from any suburban state, being swept 252 to 0 by Johnson, who was en route to an Electoral College landslide of 486 to 52. One of Nixon's major accomplishments in 1968 was to reverse Goldwater's miserable performance and restore the GOP to suburban preeminence.

Times were different, to be sure. Goldwater had faced the difficult task of stirring Americans numbed by the recent Kennedy assassination; Nixon found voters in a more receptive mood after Watts, Newark, Detroit, and four years of Vietnam. But their styles also were different. Goldwater was blunt, caustic, and seemingly unconcerned about his image. His slogan was typically defiant: "In your heart, you know he's right." Nixon was low-key, cautious, and vague. His tagline was inoffensive: "This time, vote like your whole world depended on it."

Nixon's cooler approach played better in suburbia. He edged Humphrey by 510,000 popular votes nationwide, carrying the Electoral College by a margin of 301 to 191. Suburban states held the balance of power, giving Nixon 169 electoral votes, 56 percent of his total.*

Breaking Ties

If suburbanites thought that President Nixon could shield them from race-related controversies, they were mistaken.

The Supreme Court, which was safely beyond the president's control, also was considerably more liberal than Nixon. It ruled in a 1971 case (*Swann* v. *Charlotte-Mecklenburg Board of Education*) that school systems could adopt desegregation plans that bused students outside of their neighborhoods. White students could be sent to historically black schools; blacks could be bused to previously all-white schools. The howl of protest from the suburban middle class was instant and sharp.

Lower courts interpreted *Swann* in the broadest possible manner, insisting that city–suburban borders could not serve as barriers to racial equality. A federal judge in Virginia ordered busing between Richmond's largely black schools and its two largely white suburban counties. Another federal judge mandated busing across county lines in the Detroit area. The battle for civil rights was no longer a distant

---

*Wallace's slashing style, on the other hand, was not to the liking of most suburbanites, who still remembered his strident opposition to integration while governor of Alabama. Wallace received 13.5 percent support nationwide, but only 9.0 percent in suburban states.

drama that suburbanites watched on television. It was now a real, live issue in their own neighborhoods.[40]

The Supreme Court eventually reversed itself, ruling in the 1974 case of *Milliken* v. *Bradley* that students could *not* be bused between different governmental jurisdictions, but suburbanites were not reassured. They had chosen suburban life because it was less congested, offered a wider selection of homes, had better schools, and seemed more family-oriented than life in the big city. Perhaps the greatest advantage was the sense of control the suburbs gave them. They were able to live in stable neighborhoods where everyone was of their kind—same family structures, same income levels, same color. But *Swann* had shaken their faith. They now worried that the big city's chaotic, racially diverse lifestyle might infiltrate suburbia.

Nixon understood this concern, denouncing the federal courts with strong anti-busing rhetoric. But the Democrats blithely ignored it, holding fast to Clark Clifford's time-tested formula that focused on urban and minority voters. What worked for Truman, they thought, would work for them. The 1972 Democratic convention enthusiastically endorsed busing as a tool for desegregation. "They just lost Michigan to the Republicans today with their busing plank," moaned former Johnson aide Ben Wattenberg after a Democratic platform committee meeting. "No one seemed impressed by the fact that in Macomb County, they voted against busing in a referendum last fall by 14–1."[41]

Macomb County, Michigan, indeed deserved closer attention. Macomb, northeast of Detroit, was largely rural and marginally Democratic until the mid-1940s, when the postwar exodus began altering both characteristics. The more affluent refugees from Detroit moved northwest to Oakland County, but the working class—those assembly-line stalwarts who manned the city's gigantic auto plants—streamed into Macomb, bringing their core beliefs in the United Auto Workers and the Democratic Party. Their impact on the county's political makeup was unmistakable, as John Kennedy received almost 63 percent of the vote in Macomb in 1960, Lyndon Johnson almost 75 percent in 1964.

Macomb County evolved into such a Democratic stronghold that it virtually mirrored the results from Wayne County, which included Detroit. The gap between Johnson's shares in the two counties in 1964 was just 1.5 percentage points:

Dem Percentage of County Vote

Election	Macomb	Wayne	Gap (in percentage points)
1940	53.8	61.6	7.8
1944	52.1	63.4	11.3
1948	53.0	57.9	4.9
1952	49.1	57.4	8.3
1956	51.7	57.9	6.2
1960	62.8	66.0	3.2
1964	74.5	76.0	1.5
1968	55.2	63.2	8.0

Source: Author's analysis of official election returns.

The controversy over cross-county busing abruptly ended the affair between Macomb and the Democrats. Richard Nixon, who had been brusquely dismissed by the county's voters in 1960 and 1968, suddenly became their champion. They rewarded him in 1972 with a 65,000-vote margin over George McGovern. Never again would Macomb march in lockstep with the Democrats of Detroit and Wayne County:

Dem Percentage of County Vote

Election	Macomb	Wayne	Gap (in percentage points)
1972	34.9	53.3	18.4
1976	46.9	60.1	13.2
1980	40.4	58.6	18.2
1984	33.3	57.2	23.9
1988	38.8	60.2	21.4
1992	37.4	60.4	23.0
1996	49.5	69.0	19.5

Source: Author's analysis of official election returns.

The Michigan Democratic Party grew to be so worried by its precipitous decline in Macomb County that it commissioned a study in 1985. Analyst Stanley Greenberg combed through election returns, conducted polls, and convened five focus groups. He concluded that Macomb's white suburbanites had become bitterly disillusioned with their former party because they believed it was more concerned about African-Americans than about the white middle class.

"Blacks constitute the explanation for their vulnerability and for almost everything that has gone wrong in their lives," Greenberg wrote of the county's lapsed Democrats. "Not being black is what constitutes being middle class; not living with blacks is what makes a neighborhood a decent place to live."[42]

Too Late to Operate

Big cities had been losing momentum ever since World War II, much as a freight train loses speed on a steep uphill grade. The total population of America's ninety-three mother cities increased by 12.4 percent during the 1940s, 5.2 percent in the 1950s, and 3.0 percent in the 1960s. Optimists could argue that cities were continuing to grow, but most observers noted the ominous trend.

The urban express ground to a halt in the 1970s, then reversed engines. Mother cities were being drained by white flight in the post-Watts, post-*Swann* era. They collectively lost 2.85 million residents between 1970 and 1980, a decline of 6.1 percent. The population of New York City plummeted by 824,000; Chicago by 364,000; Detroit by 311,000; Cleveland by 177,000; and Saint Louis by 169,000 in just ten years.

Suburbs, meanwhile, continued to expand briskly, adding 16.6 million residents in the 1960s and 12.5 million in the 1970s. Nearly four of every ten Americans were suburbanites by 1980; less than two of ten lived in mother cities:*

	Population			Share of U.S. Total (%)		
	1960	1970	1980	1960	1970	1980
Inner America						
Mother cities	45,157,927	46,494,108	43,642,039	25.2	22.9	19.3
Suburbs	60,082,442	76,697,744	89,156,019	33.5	37.7	39.4
Outer America						
Fringe metros	31,362,899	36,583,622	44,462,365	17.5	18.0	19.6
Nonmetro areas	42,719,907	43,436,452	49,285,382	23.8	21.4	21.8

Source: Author's analysis of U.S. Census Bureau data.

Mother cities were losing in several other ways.

- They were losing corporate headquarters. *Fortune* magazine annually compiles a list of the nation's 500 largest companies. Fully 140 were based in New York City in 1956. Only ninety-eight remained by 1974; the others slipped off to suburbia or fringe metros. This exodus was repeated across the nation. In 1956 Chicago headquartered forty-seven *Fortune* 500 companies, but this number dropped to thirty-three in 1974. Pittsburgh went from twenty-two to fifteen, while Detroit fell from eighteen to six.[43]
- They were losing jobs. Many large downtown-based companies

---

*See Appendix D for another way of demonstrating the rapid pace of suburban development.

were spinning off accounting, data processing, and other back-office functions to suburban offices; others moved completely. Suburbia, as a result, was supplying a majority of the jobs in nine of the nation's fifteen largest metro areas by 1970.[44]

- They were losing stores. What author Joel Garreau referred to as the "malling of America" reached its zenith in the 1970s.[45] Retailers scrambled for suburban locations that would offer easy access to their customers, especially the affluent residents of exclusive suburbs. Downtown was dismissed as an unsafe and inconvenient destination for shopping.
- They were losing political clout. The District of Columbia, Hawaii, New York, and Tennessee were the only city states in 1972. Suburban states reached a critical milestone the same year, extending their domain to 277 electoral votes, thereby attaining a majority in the Electoral College for the first time. There were twenty-one suburban-dominated states by 1980, wielding 281 electoral votes.[46]

These demographic, economic, and political shifts shredded the bonds that once linked cities and suburbs. The Detroit area, for example, had been reasonably unified as late as 1960. The urban core still had much in common with its outlying communities. Their populations were comparable: Detroit, 1.67 million; suburbs, 2.09 million. They both had sizable white majorities: 71 percent of city residents, 96 percent of suburbanites. And the aggregate income for all Detroiters ($3.35 billion) was competitive with the total for suburban residents ($4.73 billion).[47]

But any sense of shared purpose vanished after the 1967 riot and the controversy a few years later over city-suburban busing. Detroit shrank to less than half the size of its suburbs by 1980. Nearly two-thirds of city residents were black by then, contrasting sharply with lily-white suburbia. And Detroit's economic clout had eroded to less than 22 percent of the metro area's aggregate income:

	Detroit			Suburbs		
	1960	1970	1980	1960	1970	1980
Population (millions)	1.67	1.51	1.20	2.09	2.69	2.84
White residents (%)	70.8	55.5	34.4	96.2	96.0	93.7
Adults with college degrees (%)	5.3	6.2	8.3	8.3	11.5	16.9
Aggregate income (billions)	$3.35	$3.83	$7.48	$4.73	$11.87	$27.10
Unemployment rate (%)	9.9	7.2	18.5	5.9	4.8	9.3

Source: Author's analysis of U.S. Census Bureau data.

Suburban commuters unsurprisingly found the decaying central business district less and less attractive. Thirty-four percent of all workers who lived in Detroit's suburbs in 1960 worked in the city; only 17 percent had that distinction in 1980. More alarming was the evolution of a reverse commuting pattern, which once would have been impossible to imagine. Fully 35 percent of the workers who lived in Detroit in 1980 traveled to jobs in the suburbs.[48]

Detroit was not alone. The same depressing story was unfolding to various degrees in mother cities across the country. Officials in Saint Louis—which would lose 40 percent of its population between 1960 and 1980—turned to the Rand Corporation in desperation in 1973. Rand's experts advised surrender, contending that the city of Saint Louis would never regain regional dominance. They recommended that the city strive to be "one suburb among many in metropolitan Saint Louis," no better and no more powerful than its neighbors.[49]

That was tough medicine to take. An even more distasteful prescription was written for New York City, whose tax base was shrinking as rapidly as its expenses were increasing. The once-proud city was forced into bankruptcy in 1975, reduced to begging for state and federal bailouts. "Make the patient as comfortable as possible; it's too late to operate," grumbled historian Lewis Mumford, who loved cities.[50] An even harsher assessment came in 1980 from George Sternlieb, director of the Rutgers University Center for Urban Policy Research. "It takes a man who's been shot in the head a while to realize he's dead," he wrote. "New York may not realize it, but if you look at the numbers, it's clear that New York is dead."[51]

An Era of Limits

Enter Ronald Reagan.

The amiable Californian had run for president twice before—briefly in 1968, intensely in 1976—falling short of the nomination both times. But 1980 was his year. Reagan defeated a small army of foes for the GOP nomination, then buried the Democratic incumbent, Jimmy Carter, in a November landslide. Reagan rolled up 489 votes to Carter's 49 in the Electoral College. His margin in suburban states was 253 to 28.

Reagan, the fourth postwar Republican president, was unlike his three predecessors. Eisenhower had been apolitical, serenely willing to accept Democratic social programs. Nixon had talked tough, but was surprisingly generous with cities, increasing their direct federal aid from $14 billion in 1969 to $26.8 billion in 1974.[52] Gerald Ford had reached his political maturity in Congress, where bipartisan cooperation was prized above all else.

Reagan did not look to any of these men for guidance; his spiritual father was Barry Goldwater, the Republican nominee who had performed so abysmally in 1964. Reagan, like Goldwater, was a staunch conservative, an outspoken critic of federal social programs, and a happy warrior in partisan politics. The sharpest difference between the two was in the effectiveness of their campaigns against Democratic presidents. Suburbanites curtly rejected Goldwater, but warmly embraced Reagan:

Area	1964 GOP Margin	1980 GOP Margin	Reagan Gain
Baltimore suburbs	Lost by 57,689	Won by 50,509	108,198
Denver suburbs	Lost by 45,013	Won by 147,250	192,263
Detroit suburbs	Lost by 419,768	Won by 190,155	609,923
New York City suburbs	Lost by 493,899	Won by 648,691	1,142,590
Philadelphia suburbs	Lost by 209,215	Won by 261,785	471,000
Saint Louis suburbs	Lost by 187,784	Won by 110,908	298,692
Washington suburbs	Lost by 151,923	Won by 115,348	267,271

Source: Author's analysis of official election returns.

Why the large disparity? Style was a factor, of course. Goldwater came across as a curmudgeon, Reagan as a kindly uncle. The political climate also was important. Goldwater had the misfortune of facing Lyndon Johnson shortly after the Kennedy assassination, Reagan the good luck of challenging Jimmy Carter when unemployment was over 7 percent, interest rates were soaring, and the public was deeply frustrated by the taking of American hostages in Iran.

But a deeper force also had been at work for several years.

Arab nations, angered by U.S. support of Israel during the 1973 Yom Kippur war, had slapped an embargo on oil shipments that October. America weathered the crisis only by taking extreme measures, including limited gas rationing, higher gasoline prices, and lower speed limits. These were bitter pills for a society that relied so heavily on the automobile. Even worse was the resulting inflationary pressure. Oil prices doubled between 1973 and 1975, forcing up the costs of transporting food and manufactured goods to market—hitting everyone in the pocketbook. A salary of $10,000 in 1973, a decent wage at the time, was worth the equivalent of just $4,880 by 1981.[53]

The suburban middle class, whose very existence depended on the automobile and an expanding economy, quite naturally felt threatened. Its concerns were heightened when oil prices soared again between 1978 and 1980, reigniting the inflationary spiral.

Nor was that all. American pride suffered two serious wounds in the early 1970s. The Vietnam War slogged to an unsatisfactory conclusion, bitterly dividing the country and destroying America's myth of military invincibility. The Watergate crisis soon followed, raising serious doubts about the effectiveness of the political system, not to mention the honesty of elected officials. These events stripped Americans of their customary optimism, leaving them confused about their nation's course and worried about its prospects.

A new breed of politician emerged from this malaise. The first to attain prominence was Jerry Brown, a somewhat eccentric Democrat who in 1974 was elected governor of California, where 60 percent of voters lived in suburbs. He insisted that America had entered an "era of limits." It was a mistake to believe that government could solve all of the nation's problems, said Brown, who advocated balanced budgets and a leaner bureaucracy. The nation was unaccustomed to hearing such pronouncements from a leading Democrat—an heir, as it were, to Franklin Roosevelt's New Deal and Lyndon Johnson's Great Society—but it shared Brown's scorn for traditional political labels. "Is it a liberal program? Is it a conservative program?" he asked. "It's *my* program." Suburban voters applauded.[54]

Another new-style Democrat, Jimmy Carter, emerged from obscurity to win the presidency in 1976. He was the beneficiary as Americans sought to punish the Republicans for Nixon's Watergate sins, yet his victory was surprisingly fragile. The former Georgia governor forged an unusual coalition of voters from big cities, fringe metros, and the rural South to edge Gerald Ford in the Electoral College, 297 to 240. Carter actually lost the suburban states, 171 to 109, the first victorious candidate since Truman in 1948 to do so.*

The new president accepted Brown's theory of an era of limits. "Government cannot solve our problems," Carter declared. "It can't set our goals. It cannot define our vision. Government cannot eliminate poverty or provide a bountiful economy or reduce inflation or *save our cities*."[55] Big-city mayors rightly considered these words ominous. Carter would scale back or eliminate several federal aid programs for cities, starting a process that his successor would accelerate.

The president was reflecting his times. The middle class, feeling safe and secure in the early and mid-1960s, had not objected when

---

*It is worth noting that Truman's and Carter's coalitions dissolved soon after their victories. Both ended their terms with low popularity ratings, and both were repudiated in the next election. Truman's designated heir, Adlai Stevenson, was routed in 1952; Carter himself was defeated handily in 1980. So much for the advisability of governing without suburban support.

Kennedy and Johnson greatly expanded the federal government. But its equanimity disintegrated during the chaotic 1970s. Suburbanites now were worried about their own survival; they had no interest in America's cities, nor in the minorities and poor people who lived within them. California reflected the national mood when it approved Proposition 13 in June 1978, mandating a statewide rollback of property tax rates (which, in turn, would lead to cuts in social services) and launching a coast-to-coast tax revolt. Sixty-seven percent of suburban voters supported Proposition 13, supplying three-quarters of its statewide margin of 1.95 million votes.[56]

Carter knew his best strategy in such a climate was to hew to the middle of the road, but two competitors pushed him leftward during the 1980 campaign. The first was Senator Edward Kennedy, who unsuccessfully challenged the president for the Democratic nomination, but had better luck spicing up the party's platform. "The result was that some planks in the platform were much more liberal than either the general public or I wanted," Carter later lamented.[57] Independent candidate John Anderson carried the liberal torch in the fall, espousing a wide range of causes that appealed to Kennedy supporters. Carter feared that if he steered his party too far in a moderate direction, millions of Democrats might jump on the Anderson bandwagon.

The stage was set for Reagan's ascension. John Kennedy had ushered in the 1960s with a challenge. "And so, my fellow Americans," he implored in his inaugural address, "ask not what your country can do for you; ask what you can do for your country." But such idealism could not sway the nervous, disillusioned suburbanites of 1980. They were less interested in national issues, more concerned with themselves. Reagan accurately sensed their mood, asking voters, "Are *you* better off than you were four years ago?"

Carter's chief aide, Hamilton Jordan, did not mask his contempt for Reagan's tactics. Yet Jordan ruefully conceded that Carter, in a sense, had paved the way for his successor. "What a narrow and selfish premise, I thought, asking people to choose their president based solely on their present condition," he later wrote. "Nevertheless, it was our idea, and now Reagan had turned it against us."[58]

The Reagan Revolution

Ronald Reagan took Washington by storm. Not since Franklin Roosevelt had a new president been so determined to change profoundly the way America was run. "We are a nation that has a government—not the other way around," Reagan declared in his first inaugural address. "It is time to check and reverse the growth of government which shows signs of having grown beyond the consent of the governed."[59] Democratic congressional leaders pledged to block his efforts, but Reagan eventually achieved several of his revolutionary goals:

- He stepped up the urban-aid reductions that Carter had initiated. The cumulative impact on city treasuries was devastating. Baltimore, for example, funded 20 percent of its 1978 budget with federal money, a figure that dropped to 6 percent by 1985. Chicago's share fell from 27 percent to 15 percent during the same period, while Cleveland's dropped from 33 percent to 20 percent.[60]
- He gutted the public housing program. Federal agencies constructed 68,500 units in 1978, mostly in inner cities. The grand total for 1985 was a paltry 1,426.[61]
- He scaled back social programs for the poor and disadvantaged. Twenty-two percent of Carter's final budget had been earmarked for such discretionary domestic spending; the 1989 share was less than 15 percent. Reagan transferred authority for some social programs to the states without corresponding funding; he killed others outright.[62]
- He cut taxes for those in upper income brackets. A study by H&R Block, the nationwide tax-preparation company, found that the average tax bill for someone earning $50,000 had increased 7.75 percent between 1977 and 1990. The bill for someone earning $200,000 had dropped 27.75 percent.[63]

A 1985 *Los Angeles Times* study quantified the impact of the Reagan revolution, showing clearly that the suburban middle class was prospering while the urban poor were suffering. The *Times* compared a fictional family headed by two adults who jointly earned $40,000 to $80,000 a year with a single worker who was paid less than $10,000 annually. The middle-class couple saved $3,080 from tax cuts during Reagan's first four years, but lost only $170 in government benefits due to spending cuts. Its net gain: $2,910. The low-income worker, on the other hand, gained only $20 from tax cuts, but saw $410 in benefits slip away. His net loss: $390.[64]

Outraged liberals resolved to turn the 1984 election into a referendum on Reagan's policies. Their champion—and the eventual Democratic nominee—was former Vice President Walter Mondale, whose voting record in the Senate had mirrored that of his mentor, Hubert Humphrey, a patron saint of American liberalism. "They were

Tweedle-Dum and Tweedle-Dee," recalled a Minnesota congressman. "It would have taken major surgery to separate the two."[65]

Mondale drew the issues sharply, blasting the Reagan administration for providing "government of the rich, by the rich, and for the rich." He condemned the "utter moral bankruptcy" of Reagan's efforts to dismantle the network of social programs constructed by Democratic presidents from Roosevelt to Johnson. He even did the unthinkable, pledging to raise taxes.[66] The president countered serenely that it was a time for optimism—and certainly not the time for tax hikes. "America is coming back," he declared, "and is more confident than ever about the future."[67]

Suburbia left no doubt where it stood, supporting Reagan overwhelmingly. The president received 65 percent of the vote in the suburbs outside New York City, 64 percent outside Baltimore, 63 percent outside Philadelphia, and 62 percent outside Saint Louis. Reagan's massive suburban majorities obliterated the smaller margins that Mondale accumulated in mother cities:

	Winner's Margins	
Metro Area	Mother Cities	Suburbs
Baltimore	Mondale by 122,157	Reagan by 163,982
Detroit	Mondale by 246,103	Reagan by 449,077
New York City	Mondale by 491,558	Reagan by 923,631
Philadelphia	Mondale by 234,191	Reagan by 362,267
Saint Louis	Mondale by 51,298	Reagan by 212,679
San Francisco	Mondale by 103,059	Reagan by 117,513

Source: Author's analysis of official election returns.

Never had the emerging political power of suburbia been so starkly demonstrated. Reagan won 278 electoral votes from suburban states alone, eight votes above the threshold for victory. Mondale's campaign, eager to prove the vitality of urban liberalism, instead had exposed its utter weakness.

The Democratic Party, battered and dispirited in the wake of the 1984 election, now faced the crucial question of choosing its future direction. Competing schools of thought emerged, each headed by a candidate who had challenged Mondale unsuccessfully in the 1984 primaries.

Colorado Senator Gary Hart advocated a turn away from traditional liberalism. "The New Deal has run its course. The party is over," he insisted.[68] Hart had much in common with Jerry Brown. Both were Westerners; both represented suburban states; both were political loners who had attained high office in 1974, the first post-Watergate election.

Hart and Brown generally agreed that the party should steer a moderate course. They believed the federal government should be fiscally prudent, environmentally aware, and technologically oriented. They weren't conservatives, but they doubted the effectiveness of the massive social programs that were a Democratic hallmark. Perhaps the biggest difference between them was that Hart placed a much greater emphasis on generational politics. "It is time for the old order to pass, for the old establishment politicians to give way," he said. "It is time for our voices to be heard at last."[69]

Jesse Jackson, a black political activist from Chicago, issued a similar call. "It's time for a change," he told his supporters. "Our time has come!" But Jackson did not share Hart's aims. He embraced the Democratic Party's urban liberal tradition, contending that government had a moral duty to help minorities, the poor, and the disadvantaged.

Jackson's message galvanized the African-American electorate in 1984, but failed to draw more than 9 percent of the white vote in any primary. Such political considerations were irrelevant, he insisted. What mattered was whether the party lived up to its obligations. "I am troubled by those who have shifted us away from the moral center, who leave working-class people full of anxiety and the real poor without a safety net," he would say years later. "Within the Democratic Party, there will be a struggle for its soul, and its soul must not be a poll."[70]

Suburbia in Command

The anticipated battle for the Democratic Party's soul was disappointingly anticlimactic. Hart, the early frontrunner for the 1988 nomination, was derailed by a tawdry sex scandal before the primaries began. Jackson improved upon his 1984 performance—even winning the primary in virtually all-white Vermont—but he never could convince party leaders to take him seriously.

Most of the remaining contenders scrambled for Hart's mantle. Bruce Babbitt, Joseph Biden, Richard Gephardt, and Al Gore all presented themselves as advocates of new ideas, representatives of a new generation. Jackson and Paul Simon were the only remaining champions of traditional, Clark Clifford-style liberalism.

That left the political center to the governor of Massachusetts, Michael Dukakis, who ran a strangely hybrid campaign. Dukakis had been unswervingly true to liberal causes throughout his career: upholding the right to abortion, opposing the death penalty, speaking out against nuclear proliferation. "We have a responsibility to create

... a society in which every citizen—and I mean every citizen—can have the kind of opportunity that is part and parcel of the American dream," he said in words that Jackson himself might have used.[71] Yet Dukakis also was somewhat of a technocrat, reveling in the arcane details of government management. He maintained publicly that he, too, belonged to the new breed.

Dukakis had a foot in each camp, yet belonged to neither. He offered the Democrats a bridge, an opportunity to defer internecine war and make common cause against Reagan's Republican successor, Vice President George Bush. He secured the nomination with little difficulty.

The Democrats entered the fall campaign with high hopes. Opinion polls showed Dukakis comfortably ahead in several suburban states; he maintained a nationwide lead of more than 10 percentage points over the vice president. Yet, as the November election drew closer, the Republicans went on the offensive and began to close the gap:

- They effectively tied the Democratic nominee to fellow Massachusetts politicians Ted Kennedy and Tip O'Neill, both devotees of big government. The message: Dukakis was a typical tax-and-spend liberal.
- They claimed that Boston's waterfront was "the dirtiest harbor in America." The message: Dukakis not only governed a big city, but he did it ineffectively.
- They blasted the governor for furloughing Willie Horton, a black convicted murderer who committed rape and assault after being let out of prison. The message: Dukakis was soft on crime, not to mention chummy with minorities.

Bush had pledged a "kinder, gentler" approach to government, a promise now conveniently forgotten. The vice president lashed out at Dukakis, depicting him as a zealot who threatened America's social stability. "I'm not going to let that liberal governor divide this nation," Bush declared defiantly. "His attempt to divide Americans by class is going to fail."[72]

Dukakis had no such designs, of course, but he strangely refused to counterattack, allowing the Republicans to cement his image as a classic big-city liberal. His suburban support eroded accordingly. Dukakis had entered the summer with a 14-point lead in New Jersey—where 88 percent of all voters were suburbanites—but it melted under the Bush attack. Suburban voters generally were satisfied with America's direction; they wanted no return to liberal policies they considered failures. "Bush has a quasi-incumbent status now; people see him as part of

Ronald Reagan's success," said New Jersey pollster Cliff Zukin. "If I'm a voter and I don't have any real reason not to, I'm going for George Bush."[73] And so they did. Bush won in New Jersey by 420,000 votes.

Dukakis's hopes vanished for a breakthrough in suburbia, and with them went the election. Suburban states gave Bush 240 electoral votes, Dukakis just 48. The vice president carried the Electoral College with ease, 426 to 111.

The Democrats had been disheartened by Mondale's loss four years before, but consoled themselves that nobody could have beaten a president as popular as Reagan. They found no such solace in 1988: Bush wasn't the incumbent, nor was he charismatic. His victory could be attributed only to a campaign strategy that had targeted the suburban white middle class, simultaneously scaring it with predictions of Democratic liberalism run amok and enticing it with pledges to restrain taxes, promote education, and protect the environment.

Dukakis struggled to satisfy several key interest groups—urban liberals, minorities, organized labor—but Bush had the luxury of focusing on suburbia, the new mother lode of American politics. Big cities didn't even warrant his attention; the exodus of the white middle class had virtually drained them of Republicans. The city of Baltimore, for example, accounted for just 13 percent of all GOP votes within its metro area by 1988:*

Votes in Baltimore Metro for GOP Nominee

Election	Baltimore	Suburbs	City Share of GOP Metro Total (%)
1940	112,364	56,247	66.6
1944	112,817	66,120	63.0
1948	110,879	72,141	60.6
1952	166,605	136,171	55.0
1956	178,244	166,904	51.6
1960	114,705	160,114	41.7
1964	76,089	131,683	36.6
1968	80,146	186,019	30.1
1972	119,486	313,237	27.6
1976	81,762	269,295	23.3
1980	57,902	277,526	17.3
1984	80,120	373,137	17.7
1988	59,089	384,094	13.3

Source: Author's analysis of official election returns.

Baltimore's political evolution was typical. Mother cities—a powerful force in both parties in 1940—had become virtually impotent.

---

*Baltimore technically is part of the Washington-Baltimore metro area (see Appendix C), but this book recognizes Anne Arundel, Baltimore, Carroll, Harford, Howard, and Queen Anne's counties as Baltimore suburbs.

They lacked any influence in the Republican Party, and they no longer supplied enough votes to carry the Democrats to victory. Suburbia was in command.

The 1990 census would dramatize the point, reporting that more than 102 million Americans were living in suburbs, only 44.5 million in mother cities. Suburban population had expanded at the breathtaking pace of 229 percent since 1940; mother cities were up by less than 17 percent. Suburbia, as a result, was home to 41 percent of all Americans in 1990. The other three population sectors—mother cities, fringe metros, and nonmetro areas—were far behind, each accounting for roughly one-fifth of the nation's residents:

	Population		Growth Rate (%)	Share of U.S. Total (%)	
	1940	1990	1940–1990	1940	1990
Inner America					
Mother cities	38,167,315	44,486,735	+ 16.6	28.9	17.9
Suburbs	31,133,540	102,305,750	+228.6	23.6	41.1
Outer America					
Fringe metros	20,128,851	51,313,129	+154.9	15.2	20.6
Nonmetro areas	42,734,863	50,604,259	+ 18.4	32.3	20.3

Source: Author's analysis of U.S. Census Bureau data.

Democrats had ignored these changing demographics for too long, clinging to liberal, urban-oriented policies that led inevitably to a series of landslide defeats. Carter was saddled with Ted Kennedy's platform in 1980, Mondale defiantly advertised his liberalism in 1984, Dukakis made no effort to moderate his image in 1988—and the Republicans buried them by the combined margin of 32.4 million popular votes. The outcome was even worse in the Electoral College: 1,440 electoral votes for Reagan and Bush, 173 for the three Democrats. Suburban states supported the GOP by a count of 771 electoral votes to 86.

Columnist George Will, surveying the wreckage of the Dukakis campaign, wondered if the Democrats would ever update their tactics to meet the new realities of American politics. "How many times does the electorate have to hit the Democratic Party across the bridge of the nose with a crowbar before the party gets the point?" he asked.[74]

It was an awfully good question.

3 No Longer Sub to the Urb: 1991–1996

Most members of Congress headed up Capitol Hill on the morning of January 12, 1991, with mixed feelings of excitement and dread.

Their excitement was natural. This, after all, would be their day of reckoning. They were being asked to authorize military action to drive Iraqi troops from Kuwait. It was just the tenth time since 1789 that Congress had faced the question of sending American troops into battle, and Senator Robert Byrd, for one, felt the pressure of history. "I've cast 12,822 votes during my thirty-nine years in Congress," Byrd told his colleagues. "But this vote is the most important vote that I shall have cast in my career."[1]

Their dread was understandable, too. The ghosts of Vietnam still swirled through the Capitol. Congress had approved the 1964 Tonkin Gulf resolution with virtually no dissent, paving the way for a decade of bloodshed in Southeast Asia. Would today's vote have the same unhappy result? Would thousands of American soldiers return from the Persian Gulf in body bags? Would angry constituents eventually punish those politicians who approved the use of force?

George Bush sought to allay Congress's fears by portraying the issue in stark shades of black and white. Iraq's invasion of Kuwait in August 1990 was an immoral act, the president said, and the United States and its allies were obligated to undo it. He likened Iraqi dictator Saddam Hussein to Adolf Hitler, warning that Hussein would commit further atrocities if Congress refused to act. Roughly 400,000 American troops had been sent to Saudi Arabia during the previous five months. They were ready to move toward Kuwait, pending approval from the House and Senate. "The facts are clear," Bush wrote three days before the vote. "The choice unambiguous: Right versus wrong."[2]

At least half of Congress seemed to favor Bush's call for military action, but few members believed the decision would be as simple as the president described it. "Standing up for our principles is an American tradition," Bush declared.[3] But what principle was involved? Small wars raged constantly around the globe. The United States stayed ideologically neutral in most of those conflicts—and did not commit its troops to any. What made Kuwait so special?

Oil.

America depended on foreign sources for almost half of the oil it consumed; Kuwait and Saudi Arabia were leading suppliers. The men and women assembling in the Capitol that January morning knew the consequences if the flow of oil from the Middle East were disrupted. They remembered how the energy crises of 1973–75 and 1978–80 had triggered sharp increases in gasoline prices, which in turn had fueled rampaging inflation. And, most of all, they recalled how the electorate had turned against those politicians who tried, and failed, to solve America's energy problems. Jimmy Carter's unhappy fate was on the minds of many.

Bush continued to preach about protecting "the integrity" of Kuwait and Saudi Arabia. He insisted that American action in the Middle East would "define who we are and what we believe." But his words could not obscure one simple fact: The Persian Gulf War was about oil.[4] It was about safeguarding the energy sources that allowed people in the United States to own large houses and commute long distances to work. It was about maintaining Americans' freedom to live where they wanted, keep their homes as warm and bright as they wanted, and drive their cars when and where they wanted.

It was, in essence, about protecting the suburban way of life, an objective that almost everyone understood:

- Republican leaders knew what was at stake. Senator John McCain, a plain-spoken Arizona Republican who had been a prisoner of war in North Vietnam, wholeheartedly supported Bush's request, but not for Bush's stated reasons. McCain said that America's top priority was to stop Hussein before he gained control of the world's oil supplies. "We cannot risk putting that capacity in his hands, the capacity of destroying the world's economies," he said.[5]
- Their Democratic counterparts knew. The chairman of the House Armed Services Committee, Wisconsin Democrat Les Aspin, detected the kernel of self-interest beneath the president's rhetorical fog. "This is much more important than (previous U.S. military actions in) Panama, Libya, or Grenada," he said in August 1990. "What we are talking about is our economic well-being."[6]
- Bush's cabinet members knew. Secretary of State James Baker, in an unguarded moment, was asked to express the rationale for the war as simply as he could. "Jobs," he replied.[7]
- Impartial analysts knew. Tom Mann, director of governmental affairs at the Brookings Institution, said economic considera-

tions had persuaded him that America must act. "This is bald self-interest we're talking about here," he said.[8]

- Washington columnists knew. George Will laughed at Bush's high-minded references to principle. Will wrote: "That is principle, spelled p-e-t-r-o-l-e-u-m."[9]
- And average citizens knew, too. Fifty percent of Americans believed the president's Middle Eastern strategy was motivated by his desire to protect oil supplies, according to a bipartisan survey conducted in December 1990 by former pollsters for the Bush and Dukakis campaigns. Just 28 percent thought that Bush's goal was the liberation of Kuwait, while 14 percent said the aim was to neutralize Iraq's military capability.[10]

One of these typical Americans—James Weihing of Portland, Oregon—offered perhaps the best analysis of America's stance in the Middle East. The sixty-four-year-old Weihing sat with a *Los Angeles Times* reporter on a bench overlooking Portland's Pioneer Square in the chill of early January. The reporter posed a predictable question about the nation's mood on the eve of war, and Weihing responded with two questions of his own. "If Kuwait had nothing but carrots," he asked, "would Iraq be there? Or the U.S.A.?"[11]

Everyone—even George Bush—knew the answer.

Choosing Sides

The congressional debate that January 12 was more intense and emotional than any session since the Vietnam era. Senators rose in turn at their desks to cast their votes, a formal procedure used only on the most important occasions, such as impeachments. Vice President Dan Quayle announced the final tally to a hushed chamber: fifty-two in favor, forty-seven against. The House echoed approval from its side of the Capitol, 250 to 183.

It came as no surprise that Republicans solidly supported the president. There were just five dissenting votes from the GOP: two in the Senate and three in the House. But the Democrats were sharply divided. The party's liberal wing had stood as a single bloc against a Republican president's controversial war in 1971; it equivocated under similar circumstances in 1991. A majority of Democrats eventually voted against the Gulf War, but ten senators and eighty-six House members broke ranks to back military action.

Victory on the battlefields of the Middle East followed so quickly—

and casualties were so few—that a relieved electorate soon forgot the tensions that accompanied the January roll calls. President Bush's popularity ratings soared into the political stratosphere by winter's end, briefly hovering around 90 percent. He seemed invincible.

The Democratic Party, on the other hand, was hampered by the now-widespread belief that it had opposed a just and patriotic war. "What that war vote does is reinforce the perception that Democrats are unwilling to defend the national interest," complained Al From of the Democratic Leadership Council.[12] The party's new heroes were those pragmatists who had supported military action, like Senator Joseph Lieberman. Those who had voted no, such as Sam Nunn, fell into disfavor.

Lieberman and Nunn had much in common. Both were Democratic senators from suburban states: Lieberman from Connecticut, Nunn from Georgia. And both knew the importance of foreign oil. Lieberman represented thousands of suburbanites who made agonizingly long commutes into New York City or Hartford; Nunn's suburban constituents fought dense traffic into Atlanta. Connecticut and Georgia consumed more petroleum per capita than larger states like California, New York, and Illinois did.[13]

But the two lawmakers were worlds apart philosophically. Lieberman was a liberal, certified as such by Americans for Democratic Action, which in 1990 gave him an impressive rating of 83 on its 100-point scale of liberal purity. Nunn was a conservative, still haunted by memories of his first Senate campaign in 1972, when he had struggled to keep his distance from the party's liberal national ticket. "My main tactic was to go around separating the Nunn and McGovern signs," he recalled.[14] The two men also differed in the amount of influence they wielded. Lieberman, a Senate newcomer, had little. Nunn chaired the powerful Senate Armed Services Committee.

But their votes on the war tilted the balance. Lieberman, the liberal, nonetheless decided to support the president. He suddenly was in demand, appearing on thirteen network news programs in the first four months after the fateful roll call. ABC's *Nightline* identified him as one of the biggest political winners emerging from the war. "There's a higher level of awareness about him in Washington than there is with other newcomers," said Democratic analyst Robert Beckel. The impact was obvious at home, too. Lieberman suddenly became the most popular politician in Connecticut, according to a *Hartford Courant* poll.[15]

Nunn, on the other hand, struggled to recover from his seemingly out-of-character vote against the war. Polls in Georgia showed his popularity plummeting by 10 points overall, by 20 points among young white males. Republicans who previously feared him now mocked him. Insiders who once touted him for president no longer mentioned his name. "I think the ground has gone out from under him," said analyst Kevin Phillips. "He was the Democrats' high-powered military expert. He was wrong, militarily."[16]

Politically, too.

The Pennsylvania Miracle

The Gulf War exposed the political perils awaiting those who ignored suburbia's wishes. Suburbanites held the balance of power in twenty-three states by 1991; they controlled about 40 percent of the House of Representatives, nearly half of the Senate, and almost 60 percent of the Electoral College. This new ruling class generally wasn't motivated by ideology; suburban voters didn't seem to care much about labels like "liberal" or "conservative." What mattered to them was whether their government supported their way of life—the *suburban* way of life—as Joe Lieberman and Sam Nunn could attest.

This lesson was reinforced by a second event a few months after the Gulf War. Pennsylvania Senator John Heinz, a popular Republican, died in an airplane-helicopter crash in April 1991. State law required the governor to appoint someone to warm the seat until November, when voters would elect Heinz's permanent successor.

Observers expected the appointed senator, Harris Wofford, to enjoy a few quiet months in Washington before turning his office over to Richard Thornburgh, the favorite in the fall campaign. Thornburgh was a dynamic, popular veteran of Pennsylvania politics, a former governor who also had served as George Bush's attorney general. Wofford, in contrast, was a scholarly man accustomed to working in the background; he had helped create the Peace Corps and later served as Pennsylvania's labor secretary. His gentle manners seemed unsuited for the rough and tumble of partisan politics.

A statewide poll in late spring confirmed the conventional wisdom, showing Thornburgh ahead of Wofford by the seemingly insurmountable margin of 47 percentage points. Wofford's strategists, James Carville and Paul Begala, knew their man could not close the gap—let alone win—unless he ran an unconventional campaign. Typical Democratic appeals to big cities and minorities could not derail Thornburgh. The appointed senator's only hope was to focus on the middle class, especially in the sprawling suburbs outside Philadelphia and Pittsburgh, which is what he did.

Wofford's reputation was that of a liberal in the mold of John

Kennedy and Lyndon Johnson, but he now spurned the label, calling himself a "Democrat with no prefixes." He soft-pedaled his party's advocacy of programs for the poor, contending that the best programs were those that helped *all* Americans, like the G.I. Bill that had put him through college. His goals, he promised middle-class voters, included a more efficient federal government and a tax cut. "It's time to take care of our own," he said over and over.[17]

Pennsylvanians began to get the message as the calendar flipped to October and then November. "I began to feel a surge," Wofford later told reporters. "I couldn't believe it."[18] Neither could Thornburgh, who lost an unlosable race by 10 percentage points:

	(%)		
	Wofford	**Thornburgh**	**Margin**
Statewide	55.0	45.0	Wofford by 338,774
Components (share of state vote in percent)			
Philadelphia and Pittsburgh (16.2)	74.4	25.6	Wofford by 268,230
Suburbs of two cities (37.4)	54.5	45.5	Wofford by 114,684
Other metro areas (31.4)	48.6	51.4	Thornburgh by 29,900
Nonmetro counties (15.0)	48.6	51.4	Thornburgh by 14,240

Source: Author's analysis of official election returns.

Wofford was just the fourth Democrat to be elected to the Senate from Pennsylvania in the twentieth century, thanks to hundreds of thousands of suburban Republicans who crossed party lines to support him. Democrats always won Philadelphia and Pittsburgh—as Wofford did—but historically were submerged by a suburban Republican tide. Michael Dukakis, for example, had carried Philadelphia by 230,000 votes in the 1988 presidential election, but lost its suburbs to Bush by 287,000 and lost the state as well.

Thornburgh had every reason to expect the same suburban Republican bounce in 1991. He needed just 59 percent support in the suburbs of Philadelphia and Pittsburgh to win the election, a threshold he had crossed in his races for governor, but his share of the suburban vote in the Senate race was a measly 45.5 percent.

Analysts struggled to explain the shocking turnaround in Wofford's fortunes. Most agreed that his advocacy of national health insurance had struck a chord with the middle class. (A new presidential candidate named Bill Clinton would accept this assessment, to his later regret.) But a few sage observers knew that larger forces were tugging at voters in Pennsylvania, whose economy had stagnated during the Bush presidency. The state's employment base expanded by just 0.7 percent between 1988 and 1992, compared to the national growth rate of 3.1 percent.[19] Middle-class homeowners in the Philadelphia and Pittsburgh metros had good reason to be worried.

The *Harrisburg Patriot-News* was among the few to divine the national implications of Wofford's victory. "If they have any hope of regaining the White House soon," it suggested in a post-election editorial, "Democrats must return to their traditional constituency, America's hard-pressed working people and middle class, who were the focus of Wofford's successful appeal."[20]

James Carville, soon to join the Clinton campaign, agreed. Reporters surrounded him at the victory celebration in Philadelphia, hounding him for the secret of Wofford's success. Most wanted to know if national health insurance had been the key. "The health-care issue showed that he was willing to do something different, that he was willing to talk about something different," Carville said. "*And I don't think the Republicans ever understood that it wasn't about a plan.* But it was about somebody that was willing to talk about something that mattered to people."[21]

The Death of Regionalism

It is a truism that commanders, when leading their troops into battle, tend to fight the previous war, relying on tactics that worked the last time they took the field. History tells of generals who thought the sword mightier than the musket, who unleashed cavalry against tanks, who believed that aircraft had no military use. Thus the French clung to the Maginot Line in 1940, even as the Germans outflanked it and seized Paris. Thus the Pentagon implemented a conventional strategy in Vietnam, even though it was fighting an unconventional war.

Most politicians have the same weakness, tending to imitate success stories from previous campaigns. John Kennedy contested every primary election in 1960, an unusual tactic at the time. Primaries—and candidates to run in them—proliferated after Kennedy's success. George McGovern hit the streets two years before the 1972 Democratic convention, well in advance of any other contender. Multi-year campaigns became the rule after McGovern secured his party's nomination. Jimmy Carter focused his efforts on Iowa for an entire year before its 1976 caucuses, a narrowly based strategy that held no appeal for his opponents. Iowa jumped to the top of every candidate's list of priorities after Carter reached the White House.

This tendency to live in the past never was more evident than when politicians talked about regions. They would describe each section of

America as a monolithic bloc inhabited by two-dimensional charac-
ters: the Midwest's stolid conformists and the West's rugged individuals, Eastern liberals and Southern conservatives. The South, indeed,
was the most stereotyped of the bunch. Democrats relied for decades
on the electoral votes of the "Solid South." Richard Nixon employed
his ballyhooed "Southern Strategy" to nudge it toward the Republican
column in 1968. Democratic analysts Richard Scammon and Ben Wattenberg quickly countered that America's political fate rested not with
the South, but with a new region—an anti-South, as it were—that they
named Quadcali, a combination of Northeastern and Midwestern
states (forming a *quad*rangle) and California.[22]

Politicians continued to make regional calculations into the 1990s,
even though the concept had become sadly outdated. The South
again offers the best case history. A wide electoral gap once separated
the region from the rest of America. Franklin Roosevelt, for example,
received 72.5 percent support within the South in 1940, compared to
52.0 percent outside it, a difference of 20.5 percentage points. But
Southern voters drew closer to the national trendline upon the 1976
election of Carter, their favorite son. And the rest of the nation grew
more conservative in the 1980s, increasing its sympathy for the South's
dominant philosophy. Five of the six presidential elections since 1976,
as a result, have seen a difference of less than five points between
Democratic support in the South and the rest of America:

Election	Dem Percentage of Regional Popular Vote		Gap (in percentage points)
	South	Rest of U.S.	
1940	72.5	52.0	20.5
1944	67.4	51.2	16.2
1948	52.5	49.1	3.4
1952	51.0	43.0	8.0
1956	47.3	40.9	6.4
1960	49.4	49.8	0.4
1964	51.0	63.6	12.6
1968	31.4	46.1	14.7
1972	29.0	40.0	11.0
1976	53.7	48.8	4.9
1980	44.2	39.8	4.4
1984	37.0	41.9	4.9
1988	41.0	47.4	6.4
1992	41.0	43.8	2.8
1996	45.9	50.7	4.8

Sources: Author's analysis of official election returns.

Regionalism, as any astute politician could see, was a dead issue by
the 1990s. It once made sense for a presidential candidate to tailor his

platform to win a particular section of America, but not now. Such a regional strategy could not succeed in the homogenized age of *USA Today,* Cable News Network, and the Internet.

America's sharpest division no longer was East versus West or Midwest versus South. It was city versus suburb. The candidates preparing for the 1992 election would be focusing on the twenty-three suburban states and their 320 electoral votes. Big cities controlled a paltry thirty-six electoral votes:

	States	Electoral Votes (EV)	Share of EVs (%)	EVs per State
Inner America				
City states	2	36	6.7	18.0
Suburban states	23	320	59.5	13.9
Outer America				
Fringe states	8	82	15.2	10.3
Nonmetro states	18	100	18.6	5.6

Source: Author's analysis of U.S. Census Bureau data.

A suburban strategy obviously offered the best chance of success in 1992. It had worked in the past for the Republicans; Ronald Reagan drew enough electoral votes from suburban states alone to win the 1984 election. It had worked for the Democrats; Harris Wofford's Senate seat was proof.

The only question was whether the contenders lining up for 1992 had been paying attention.

Rise of the Chameleon

Lanny Davis knew better than most what was at stake in 1992. Davis was a Democratic National Committee member from Maryland. His party historically had dominated his state; Democratic nominees carried Maryland in five of six presidential elections between 1960 and 1980. But Maryland voters subsequently drifted to the right, backing Reagan in 1984 and Bush in 1988. "We have a major problem as a party in the suburbs," Davis told a reporter as the 1992 campaign unfolded. "It's the formerly liberal '60s kids who moved to the suburbs and got progressively more conservative. We have to win those back."[23]

It was a tall order. The Democrats had not won a presidential election since 1976, and they hadn't carried suburbia since 1964. The party's recent nominees had fared poorly outside of big cities: Jimmy Carter received a scant 39.9 percent of the popular vote in suburban states in 1980, Walter Mondale drew 41.7 percent in 1984, Michael Dukakis 46.5 percent in 1988.

A typically large pack of contenders entered the 1992 race for the Democratic nomination. Three survived the early skirmishes:

- Jerry Brown, the populist gadfly who had been governor of California from 1975 to 1983, was making a comeback after nearly a decade in the political wilderness. He staked out the party's left wing. "The ruling class has lost touch with the American people," he declared. "They have lost touch because they swim in a world of privilege, power, and wealth."[24]
- Paul Tsongas, a former Massachusetts senator, seemed comfortable with the very people that Brown attacked. He placed a high priority on cutting the federal deficit and granting tax incentives to struggling companies, neither a typical Democratic cause. Critics within the party considered him too chummy with big business.
- Bill Clinton, the governor of Arkansas, positioned himself between his two opponents, insisting that he was "neither liberal nor conservative." His campaign stressed middle-class concerns, taking a tougher stand on social issues than either Mondale or Dukakis had. "No more something for nothing," was one of Clinton's constant refrains.[25]

The dilemma facing these three finalists was the one that had bedeviled all Democratic presidential contenders since the late 1960s: How could they win the favor of a generally liberal electorate in the spring, then woo a substantially more conservative group of voters in the fall? The Democratic nomination would go to the candidate who triumphed in a long series of primary elections in which urban liberals and minorities still wielded substantial clout. But the lucky nominee would need to shift gears abruptly after Labor Day to appeal to the dominant force in the general election—white, middle-class, suburban voters, most of whom were Republicans or unaffiliated with any major party.

This dichotomy was most pronounced in New York, whose Democratic primaries were dominated by its largest city. Fully 52.1 percent of the votes in the 1992 statewide Democratic primary were cast by New York City residents, compared to just 19.9 percent by voters in the adjacent suburbs. But the city's influence was muted considerably in the 1992 general election, when suburban Republicans and independents swelled the pool of voters. New York City supplied just 30.6 percent of the state's votes, 21.5 percentage points less than in the primary and barely enough to counteract its suburbs. Other mother cities suffered similar declines in political power that November, though of lesser magnitude:

	Share of 1992 Statewide Popular Vote (%)		
	Dem Primary	General	Gap (in percentage points)
Colorado			
Denver	20.3	13.9	− 6.4
Denver suburbs	44.5	46.6	+ 2.1
Maryland			
Baltimore	16.9	12.3	− 4.6
Baltimore suburbs	36.8	38.2	+ 1.4
New York			
New York City	52.1	30.6	−21.5
New York City suburbs	19.9	28.3	+ 8.4
Pennsylvania			
Philadelphia	17.2	12.9	− 4.3
Philadelphia suburbs	11.2	20.2	+ 9.0

Source: Author's analysis of official election returns.

The key was to be liberal enough to secure the Democratic nomination, but moderate enough to win the general election. Brown, a darling of suburban voters in his previous incarnation, was the most liberal of the three 1992 contenders and logically should have been the most appealing choice for urban Democrats. But he made no real effort to connect with the mosaic of racial and ethnic minorities that constituted America's big cities. Nor did Tsongas, whose base of support essentially was suburban. Clinton consequently became the urban favorite largely by default. This governor of a rural Southern state, this man who promised to remake a liberal party in a moderate image, won the crucial New York primary by rolling up a 109,000-vote margin in New York City:

	(%)			
	Brown	Clinton	Tsongas	Margin
Statewide	26.2	40.9	28.6	Clinton by 124,019
Components (share of state vote in percent)				
New York City (52.1)	25.3	46.0	24.5	Clinton by 109,008
New York City suburbs (19.9)	23.0	37.1	36.4	Clinton by 1,407
Rest of state (27.9)	30.3	34.1	30.7	Clinton by 9,773

Source: Author's analysis of official election returns.

Tsongas fought Clinton to a draw in the New York City suburbs and decisively defeated him among suburban voters in other states, such as

Maryland, where polls showed him to be the clear favorite of affluent, well-educated Democrats.[26] Tsongas won Maryland easily, carrying the Baltimore suburbs by 30,000 votes and the outlying parts of the state, including the Washington suburbs, by another 20,000. Clinton did well only in the city of Baltimore, home to one of every six primary voters:

	(%)			
	Brown	Clinton	Tsongas	Margin
Statewide	8.2	33.5	40.6	Tsongas by 40,584
Components (share of state vote in percent)				
Baltimore (16.9)	8.3	44.6	33.8	Clinton by 10,337
Baltimore suburbs (36.8)	9.0	29.2	43.8	Tsongas by 30,524
Rest of state (46.2)	7.5	32.9	40.6	Tsongas by 20,397

Source: Author's analysis of official election returns.

Tsongas, in some respects, seemed the best choice to carry the Democratic standard in the fall campaign. He possessed an impressive ability to attract suburban support, a quality sadly lacking in the party's recent nominees. Clinton had scored points with liberal Democrats by attacking Tsongas as "the best friend Wall Street has ever had," but most suburbanites saw nothing wrong with electing a president who was friendly with the financial elite.[27] Voters in the suburbs of Baltimore and Washington obviously didn't mind.

Tsongas, however, had several weaknesses. He was not as charismatic as Clinton, nor could he match the Arkansas governor's campaign treasury or organization. But Tsongas's biggest shortcoming was that he was not a political chameleon; he preached the same dry, technocratic sermon to all Democrats, even to city residents who generally found it unappealing. Clinton, on the other hand, courted liberal voters in New York City, Baltimore, and other big cities with unexpected skill, yet also remained tight with the party's moderate wing. He had been a co-founder of the Democratic Leadership Council (DLC) in 1985, helping to pull the party back toward the center after Walter Mondale's landslide defeat the year before, and had become the DLC's chairman in 1990.[28]

Clinton rolled to the nomination with ease, eliminating Tsongas and Brown weeks before the Democratic convention and turning his sights on the Republican incumbent, George Bush. Clinton seemed to be a rare Democratic nominee, more moderate than Mondale, more flexible than Dukakis, a man equally comfortable speaking the languages of urban liberals or suburban moderates. A man who could win.

It appeared he was exactly the kind of candidate Lanny Davis had been hoping for.

A New Breed of Democrat

Three promises were central to Bill Clinton's fall campaign:

- He promised to change the way Washington operated, vowing to "give this capital back to the people." He said that he would make the federal government less bureaucratic and more responsive.
- He promised to implement policies to help families. He said, for example, that he would guarantee workers time off from their jobs to handle family crises and would strive to make college more affordable.
- He promised to improve the economy.[29]

The last point was by far the most important. The national economy had slumped badly on Bush's watch. Employment, which had expanded at the impressive rate of 1.9 percent per year during the Reagan administration, was edging up just 0.8 percent a year under Bush. Several suburban states were doing even worse; Connecticut, Maryland, Massachusetts, and New Jersey actually had fewer jobs in 1992 than in 1988.[30] Bush seemed unbeatable in 1991 after his triumph in the Gulf War, but his popularity ratings unraveled so badly by the summer of 1992 that the Democrats and wealthy, independent, Texas businessman Ross Perot were eager to take him on.

Clinton was ever mindful of the issue that was foremost with voters. "It's the economy, stupid," his advisers reminded each other whenever they strayed from their main theme. But Clinton's entire platform, no matter the issue, was remarkable for the depth of its concern for the suburban middle class, concern unprecedented in recent Democratic campaigns. The nominee's inclination to hew to the middle of the road had been reinforced by his long trek through the primaries; Tsongas had proven to him that a moderate Democrat could inspire suburban support. And Clinton, a more pragmatic candidate than Mondale or Dukakis, knew exactly where the election would be won or lost.

The cornerstone of Clinton's suburban strategy was his eagerness to show that the Democratic Party would not be controlled by urban liberals or minority groups, even though they had helped him win the nomination. He kept liberals at a distance by taking moderate-to-conservative positions, pledging to cut taxes, reduce the size of government, and reform the welfare system. He neutralized the racial issue by making few appearances before African-American organizations and hiring few black staffers. He gave Jesse Jackson only a limited role in his fall campaign. And, in a highly publicized speech to Jackson's Rainbow Coalition, he blasted African-American rap singer Sister Souljah for making comments that had been widely perceived as a call to arms against white people.[31]

Clinton's actions inevitably alienated black voters. An autumn poll by the Joint Center for Political and Economic Studies published in the *Washington Post* found that 30 percent of black respondents believed Clinton had been "cooler and less friendly to black leaders" than past Democratic nominees had been.[32] Roger Wilkins, a civil rights official in the Johnson administration, was among those who watched with dismay. "The whole tenor of the campaign was to say we are new Democrats, we are different Democrats," he said a week after the election, "and the next thing was to say we're hard on crime and we're hard on welfare." Clinton's intent, as Wilkins saw it, was to say, "We don't cater to black people."[33]

The political genius of Clinton's strategy was that African-American voters had no alternative. Bush essentially ignored them, and Perot had no idea how to approach them, repeatedly referring to blacks as "you people" during an awkward appearance before the NAACP national convention. Exit polls reported that 83 percent of black voters pulled the Democratic lever, while only 11 percent voted for Bush and 7 percent chose Perot.[34] Clinton, despite taking a more conservative line than Dukakis, actually improved upon his predecessor's performance in urban centers, picking up an additional 477,000 votes in six selected mother cities:

City	1988 Dem Margin	1992 Dem Margin	Clinton Gain
Baltimore	Won by 111,724	Won by 145,028	33,304
Detroit	Won by 217,197	Won by 268,061	50,864
New York City	Won by 675,388	Won by 949,361	273,973
Philadelphia	Won by 230,513	Won by 301,576	71,063
Saint Louis	Won by 69,170	Won by 76,915	7,745
Washington	Won by 131,817	Won by 171,921	40,104

Source: Author's analysis of official election returns.

Clinton's strategy paid rich dividends in suburbia, where voters were troubled by Republican economic failures and pleased by the Democratic nominee's moderate course. Perot's populist campaign almost spoiled his calculations, siphoning off those suburbanites who were most disenchanted with the state of the union. Perot drew 19.8 percent support in suburban states, compared to 17.4 percent in the rest of the nation. But Clinton nonetheless scored a major breakthrough, bettering Dukakis by 1.7 million votes in the suburbs around the six selected cities, an increase three-and-a-half times larger than his gain in the cities themselves:

Area	1988 Dem Margin	1992 Dem Margin	Clinton Gain
Baltimore suburbs	Lost by 137,049	Lost by 14,204	122,845
Detroit suburbs	Lost by 234,343	Won by 52,826	287,169
New York City suburbs	Lost by 638,863	Lost by 92,419	546,444
Philadelphia suburbs	Lost by 287,427	Won by 19,966	307,393
Saint Louis suburbs	Lost by 55,612	Won by 116,755	172,367
Washington suburbs	Lost by 105,797	Won by 165,291	271,088

Source: Author's analysis of official election returns.

The Republicans long ago had fallen into the habit of relying on suburbia. They carried the bloc of suburban states in six straight elections from 1968 through 1988, winning 1,373 electoral votes from those states, while the Democrats received just 304. But Clinton disrupted the pattern. He was the first Democratic nominee to target suburban voters, and his strategy won him the presidency. He took 258 electoral votes from suburban states—just twelve short of the threshold for victory—while Bush carried only sixty-two. The rest of the nation was closely divided, giving Clinton a 112 to 106 edge in the Electoral College.

The president-elect benefited greatly from discontent with the sluggish economy. Exit polls showed that among those who based their votes on economic issues, 53 percent backed Clinton and only 24 percent went for Bush. But money and jobs weren't the only issues. Clinton also attracted support because he was tougher than previous Democratic nominees on social issues and was more willing to address the spoken and unspoken concerns of middle-class Americans. Suburbanites had come to realize that Bill Clinton was different from Walter Mondale and Michael Dukakis. He was a winner.

Drifting Off Course

The Democratic Leadership Council (DLC) had good cause to be excited. One of its founders—one of its former chairmen, no less—was moving into the Oval Office. President Clinton would have the power to implement the DLC's policy objectives. He would be able to demonstrate to a skeptical nation that a Democrat could be tough on crime, frugal with the public's money, and independent of special interest groups.

The DLC's brain trust believed that the new president needed to signal his intentions early in his administration. It pushed him to tackle welfare reform. Clinton, after all, had promised during the campaign to "end welfare as we know it," to get lifelong recipients off of public assistance and into productive jobs. Welfare reform, in the DLC's view, would galvanize middle-class voters who were waiting to see if Clinton could convert his moderate rhetoric into action.[35]

But the new president wandered from his agenda almost immediately, devoting much of his time to matters of little or no interest to the suburban middle class that had elected him:

- He launched his administration inauspiciously, spending his first days in Washington embroiled in a controversy over allowing gays to serve in the military.
- He quietly abandoned his promise of an immediate middle-class tax cut, instead agreeing to increases in gasoline and diesel-fuel taxes. "It would be irresponsible for any president of the United States ever not to respond to changing circumstances," he said.[36]
- He tried to placate the African-American community he had ignored during the campaign, appointing Lani Guinier, a controversial law professor, to head the Justice Department's Civil Rights Division. Guinier's radical proposals to magnify the electoral clout of minority groups did not square with the traditional beliefs of most congressional Democrats, and she eventually was forced to withdraw her name.*

The DLC was troubled by Clinton's flirtations with the Democratic Party's liberal elements, notably gays and blacks. Its concerns grew when the president finally selected the signature issue for his first term, deciding to tackle not welfare, but the health care system. Clinton told advisers he intended to prove to the middle class that its taxes were being used wisely, that the government was looking out for the American family's best interests. He felt health care reform offered the best chance to make his point.

The president proposed to revamp the existing system by organizing consumers into vast "alliances" that would shop for the best

---

*Guinier had written several articles advocating "cumulative voting," a process that would allow a citizen to cast more than one vote for any given candidate for local office. Suppose, for instance, that there was an election for city council in which the three leading candidates would win council seats. Guinier proposed that each voter be given three votes to distribute as he or she saw fit, even to the point of casting all three for one candidate. Such a system theoretically would allow minority voters to concentrate their ballots to elect minority candidates. (See Andrew Hacker, *Two Nations* [New York: Ballantine, 1995], pp. 212–13, for additional information.)

health insurance plans. Each person would receive a national health security card, much like an automated teller machine card. All Americans would have comprehensive coverage for doctor and hospital bills; no one would be turned away. "This is a moment in history which we have to seize in order to take care of ourselves," said First Lady Hillary Rodham Clinton. "None of this comes without controversy; none of this will be easy."[37]

She was right.

Polls showed that most Americans supported the *concept* of health care reform, but they were not so sure about the president's plan, whose very complexity left it vulnerable to political attacks. Critics quickly moved in. Moderate and conservative Democrats joined Republicans in charging that Clinton's proposal would create vast new bureaucracies on the federal and state levels. They asked how the president could possibly restrain federal spending and streamline the government, as he had pledged during the campaign, while also implementing such a massive program.

Clinton's hopes rested on a misreading of recent history. He believed the middle class was so powerfully attracted to the idea of health care reform that it would insist on passage of his legislation. Hadn't Harris Wofford ridden this very issue to victory in Pennsylvania in 1991? Conventional wisdom agreed that he had; a closer look showed that other factors had been more important. "It wasn't about a plan," James Carville, then a Wofford staffer, had admitted on the night of the senator's miraculous victory.[38] Yet Carville now was helping to lead the battle for Clinton's plan—and was having surprisingly little success.

The suburban middle class slowly, inevitably turned against health care reform, pushing Congress to do the same. Suburbanites quite simply had less at stake than other Americans. Fully 77.6 percent of suburban residents had been covered by private or government health insurance throughout a thirty-two-month study period from 1991 to 1993, according to a Census Bureau report, while only 3.1 percent were uncovered the entire time. People living in central cities and nonmetro areas had more to gain from the Clinton plan, since they were less likely to have health insurance:

| | | (%) | |
Coverage	Central Cities	Suburbs	Nonmetro Areas
All 32 months	69.9	77.6	69.8
13–31 months	18.2	14.5	18.2
1–12 months	7.6	4.8	7.1
No coverage	4.3	3.1	4.9

Source: Author's analysis of U.S. Census Bureau data.

The unraveling of his health care proposal was Bill Clinton's worst setback during his rocky two-year presidential initiation. It made him look weak; he had been unable to push critical legislation through a Congress dominated by his own party. It made him look politically inept; he had failed to understand the shallowness of the middle class's commitment to reform. And, perhaps worst of all, it made him look like a liberal—a stereotypical big-spending, big-government-loving Democratic liberal.

Suburbia had invested its hopes in Clinton in 1992. He was supposed to be its man in Washington—cutting taxes, trimming bureaucracy, implementing policies to make it easier to raise a family in a hectic age. But these expectations had been dashed by mid-1994. The white middle class no longer knew if the president could be depended upon, or indeed, if he had any fixed beliefs at all. It began to hunt for a new hero.

Changing Horses

The best way for disaffected voters to reprimand Clinton, in theory, would be to transfer control of Congress to the Republicans. But it was difficult to imagine them doing something so extreme. The GOP had been the majority in the Senate for just six years of the past forty, in the House of Representatives not at all since 1955. Republicans occupied barely 40 percent of the seats in the current House, holding eighty-two seats fewer than the Democrats.

Newt Gingrich, however, had big plans to end his party's minority status in 1994. He had personal reasons for aiming so high; he would become Speaker if the Republicans achieved a House majority. But he also was motivated by ideology. Gingrich represented a white, conservative district in the Atlanta suburbs and believed the nation should be governed by the same principles his constituents held dear. "I am a transformational figure," he boasted. "I think I am trying to effect a change so large that the people who will be hurt by the change, the liberal machine, have a natural reaction."[39]

Gingrich's most inspired decision was to publicize the Contract with America, a ten-point Republican platform that duplicated some of Clinton's 1992 promises, such as cutting taxes and reforming welfare, and added a few pledges of a more conservative bent, like balancing the federal budget and hiking defense spending. Most Republican House candidates signed the contract as the fall campaign began. Middle-class voters might not agree with all ten planks—and surveys showed many didn't—but they did applaud the GOP's willingness to commit to specific causes, a willingness that Clinton seemed to lack.[40]*

The unveiling of the Contract with America was the turning point in the fall campaign. Polls began to indicate in October that the unthinkable might happen, that voters might pass congressional control to the Republicans. And that indeed was what happened, as the GOP gained fifty-four seats in the House to take a comfortable twenty-six-seat majority:†

| | Seats | | Share of Two-party Popular Vote (%) | | |
	Rep	Dem	Rep	Dem	92–94 Change in Rep Seats
Nationwide	230	204	53.6	46.4	+54
Inner America					
City districts	21	75	37.5	62.5	+ 8
Suburban districts	108	61	56.9	43.1	+17
Outer America					
Fringe districts	56	28	60.8	39.2	+13
Nonmetro districts	45	40	54.0	46.0	+16

Source: Author's analysis of official election returns.

Public dissatisfaction with Clinton was so intense by November 1994 that the Republican Party picked up seats in all four categories, even adding eight in city districts. But its largest gain, seventeen seats, took place in suburbia. And it was there that the new congressional majority would find its inspiration: 47 percent of the Republicans in the next House—108 of 230—would represent suburban districts; only 9 percent were from mother cities. It marked the first time in history that the House's majority party—and consequently the House itself—would be run by suburbanites. Gingrich himself would be the first

---

*The ten planks of the Contract with America included Republican promises to (1) balance the federal budget, (2) enact tougher anti-crime measures, (3) reform the welfare system, (4) reinforce the family structure with tax incentives for adoption and better enforcement of child-support orders, (5) approve a $500-per-child tax credit, (6) increase defense spending, (7) raise earnings limits for Social Security recipients, (8) cut capital-gains taxes, (9) reform the legal system by limiting punitive damages and modifying product liability laws, and (10) place limits on the number of terms served by senators and congressmen.

†This book categorizes House of Representatives districts exactly as it does states, putting them in four categories according to their population patterns: A *city district* is one in which mother cities have the most residents. A *suburban district* is one in which the suburbs have the population edge. A *fringe district* is dominated by fringe metros, a *nonmetro district* by nonmetro areas. All popular votes in a particular district are allocated to its designated category.

Speaker of the House to hail from the suburbs. The minority Democrats retained their urban focus: 37 percent were from city districts, 30 percent from suburbia.[41]

A post-election poll by the *Washington Post* showed that the middle class wanted someone, anyone, to slash government spending and bureaucracy. "It was a tougher version of the message many voters thought they delivered two years ago," wrote *Post* reporter Richard Morin.[42] The item at the top of the electorate's wish list, according to the poll, was not health-care reform, not even a tax cut. It was welfare reform, the very issue the Democratic Leadership Council had urged on Clinton at the beginning of his term.

The prognosis for the president was grim, but not terminal. Edward Bohne, a thirty-eight-year-old lawyer in suburban Saint Louis, spoke for a majority of poll respondents when he said that Clinton still had a chance to regain the middle class's favor.

" 'New Democrat' was the term I think he used, but when he was sworn in, the first thing he looked at was far from the mainstream— gays in the military, (trying) to placate fringe groups with nominations (like) Lani Guinier," Bohne told a *Post* interviewer. "If Democrats, and by this I mean mainly the executive branch, realizes [*sic*] what the population has said . . . and moves [*sic*] back to the mainstream issues he said he was going to work on, I think it will be all right."[43]

The Suburban Age

Bill Clinton had been in this position before.

He first came to national attention in 1978, when he was elected governor of Arkansas at the tender age of thirty-two. Clinton's platform was unusually liberal for such a conservative state, and he vigorously set out to implement it. "We were going to redo the world in two years," Hillary Clinton would recall.[44] Arkansas voters registered their unhappiness in 1980 by tossing her husband out of office, something they almost never did to an incumbent Democrat.

Clinton learned from his defeat. Political insiders found him humbler, more willing to listen to his constituents. They also noticed that he had moderated his positions. He later acknowledged his metamorphosis, saying the 1980 election taught him that "you have to spend a lot of time listening to people and can't let your policies get too far ahead of what they'll accept." Others were not as kind. "I think he learned his lessons too well from that defeat," said John Brummett, a political columnist who first met Clinton in 1975. "He became stronger, harder to beat, for sure, but I think he also became too cautious and too willing to compromise."[45]

The new, improved Bill Clinton was a more successful politician. He ran for governor again in 1982, dismissing his more radical aides and pledging to concentrate on nuts-and-bolts issues like economic development. He won easily and thereafter maintained a harmonious relationship with the state's largest business interests, much to the disappointment of the same liberals who once supported him so enthusiastically.

It was entirely in character for Clinton to react to the 1994 Republican victory in a similar manner. The president and his advisers wasted little time mapping strategy, beginning a not-so-subtle shift to the right early in 1995:

- Clinton endorsed a plan to balance the federal budget within seven years. "The era of big government is over," he declared in his 1996 State of the Union address.
- He promised to develop a plan to reform the nation's welfare system.
- He took a strong stand against sex and violence on television, saying that V-chips should be implanted in TV sets to allow parents to block programs they considered offensive.
- He advocated having public school students wear uniforms to class.
- He supported a ban on same-sex marriages.
- He endorsed a Republican bid to repeal the very gas-tax hike that he had steered through Congress in 1993.
- He took a hard line with Cuba after it shot down two civilian planes piloted by Cuban exiles.

"He's terrific. People said that Ronald Reagan was good, but this guy's a better politician," marveled Jim McLaughlin, a Republican adviser and pollster. Analyst Kevin Phillips agreed that Clinton was making the right moves: "I think he's being very shrewd. The Democrats finally recognize that the public is slightly right of center on certain social issues." Bob Dole, who would be the 1996 GOP nominee, was considerably less gracious as he watched the Democratic president latch on to Republican causes. Clinton's transformation, Dole said sourly, was nothing less than "grand theft."[46]

The Democratic Leadership Council, which had not concealed its displeasure with Clinton's leftward veer in 1993, was delighted by his return to its "new Democratic" principles. Moderates controlled the president's reelection campaign. Two former DLC staffers were tapped to write the party's 1996 platform. And Indiana Governor Evan Bayh, the president's choice to deliver the keynote address at the Democratic convention, was described by DLC President Al From as a "new Democrat poster boy."[47]

Liberal Democrats, unhappy though they might be with Clinton, found the alternatives—Dole and the second coming of Ross Perot— even less appealing. "Certainly the moral line is not what drives some of these decisions," Jesse Jackson said of Clinton's moderate, sometimes even conservative, strategy. "He hopes that the end will justify the means. That's his calculation. I think fundamentally Clinton is a good person. He thinks he's having to govern, and his governing requires that he *expand the base*, and one has to say that to some extent he has been successful."[48]

That was an understatement.

Clinton revived his seemingly moribund career by reconnecting with the same suburban voters who first elected him in 1992 and then repudiated him in 1994. Dole might call the president a liberal, Perot might accuse him of weakness, but the suburban middle class was more interested in the fact that the economy was booming once again. America had added 10.9 million jobs during Clinton's first term, compared to a puny 3.4 million under Bush, and the average unemployment rate had settled at 5.4 percent by 1996, down from 7.5 percent in 1992.

Suburbanites also were gratified that Clinton again was giving top priority to their needs and concerns. Once more he was talking like a moderate, like someone who could keep the government under control, resist the extremists in *both* parties, and make it possible for parents to raise their families in peace. Dole and Perot were outmatched. The stretch drive in October resembled a coronation more than a real campaign.*

This book already has explored the dimensions of Clinton's triumphant reelection. He defeated Dole by a margin of 8.2 million popular votes, translating to a 379 to 159 landslide in the Electoral College. Suburban states gave Clinton 237 of those electoral votes, just thirty-three fewer than the total needed for victory.

Dole's inability to close the gap during the campaign's final weeks undoubtedly reduced interest in the election; the number of voters in 1996 dropped 8.1 million below the figure for 1992. Yet Clinton managed to boost his level of support despite the smaller pool of voters,

---

*The 1996 election is discussed in considerably more detail in chapter 1.

drawing 47.4 million votes in 1996, up nearly 2.5 million from his 1992 total. He recorded his biggest improvement—almost 1.4 million votes —in suburban-dominated states. Dole eked out a slight gain of his own in suburbia, while Perot went into an electoral free fall, losing almost 8 million votes in suburban states and 11.6 million overall:

	Change in Popular Votes from 1992 to 1996*			
	Total Votes	**Clinton**	**Dole**	**Perot**
Nationwide	−8,150,450	+2,491,859	+ 93,587	−11,656,363
Inner America				
City states	− 652,642	+ 277,328	−416,516	− 593,333
Suburban states	−5,704,477	+1,366,206	+199,813	− 7,977,091
Outer America				
Fringe states	− 457,996	+ 714,739	+194,533	− 1,402,628
Nonmetro states	−1,335,335	+ 133,586	+115,757	− 1,683,311

*Dole is compared to George Bush's performance in 1992.
Source: Author's analysis of official election returns.

The Republicans, meanwhile, scrambled to maintain their grasp on Congress. "I am not prepared to compromise," a defiant Newt Gingrich had declared after the GOP took control of the House in 1994. And the new Republican majority had lived up to his words, reducing funding for Medicare, Medicaid, and environmental programs (cuts that Clinton vetoed), condemning abortion and gun control, and precipitating two federal government shutdowns in late 1995 and early 1996. The white middle class, which had counted on the Republicans to restore sanity to Washington, was disillusioned by the party's extreme positions and confrontational tactics.[49]

It obviously was time for a change in strategy. Out went the cockiness and exuberance of 1994; in came a calmer legislative style, an approach more in line with suburban expectations. It was a softspoken, conciliatory Gingrich who watched the Republicans scrape out a smaller majority in 1996. "There is no reason we can't find common ground," the Speaker now said of his relationship with the president.[50]

The GOP picked up six House seats in nonmetro areas and essentially broke even in city and fringe districts. But suburbia emphatically registered its discontent with the harsher aspects of Gingrich's conservative agenda. The Republican Party entered the 1996 election with 108 suburban seats, but left with only 98:

	Seats*		Share of Two-party Popular Vote (%)		94–96 Change in Rep Seats
	Rep	Dem	Rep	Dem	
Nationwide	226	207	50.1	49.9	– 4
Inner America					
City districts	22	74	34.3	65.7	+ 1
Suburban districts	98	71	52.6	47.4	–10
Outer America					
Fringe districts	55	29	56.5	43.5	– 1
Nonmetro districts	51	33	52.0	48.0	+ 6

*Two independents were elected to the House in 1996.
Source: Author's analysis of official election returns.

The political battles of the mid-1990s ushered America into a new age—the Suburban Age. The 1994 election brought to power the first House majority to be dominated by suburban representatives, led by the first Speaker of the House from a suburban district. The 1996 election featured the triumph of the first Democratic president to target his campaign at moderates in suburbia, not liberals in big cities.

Both parties—the Democrats in the White House, the Republicans on Capitol Hill—undeniably owed their success to suburban voters. And both knew the consequences of straying from the suburban agenda, a lesson learned by Clinton upon losing Congress in 1994 and by Gingrich after nearly losing his House majority two years later. "Suburban voters are the balance of power in American presidential elections," conceded Ann Lewis, deputy manager of the Clinton organization, as the 1996 campaign entered its final days. "They are less partisan than people living in the cities," she said. "They're more likely to make up their minds at each election. And that makes them very powerful."[51]

The Great Divide

The prefix was the key. Suburbs, by definition, were inferior to urban centers. They lacked self-sufficiency; suburban residents depended on mother cities for jobs, stores, places to go, and things to do. Suburbs, above all else, were supposed to be *sub*.

So said the dictionary, but the reality of the Clinton years was dramatically different. Suburbia had taken charge of America. Suburbs, not mother cities, controlled the nation's political and economic systems. Dozens of suburban communities had quietly emerged as employment, entertainment, and retail centers for their regions,

usurping the role once reserved for major cities. Author Joel Garreau
came up with a name for these new hubs: *edge cities.* "These are not
suburbs," he wrote. "They are not sub-anything. They are their own
urbs. At 9 o'clock in the morning, more people are going to work in
these places than are heading away from them."[52] Geographer Peter
Muller, who observed the same trend, expressed it more succinctly:
"The suburbs are no longer sub to the urb."[53]

It was impressive enough that there were twenty-three suburban
states by 1996, and that they had a total of 320 electoral votes. But even
more amazing was the extent to which suburbia dominated most of
these states, accounting for a majority of the residents of fourteen of
them, topped by 89 percent in New Jersey. In only four states—Hawaii,
Missouri, Indiana, and Texas—could the next-largest population
sector come within 10 percentage points of suburbia's share:

Suburban State	Electoral Votes	Residents in Suburbs (%)	Next Pop Sector (%)
New Jersey	15	89.0	Mother cities, 11.0
Maryland	10	78.0	Mother cities, 13.3
Rhode Island	4	77.1	Mother cities, 14.7
Connecticut	8	72.7	Mother cities, 10.9
Massachusetts	12	71.9	Mother cities, 21.0
California	54	62.4	Mother cities, 20.3
New Hampshire	4	62.3	Nonmetro areas, 37.7
Virginia	13	59.9	Nonmetro areas, 22.1
Washington	11	56.4	Nonmetro areas, 17.2
Delaware	3	54.9	Nonmetro areas, 18.0
Ohio	21	54.5	Mother cities, 21.1
Utah	5	52.4	Nonmetro areas, 23.1
Michigan	18	52.2	Nonmetro areas, 17.6
Illinois	22	50.7	Mother cities, 23.6
Minnesota	10	46.9	Nonmetro areas, 30.3
Colorado	8	46.5	Fringe metros, 24.6
Georgia	13	44.4	Nonmetro areas, 31.5
Pennsylvania	23	44.1	Fringe metros, 23.2
Hawaii	4	40.9	Mother cities, 32.6
Oregon	7	40.9	Nonmetro areas, 29.9
Missouri	11	40.6	Nonmetro areas, 32.1
Indiana	12	33.6	Nonmetro areas, 28.3
Texas	32	31.6	Fringe metros, 30.4

Source: Author's analysis of U.S. Census Bureau data.

Mother cities, on the other hand, were politically impotent—con-
trolling just two states—and were economically weak, as well. Urban
bosses of the 1940s had wielded enough clout to influence and sometimes even dictate national policy; big-city mayors of the 1990s were
reduced to begging for scraps from a Congress and state legislatures
dominated by suburbanites. "All of America's major cities are on
greased skids," University of Pennsylvania urbanologist Ted Hershberg
said wearily in 1994. "What differentiates one from another is the

angle of descent. You may slow the descent, but unless there's a major shift in public policy, America will lose all its major cities."[54]

The inevitable result was an ever-widening city-suburban gap that manifested itself in nine distinct ways during the 1990s.

1. Race

The most obvious distinction—one hardly in need of elaboration— was racial. Minorities were approaching population parity in mother cities by 1990, comprising 49 percent of all urban residents. But their numbers still were weak in white-dominated suburbia:*

		(%)	
Race	Mother Cities	Suburbs	Rest of Nation
White	50.9	80.7	81.5
Black	27.6	7.1	9.5
Hispanic	16.0	8.4	6.6
Asian	5.1	3.5	1.1
Native American	0.4	0.4	1.2

Source: Author's analysis of U.S. Census Bureau data.

Of the eight cities that had more than a million residents in 1990, only Philadelphia and San Diego still had white majorities. Racial minorities accounted for 57 percent of the residents in New York City, 62 percent in Chicago, 63 percent in Los Angeles, and 79 percent in Detroit.[55]

This imbalance was magnified in the public schools, since a substantial number of white city dwellers opted to educate their children in private institutions beyond the reach of the urban poor. Just 4 percent of all students in Washington, D.C., public schools in the early 1990s were white. The corresponding figures were 10 percent in Newark and 13 percent in Los Angeles.[56]

2. Family Stability

White Americans smugly believed that the African-American family structure was disintegrating. They read the cascade of statistics in their daily newspapers: Only 39 percent of black families included two parents in 1990; 68 percent of black babies were born out of wedlock in 1992; 58 percent of black households were headed solely by women in 1993.[57] It was shocking stuff.

---

*See Appendix E for the racial compositions of mother cities and their suburbs in 1990.

The problem, in reality, was not confined to a single racial group. The entire urban family structure was crumbling. Households in big cities, regardless of race, were less likely than their suburban counterparts to be headed by married couples and more likely to lack father figures:

	(%)		
	Whites	Blacks	Hispanics
Households			
Comprised of married-couple families			
Central cities	46.2	29.5	49.0
Suburbs	62.1	42.8	61.9
Headed by a female householder (no husband present)			
Central cities	4.7	20.4	13.8
Suburbs	4.3	16.3	9.1

Source: Author's analysis of U.S. Census Bureau data.

This gap in family stability was evident in all of America's major metro areas. Atlanta was typical. Fully 74 percent of the children in the Atlanta suburbs lived at home with both parents in 1990; the same was true of just 36 percent of children in the city itself.[58]

3. Education

Jeffrey Hayden spent two years in the mid-1990s visiting schools in Ohio for a PBS documentary he was producing on the quality of American education. He was awed by the state-of-the-art facilities in the suburbs of Cleveland and Columbus. "They are magnificent architecturally, magnificent in supplies," he said. "If there are 600 students in schools, there are 600 computers. The science labs are like nothing I have ever seen in my experience."

But Hayden also was haunted by the decaying buildings that he found in the rest of Ohio. "We cannot keep sending our children to these inner-city and rural schools," he said. "They are unhealthy; they are unsafe. They violate building codes. You get into these schools and say, 'Wait a minute, this is unreal.' "[59]

The same disparities existed in New York, where suburban districts spent $9,688 per pupil in 1994, 18 percent more than the $8,205 spent per student in New York City and 6.2 percent above the average of $9,117 in the state's other mother cities. This spending gap, in turn, contributed to gaps in supplies and test results. New York City schools had only 9.4 library books per pupil, while suburban and rural districts averaged 20.0 per student. And only 21 percent of 1995 high school graduates in mother cities earned Regents diplomas, awarded to those who passed a broad range of college-preparatory courses.[60] Half of all suburban seniors were Regents grads:

	(%)		
	New York City	Other Large Cities	Suburbs
Graduates with Regents diplomas	21	21	50
Students passing statewide exams			
English	20	32	61
U.S. history	17	29	61
Mathematics I	30	26	65
Biology	17	23	58

Source: The State of Learning: A Report to the Governor and the Legislature on the Educational Status of the State's Schools (Albany: New York Education Department, 1996), pp. 72–77.

Urban–suburban inequality was the rule even for the newest of educational technologies. A 1996 U.S. Education Department study found that 59 percent of suburban schools were connected to the Internet, compared to just 47 percent of city schools.[61]

4. Public Safety

Television newscasts in America's major cities typically featured a nightly series of horror stories, a rapid succession of murders, assaults, rapes, arsons, and robberies. It was no wonder that most suburban viewers considered urban centers to be nearly as dangerous as war zones.

TV exaggerated the menace, of course, but there still was considerable truth behind the stereotype. Nearly half of all murders in the United States in 1992 were committed in mother cities, even though they were home to fewer than 18 percent of Americans. FBI statistics showed that suburbia was considerably less exposed to all types of crime. Rape rates were 56 percent lower in suburbs than in large central cities in 1992, robbery rates were 88 percent lower, assault rates 68 percent lower, and burglary rates 51 percent lower.[62]

The mid- and late 1990s offered hope that urban violence might be receding. Murder rates hit a twenty-year low in Los Angeles and a thirty-year low in New York City in 1997. A federal report issued the same year determined that the violent crime rate for all American cities declined 10.7 percent between 1994 and 1995, good news indeed. But the suburban crime rate dropped even more—15.1 percent —meaning that the public safety gap actually continued to widen.[63]

5. Business

It was easy to choose a site for a corporate headquarters in the 1940s. Downtown was the only sensible place to put a head office; it was the only location offering the space and services that busy executives needed.

That was no longer the case by the 1990s. Large corporations had been slipping away to suburbia for half a century, attracted by lower rents, easier access, and free parking. New York City was a leading victim of this trend. Ninety-eight *Fortune* 500 companies were head-quartered in the city in 1975, a total that was slashed to forty-nine by 1995 as companies fled to the suburbs or the Sunbelt.[64] The city's share of all *Fortune* 500 head offices within its metro area dropped from two-thirds to slightly less than one-half during the same twenty years:

	1975		1995	
	Companies	Metro Share (%)	Companies	Metro Share (%)
New York City metro	145		99	
Components				
New York City	98	67.6	49	49.5
Other mother cities	2	1.4	3	3.0
Suburbs	45	31.0	47	47.5

Source: Author's analysis of data from *Fortune* (May 1975 and May 15, 1995).

Erosion of the urban corporate base was even more pronounced in the Chicago metro area, which in 1996 boasted 919 companies with annual revenues of at least $100 million. Almost two-thirds of those businesses were based in the suburbs. Just 29 percent were at home in the Loop, Chicago's downtown.[65]

6. Employment

It followed logically that if corporate offices were moving out of mother cities, jobs were moving, too. Five of every six jobs created in the nation's thirty-five largest metropolitan areas between 1960 and 1990 were created in the suburbs. Those same suburban communities, as a result, contained 62 percent of all jobs within their metros by 1990.[66]

Washington, D.C., mirrored the national trend. The city added 136,800 jobs between 1949 and 1996—a decent enough figure, but one that paled in comparison to an increase of 1.71 million jobs in suburban Washington. Employment growth in the suburbs outpaced the city regardless of who was in the White House—Republican or Democrat, rugged individualist or big-government advocate:*

Administration	Change in Jobs		Annual Job Growth Rate (%)	
	Washington	Suburbs	Washington	Suburbs
Truman (second term)	+42,500	+ 32,300	+2.8	+10.8
Eisenhower	−29,500	+127,700	−0.7	+ 9.4
Kennedy	+45,800	+ 63,400	+2.9	+ 7.8
Johnson	+39,200	+211,100	+1.4	+10.9
Nixon	−10,300	+224,500	−0.3	+ 6.1
Ford	− 5,700	+ 44,200	−0.5	+ 2.9
Carter	+44,900	+236,500	+1.9	+ 6.7
Reagan	+57,900	+584,300	+1.1	+ 5.8
Bush	− 3,100	+ 11,300	−0.1	+ 0.2
Clinton (first term)	−44,900	+178,200	−1.7	+ 2.6

Source: Author's analysis of U.S. Bureau of Labor Statistics data.

Nor was there any reason to believe the city's decline would be reversed. A total of 33,800 people dropped off Washington's employment rolls in the twenty-four months between July 1994 and July 1996. "The only rates that were close to this were after the 1968 riots," said Charles McMillion, chief economist for MBG Information Services in Washington. "We don't know who these people are, but the general feeling is that it's the middle class."[67]

7. Retail Sales

Urban expert George Sternlieb foresaw the demise of downtown shopping in the early 1960s, years before the mall became king. He blamed transportation difficulties in the central city: "We are asking the customer to pay a penalty to visit the downtown store—either to use the mass transit system which she has voted against or an automobile in an environment which cannot comfortably accommodate it."[68]

Sternlieb's prediction, as everyone knows, became stark reality. A study of the nation's eighty largest metropolitan areas found that suburban stores attracted $728 of every $1,000 of retail spending in 1992, leaving just $272 for their city counterparts. And the suburban share

---

*Washington technically is part of the Washington-Baltimore metro area (see Appendix C), but this book recognizes five counties in Maryland, eleven counties and six independent cities in Virginia, and two counties in West Virginia as Washington suburbs. This chart compares the average annual employment totals during the final year of the previous administration with the final full year of the administration under study. The Eisenhower row, for example, compares the number of jobs in 1952 and 1960.

was bound to keep growing; it had increased in seventy-seven of the eighty metros between 1982 and 1992.[69]*

8. Income

It wasn't too many years ago that cities actually were wealthier than their suburbs, impossible though that now may seem. The average income of city residents in 1960 was a full 5 percent higher than the corresponding figure for suburbanites. But the flight of the white middle class—and the businesses, jobs, and stores that went along— took its toll on urban centers. City incomes fell 4 percent below suburban incomes by 1973, a disparity that widened to 11 percent in 1980 and 17.5 percent in 1989. The per capita income for mother cities in the latter year was $14,069, compared to $17,051 in the suburbs.[70]†

The financial gap was considerably worse in several metro areas. The typical Detroit resident had a per capita income of just $9,560 in 1989, 45 percent below the average of $17,282 in surrounding suburbia. The differential between city and suburbs was an identical 45 percent in Hartford, 37 percent in Cleveland, 35 percent in Milwaukee, and 34 percent in Philadelphia. These five metros were among nine that had "reached the extremes where both poor and affluent are tending toward isolated enclaves, spatially distant from one another," in the words of a 1996 Case Western Reserve University study. (The other four were Baltimore, Chicago, Cincinnati, and Memphis.)[71]

It was undeniable that more cities would be joining the list. The disparity between urban and suburban incomes continued to widen no matter which political party was in charge, accelerating during the Reagan-Bush years and then growing progressively worse after Bill Clinton became president. "We have entered a new era of inequality, where the privileges of the rich and the disadvantages of the poor will increasingly be amplified and reinforced through a powerful process of geographic concentration," said University of Pennsylvania sociologist Douglas Massey.[72]

---

*Sports marketers demonstrated an acute understanding of how far urban retail power had fallen by the end of the twentieth century. Major League Baseball granted expansion teams to Denver, Miami, Phoenix, and Saint Petersburg in the 1990s, but all four franchises declined to use the names of their home cities. They opted instead for state or regional names that suburban consumers found more appealing: Colorado, Florida, Arizona, and Tampa Bay, respectively.

†See Appendix F for the per capita incomes of mother cities and their suburbs in 1989.

9. Politics

This book has documented the erosion of urban power and the con-current rise of suburban influence, showing them to be the inevitable results of a massive population shift during the past half-century.

Two factors have magnified these trends. The first is voter turnout. Suburbanites quite simply are more likely than city residents to vote, as analyst Kevin Phillips found while studying the 1988 election. "The actual lever-pulling electorate," he wrote, "was disproportionately Buick-owning and Book-of-the-Month Club."[73] The same was true in 1996, when whites and college graduates voted in disproportionately high numbers. Whites, for example, accounted for 84.1 percent of the voting-age population, but 86.9 percent of actual voters. Blacks and other minorities consequently were underrepresented, as were those people who had not gone to college:

| | Voting-Age Population | | Actual 1996 Voters | |
	Persons	Share (%)	Persons	Share (%)
Race				
White	162,779,000	84.1	91,208,000	86.9
Black	22,483,000	11.6	11,386,000	10.8
Other	8,389,000	4.3	2,423,000	2.3
Education				
Not a high school grad	34,988,000	18.1	11,287,000	10.7
High school graduate	65,208,000	33.7	32,019,000	30.5
Some college	50,939,000	26.3	30,835,000	29.4
Bachelor's degree or higher	42,517,000	22.0	30,877,000	29.4

Source: Author's analysis of U.S. Census Bureau data.

Suburbia has further intensified its political power by taking con-trol of key government positions. The House of Representatives, for example, was run for nearly three decades by Speakers from mother cities: John McCormack (1962–71) of Boston; Tip O'Neill (1977–86) of Cambridge, Massachusetts; Jim Wright (1987–89) of Fort Worth; and Thomas Foley (1989–94) of Spokane, Washington.* All were champions of liberal, urban-oriented legislation.

Newt Gingrich, the first suburban Speaker, took the gavel in 1995, bringing with him a host of like-minded conservative colleagues. Sub-urbanites previously had not occupied more than three of the House's twenty power positions at one time, but they held ten in 1995. City dis-tricts were shut out for the first time:†

---

*Their streak was interrupted only by Carl Albert (1971–76) from rural Oklahoma.

†The House's power positions are Speaker, Majority Leader, Majority Whip, and the chairmen of the seventeen standing committees that have existed since 1965.

	House of Representatives Leaders			
	1965	1975	1985	1995
City districts	6	5	10	0
Suburban districts	3	3	3	10
Fringe districts	6	7	3	6
Nonmetro districts	5	5	4	4

Source: Author's analysis of data from Congressional Directory (Washington, D.C.: U.S. Government Printing Office, 1965, 1975, 1985, and 1995).

The sharp change in 1995 stemmed largely from the Republicans' success in breaking the Democrats' forty-year stranglehold on the House. But the winds of change were blowing through the Democratic Party, too. Eight of its nineteen floor leaders and ranking committee members in 1995 represented suburban districts; only six were from mother cities.

Coda

The ever-widening chasm that separated America's cities and suburbs saddened Jimmy Carter, but it did not surprise him. The former president had witnessed the damaging effects of racial segregation during his boyhood and early political career in Georgia. It seemed to him that the division between haves and have-nots in the nation's metro areas could be considered a different type of segregation, as he told CNN's Larry King on the January 13, 1993, airing of Larry King Live just a week before Bill Clinton's first inauguration.

"I would say that our society now is about as segregated as it was thirty years ago, not based on race, necessarily, certainly not based on legal race," Carter told King. "Based on wealth and based on power and the making of decisions that affect a person's life.

"On the one hand, you've got rich persons, like you and me. I'm not talking about bank account, but a rich person is one that has a home to live in and has a chance of a job and a modicum of education and health care, who lives in a neighborhood where they believe it's reasonably safe to go outdoors, and who thinks the police and the judicial system are on their side.

"On the other hand are the ones who don't have any of those things, who live side-by-side with us in our major cities, in particular. Atlanta is two cities. Atlanta is a great city—one of the best—but there are two Atlantas; there are two Washingtons; there are two New Yorks; there are two Los Angeles."

"And one doesn't see the other, right?" interjected King.

"The one doesn't even—is not even aware of the other," Carter replied. "In fact, I think now that the powerful people in our society ignore the suffering people in our society perhaps as much as the white leaders did thirty years ago ignore the blacks."

"Why?"

Carter paused. "We don't want to see it," he said.[74]

Two Americas: Into the Twenty-First Century

Tom Peters and George Gilder got together in 1995 to discuss the future of America's great cities.

Theirs was no casual conversation. It was arranged by the magazine *Forbes ASAP*, which hoped to entertain its readers by staging a debate between two of America's sharpest minds. Peters and Gilder were ideal choices. Each was a respected, best-selling author, as well as an acute observer of the national scene.

Peters was the more famous of the two, having made his mark as a management consultant who dared to challenge the traditional beliefs of business executives. "Destroy all organization charts," he urged. "Thrive on the chaos." He enunciated his liberal, power-to-the-people philosophy in a steady stream of books, the best-known being *In Search of Excellence*. Peters was in such demand by the mid-1990s that he could charge $65,000 just to lead a two-hour seminar.[1]

Gilder built his reputation as a pioneering advocate of supply-side economics. His breakthrough came in the early 1980s with *Wealth and Poverty*, a book often quoted by Ronald Reagan, whose endorsement secured Gilder's place in the conservative pantheon. Technology plainly fascinated him. "One person at a computer work station," Gilder was fond of saying, "can command the creative power of a factory tycoon of the Industrial Era and the communications power of a broadcast tycoon of the Television Era."[2]

Forbes ASAP had made its selections well. The men who settled in front of its tape recorder—Peters, the liberal who stressed the worth of the individual; Gilder, the conservative who believed in the power of technology—presented dramatically different visions of what lay ahead for urban America.

Peters expressed confidence that cities would continue to attract talented people and to thrive as producers of goods, information, and services. He conceded that Americans had been fleeing densely settled communities for half a century, but nonetheless insisted that cities such as New York and quasi-cities like California's Silicon Valley would prosper in the future. "These clusters of exuberant variety are at the heart of entrepreneurship and progress," said Peters. "Technology is great, but humans like to schmooze."[3]

Gilder was not persuaded. "I think we are headed for the death of cities," he said. "That is, the death of the current configuration of cities as we know them all today." He based his prediction on Moore's Law, which holds that the number of transistors a manufacturer can fit on a microchip tends to double every eighteen months, yielding computers that are progressively more powerful and cost-effective. The inevitable result of Moore's Law, in Gilder's mind, would be the further decentralization of American society. People would be able to work—and live—anywhere. "Big cities are leftover baggage from the industrial era," he said.[4]

The conversation clearly pivoted on a single question: Which force would have the greater impact on the future—human nature or modern technology? It was Peters's view that people and companies were most innovative when they enjoyed the social interaction available in cities. "I think we need the physical mixing and blending and bustling of Silicon Valley and other such clusters," he insisted. Gilder countered that faster computers would be able to simulate an urban environment in the most bucolic of settings. "The telecosm can destroy cities," he said, "because then you get all the diversity, all the serendipity, all the exuberant variety that you can find in a city in your own living room."[5]

It was inevitable that men with opinions so divergent would interpret the fifty-year rise of suburbia in vastly different ways. Peters was unimpressed. He contended that suburbs lacked sufficient population density to foster creativity, yet were too densely populated to offer tranquility. "As far as I am concerned," he said, "the greatest thing in the world would be the dispersion of the suburb. You should either be in places where there are two people per square mile or places where there are two million per square mile."[6]

Gilder scoffed that such beliefs defied the logic of history. The age of great cities was over, to his way of thinking. Urban centers would not be America's driving force in the twenty-first century; they would be its greatest burden. "The problem with the cities today is that they are parasites," he said. "We've got these big parasite cities sucking the lifeblood out of America today. And those cities will have to go off the dole."[7]

The tape recorder eventually was turned off, leaving the two debaters far from common ground. The truth undoubtedly lay somewhere between their extreme positions. It seemed likely that Peters was correct in saying the future would favor communities whose population densities at least reached moderate levels, and that Gilder was correct, too, in saying the future would smile on places whose residents were best prepared to capitalize on scientific progress.

It seemed likely, in other words, that the future would belong to suburbia.

A New Electronic Heartland

The irony was that America's mother cities, which Gilder believed were doomed by technological advances, had been products of modern technology themselves.

The arrival of the typewriter in the 1870s, accompanied by the spread of high-speed stenography and mechanical systems of audit and control, gave executives new power to rule vast commercial empires from offices in big cities. It suddenly became possible for a single corporation to administer distant factories and to trade with distant partners. Skyscrapers sprouted toward the heavens to house ever-expanding corporate workforces; streetcar lines stretched toward the horizon to transport employees between home and work. Downtowns grew rapidly as a result; so did nearby residential neighborhoods.

Even more power was concentrated in mother cities in the late nineteenth and early twentieth centuries as new technologies spawned modern white-collar industries. Finance, insurance, and advertising firms—labeled the "new trinity" by Lewis Mumford—invariably chose downtown locations.[8] These young businesses not only added to the burgeoning employment base of their home city, but also increased its economic control over nearby small towns and rural counties.

Technology therefore served as a powerful centralizing force into the early 1900s, fueling the growth of major cities. It promoted size; skyscrapers were the best buildings for large corporate offices. It encouraged concentration; streetcars carried people from disparate neighborhoods to the downtown hub. And it bred dominance; businesses headquartered in big cities now exercised substantial influence over vast regions.

Such an environment left corporations no choice but to locate in the central city. Downtown was where their colleagues, customers, and competitors were based; it was where the action was. Their impulse to congregate was unchanged from the 1700s, when London's leading merchants and bankers had crowded into a single square mile. "London thrived as a center of trade: *in other words, as a center of information*," historian Robert Fishman wrote. "Its leading merchants depended on rapid knowledge of markets throughout the world, a knowledge that was available to them only through a multitude of face-to-face contacts."[9] Such was the case in 1900, as well.

H. G. Wells, the famous British author, was among the first to discern that change was coming. He predicted in 1900 that emerging technologies would make it easier to transmit information and transport people, thereby reducing the importance of location. Three advance agents of decentralization proved him correct by the 1920s, when each came into widespread use:

- The automobile allowed people to go where they wanted when they wanted, freeing them from dependence on streetcars that primarily shuttled to and from downtown.
- The telephone made it possible for businesspeople to talk to anyone at any time, reducing their need for in-person meetings.
- Electricity was extended rapidly into suburban and rural areas, opening those regions for commercial and residential development.

The moral couldn't be more obvious: Technology, which did so much to create and shape America's great cities, was not their friend during most of the twentieth century. Nor will it be in the twenty-first.

Recent and anticipated technological developments will accelerate decentralization. Futurists talk confidently about the advent of the "virtual office," which in fact will not be an office at all. Employees will be able to work anywhere—at home, on the road, in a satellite office—connected by wireless phones, fax machines, laptop computers, and the Internet. They will become "telecommuters." A few companies had implemented this concept on a broad scale by the mid-1990s, including Primetime Publicity & Media, a firm that employed sixteen professionals across America, but had no headquarters as such. Primetime's chief executive officer, Dick Grove, lived on a ranch in Kansas, rarely meeting face-to-face with his staff. "I invest in people and technology, not fancy offices," he told a reporter.[10]

The virtual office, of course, isn't suited to every line of work. We won't be seeing virtual factories or virtual grocery stores. But the communications revolution has the potential to change the lives of millions of office workers, the very people who still drive each day from suburban homes to urban skyscrapers. Many undoubtedly will find telecommuting an appealing alternative to rush-hour traffic and $200-a-month downtown parking bills. And their employers, hoping to benefit from reduced overhead, can be expected to encourage them, especially after telephone and cable TV companies build efficient digital networks that can carry video, still pictures, and text to distant computers faster than the blink of an eye.

The demographic implications are stunning. Futurists John Naisbitt and Patricia Aburdene predicted as early as 1990 that telecommuting professionals will create "a new electronic heartland" as they choose to live and work on the fringe of suburbia or beyond, thereby escalating the exodus of residents and jobs from the central city. "Quality-of-life rural areas are linked to urban centers, as are other cities," they wrote. "This megatrend of the next millennium is laying the groundwork for the decline of cities."[11]

Decline, yes. Death, certainly not. Several experts have been guilty of overstating the impact of new technology. George Gilder, as we have seen, envisioned urban doom, and Marvin Cetron, a noted futurist, forecast that one of every five workers would be telecommuting by the year 2000. The truth, of course, is that humans are social animals. Surveys indicate that men and younger workers, in particular, would miss the personal contacts they make in the office, contacts on which business—and professional advancement—depends. "I don't know how big (telecommuting) will be in reality. Working in a virtual office may be virtual death to your career," said Neal Thornberry, a Boston business consultant.[12]

Realistic predictions are that 3 to 5 percent of the nation's workers will become telecommuters—still a significant number, to be sure, but not large enough to drain the central city by itself. The real danger posed by new technology is that it will offset most of the remaining advantages of a downtown location. It will allow almost any type of office to move from the central city to the suburbs—where rents are cheaper, parking is free, and the homes of employees and customers are close—without losing essential contacts with other businesses. Thousands of companies already are clustered in Joel Garreau's edge cities and more are coming everyday, achieving a critical mass previously available only in big cities. The chamber of commerce in suburban Fairfax County, Virginia, for example, boasted 2,000 member firms in 1997, compared to just 1,150 belonging to the Greater Washington Board of Trade, the largest business association in Washington, D.C., itself.[13]

Even those businesses that still congregate downtown—law firms, stock brokerages, accounting firms, and Mumford's trinity of advertising agencies, banks, and insurance companies—will be freed to locate wherever they please. Major law offices won't need to be near the local courthouse; they will be able to obtain court documents on the Internet and to submit filings the same way. Ad agencies will transmit copy by modem to clients and media outlets. Banks will handle all transactions with corporate customers electronically, no longer using couriers to carry large sacks of paper money. "Such deep changes in the money system cannot occur without threatening entrenched institutions that have, until now, enjoyed positions of extraordinary power," wrote futurist Alvin Toffler. "At one level, the substitution of electronic money for paper money is a direct threat, for example, to the very existence of banks as we know them."[14]

Urban officials, try as they might, will be unable to prevent the further dispersion of downtown offices to the suburbs. The communications revolution, in a sense, will flatten the central city, in the opinion of Edward Cornish, president of the World Future Society. "Large office towers in New York City now stand empty, or nearly so. Big American corporations have turned their back on skyscrapers," he wrote. "Wal-Mart's headquarters in Bentonville, Arkansas, is two stories high. The roof of Microsoft's headquarters in Redmond, Washington, doesn't clear the tree tops. And Sears Roebuck, which built the world's tallest building in Chicago in 1974, has moved to a low-rise campus in the suburbs."[15]

Outward, Ever Outward

Critics long have tossed a favorite epithet at suburbia: *sprawl.* Lewis Mumford insisted way back in the 1940s that suburbs would turn out to be inefficient and uninteresting simply because they had too few residents on too much land—in other words, because they sprawled. A chorus of architects, sociologists, and urban planners kept Mumford's complaint alive during the half-century that followed.

This criticism, of course, did nothing to stem the exodus of the white middle class from mother cities. "Sprawl is what you do on Sunday afternoons on the couch. It's comfortable and it's got some room. Efficiency is when you get the middle seat on USAir with the crying baby next to you," laughed James DeFrancia, a housing developer in suburban Washington.[16] Others detected an element of elitism in those who derided sprawling development patterns. "There is this strange conceit among architects that people ought to live in what they design," said Peter Gordon, a University of Southern California economics professor. "If you look at how people really want to live in this country, suburbanization is not the problem, it is the solution."[17]

There is no reason to believe that the American people will turn their backs on suburbia anytime soon. Sprawl will remain a central fact of life well into the twenty-first century, according to a computer model that shows the suburbs increasing their share of the nation's population from 41.1 percent in 1990 to nearly 44 percent by 2020. Mother cities will slip almost three percentage points during the same period:*

	Projected Share of U.S. Population (%)			
	Mother Cities	Suburbs	Fringe Metros	Nonmetro Areas
1990	17.9	41.1	20.6	20.3
2000	16.0	42.4	21.7	19.9
2010	15.5	43.1	22.2	19.2
2020	15.3	43.7	22.4	18.5

Source: Author's projection of population trends.

The raw numbers behind these percentages are equally compelling. Suburbia's total population is projected to soar from 102.3 million in 1990 to 141.1 million in 2020, while mother cities will inch up from 44.5 million to 49.5 million residents during the same thirty-year period. Suburbanites will outnumber city dwellers by almost 92 million in 2020.†

Sprawl will be unabated in the future despite the howls of critics and government planners; housing developments will continue eating up rural land on the suburban fringe, moving ever farther from the already distant central city. This decentralization will be driven not only by technology, but also by prevailing attitudes. Surveys indicate that suburban residents enjoy the moderate concentration of services provided by shopping malls, strip plazas, and office parks, but dislike the heavier densities of the typical downtown. And they will oppose strongly any efforts to transform their uncrowded neighborhoods into copies of the congested urban model. A poll of Orange County, California, residents in 1982, when population pressures in the Los Angeles area were much less severe than they are today, found that 65 percent already favored restrictions on suburban growth.[18]

The only course open to developers will be to keep pushing outward from the stagnant urban core. The population of Washington,

---

*The author developed a statistical model to predict population trends and changes in racial composition through 2024. The model used thirty-two variables to generate estimates for 841 metropolitan counties and independent cities, as well as all ninety-three mother cities. Among the factors taken into account were local growth rates since 1980, county-by-county racial patterns, and the U.S. Census Bureau's own state-by-state population projections. Projecting the future admittedly is as much an art as a science, and sometimes an inexact art at that, yet it can offer a fairly reliable glimpse of the years to come. These projections will be used in the rest of this book to predict America's demographic and political future.

†See Appendix A for projections for mother cities, Appendix B for projections for Inner America's metro areas, and Appendix H for projections for states.

D.C., for example, will be virtually unchanged between 1990 and 2020. Its first ring of suburbs, consisting of those counties and independent cities that adjoin Washington, will grow at a healthy pace of 44.3 percent. But the fastest rates of expansion will occur far from the city. The second suburban ring and the even-more-distant belt of outlying counties will increase their populations by more than 60 percent:

	Population		Growth Rate (%)	Share of Metro Total (%)	
	1990	2020	1990–2020	1990	2020
Washington metro	4,223,485	6,034,813	+42.9		
Components					
Washington	606,900	623,000	+ 2.7	14.4	10.3
First ring	2,616,198	3,774,577	+44.3	61.9	62.5
Second ring	639,240	1,055,463	+65.1	15.1	17.5
Outlying ring	361,147	581,773	+61.1	8.6	9.6

Source: Author's projections of population trends.

Loudoun County, Virginia, and Charles County, Maryland, are among the second-ring suburbs that are primed for rapid growth. Loudoun will balloon from a 1990 population of 86,100 to a 2020 total of 153,700; Charles will increase from 101,100 to 155,300. Virginia's Spotsylvania County, until recently a typical farming county in the outlying belt, will soar from 57,400 residents in 1990 to 125,400 in 2020.[19]

The city of Washington is too far from these booming counties to serve as their commercial hub. It would take a Spotsylvania County commuter more than an hour to reach Washington under the best of conditions, perhaps two hours when traffic is snarled. But several suburban edge cities are much more convenient, offering a large and ever-expanding array of high-paying jobs. The employment base in Washington's Virginia suburbs grew by 6.2 percent between 1994 and 1996, while the city itself was losing 5.4 percent of its jobs.[20]

Bethesda, Maryland, is typical of the suburban hubs that encircle the District of Columbia. It once was a bedroom community, but now is a shopping and employment center for hundreds of thousands of people living northwest of Washington. Downtown Bethesda boasts more than 7 million square feet of office space, compared to just 4 million in the early 1980s. Restaurants and shops thrive by serving two prosperous clienteles: office workers by day and local residents at night and on weekends.

Bethesda's strength is that it offers urban diversity in a suburban setting. It is not as difficult to reach as Washington, nor is it as expensive or as dangerous. "Our market is mostly women, and we didn't feel that they wanted to shop in Washington," said David Ginsberg, co-owner of a home furnishings boutique in Bethesda. "We looked carefully at (the Washington neighborhood of) Georgetown, and we decided against it because we felt that our target audience felt uncomfortable there."[21]

Selective Renaissance

The truth is that Americans have never liked cities.

The founding fathers preferred rural life, which they believed to be ennobling. "I view large cities as pestilential to the morals, the health, and the liberties of man," Thomas Jefferson wrote. He also said: "The mobs of great cities add just so much to the support of pure government as sores do to the strength of the human body."[22] American literature typically reflected the founders' biases by deifying nature and scorning the big city.

These attitudes remained prevalent even after America had been transformed into an urban nation. The Gallup Poll in 1949, when mother cities still were near their peak, asked respondents who was happier, someone who lived on a farm or someone in a city. Sixty-five percent voted for the farmer, only 21 percent for the city dweller. People who themselves lived in large cities did not differ much from the national consensus: 55 percent agreed that farmers were happier. Gallup posed similar questions through the years, consistently proving the unpopularity of cities.[23] A 1989 poll, for example, offered respondents the hypothetical choice of living in any of four types of communities. The city did better than in previous surveys in the 1960s and 1970s, but still finished last:

Small town	34%
Suburban area	24%
Farm	22%
City	19%

Source: "Cities Enjoy New Popularity," *The Gallup Report* (October 1989): 27.

What was striking about these surveys was that people in suburban and rural areas were not alone in disliking cities; millions of urban residents shared the sentiment. A variety of local polls in the late 1980s and early 1990s confirmed that sizable groups of city dwellers wanted to escape if they could find the means to do so: 43 percent in Boston expressed a desire to leave their city, as did 48 percent in Los Angeles, 53 percent in Detroit, and 60 percent in New York City.[24]

This widespread disdain for city life will be the biggest impediment to any future plans to rebuild America's urban centers. Suburbanites steadfastly will oppose spending the billions upon billions of tax dollars that would be required to return cities to their former glory, if such a thing indeed were possible. A large proportion of city dwellers will understand their opposition, and even agree with it.

The best that can be accomplished in such a climate will be a selective urban renaissance. The days when affluent mother cities were able to fund their own projects are long past. Shrinking tax bases and skyrocketing expenses have forced them to depend heavily on county, state, and federal funds, all of which are controlled by suburban lawmakers. Cities, as a result, will be allowed to build or renovate primarily those structures that suburbanites will use personally—and therefore will be willing to subsidize. New downtown stadiums, arenas, convention centers, and museums will be embraced enthusiastically, since they are magnets for suburban consumers. Expressway improvements and state-of-the-art parking garages will be approved as well, since they are amenities for suburban commuters. But massive aid will not be forthcoming to tackle more urgent problems within the city, like pockmarked side streets in need of repaving or dilapidated housing in need of renovation.

Mayors and journalists alike can be counted upon to ignore this dark truth about the city's economic and political impotence. They will herald each arena, each museum, each parking garage as evidence of an urban comeback, indulging an impulse that historian Jon Teaford noted in his study of development trends during the Carter and Reagan years. Teaford found that politicians and the press joined in "an era of unprecedented urban hype" to overhaul the tired images of major cities, regardless of whether such positive publicity was warranted. "During the late 1970s and the 1980s, Cleveland had to be proclaimed a comeback city even if it was not," he wrote, "and Baltimore had to be painted pink by image makers even though much of it was dull gray."[25]

Cleveland, in fact, provides a perfect case history of a selective renaissance. The national media hailed Cleveland as the comeback city of the 1990s because of its modernistic Rock 'n' Roll Hall of Fame and sparkling Jacobs Field, the latter a stadium that housed baseball's resurgent Cleveland Indians. But the glowing stories omitted important details about the desperate condition of the city's neighborhoods. Cleveland's population had declined 42 percent since 1940, and 43 percent of its children were living below the poverty level. "The corporate leadership and political leadership came together with important things to strengthen the downtown," said researcher Claudia Coulton of Case Western Reserve University. "But that has done nothing to change the distribution of affluent and poor people."[26]

Detroit also aspired to a rebirth in the 1990s, with new office buildings going up and new football and baseball stadiums on the drawing boards. But residential construction was virtually nonexistent, a sure sign that the city was continuing to lose population. A total of 23,338 housing permits were issued in the seven counties of southeastern Michigan in 1996, but just eighty-six were in Detroit. "You see in Detroit new construction in the (neighborhood around the) Medical Center or in Harmonie Park, but that's offset by demolition and the reductions of values elsewhere," said Comerica Bank economist David Littmann. "Out in (the suburbs of) Troy or Bloomfield, you don't have those offsets, so it's all gravy."[27]

The sad fact is that mother cities like Cleveland and Detroit no longer offer something for everyone; they now fulfill a few specialized needs, such as employment and entertainment. They essentially play the role of one suburb among many, exactly as the Rand Corporation suggested Saint Louis do a quarter-century before. This transformation was dramatized by a 1996 survey of 400 downtown Buffalo business leaders, two-thirds of whom lived in the suburbs. These executives were asked to identify the "extracurricular" activities that attracted them back to the city's core. Their top five answers confirmed downtown's role as an entertainment hub: performing arts (66 percent), sports (63 percent), festivals and special events (60 percent), bars and restaurants (58 percent), and music at clubs and concerts (40 percent).* But almost no one mentioned other services that downtown once provided—such as shopping or housing—that now are the province of suburbia.[28]

The irony is that by emphasizing massive downtown projects over neighborhood revitalization, urban leaders are placing a higher priority on the wishes of suburban commuters than on the needs of those people who actually live in the city. Such policies will broaden the political impotence of mother cities and further polarize their residents. Author John Herbers, who studied development patterns in the 1980s, envisioned the day when cities would be dangerously divided between those who lived in trendy neighborhoods and those who merely served downtown workers and visitors. "The city (will become) home mostly for professionals, skilled white-collar workers who draw high wages, and low-paid service workers needed to maintain the downtown communications-finance-entertainment-tourist complex," he predicted.[29] The result cannot be positive. Twenty-six of the ninety-

---

*Responses add to more than 100 percent because multiple answers were allowed.

three mother cities will lose population between 1990 and 2020; only seven of the rest will grow faster than their suburbs.[30]*

The Domino Theory

Frederick Law Olmsted saw it coming long, long ago.

Olmsted was America's pioneer landscape architect, designing several of the nation's grandest public spaces during the mid- and late 1800s, including New York City's Central Park and the grounds of the U.S. Capitol. He was an early apostle of green space, believing that woods and fields offered precious tranquility to harried city residents. Those same people, he believed, would be greatly attracted if small, park-like communities were built on the periphery of the city. Thus Olmsted—as early as 1860—envisioned the flight of affluent city dwellers and the rise of the modern suburb. But he also sounded a warning, predicting that these refuges would fall short of their promise if they failed "to offer some assurance to those who wish to build villas that these districts shall not be bye and bye invaded by the desolation which thus far has invariably advanced before the progress of the town."[31]

Olmsted's words have become reality. Urban decay, blind to artificial borders, has spread from cities to suburbia. Hundreds of inner suburbs, the very magnets that first drew the middle class away from mother cities, now share their fate. They have become rundown and unfashionable, losing wealth and population.

This decline seems inevitable in retrospect. The large families that crowded into first-ring suburbs in the two decades following World War II have long since dispersed. The children have grown up and moved away, often to newer, more stable suburbs farther from the central city. Their parents, now elderly, rumble around in quiet, empty houses. "It's the same phenomenon that brought down central cities," said Thomas Bier, an urbanologist at Cleveland State University. "Suburbanites never dreamed it could catch up to them."[32]

This trend surfaced in the 1970s, when the inner suburbs of Boston, Cleveland, Pittsburgh, and Saint Louis stunned demographers by losing more than 10 percent of their residents. But the Detroit area offered the best example of suburban decay.[33] The twenty-one first-ring communities adjoining Detroit lost 19 percent of their population between 1970 and 1990, a net decline of almost 170,000 people.

---

*Charlotte, Columbus, Duluth, Milwaukee, Omaha, Portland, and Providence.

Their loss was not as severe as Detroit's 486,000, to be sure, but it was shocking nonetheless:

	Population Change	Growth Rate (%)	Share of Metro Total (%)	
	1970–1990	1970–1990	1970	1990
Detroit metro	Loss of 128,738	–2.4		
Components				
Detroit	Loss of 486,089	–32.1	28.5	19.8
First ring	Loss of 169,657	–19.1	16.7	13.8
Second ring	Gain of 364,877	+20.2	33.9	41.8
Outlying ring	Gain of 162,131	+14.6	20.9	24.6

Source: Author's analysis of U.S. Census Bureau data.

Urban decay had not seeped beyond the first ring of suburbia by 1990. Metropolitan Detroit's two outer belts continued to prosper, adding 527,000 residents between 1970 and 1990. Some of the distant suburbs, in fact, were growing at rates that would have made Sunbelt communities envious. Rochester Hills increased its population by one-half in the 1980s alone; Novi grew by one-third.[34]

It seemed possible that the decline of Detroit's inner suburbs might serve as an alarm, startling outer suburbanites into facing reality. If urban blight could penetrate Dearborn and Warren, after all, perhaps it eventually could reach Rochester Hills and Novi. But residents of the outer rings appeared unworried. Detroit, even when combined with the inner suburbs, was not much of a factor in their lives. The city and its first suburban ring had accounted for 45 percent of the metro area's population in 1970, but their share dropped below 34 percent by 1990. The economic imbalance was even worse. Residents of Detroit and its inner suburbs had an aggregate income of $21 billion in 1989; the two outer rings pulled in a hefty $59 billion.[35]

This pattern undoubtedly will be duplicated in varying degrees from coast to coast. The urban poor will move in growing numbers to inner suburbs, in turn pushing affluent suburbanites even farther from the central city. Most first-ring suburbs will be defenseless against economic decline, since they lack the downtowns, cultural attractions, and major hospitals on which mother cities are basing their own meager hopes for rebirth. Bier has conceded the likelihood that "urban problems will continue taking down suburb after suburb in a domino fashion."[36] This deterioration will not be stopped, but Detroit's history suggests that the population loss in the first ring will remain much smaller than the rate of expansion on the suburban fringe.

The Fire This Time

Hovering over any discussion of America's future is the issue that divides cities and suburbs more sharply than any other. Race.

The public eye uses color to distinguish between the two types of communities. It sees cities in shades of black and brown and yellow, suburbs in white. This stereotype reflects a substantial amount of truth, as stereotypes often do, but it will be increasingly inaccurate as the twenty-first century unfolds.

The truth first. It hardly comes as news that minority groups are concentrated in urban centers. The 1990 census classified nearly half of all mother-city residents—49.1 percent, to be exact—as minorities. Included were 12.3 million African-Americans, 7.1 million Hispanics, and 2.3 million Asian-Americans. Whites barely qualified for majority status within mother cities, accounting for 22.6 million residents, 50.9 percent of the total.

It is equally unsurprising that whites dominate the suburbs. The Census Bureau counted 82.6 million whites in suburbia in 1990, equaling 80.7 percent of all residents. The ranks of suburban minorities seemed puny in comparison: 8.6 million Hispanics, 7.2 million blacks, 3.5 million Asians.

But change is coming, dramatic change in the way the races are distributed in cities and suburbs. Some experts predict that today's minority groups will comprise roughly half of all Americans by the middle of the twenty-first century. "The United States is undergoing a transition from a predominantly white population rooted in Western culture to a society composed of diverse racial and ethnic minorities," observed demographer William O'Hare.[37] The nation's political and economic systems inevitably will change as well.

Mother cities will add approximately 5 million residents between 1990 and 2020, as minority groups grow in size and influence. The number of whites in mother cities will drop by 7.9 million as their exodus to suburbia continues; immigration and relatively high birth rates will drive the number of urban minorities up by almost 13 million. Whites will lose their tenuous majority as a result, sinking to just 29.7 percent of total city population by 2020. Hispanics and blacks will increase their proportions—the former more rapidly than the latter—until both groups reach statistical parity with urban whites. Each of these three blocs will contain approximately 30 percent of mother-city residents by 2020:

| | Share of Total Mother City Population (%) | | | | |
	White	Black	Hispanic	Asian	Native American
1990	50.9	27.6	16.0	5.1	0.4
2000	41.6	29.8	21.1	7.1	0.4
2010	35.3	30.4	25.2	8.7	0.4
2020	29.7	30.6	29.2	10.0	0.5

Source: Author's projections of population trends.

Whites still held population majorities in almost two-thirds of mother cities in 1990—sixty-one in all—but the total will drop to thirty-eight cities within three decades. Blacks will constitute the racial majority in eighteen mother cities by 2020, as will Hispanics in ten and Asians in one. The remaining twenty-six cities will be up for grabs, with no single group accounting for half of all residents.[38]

This demographic shift will alter cities like Philadelphia in striking ways. Whites retained a sizable edge in Philadelphia in 1990, with 52 percent of the city's population. Blacks, at 39 percent, were the only significant minority group. But Philadelphia will evolve into a multi-cultural community by 2020: 46 percent black, 34 percent white, 12 percent Hispanic, 8 percent Asian. Other cities that had white majori-ties in 1990 will become similarly diverse. Milwaukee, for example, will be 46 percent black, 36 percent white, 12 percent Hispanic, and 5 per-cent Asian in 2020. Sacramento will be 41 percent white, 23 percent Asian, 20 percent Hispanic, and 15 percent black.[39]

The key factor in determining the future of America's urban cen-ters will be the manner in which these disparate racial groups interact. Will they pool their political clout and economic resources to run their cities cooperatively? Or will they engage in bitter battles for undisputed control?

The unhappy fact is that the latter scenario seems more likely. It is true that a few cities with white majorities have elected black mayors, including Denver, Minneapolis, Rochester, and Seattle, but sharp racial divisions are the general rule in municipal elections. Harold Washington, an African-American who was the Democratic nominee for mayor of Chicago in 1983, was supported by just 12 percent of white voters, even though most Chicago whites were registered Demo-crats. This outcome was repeated in New York City six years later, after the Democratic Party nominated a black candidate, David Dinkins, for mayor. Republican Rudolph Giuliani was backed by 71 percent of white voters, including hundreds of thousands of Democratic defec-tors. Dinkins received 91 percent of the black vote.[40]

Nor are racial tensions confined to elections pitting blacks against whites. The 1996 campaign for mayor of metropolitan Miami matched

Arthur Teele, an African-American, against Alex Penelas, an Hispanic. Polls found that white voters were almost evenly divided between the two candidates, thereby shifting the balance of power to minority voters. Further complicating the election was the fact that neither contender reflected his race's political leanings. Most blacks in Miami were Democrats, but Teele was the Republican nominee. Cuban-Americans, on the other hand, had a strong affinity for the GOP, yet Penelas was the Democratic candidate. The election shaped up as a classic test of competing loyalties to party and race.

Race won out. Fully 95 percent of black voters supported Teele, while 92 percent of Hispanics opted for Penelas, who won the election. A widely published photo the next morning showed a jubilant Congresswoman Ileana Ros-Lehtinen embracing Penelas at his victory celebration. Her joy knew no political bounds, since she was a Republican and the mayor-elect was a Democrat. What mattered most was that both were of Cuban heritage.[41]

Such ethnic divisions, of course, are as old as American cities themselves. The earliest immigrants congregated according to nationality: Italians in one neighborhood, the Irish in another, Germans in yet another. And they voted accordingly, favoring candidates from their homelands. Tammany Hall, New York City's Democratic machine, eventually learned to harness these prejudices by balancing its tickets, making sure to have at least one nominee from every major ethnic group.

But racial politics can be considerably more volatile. Italians, Irishmen, and Germans had their whiteness in common; their descendants gradually blended in the melting pot. But the multicultural city of the future will be divided on the irreducible basis of skin color. Whites, African-Americans, Hispanics, and Asians never can be completely alike; they always will be aware of the overriding characteristic that makes them distinct.

This self-consciousness almost certainly will trigger a rise in urban tensions. Some whites living in mother cities—young professionals, for instance—can be expected to embrace multiculturalism. But the working and middle classes, who once worried so intensely about the rise of black power, will grow increasingly uncomfortable as Asians and Hispanics also gain demographic, political, and economic influence. This stress already is being felt in many mother cities, even in relatively small Reading, Pennsylvania, where one of every five people is Hispanic. "Oh Lord, we've been inundated with them. I wish (they) would make more of an effort to learn the English language and not expect us to cater to them," said Betty Hangen, a sixty-eight-year-old white

Reading resident, to a reporter. Her complaint was received bitterly by twenty-one-year-old Michelle Perez, who lived nearby. "They see Spanish people," she said, "and they think troublemakers, roaches, rice, and beans."[42]

Minorities will feel a greater sense of competition not only with whites, but also with each other, following the Miami model. African-Americans, historically the largest minority group in mother cities, struggled for decades to achieve equality with whites, but now see others grasping for urban power. Asian-Americans already outnumber blacks in San Francisco and Seattle. Hispanics moved ahead of blacks in Houston, Los Angeles, and San Antonio before the 1990 census and passed them in New York City in the mid-1990s. This upheaval in population rankings will become more chaotic after the turn of the century. The number of Asians in mother cities is projected to grow by 118 percent between 1990 and 2020, while the number of Hispanics is expected to increase 104 percent. The growth rate for urban blacks will be only 24 percent.[43]

It is entirely possible that a mayoral election in the typical mother city of the future could be virtually deadlocked, with white, black, and Hispanic contenders being supported by most members of their respective racial groups, yielding about one-third of the total vote for each. The white candidate might slip through to become leader of a city heavily populated by minorities.* Or a black or Hispanic mayor might take office despite the opposition of the other two major races. How will the losers react? And, more importantly, how will the winner, no matter his or her color, govern effectively?

This turmoil will be compounded by the declining value of the objective—political control of mother cities. Racial groups will be battling for pieces of an ever-shrinking pie, a situation that is guaranteed to increase urban levels of frustration and desperation. Each successive federal census has found a smaller percentage of Americans living in central cities; each has reported a higher proportion of city residents living in poverty; each has detected a widening of the income gap between mother cities and suburbs. None of these trends will be reversed in coming decades, as jobs and wealth migrate even farther from the urban core.

The forecast for urban America admittedly is a gloomy one, beginning with the largest urban center of all, New York City. A special panel,

---

*The precedent exists. Both New York City and Los Angeles elected white mayors in the 1990s even though 57 percent of New York City residents and 63 percent of Los Angeles residents were minorities.

the Commission on the Year 2000, analyzed the city's condition in 1987 and concluded that "without a response to the problem of poverty, the New York of the twenty-first century (would) be not just a city divided, not just a city excluding those at the bottom from the fullness of opportunity, *but a city in which peace and social harmony (might) not be possible.*"[44] Similarly frightening predictions could be made for most of the nation's mother cities. "As poverty becomes even more concentrated, we have no reason to believe that the possibility for urban unrest will decline," said Michael Dawson, director of the University of Chicago's Center for the Study of Race, Politics, and Culture.[45]

This anger certainly will spill over into contentious political campaigns, but it also might seek dangerous outlets. The problems of urban poverty and frustration are every bit as severe now as when Watts, Detroit, and Newark burned in the 1960s. And the outcome could be similar, too, predicted columnist Carl Rowan in his 1996 book, *The Coming Race War in America.* He contended that poor blacks had no meaningful stake in America's future. Their despair, coupled with the rise of white hate groups, seemed to Rowan to be a deadly prescription for violence. "Too much rage has built up in the minds of young blacks who are trapped in the corridors of resentment and hopelessness for me to assume that they will not strike out with firepower, especially if provoked," he wrote.[46]

Suburban Havens

Suburbanites will watch this urban disorder with a combination of fascination and anxiety. They already considered cities to be foreign places in the 1990s, but they will think them even stranger in the future, especially when viewing them from the safety of their middle- and upper-class enclaves.

Whites typically overstate the size and influence of minority groups, an inclination revealed by a 1995 *Washington Post* poll. The *Post* asked white respondents to guess what percentage of Americans were black, Hispanic, or Asian. The average answer put 49.3 percent of the nation's residents into those three minority classifications, more than double the correct figure of 24.4 percent.[47]* One can only imagine what the answers will be if the *Post* repeats its survey in 2020,

---

*Minorities had similar misperceptions. Blacks estimated that 45.5 percent of Americans were white. Hispanic respondents put the figure at 46.7 percent, Asians at 54.8 percent. The correct answer was that roughly 74 percent of Americans were white.

when fully 36 percent of all Americans and 70 percent of mother-city residents will be minorities.[48]

Suburbanites also tend to believe that racial harmony is unattainable. A 1995 Gallup Poll asked respondents of all races whether they believed black–white relations will always be tense or eventually will be normalized. Urban residents showed a surprising level of optimism in splitting their votes almost evenly: 49 percent said race relations will remain difficult, but 46 percent expressed faith in a solution. Suburbanites, on the other hand, demonstrated an unmistakable pessimism: 58 percent said that racial problems always will exist, while just 38 percent suggested they will be worked out.[49]

These two beliefs—that minorities are more numerous and powerful than they really are, and that whites and minorities cannot live in harmony—will inspire white Americans to maintain, as best they can, their suburban havens from twenty-first century urban turmoil. They generally will succeed, though not as well as many might like. Suburbia will not be immune from the diversification of America. The number of minorities living in the suburbs will grow by 26.6 million between 1990 and 2020, easily outpacing the corresponding increase of 12.2 million suburban whites. But whites nonetheless will remain dominant, accounting for two-thirds of all suburbanites in 2020:

	Share of Total Suburban Population (%)				
	White	**Black**	**Hispanic**	**Asian**	**Native American**
1990	80.7	7.1	8.4	3.5	0.4
2000	76.0	8.0	10.9	4.8	0.4
2010	71.4	8.7	13.4	6.1	0.4
2020	67.2	9.1	16.0	7.3	0.4

Source: Author's projections of population trends.

White hegemony was unchallenged in 1990, as white majorities controlled sixty-six of Inner America's sixty-seven suburban regions. The sole exception was Honolulu, where 53 percent of suburbanites were of Asian heritage. The situation will be much the same in 2020, with whites continuing to exercise suburban power in all but three metros. Asians will remain dominant in suburban Honolulu in 2020, and Hispanics will have achieved pluralities in the suburbs of Los Angeles and Miami, two regions where they already claimed about one-third of all residents back in 1990.

Most of Inner America's suburban regions will retain substantial white majorities well into the future, even though nearby mother cities will be undergoing radical changes. Ninety-three percent of the residents of suburban Pittsburgh in 2020 will be white, as will similarly high proportions in other suburban regions: 85 percent outside Detroit, 79 percent outside Philadelphia, 74 percent outside Sacramento, 71 percent outside Chicago, and 68 percent outside New York City.

These suburban whites feel little kinship with their urban neighbors, and they will feel even less as the racial balance tips in the next century. Just 12 percent of all white Americans lived in mother cities in 1990; this tiny share will decline to 7 percent by 2020. Suburbia, on the other hand, contained 44 percent of the nation's white residents in 1990, a share that will expand to 46 percent by 2020.[50]

It is a simple fact that whites are losing any sense of connection with big cities; their alienation is reflected in their reluctance to support urban charities. The American Association of Fund-Raising Counsel reported that donations to universities, hospitals, and museums—favorite causes of the suburban middle class—grew a healthy 80 percent between the late 1980s and the late 1990s. But contributions increased only 48 percent to agencies helping the poor and homeless. "There has been a shift in the attitudes of a lot of people toward urban poverty," said Richard Hirsch of Covenant House, a New York City shelter and counseling service. "There is a lot less sympathy out there for this kind of work."[51]

The bulk of the diversification that does occur within suburbia in coming decades will be concentrated in the inner suburbs, many of which already are assuming an urban character. The Washington, D.C., metro will be typical. Fully 86 percent of the increase in the black, Hispanic, and Asian populations of suburban Washington between 1990 and 2020 will occur in the first ring, consisting of those counties and independent cities that adjoin the mother city. Only 2 percent of all new minority settlers will choose the outlying suburban belt about fifty miles away from Washington. Most whites, on the other hand, will opt to be as far from the city as possible. Just 34 percent of the increase in white suburban population will occur in the first ring, compared to 40 percent in the second ring and 26 percent in the outlying belt.[52]

This is not to say that suburban segregation will be unchallenged as the twenty-first century unfolds. It will erode fairly rapidly in the inner suburbs, more slowly in the outer rings. The pace of integration will be linked to economic progress within individual regions, according to a 1994 University of Michigan study. The more prosperous the metro area, it said, the better the opportunities will be for minorities in the suburbs. "There are sometimes very few things that are hopeful in race relations," wrote Reynolds Farley, a Michigan research scientist. "But where there has been rapid new construction, segregation has fallen modestly, in general. In some areas, it has fallen quite substantially."[53]

The rapid expansion of the minority middle class will add to the pressure for suburban desegregation. Press reports focus on the urban poor, but millions of African-Americans, Hispanics, and Asian-Americans earn good salaries and wish to live accordingly. They seek to escape cities for the same reasons that whites are leaving—crime, poor schools, declining services. Many already have made the move. "Huge concentrations of affluent minorities live in edge cities," reported Joel Garreau, pointing to suburban enclaves such as the Southfield-Northland Mall area near Detroit and the Lanham-Landover area near Washington, both of which were more than 70 percent black in 1990.[54]

Most minority residents of suburbia, however, do not have neighbors of the same color. They have been forced to integrate themselves into white communities as best they can, often suffering a severe identity crisis in the process. Suburban minorities clearly are different from the whites next door—a fact of which they are reminded every day—yet they also have surprisingly little in common with urban minorities. Blacks in well-to-do Oakland County, Michigan, for example, earn twice as much as blacks in nearby Detroit, yet they are paid 17 percent less than their fellow Oakland County residents who happen to be white. These suburban blacks likewise are caught in the middle in terms of education and employment—substantially better off than city blacks, but a few steps behind suburban whites:

	Detroit		Oakland County	
	Whites	Blacks	Whites	Blacks
Population				
Total	212,804	778,456	959,618	77,255
Blacks per 100 whites	100	366	100	8
Income				
Median family income	$27,122	$21,283	$51,502	$42,904
Per $100 by whites in same locality	$ 100	$ 78	$ 100	$ 83
Per $100 by Detroit blacks	$ 127	$ 100	$ 242	$ 202
Education				
Adults with high school diplomas (%)	61.9	62.6	85.1	79.0
Adults with bachelor's degrees (%)	12.3	8.4	29.9	25.2
Employment				
Management or professional specialties (%)	21.5	17.7	35.0	30.8
Unemployment rate (1990; %)	11.6	22.2	4.8	10.9

Source: Author's analysis of U.S. Census Bureau data.

Straddling two starkly different Americas—and not being wholly accepted by either—can take its toll on suburban minorities. A *Wall Street Journal* reporter encountered several African-American teenagers who lived in Detroit suburbs, yet were strongly attracted to the inner city, no matter how impoverished and dangerous it might be. "I feel like I've been deprived of knowing myself," said thirteen-year-old Rebecca Allen. "When I go into the city, there is a different way of talking among blacks, a different way of dressing. I want to educate myself about that." But her wish was not one that could be fulfilled easily. Chante Butler, a twenty-four-year-old woman from Farmington Hills, Michigan, said her experience had been that city blacks often looked down on suburban blacks like herself, calling her "a snob, a sellout, an Oreo."[55]

The key question, as far as politicians are concerned, is which way the expanding ranks of suburban minorities will vote. The gospel of American politics insists that people are most strongly influenced by the prevailing views of the place they live. A city Democrat who moves to the suburbs might not change his registration, goes the conventional wisdom, but he or she will be more likely to vote Republican nonetheless.

It remains unclear whether this rule will extend to minorities still fighting for their share of the suburban dream, especially when most Republicans seem to have little sympathy for their struggle. GOP candidates have made a few breakthroughs, to be sure. Fully 62 percent of black voters supported Republican Tom Kean, a liberal on racial issues, in the 1985 governor's race in New Jersey. But more typical are the results of the 1996 presidential election, where 82 percent of suburban blacks backed Bill Clinton and just 13 percent voted for Bob Dole.[56]

Whites, for their part, will stay comfortably in charge of suburbia— and hence the nation—well into the twenty-first century. They will retain local control of the things that really matter to them, like schools, roads, and recreation facilities. And they will strive to keep mother cities and their urban woes at arm's length or even farther if possible.

But that doesn't mean they will exclude blacks, Hispanics, and Asians from future political debate. Racial prejudices in the voting booth can be expected to erode—slowly, to be sure—as whites come into daily contact with the growing numbers of middle-class minorities in suburbia. Assisting this process of electoral integration will be the fact that young, college-educated whites—the next generation of suburban leaders—show a willingness to accept political diversity. A 1998 Harris Poll of 2,000 college freshmen found that nearly three-quarters believed a member of a minority group will be elected president in their lifetimes.[57]

There already have been a few instances of suburban whites supporting minority candidates. Douglas Wilder, an African-American, was elected governor of the suburban state of Virginia in 1989. Gary Locke, the son of Chinese immigrants, won the 1996 election for governor of Washington, a suburban state where 88 percent of voters were white and only 5 percent were Asian.

The surprising fact in both campaigns was that remarkably few voters seemed to care that Wilder and Locke were not Caucasian. What mattered was that both candidates de-emphasized racial issues— "I've got to be a governor for *everybody*," said Locke—while advocating moderate policies and pledging allegiance to the middle class.[58] What mattered, in other words, was that they articulated the suburban agenda. "Race is always there, but it isn't the great fault line it is in the South or California," said University of Washington political scientist Andrea Simpson after Locke's win. "Whites aren't nervous that this politician will only represent blacks or Asians. *I get the sense the divisions here are more urban–rural or urban–suburban.*"[59]

The Growing Divide

Race will draw the sharpest distinction between mother cities and suburbs in coming years, but not the only one.

Jesse Jackson, who has focused on civil rights throughout his long career, discussed the broader picture in 1997 on the forty-third anniversary of the Supreme Court's landmark *Brown* v. *Board of Education of Topeka* school-desegregation ruling. "The race gap, in some instances, is wider," he admitted. But he cautioned that much more was at stake, that the nation was dividing into two Americas, one suburban and prosperous, one urban and poor. "The investment gap, the class gap, the opportunity gap, is greater than in 1954," he said. "And now, with the advent of computers, it is getting greater still."[60]

Similar concerns troubled Daniel Patrick Moynihan, the renowned social analyst and U.S. senator from New York, who watched with dismay as urban America deteriorated in the 1980s and 1990s. He warned fellow delegates to the 1996 Democratic convention that, by all indications, things were going to get worse in the future, not better. "The condition of our cities," he said, "is going to be a problem beyond anyone's comprehension."[61]

A wide array of evidence suggests that Jackson and Moynihan are correct. The chasm between the two Americas will widen substantially in the twenty-first century, not only racially, but also in terms of the other city–suburban gaps that were discussed in chapter 3.

Family Stability

Pressures on urban families are intensifying. The U.S. Conference of
Mayors surveyed twenty-nine cities in 1997 and learned that the
demand for emergency food and housing had increased for the thir-
teenth straight year. The study's most striking discovery was that 60
percent of the hungry and 36 percent of the homeless were not anony-
mous drifters, but were members of families.[62]

This situation undoubtedly will worsen, given the new, tight restrictions on welfare eligibility and the slow decline in the number of
urban jobs offering decent pay. "Having a job does not protect people
from being hungry," said Ellen Parker, director of a Boston food bank.
"We're fighting an uphill battle."[63]

Education

Blacks and Hispanics might be rising to political control in dozens of
mother cities, but they remain stranded at the bottom of the educational ladder. A Census Bureau study of adults between the ages of
twenty-five and forty-four found that just 14 percent of blacks and 10
percent of Hispanics had college degrees as of 1992. The corresponding figure for white twenty-five-to-forty-four-year-olds was 28 percent.[64]

Future generations of urban minorities will suffer from the same
educational imbalance, as indicated by current dropout rates. Black
students are almost twice as likely as their white counterparts to leave
high school without graduating, according to federal data, while the
dropout rate for Hispanic students is three times the rate for whites.
"This is a time bomb waiting to happen. This will be a disaster for the
U.S., if a large percentage of the labor force doesn't have a high school
education," said Jorge del Pinal, a Census Bureau demographer. His
worries were echoed by Walter Secada, an education professor at the
University of Wisconsin: "It's a recipe for social and economic disaster
that will make . . . the Watts riots look like Disney World."[65]

The decay of urban educational standards, if anything, seems
likely to accelerate. Studies already point in that direction. Eighty-six
percent of suburban teachers surveyed by Metropolitan Life in 1995
characterized their schools as excellent or good, up five percentage
points from 1984. But the number of city teachers who felt positively
about their schools was lower (77 percent) and had dropped two
points in a decade.[66]

Public Safety

It won't matter much if big-city crime rates rise or fall in coming years. Perception will be as important as reality, and the suburbanites of the future undoubtedly will continue to perceive mother cities to be dangerous.

Most of the blame will belong to tabloid-style television newscasts and their lurid fascination with violence. "Crime has become a hot issue for a number of reasons, beginning with the media. The public's concern with crime rises and falls in lockstep with media reporting about the issue," wrote demographic analyst Cheryl Russell. Her conclusion was backed by a 1994 *Los Angeles Times* poll that asked Americans how their attitudes about public safety had been shaped. Sixty-five percent said the media had wielded the most influence on their perceptions of crime, 21 percent said personal experience had been more important, and 13 percent cited both factors.[67]

The moral? If TV newscasts were to reduce their bloated diets of crime stories, suburbanites might have a more realistic view of public safety in big cities. The likelihood of it happening? Virtually none.

Business

Future technological developments, as we have seen, will accelerate the decentralization of metro areas. Mother cities are bound to suffer. Corporate headquarters will continue streaming to the suburbs, as will businesses that historically have favored downtown locations, such as law firms, stockbrokerages, advertising agencies, and banks.

A second factor will contribute to this exodus. Most bosses, quite simply, prefer the suburbs. Author William Whyte studied the moves of thirty-eight major corporations out of New York City over a ten-year period, finding that thirty-one moved close to the suburban homes of their chief executive officers. "It's a wonder executives keep a straight face," he wrote. "Life-style needs of employees? Companies don't have to spend all that money researching them. They don't have to compare area A with area B and area C. All they have to do is look in the phone directory. Where does the boss live? That is where the company is going."[68]

Employment

As the urban–suburban education gap widens, so will the employment gap. A 1995 Census Bureau report demonstrated conclusively that earnings are related directly to the amount of schooling received by a family's chief breadwinner. Median household incomes progressed from $18,300 for a high school dropout to $31,400 for a high school graduate, $37,200 for a college dropout, $52,900 for a college graduate, and $80,000 for someone with a doctorate.[69] "The new economy is skill-based and more and more high-tech oriented," said Ron Boster of the Committee for Economic Development, an independent research firm. "Those who have skills do very well. Those who do not, fall through the cracks in terms of income and, very importantly, in terms of opportunity."[70]

Heavy industry once provided the urban working class with middle-class wages. But the number of manufacturing jobs in big cities will continue declining as some factories move to the suburban fringe, others flee to foreign countries, and still others become automated. "In short, if it can be done by a machine, it soon will be," wrote futurist Marvin Cetron. "Most of the new jobs that appear, not just in the 1990s but from now on, will fall into only two categories: the ones you don't want and the ones you can't get—not, at least, without extensive preparation."[71]

Retail Sales

The golden age of downtown shopping is long gone, and it won't be returning.

Analysts Christopher Leinberger and Charles Lockwood noted as far back as 1986 that the typical metro area was realigning around "urban villages," their name for burgeoning suburban amalgamations of office parks and shopping centers. "Each urban village has its core—a kind of new downtown—where the buildings are tallest, the daytime population largest, and the traffic congestion most severe," they wrote.[72] These edge cities, as Joel Garreau later named them, will dominate the future, drawing more than three-quarters of all the retail spending in Inner America.

Income

The United States reached an unhappy milestone in 1994, marking the first time that the richest 20 percent of households had a larger combined income than the middle 60 percent. This imbalance hit cities hardest of all. "The problem of this disparity is not just with the lowest-class people," said Baltimore Mayor Kurt Schmoke. "The working-class and middle-class folks are going to feel the same pinch."[73]

The income gap between cities and suburbs has been widening ever since the late 1960s, and it undoubtedly will continue doing so. Hopes for an urban renaissance will be dashed by the widespread poverty that plagues big cities, especially their minority residents. Four of every ten black and Hispanic children—the future leaders of so many mother cities—were being raised in substandard conditions in 1995:

Share of Each Racial Group Living Below the Poverty Level (%)

	Whites	Blacks	Hispanics	Asians
All persons	11.2	29.3	30.3	14.6
Persons under 18	16.2	41.9	40.0	19.5

Source: U.S. Census Bureau data.

Urban analyst David Rusk insisted that if suburbanites would be willing to tackle the problem of urban poverty, they could help narrow the income gap. "Inner cities should not have to assume the role of sole providers for the poor," he said. "That must be the responsibility of the whole metro area—city and suburbs, cities without suburbs."[74] His wishes were heartfelt, but they are not likely to be fulfilled.

A Defining Moment

The ninth and final gap between suburbs and mother cities—the disparity in their political power—will be just like all the others. It will widen in the early years of the twenty-first century.

Suburban states, which controlled 320 electoral votes in 1996, will climb to a projected peak of 362 in 2004, then settle back to 332 by 2020, easily dwarfing the other three categories of states. The paltry ranks of city states will be thinned from two to one when New York temporarily falls into the suburban sphere in 2000, leaving only the District of Columbia and its three electoral votes in the urban column. An upswing in New York City's population will restore New York's designation as a city state by 2008.*

A comparison of the political landscapes in 1996 and 2020 shows that suburbia will tighten its control of America ever so subtly during the intervening years. Suburban states provided 62.5 percent of all popular votes and 59.5 percent of the electoral votes in 1996. Both shares will increase slightly more than two percentage points by 2020:

---

*See Appendix I for the projected allocation of electoral votes between 2000 and 2024.

	States*	Projected Pop-ular Votes (PV)	Share of PV (%)	Projected Elec-toral Votes (EV)	Share of EV (%)
Nationwide (2020)	51	116,082,369	—	538	—
Inner America					
City states	2	6,952,205	6.0	32	5.9
Suburban states	24	75,184,647	64.8	332	61.7
Outer America					
Fringe states	9	21,477,373	18.5	98	18.2
Nonmetro states	16	12,468,144	10.7	76	14.1

*Recall that Washington, D.C., is classified as a state.
Source: Author's projections of election trends.

Mother cities will be far and away the weakest political players in twenty-first century America. Suburban states will be about ten times as powerful as city states by 2020. Fringe and nonmetro states, though weaker than suburbia, still will have considerably more muscle than big cities. Presidential candidates and congressional leaders, mindful of this hierarchy, can be expected to stress policies that will appeal to the suburban majority. It will be a rare politician indeed who places top priority on addressing the severe economic and social problems of America's cities.

Congress offered a preview of this brave new world in July 1996, when it debated legislation to reform the welfare system. The Republican-sponsored bill stipulated that welfare recipients would have to find jobs in two years or lose any future benefits. It also mandated that no individual could receive more than five years of welfare payments during his or her lifetime.

The Urban Institute, a nonpartisan research organization, estimated that the proposed legislation would plunge into poverty another 1.1 million children, most of whom lived in urban areas. "This is going to hit cities very hard, and we don't hear a lot about that," warned the Urban Institute's Sheila Zedlewski. "Most new jobs are in the suburbs, and it's not going to be easy for everyone to take a fast-food job fifteen miles from their home."[75]

Bill Clinton found himself in an uncomfortable position as the crucial roll call approached. He had been elected president in 1992 on a promise to "end welfare as we know it," yet had been unable to craft a bill acceptable to the liberal wing of the Democratic Party during his first two years in office. Republicans seized the initiative in 1995, offering a series of welfare proposals that were much tougher than the president would have liked. Clinton vetoed two Republican bills, and he wasn't much happier with this latest version, which he admitted had "serious flaws." But his chief political consultant, Dick Morris, warned that a third veto might be catastrophic politically.[76]

Daniel Patrick Moynihan viewed the president's political dilemma without sympathy. Moynihan was that rarest of birds in the 1990s, a senator from a city state, and he believed the Democratic Party had a responsibility to help the urban poor. He had spoken caustically in late 1995 when Clinton vetoed an earlier welfare bill only after much anguish. "A 'liberal' executive and a 'conservative' Congress were quite prepared to enact legislation that verged on vengeance against children whose existence is seen as an affront to the values of a threatened society," Moynihan charged. "When fear takes hold, *even so piteous a fear as that of losing an election,* expect no mercy."[77] The election seemed even more fearsome to Clinton and most politicians by late July 1996, since it was less than 100 days away.

The welfare-reform package sailed through the House of Representatives with surprising ease. The final vote was 328 to 101. Speaker Newt Gingrich described the victory as a "major, major achievement" accomplished by "a bipartisan majority" of 230 Republicans and 98 Democrats.[78] What was most striking about the roll call was the sharp division between urban and suburban representatives. Congressmen from mother cities voted against welfare reform by a count of nearly 2 to 1, but their counterparts from suburbia carried the day, favoring reform by an overwhelming margin of 6 to 1. This split was mirrored within the Democratic Party itself. City Democrats cast 59 votes against welfare reform and just 14 for it, but suburban Democrats offered 37 yes votes and only 23 no votes:*

	Total Vote		Republicans		Democrats	
	Yes	No	Yes	No	Yes	No
House	328	101	230	2	98	98
Components						
City districts	33	61	19	2	14	59
Suburban districts	144	23	107	0	37	23
Fringe districts	76	8	58	0	18	8
Nonmetro districts	75	9	46	0	29	8

Source: Author's analysis of congressional roll call (July 31, 1996).

The president quickly announced that he would sign the bill when it reached his desk. "There was significant disagreement among my advisers about whether this bill should be signed or vetoed," he said of the intense debate within the White House. "It was a very moving thing."[79]

---

*This roll call chart—and similar charts in subsequent chapters—does not break down the votes of congressmen outside the Democratic or Republican parties. But votes cast by these independents are included in the "Total Vote" columns.

Clinton's decision was widely regarded as a political watershed. A Democratic president and a majority of suburban Democratic representatives had turned their backs on the party's New Deal tradition, and city congressmen had been too weak to prevent it. "This is a defining moment for the president and the party," cheered Ed Kilgore, political director of the Democratic Leadership Council. "We certainly believe that taking positive action on welfare reform is kind of a threshold credibility issue for anyone trying to show they're a new Democrat."[80]

The strongest voice in opposition, not surprisingly, was that of Pat Moynihan. He blasted the bill as "welfare repeal," not welfare reform, and insisted it was the first step toward dismantling America's social contract with its disadvantaged citizens, a pact that Franklin Roosevelt had initiated more than sixty years earlier. The consequences, he predicted, would be devastating for the poor, for cities, and for the Democratic Party itself.

His fellow senators listened impatiently to this forecast of doom; they had heard it before. Moynihan, after all, had used even stronger language a few months earlier in cautioning his fellow Democrats against welfare reform. If they ever supported the Republican legislation, he told them, they would hasten urban deterioration. "Should it do so, the Democratic Party will be to blame, and blamed it will be. It will never again be able to speak with any credibility to the central social issue of our age," Moynihan warned darkly. "We have fashioned our own coffin. There will be no flowers."[81]

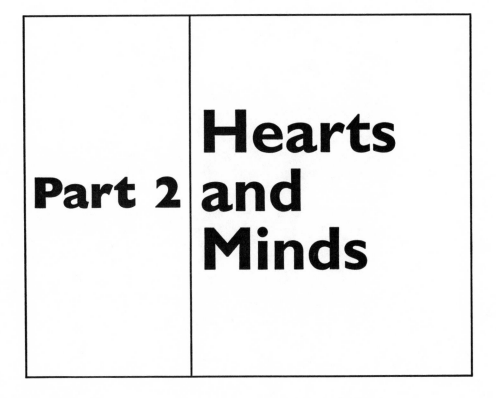

Part 2 Hearts and Minds

5 Levittown's Children: The Suburban Viewpoint

America's suburban pioneers were drifting into their golden years as the twentieth century neared its end. The young, enthusiastic veterans who had gathered up their families and streamed out of big cities in the 1940s and 1950s were growing old. They no longer rushed to work each morning on expressways and commuter trains, nor did they hurry back each night to subdivisions teeming with children. Their paychecks now came from the Social Security Administration, and their kids were off raising kids of their own.

Curators at the Smithsonian Institution knew that an era was ending. It was their task to preserve Americana of all types—important scientific inventions, inaugural gowns of the first ladies, props from popular TV shows—and they felt the need to add to their collection. They decided in 1996 to seek the perfect souvenir of modern suburbia's early days.[1]

But what should it be?

The logical place to search for the answer was Levittown, the prototypical suburb that had risen from the potato fields of Long Island in the late 1940s. It was there that William Levitt had introduced assembly-line techniques to the construction industry. Old-timers still recalled how Levitt's crews built hundreds of homes simultaneously, as trucks moved slowly down Levittown's new streets, dropping off windows, siding, and toilets every sixty feet, while landscapers planted trees every twenty-eight feet, no more or no less. "We planned every foot of it," Levitt once boasted. "Every store, filling station, school, house, apartment, church, color, tree, and shrub."[2] His company built 17,447 houses, creating from scratch a community of 65,000 people. Other developers marveled at his efficiency and shamelessly copied his methods. "If imitation is the sincerest form of flattery," wrote historian Kenneth Jackson in 1985, "then William Levitt has been much honored in the past forty years."[3]

The Smithsonian decided that a few run-of-the-mill mementos could never do justice to such an historic place. It sought the very object that had lured tens of thousands of refugees from New York City, the structure that had galvanized contractors from coast to coast. It cast its dragnet for an original Levittown house, one unmodified from Levitt's design.

The searchers set to their work with an optimism that soon faded. Everyone, it seemed, had changed his or her property since the 1940s. The garages were proof of that. Levitt had not included garages in his master plan, considering them an unnecessary frill, but they had become nearly universal in Levittown by the late 1990s. One observer estimated that 90 percent of the homes in Levitt's dream town had been expanded; most of the rest had been altered more subtly. The Smithsonian, try though it might, was forced to report in early 1997 that it could not find its prize. "One of these days, there is going to be a Levitt house that will be a museum," sighed Lynn Matarrese of the Levittown Historical Society. "But I don't know when that will be, and I don't know where."[4]

Her frustration dramatized the fact that suburbia had come of age. Not only had Levittown's homes been enlarged and improved, but the town itself had changed substantially from William Levitt's original vision:

- Levittown began as a bedroom community for people with jobs in New York City, but it had become largely self-sufficient. The 1990 census found that 64 percent of all employed Levittowners stayed within suburban Nassau County to work.
- It began as a home for adults just starting out, but now included many who had achieved success. One of every four Levittown workers in 1990 was a manager or practiced a professional specialty like medicine or the law.
- It began as a place to raise young families, but had grown considerably older. Fully 27 percent of Levittown households were receiving Social Security checks as of 1990.
- It began as a town with affordable housing, but had become much more expensive. The first Levittown homes sold for $6,900 to $9,900, but their expanded, updated reincarnations went for $120,000 to $180,000 by 1997.
- It began as a haven for whites—and remained one—but now was diversifying slowly. Levittown was 99.7 percent white in 1960, a figure that inched down to 97.4 percent by 1990. The latter census found 1,403 minorities in town, most of them Asian-Americans.[5]

Perhaps the biggest change was one that could not be quantified. Levittown—and indeed, burgeoning suburbs across America—was built for a postwar generation that retained strong ties to nearby cities even after leaving them. These suburban pioneers had been born and raised in city neighborhoods; they still had family and friends there.

But their children—the ubiquitous baby boomers born between 1946 and 1964—had radically different experiences. They grew up and went to school in suburbia; most are raising their own families there today. Big cities, to them, are distant, somewhat forbidding places where one might work a day job or visit occasionally for a night out. But live in a city? Absolutely not.

It is this Suburban Generation—one without an urban focus—that now is attaining financial and political power across America. The oldest of these baby boomers will be just fifty-four in 2000—a prime age for corporate presidents and political leaders—and won't be eligible for retirement until 2011. The youngest boomers will remain in the workforce and the political arena well into the 2030s. These suburban adults are widely separated in age, but not in temperament. They hold five core beliefs in common, beliefs that will reshape America dramatically in the years ahead.

An Independent Streak

Frank Lloyd Wright concluded as early as 1958 that America's urban centers were afflicted with a terminal disease. "To look at the cross section of any plan of a big city," he scoffed, "is to look at something like the section of a fibrous tumor."[6]

The biggest problem, in the famed architect's opinion, was that cities were too densely populated. The typical mother city in 1950 crammed 8,715 persons into each square mile, the equivalent of fourteen per acre. Congestion was most severe in New York City, which had 25,046 people per square mile, translating to thirty-nine per acre.[7] "Gather so many people together, visible on every acre, and try to imagine freedom and the pursuit of happiness left to each in housing them by the square mile," Wright wrote. "Any wise recognition and definition of freedom under democracy must say that ultimate human satisfactions no longer depend upon, but *are destroyed by density of population*." He contended that the ideal settlement pattern—one that would nurture individual freedom and creativity—would be just one person per acre.[8]

The white middle class thought along the same lines. The suburban land rush of the 1950s was as much a rebellion against density as anything else, with disgruntled city dwellers scrambling to escape the congestion, traffic, and related tensions of urban life. The irony was that their exodus helped to relieve the very overcrowding they fled; all but ten of the nation's ninety-three mother cities reached their peak densities before 1961. The average square mile in the average mother city slimmed rapidly from 8,715 residents in 1950 to 6,999 just ten years later, then continued a steady decline to 4,249 by 1990.[9]

Most urban refugees didn't object to size, in and of itself. Philadelphians, for example, could take pride when their city passed the population milestone of 2 million residents in 1950. But they also could be annoyed that they and their 2 million neighbors were packed into a mere 127 square miles.[10] The city's density of 16,286 people per square mile seemed inhuman, especially at a time when suburbia had become so accessible. Hundreds of thousands living in cramped apartments and dreary row houses dreamed of a better life in the wide open spaces outside Philadelphia; many soon acted on their impulses.

Even the largest of today's suburbs reflect this aversion to high densities. A total of 115 communities have seen their populations climb above 100,000 since 1950, including dozens of suburbs such as Chesapeake, Virginia; Irving, Texas; and Rancho Cucamonga, California. These 115 young giants had a collective density of 2,034 people per square mile in 1990, less than half the average for mother cities.[11] It is intriguing to imagine what urban America might have been like if it had developed in a similar manner. New York City, for instance, would have just 628,000 residents if they were allocated at a rate of 2,034 per square mile; the city's actual population is 7.3 million. Houston would be the only one of America's largest mother cities to still have a population above 1 million under this low-density scenario:

	Actual	1990 Population If Density of 2,034 per Square Mile
All 93 mother cities	44,486,735	21,297,200
Largest mother cities		
New York City	7,322,564	628,303
Los Angeles	3,485,398	954,556
Chicago	2,783,726	462,125
Houston	1,630,553	1,098,157
Philadelphia	1,585,577	274,793
San Diego	1,110,549	659,016
Detroit	1,027,974	282,116
Dallas	1,006,877	696,442

Source: Author's projections of population trends.

New York City, of course, is in no danger of losing 90 percent of its residents, but this demographic fantasy illuminates the broad philosophical gap between mother cities and suburbs. Urban life is based on the principles of high population density, community, and coexistence; the 2.8 million people crammed into Chicago's 227 square miles have no option but to live and work in close quarters. Suburbia, on the other hand, is dedicated to open space, privacy, and autonomy; Chicago would hold just 460,000 people if it had developed along suburban lines. It is no surprise that so many suburbanites are repelled by high-density cities that are unlike their own quiet communities. Joel Garreau succinctly characterized their disdain: "If we thought downtown levels of density were functional, we'd build more downtowns, and we haven't and we don't and presumably we won't."[12]

Low population densities mesh perfectly with the individualistic tendencies of most members of the Suburban Generation. Their grandparents—especially those who were newcomers to America— derived a sense of security from the anonymity of life in crowded city neighborhoods. But suburban baby boomers grew up in more spacious environments that allowed them to assert their identities. The faceless urban crowd holds no appeal for these men and women now coming to power; they prefer a more relaxed atmosphere that allows them to do what they want, when they want. "Boomers' attitudes and values are profoundly different from those of older Americans," wrote Cheryl Russell, former editor-in-chief of *American Demographics*. "At the root of these differences is a strong sense of individualism instilled in baby boomers by their parents."[13]

This, in fact, is the first core belief of the Suburban Generation: *Suburbanites reject the underlying tenets of city life, believing in decentralization, not density, and placing a higher value on the individual than on the community.* This independent streak is the reason why suburbanites disavow the central city's long-standing claim to economic supremacy.

The downtown establishment—that informal club of executives from big law firms, banks, and other corporations—historically set local agendas throughout Inner America. These business leaders would quietly decide which politicians should be supported, which projects should be pursued, and which charities should be favored. The middle class would fall in line behind the establishment's wishes, motivated by a combination of fear and respect for these men of means.

But the Suburban Generation is neither as fearful nor as respectful. Its members are not particularly impressed by stuffy big-city corporations; they are more likely to work for smaller, unpretentious businesses in the suburbs. That's what Garreau found when he analyzed thirty-eight downtowns and 189 suburban edge cities in 1994. The twenty places with the heaviest concentrations of small businesses were edge cities.* These high-tech, high-education, high-income, low-

---

*Garreau defined a small business as one with fewer than fifty employees.

density suburbs showed little need for the urban core. "Edge cities are for entrepreneurs," Garreau concluded, "while downtowns are for old-fashioned Organization Men."[14]

His final word deserves emphasis. Men still dominate the downtown executive corps, just as they did in urban America's heyday. Garreau reported that downtown Dallas was "the most heavily male job center in America," and that nine of the ten communities most tightly controlled by men were central cities. Suburbia was considerably more up-to-date in reflecting the rise of women. Seven of the ten business centers with the highest concentrations of women were edge cities.[15]

But the Suburban Generation is not satisfied with challenging urban economic structures. It also is rejecting the traditional political liberalism of big cities.

The link between population density and voting habits is a strong one, as shown by studying the 1992 presidential election results in the 173 metropolitan counties that contain all mother cities, suburbs, and fringe metros in California, Florida, Illinois, New York, and Ohio. These counties can be grouped into five tiers according to their numbers of residents per square mile.

Support for Bill Clinton was heaviest in the most densely settled group of counties, those that were dominated by big cities. He drew 50.5 percent of the votes in this first tier, compared to George Bush's 32.8 percent. His strong performance was no surprise; Democrats historically do best in urban areas. But what was striking was Clinton's steady decline on each successive tier of the density scale. Bush actually beat Clinton by more than five percentage points in the fifth tier, consisting of those metropolitan counties that were least densely settled:

		Share of Votes within Group (%)		
	Persons per Square Mile	Clinton	Bush	Perot
All 173 counties	429	45.8	35.0	18.6
Density quintiles				
1 (most densely settled)	2,150	50.5	32.8	16.1
2	494	40.6	36.8	22.1
3	227	39.1	38.6	21.8
4	131	38.0	39.3	22.1
5 (least densely settled)	72	35.8	41.0	22.5

Source: Author's analysis of U.S. Census Bureau data and official election returns.

Clinton ran a moderate campaign in 1992, but the Democratic Party still was linked in most minds to Franklin Roosevelt's New Deal and Lyndon Johnson's Great Society, both of which had emphasized collective responsibility for minorities and the poor. This liberal tradition did not elicit much support from the individualistic residents of low-density suburban counties. They gave a higher priority to their own needs.

Ronald Reagan accurately sensed this self-absorption as far back as 1980. "Are *you* better off than you were four years ago?" he asked. Voters responded by giving him a mandate to improve their lives. Reagan understood intuitively that individualists tend to withdraw from social institutions and groups, and are not especially interested in government—except, of course, in what it can do for them.

America's preoccupation with self grew steadily through the Reagan years and beyond. It was in evidence in January 1998 when the media reported allegations that President Clinton had sex in the White House with an intern, Monica Lewinsky. Analysts confidently predicted a groundswell of public outrage; they were shocked when it failed to occur. A Gallup Poll taken days after the first lurid stories found that 60 percent of Americans approved of Clinton's performance as president, and his level of support was climbing.[16]

The same survey included additional questions that helped to clarify the public mood. Gallup asked respondents whether they agreed with a series of descriptions of Clinton:

	Yes (%)	No (%)
Can get things done	68	28
Cares about the needs of people like you	62	36
Keeps his promises	45	49
Shares your values	43	51
Shows good judgment	42	53
Is honest and trustworthy	35	58

Source: "Comparing Polls on Clinton's Approval Rating," *USA Today*, January 27, 1998, p. 4A.

Americans believed their president did not keep his promises, did not show good judgment, and was not trustworthy. Yet they nonetheless thought he was doing an excellent job, and they wanted him to stay in office. This contradiction, which so astounded political observers, was unraveled by the first two descriptions on Gallup's list. Voters felt that Clinton understood their wishes and could fulfill them. That was all the Suburban Generation cared about.

Holding the Middle Ground

Analysts Richard Scammon and Ben Wattenberg studied the American electorate during the late 1960s, one of the most turbulent periods in the nation's history. Their book, *The Real Majority*, reached the somewhat surprising conclusion that most voters were huddled near the center of the political spectrum, notwithstanding the political and social chaos at the time. "The great majority of the voters in America are unyoung, unpoor, and unblack," wrote Scammon and Wattenberg. "They are middle-aged, middle-class, middle-minded."[17] The authors conceded that liberal and conservative politicians were grabbing most of the headlines toward the end of the 1960s, but they nonetheless predicted that moderates would own the future. "A man or a party who forgets the center forgets the name of the game," they wrote. "He who forgets the name of the game loses the game."[18]

Time has proven Scammon and Wattenberg to be correct, elevating *The Real Majority* to the status of a classic work. One of the book's strengths is that it nicely captures the Suburban Generation's second core belief: *Suburbanites take moderate stands on most issues, holding the middle ground between the more liberal policies favored in mother cities and the more conservative positions espoused in Outer America.*

Political campaigns throughout 1996 showed this philosophy in action. The long year began in Oregon, which conducted a special election in January to replace retiring U.S. Senator Bob Packwood. The Republicans were confident they could keep the seat. Packwood, after all, was a moderate Republican, as was the state's other senator, Mark Hatfield. And Oregon was a strongly suburban state. Nearly 41 percent of its residents lived in suburbs, compared to just 14 percent in mother cities.

But Democrat Ron Wyden was the upset winner in Oregon, edging Republican Gordon Smith by a single percentage point. Wyden ran a centrist campaign, stressing his support for education and the environment, while Smith moved sharply to the right. "The last ad Wyden ran may have been his most effective," said Tony Williams, a strategist on the Smith team. "All he said was something like, 'If you want good schools, a clean environment, and someone pro-choice, vote for me.' " It was an approach that enabled Wyden to carry two suburban Portland counties—Clackamas and Washington—that provided his margin of victory. Said Williams admiringly: "This country is still about winning the 'burbs."[19]

And so it was. Politicians and journalists crisscrossing America on the presidential primary trail in 1996 were surprised by how contented and reasonable—indeed, how *moderate*—most suburbanites were. "We're not arch-conservatives," insisted Gayle Franzen, chairman of the county board in DuPage County, Illinois, near Chicago. Franzen was a Republican, as were a majority of his constituents, but he maintained that DuPage voters were truly conservative on just one issue. "Taxes, taxes, taxes," he said. "Everything else, don't talk to us about it."[20]

Republican pollster Linda DiVall also discovered that the middle of the road was the most direct route to suburbia's heart. Suburban respondents told her repeatedly that they were averse to extremism in all forms. "They tend to be very negative toward the liberal social agenda of Democrats on the far left," she said, "and they also react negatively to the perceived right wing of the Republican Party."[21] Exit polls in November found that at least half the voters in nine suburban states considered themselves to be moderates; at least 40 percent identified themselves that way in the remaining fourteen suburban states. Moderates outnumbered liberals and conservatives in all but Texas and Utah; the widest gap between moderates and the next-largest group was 28 percentage points in Minnesota and New Jersey:

Suburban State	Moderate (%)	Liberal (%)	Conservative (%)	Moderates' Lead
Minnesota	55	18	27	+28
New Jersey	54	21	26	+28
Illinois	53	19	28	+25
Maryland	51	23	27	+24
Massachusetts	50	26	24	+24
Michigan	51	20	30	+21
New Hampshire	50	19	31	+19
Washington	49	22	30	+19
Rhode Island	48	23	29	+19
Ohio	51	16	33	+18
Colorado	49	20	31	+18
Hawaii	47	24	29	+18
Oregon	47	21	32	+15
Delaware	50	14	36	+14
Missouri	49	15	36	+13
Pennsylvania	47	18	35	+12
California	45	22	33	+12
Georgia	47	14	39	+ 8
Connecticut	42	24	34	+ 8
Indiana	45	15	40	+ 5
Virginia	43	19	38	+ 5
Texas	41	15	44	− 3
Utah	40	10	50	−10

Source: Author's analysis of Voter News Service exit poll, November 5, 1996, as posted on CNN/Time AllPolitics website (http://allpolitics.com), November 12, 1996.

Bill Clinton's suburban-oriented campaign was received well in most of these states, as we have seen. He carried seventeen of them. Bob Dole won just six, including Indiana, Virginia, Texas, and Utah, the four suburban states where moderates had the least influence.

Further evidence of the power of the ideological center came from exit polls, which reported that 22 percent of all voters in 1996 identified themselves as suburban moderates, forming the largest single bloc in the electorate. It easily overshadowed such other groups as urban liberals (7 percent of all voters) and rural conservatives (8 percent).[22] And Clinton was the champion of this dominant bloc, drawing the support of 55 percent of all suburban moderates, while 34 percent went for Dole and 9 percent for Ross Perot. "They are pro-environment, pro-gun control, and suspicious of the conservative coalition, but they're pretty conservative fiscally," Democratic pollster Geoff Garin said of suburban voters. "By and large, they feel comfortable with Clinton on all counts."[23]

Taking Control

The Census Bureau set out in late 1997 to identify America's centers of urban growth. The bureau's demographers put together a list of twenty-five places that had registered the sharpest population increases between 1990 and 1996. Seventeen were suburbs; just eight were central cities. "This shows you where America is voting with its feet," said Robert Lang, a senior research fellow with the Fannie Mae Foundation, an organization that specializes in housing studies. "It's suburbia. *People are looking for private environments where they have greater control of their surroundings.*"[24]

He had a point. The desire for personal control had been a motive force behind suburbanization from the very beginning. The first urban refugees were attracted to suburbia because it offered them the opportunity to shape their neighborhoods as they wished. They established white, middle-class communities in their own images, barring the minorities, immigrants, and poor people who brought diversity to city life. "From its origins," wrote urban historian Robert Fishman, "the suburban world of leisure, family life, and union with nature was based on the principle of exclusion." It is a principle that remains intact today.[25]

Their eagerness to maintain the exclusivity of their neighborhoods caused suburbanites gradually to become suspicious of central authority. It was the federal courts, after all, that tried in the 1970s to desegregate suburban schools, mandating that minority students be bused in from nearby big cities. And it was large urban governments that sought to load their burdens on the backs of suburbanites, advocating the creation of metropolitan taxing districts and pushing for the construction of low-income housing in the suburbs.

A rough parallel could be drawn to the situation that Southern whites had confronted for more than a century. Northern politicians deliberately chipped away at racial segregation below the Mason-Dixon Line, insisting first on an end to slavery, then on full civil rights for African-Americans. Southern politicians contended angrily that the North's actions violated the doctrine of states' rights, which held that the Constitution had awarded most powers to the states, not to the federal government. (The Supreme Court, of course, ruled to the contrary in a series of cases spanning more than a century, ranging from *Ableman* v. *Booth* [1859], which denied the right of the state judiciary to interfere in federal cases, to *South Carolina* v. *Katzenbach* [1966], which upheld the right of the federal government to supervise the conduct of state elections.)

Suburbanites have responded in a remarkably similar way to pressures from Washington and big-city governments. They consistently advance what might be called a doctrine of localities' rights, maintaining that schools, police protection, roads, parks, libraries, and other essential services should be provided, funded, and supervised at the community level without outside interference. This bias toward local control was detected by the 1996 Survey of American Political Culture, a detailed poll of more than 2,000 Americans. Fifty-seven percent of all respondents said they were pleased with the performance of their local governments, but only 20 percent said the same about the federal government.[26] This reflects the Suburban Generation's third core belief: *Suburbanites are opposed to central authority, believing that power should be vested in individuals and the communities in which they live.*

Newt Gingrich's devotion to this philosophy was a factor in his quick rise in the nation's political hierarchy. Gingrich argued that the best model for modern government was supplied by the words and deeds of Thomas Jefferson, the founding father who considered large cities to be "pestilential" to human liberty and who spoke persuasively in favor of states' rights. "He was not for weak government, but his argument was that every additional dollar you gave the central government was power to manipulate people," Gingrich said of Jefferson. "He understood that this society is healthiest if it is a *very decentralized society* with hundreds of thousands of leaders doing their own thing."[27]

Suburbanites share this vision. The Voter News Service, which interviewed Americans as they left polling places in November 1996, asked whether respondents believed the federal government should be doing more or doing less. "Less" was the favored reply in every suburban state but New Jersey. The margins were lopsided in most cases, including such progressive states as Minnesota (where 59 percent called for government to do less, 37 percent for it to do more) and Oregon (62 percent less, 33 percent more).[28]

The demand for local oversight is strongest whenever schools are the issue. Members of the Suburban Generation insist upon the right to determine what their children learn, where their children learn, and with whom their children learn. They strive—usually with success—to keep federal and state bureaucrats as far as possible from these critical decisions. This autonomy is the direct result of suburbia's firm control over its educational purse strings, control that is unmatched in urban areas. Schools in heavily suburban states received 57.5 percent of their revenue from local taxpayers in 1991–1992.[29] The local share of school funding dropped to 46.7 percent in moderately suburban states and was just 38.4 percent in states where suburban influence was light:*

	Shares of Total Public School Revenue (%)		
Revenue Source	Heavy Suburban States	Moderate Suburban States	Light Suburban States
Federal	4.3	6.2	8.3
State	38.2	47.2	53.3
Local	57.5	46.7	38.4

Source: Author's analysis of U.S. Census Bureau data.

It stands to reason that a school superintendent would be most responsive to those who foot the largest share of the school's budget, not to mention the superintendent's salary. The fate of Detroit's financially strapped school system, for example, was tied in the 1990s to the whims of state lawmakers and administrators, rather than the wishes of parents. Fifty-nine percent of Detroit's 1991–1992 school budget was backed by state aid, dwarfing the 28 percent supplied by city taxpayers.[30]

Nearby communities, on the other hand, remained undisputed masters of their educational systems. Local funding covered at least 98 percent of school expenses in Detroit suburbs like Bloomfield Hills, Birmingham, and Grosse Pointe. It was no coincidence that these schools received substantially more support than their counterparts in Detroit did, allowing them to buy more books and to pay their teachers higher salaries. Detroit spent $5,371 per pupil during the 1991–1992 academic year, compared to $8,750 per student in Bloomfield Hills, $8,126 in Birmingham, and $6,687 in Grosse Pointe.[31]

The Suburban Generation's dislike for central authority is most pronounced on this question of educational control, but it also manifests itself in a variety of other ways:

*A heavy suburban state is one where 70 percent or more of all residents live in suburbs. A moderate state has a suburban concentration of 31 percent to 69 percent; a light state has 30 percent or less of all residents in suburbs.

- It is one reason why a majority of suburbanites are pro-choice. Paula LaBourdette, a forty-year-old Republican in Orange County, California, told a *Los Angeles Times* pollster that government should keep its nose out of the controversy over abortion rights. "Abortion has nothing to do with politics. It's a medical issue," she said. "Politicians use it as a means of getting votes, and I think that is sick."[32]
- It helps to explain why suburbanites resist governmental efforts to encourage their use of public transportation. City dwellers willingly take buses and subways; suburbanites revere the automobile as a symbol of personal freedom. Fully 22 percent of all workers living in the city of Baltimore chose public transit in 1990, as did 12.2 percent of those who lived in Saint Louis. But nearby suburbanites stuck loyally with their cars. Just 4.2 percent of the commuters in suburban Baltimore County and 1.6 percent in outlying Saint Louis County used public transportation.[33]
- It is also a factor in suburbia's disdain for affirmative action programs. Many suburbanites, to be sure, oppose racial quotas out of contempt for blacks, Hispanics, and other minorities. But others take a philosophical approach, contending that the federal government has no right to interfere in private enterprise. "I think affirmative action has seen its day," said Robert Fauteux, another suburbanite polled by the *Los Angeles Times*. "A person's qualifications and abilities should get them hired, more so than the color of their skin or gender."[34]

Critics see racism when suburbanites oppose mandatory school busing or affirmative action, moral decay when they endorse the right to an abortion, and environmental apathy when they resist public transit. But these pejorative labels ignore the common element in suburbia's positions on such diverse issues. Each stand exalts the individual over the state; each denies the power of central authority.

These impulses, in fact, explain why suburbanites tend to be broadly tolerant. They insist they have the right to conduct their own lives as they see fit, and they believe their neighbors have the same right. This laissez-faire spirit is rooted in modern suburbia's postwar origins. Author William Manchester found the suburbs of the 1950s to be "free, unstructured, and genuinely hospitable to anyone from any background, except blacks, whose time had not yet come." Another best-selling author of the period, William Whyte, was a merciless critic of suburban conformity, yet he agreed with Manchester on this point.

Whyte conceded that suburbanites exhibited "a pretty high quotient of kindliness and fundamental decency."[35]

Recent polls have documented a surprisingly high level of tolerance in suburban-dominated America, a trend obscured by the rise of the Religious Right. The Survey of American Political Culture included a section that focused on "social elites," defined as people who had at least some postgraduate education and who earned at least $50,000 a year. Such individuals, of course, were most likely to live in suburbia. The survey found that they reacted positively toward words such as *multiculturalism* and *tolerance* and negatively toward words like *Christian* or *conservative*. They also showed a greater degree of moral indifference than other Americans did to pornography, marijuana, and premarital sex.[36]

Similar findings were reported in late 1996 by a *Wall Street Journal*-NBC survey of more than 2,000 Americans.[37] Participants were asked to pretend that it was their responsibility to hire a new employee for a private company. They were shown a list of personal characteristics that had been uncovered by a hypothetical investigation of applicants. Then they were asked which items they believed should warrant automatic rejections. Only one inspired strong concern; nearly half of the respondents said that a personal history of drug abuse should not be tolerated in an employee:

Characteristic	Warrants Rejection (%)
Past record of drug abuse	49
Past record of alcoholism	18
Having a homosexual relationship	11
Having committed adultery	10
Arrest in a protest rally	3

Source: Ellen Graham and Cynthia Crossen, "God, Motherhood, and Apple Pie," *Wall Street Journal*, December 13, 1996, p. R4.

The obvious conclusion is that "live and let live" is the motto of most suburbanites—and most Americans. "People are relatively nonjudgmental and pretty tolerant in America," said Alan Wolfe, a Boston University sociologist. "They believe in virtue and morality, but they don't believe in shouting it from the rooftops."[38]

Fair Play for Workers

Many political experts declared Bill Clinton's career to be at an end after Republicans seized control of Congress in 1994. His decisive reelection two years later forced those same analysts to rely on their highly developed powers of hindsight. They attributed the president's victory to personal qualities they had previously discounted. He was remarkably resilient, some said. He was impressively charismatic, others suggested. He was a better speaker, a better debater, and a better campaigner than anyone else in politics, they all agreed.

David Kusnet and Ruy Teixeira decided to take a crack at the analysis game, too. Their credentials were solid. Kusnet had been a speechwriter for Clinton from 1992 through 1994. Teixeira was director of the politics and public opinion program at the Economic Policy Institute, a Washington-based think tank. They wrote a piece for the op-ed section of the *Washington Post* the Sunday after the 1996 election. It didn't get much attention, coming as it did during the media's lovefest for the president, but it should have.

Kusnet and Teixeira offered a unique interpretation of the 1996 election. They didn't focus on Clinton's communications skills; they concentrated on his message. The crux of their analysis was that three types of liberals were huddled together under the Democratic umbrella:

- Lifestyle Liberals were primarily interested in protecting those who lived at the edge of accepted social norms, such as homosexuals.
- Welfare Liberals aimed to protect the poor and the chronically unemployed.
- Worker Liberals believed in "fair play for those who work, who retire after a lifetime of work, who are looking for work or preparing for work, or who are unable to work through no fault of their own."[39]

Clinton's genius, according to Kusnet and Teixeira, was in targeting the third group of liberals in 1996. The Republicans had prospered by depicting previous Democratic nominees as captives of special-interest groups, the GOP's code name for those constituencies prized by Lifestyle Liberals and Welfare Liberals. But Clinton avoided the special-interest label, setting himself up as the voice of Worker Liberalism. He made job creation a top priority of his administration; he engineered an increase in the minimum wage; he shielded Medicare and Social Security from Republican threats. "It was Clinton's and the House Democrats' defense of these principles that gave the president a big victory and the House Democrats a modest comeback," the authors concluded.[40]

This analysis struck to the heart of Clinton's suburban appeal. The Democrats had been stereotyped for more than half a century as the party that prescribed a costly, bureaucratic program to tackle every social ill. Clinton shattered that image by insisting that America should bestow most of its benefits upon those who earn them. His Worker Liberalism meshed perfectly with the Suburban Generation's fourth core belief: *Suburbanites agree that all people deserve an equal place in American society, provided they are productive and responsible citizens.*

The Declaration of Independence was unequivocal. "All men," it said, "are created equal." Residents of suburbia beg to differ. They would narrow the declaration's scope by inserting both adjectives from the italicized sentence above. "All *productive* and *responsible* men are created equal," their version would say, leaving the clear implication that the millions who fall short of this standard are inferior.

Americans imagine themselves to be a generous and kindhearted people. Most, in reality, are not especially sympathetic toward those who are down and out, as shown by a national survey that the Pew Research Center for The People and The Press, a national think tank, conducted in late 1997. Respondents split almost evenly in their perceptions of poverty: 44 percent contended that most poor people were poor because of circumstances beyond their control, but 39 percent said the victims themselves were to blame because of their lack of effort. The tone of condemnation was even stronger on the topic of race. Sixty-one percent of all respondents agreed that blacks who can't get ahead in America are mostly responsible for their own lack of progress; just 25 percent said that discrimination remains a major barrier in this day and age.[41]

The white middle class obviously is in no mood for excuses, nor is it particularly eager to help. The Pew Research Center asked seven different survey groups between 1987 and 1997 whether government has the responsibility to take care of people who can't take care of themselves. Fully 71 percent of the respondents in 1987 agreed that government carries such a responsibility; the margin over those who disagreed was 47 percentage points. But the level of agreement slipped to 61 percent within a decade, and the gap between the two views shrank to 24 points. It was ironic that the public's belief in governmental responsibility was much larger during Ronald Reagan's final year in the White House (74 percent in 1988) than under Clinton's supposedly more humane presidency:

Year	Agree (%)	Disagree (%)	Margin (in points)
1987	71	24	+47
1988	74	23	+51
1990	67	29	+38
1992	69	28	+41
1993	62	35	+27
1994	57	41	+16
1997	61	37	+24

Source: Pew Research Center for The People and The Press, Deconstructing Distrust: How Americans View Government (March 10, 1998), online (http://www.people-press.org/trustrpt.htm).

The conclusion is inescapable.

The suburban middle class is not interested in funding new social programs. It wants government to devote the bulk of its time, energy, and resources to helping people who are employed or retired. Patti Jo Frey, a thirty-six-year-old marketing representative from Newport Beach, California, expressed this viewpoint as succinctly as anyone. "I'm not big on social programs and big government spending," she told a *Los Angeles Times* reporter. "I'm being selfish, but I want what's good for me in my income bracket."[42]

Frey's sentiments echoed through a *Wall Street Journal*-NBC poll taken shortly after the 1996 election. Participants were asked to study a long list of issues and then indicate which ones deserved the highest priority. Their choices, in a sense, constituted America's marching orders to President Clinton on the eve of his second term.

The top ten answers reflected the middle class's strong commitment to its own interests. Respondents urged the federal government to improve education, fight crime, create jobs, protect retirement benefits, and reduce government spending. Nowhere on this priority list was there mention of eliminating discrimination or reducing poverty:

Issue	Deserves High Priority (%)*
Improving public education	57
Reducing crime	57
Protecting Social Security	52
Protecting Medicare	48
Creating jobs and economic growth	41
Protecting U.S. jobs from moving overseas	41
Reducing the federal deficit	40
Reforming welfare	39
Reducing taxes	32
Reforming Social Security	30

*Respondents were allowed to put a high priority on as many issues as they wished.
Source: Albert Hunt, "Smarter Kids, Safer Streets," *Wall Street Journal*, December 13, 1996, p. R1.

Suburbanites, as this agenda makes clear, are relatively indifferent to many of America's ills. They believe that the federal government should play a limited role in addressing issues ranging from poverty and illiteracy to homelessness and racial discrimination. The responsibility for overcoming these problems, in their opinion, rests largely with the victims.

But it is important to note that there is little or no animosity in these stands, harsh though they might be. Suburbanites generally appear to admire poor people who pull themselves up the economic ladder and minorities who surmount racial barriers. And, more often than not, they accept such determined, successful people in their communities, as shown by the steadily increasing numbers of African-Americans, Hispanics, and Asian-Americans in suburbia.

This blend of conservatism and openness, contradictory though it seems, is in the spirit of Worker Liberalism. "These liberals understand something that Lifestyle Liberals don't: Most Americans are tolerant social conservatives," Kusnet and Teixeira wrote. "Worker Liberals stand for social inclusion of racial, religious, ethnic, and lifestyle minorities on terms that the great majority of Americans can accept: We all want to be productive and responsible citizens."[43]

Benign Neglect

The 1960s were miserable years for cities—years of riots, decay, and despair. Urban America was in such dire shape by 1969 that Eugene Raskin, a professor of architecture at Columbia University, dared to think the unthinkable. "We are shifting, not so slowly," he wrote, "to a pattern of existence that is independent of cities, that gets along just fine without cities, and to a way of life whose members, a generation or two from now, will look back upon the urban period of man's history with perhaps some romantic fondness, but certainly more than a tinge of horror."[44]

Other experts shared Raskin's apocalyptic vision. Cities would continue to exist in the decades ahead, these observers conceded, but their role in society would be diminished. Two variations of this grim forecast were offered by distinguished analysts in the fall 1971 issue of *Public Interest*, a scholarly journal. George Sternlieb predicted that the typical city of the future would be like a sandbox, where the poor and maladjusted would be told to amuse themselves and keep out of the way of productive society. Norton Long offered the model of "an Indian reservation made up of inmates and keepers, economically dependent on transfer payments from the outside society made in consideration of custodial services rendered."[45]

A generation has passed, and most Americans indeed are getting along just fine without cities, exactly as Raskin suggested. The majority of suburbanites work in suburbia, go to school in suburbia, shop in suburbia, and play in suburbia; they have little or no interest in the poor and disadvantaged residents of nearby mother cities. This isolated lifestyle has become so common that the accepted definition of *suburb* has changed. The typical American of 1969 understood a suburb to be a community that was subordinate to a big city; the average person a quarter-century later took the same word to mean that a community was not connected to its urban neighbor in any way. The difference was significant.

"Benign neglect" is the phrase that best describes the prevailing suburban attitude toward urban centers in the late 1990s. Most suburbanites feel no hatred toward mother cities, nor do they feel any affection. Cities, to them, have become irrelevant at best, an expensive nuisance at worst. "The new suburban voters do not want to cut off all government benefits to the poor or isolate the cities," said State University of New York at Albany political scientist Michael Malbin. "But they are very, very conscious of their tax burdens, and they don't want their money to be wasted."[46] Hence the Suburban Generation's fifth core belief: *Suburbanites consider cities and suburbs to be distinct entities with little in common; they consequently are not alarmed by the widening economic, educational, and employment gaps between the two.*

It cannot be denied that urban arrogance helped dissolve the ties that once bound cities and suburbs. Cities enjoyed their reign as the undisputed hubs of their metropolitan areas. They trumpeted their superiority at every opportunity, even after suburbia had gained the demographic edge. Ed Koch, the former New York City mayor, embodied the worst in urban braggadocio. "Have you ever lived in the suburbs?" he asked an interviewer in early 1982. "I haven't, but I've talked to people who have, and it's sterile. It's nothing; it's wasting your life. And people do not wish to waste their lives once they've seen New York."[47]

People also didn't like to be told that their lives were worthless. It came as no surprise when suburban voters overwhelmingly rejected Koch's candidacy for governor of New York later that same year. They preferred a lesser-known, but considerably more humble, politician named Mario Cuomo.

The evolution of political strategy was another factor that helped to widen the urban–suburban gulf. Politicians in both parties focused more of their time and money on the expanding suburban electorate, leaving less of both for city voters. Malleable candidates, aware of suburbia's indifference, began to shy away from talking about urban issues. Ronald Reagan's 1984 reelection campaign was a watershed in this regard. The president essentially had no urban policy, preferring to emphasize conservative economic theories that were popular with the suburban middle class. Reagan consequently drew more than enough electoral votes from suburban states alone to win his second term.

Bob Beckel managed the campaign of Walter Mondale, the Democrat buried in Reagan's landslide. He believed that a new era had dawned in American politics in 1984. Mondale had failed to inspire enthusiasm for social programs that once were the Democratic Party's bread and butter, while Reagan had convinced Americans to accept conservative policies they historically had rejected. "Working-class voters were persuaded that if you hitched your wagon to the poor, every time the poor moved up a rung on the ladder, they are going to take you down a rung," Beckel said. "If you hitched your wagon to the rich, every time they move up a rung, they'll take you up a step. It was a sea change in American politics."[48]

This change was driven by the demographic metamorphosis of America's metropolitan areas. Detroit and its suburbs, for example, were remarkably alike as late as 1960, as we saw in chapter 2. Nearly 45 percent of the metro area's residents lived in the city that year, as did more than a third of the area's whites and college graduates. Democrat John Kennedy not only carried Detroit by 311,700 votes in 1960; he also won its suburban region by a margin of 39,800.

This spirit of commonality vanished within a quarter-century. Mondale took Detroit by 246,100 votes in 1984, but Reagan trounced him in the suburbs by 449,000. The 1990 census showed that fewer than 8 percent of the region's whites still lived in Detroit. Urban shares of college-educated adults and aggregate income within the metropolitan area also had fallen well below 20 percent:

	1960		1990	
	Detroit	Suburbs	Detroit	Suburbs
Shares of metropolitan totals (in percent)				
Population	44.4	55.6	26.3	73.7
White residents	37.0	63.0	7.7	92.3
Adults with college degrees	36.7	63.3	12.8	87.2
Aggregate income	41.5	58.5	15.7	84.3

Source: Author's analysis of U.S. Census Bureau data.

Detroit and its suburbs could not possibly have any sense of unity or common purpose under the conditions that prevailed at the end of the twentieth century. The two sides were of different races, income levels, and political orientations. They operated independently; meaningful contact between the two was rare. The one quality they shared was self-absorption; each cared little about the other's problems. Detroit admittedly was an extreme case, but similar imbalances plagued almost every metro area to some degree. "It's led to a real erosion of a sense of shared fate," said Cleveland State University sociologist Rob Kleidman about the economic gap between cities and suburbs. "People of means increasingly are believing they can take care of their own. . . . (And) there's a large segment of society cut off from the mainstream."[49]

Which is exactly what most suburbanites prefer. A 1978 *New York Times* survey found that 76 percent of suburban New Yorkers believed their lives were not affected by events occurring in the central city. This sense of isolation has grown as urban centers have decayed. "Most Americans desired not a unified metropolis, but a fragmented one, where like-minded persons lived together untroubled by those of differing opinions, races, or lifestyles," concluded urban historian Jon Teaford in his study of postwar development trends.[50] The same attitude motivates suburbanites to favor a selective urban renaissance that creates cultural attractions and sports arenas for them to visit in the nearby city. But the larger issues of paying for the city's daily upkeep or tackling its social ills don't interest them in the least.

Buffalo is among the dozens of mother cities suffering because of this suburban ambivalence. Its downtown boasts a new baseball stadium and a new hockey arena, as well as a scattering of recently built office towers. Its downtown expressway system has been rebuilt during the past decade. But the parts of the city not used by suburbanites—its residential neighborhoods—are in serious condition. Buffalo lost 5.4 percent of its population between 1990 and 1996, the eighth-fastest decline among all American cities.[51]

Those suburban residents who still commute to Buffalo on a daily basis generally like the place, as reflected by a 1996 survey of 436 downtown executives, two-thirds of whom lived in suburbia. Respondents were given the hypothetical opportunity to relocate their offices anywhere they wished, and most voted for the status quo. Fifty-nine percent said they would prefer to stay downtown; only 36 percent opted for the suburbs.[52]

But the same survey offered two indications that the remaining links between Buffalo and its suburbs were weakening:

- Commuting time determined the likelihood that a person would be fond of working downtown. People who lived within nine minutes of Buffalo's core voted overwhelmingly to keep their offices in the central city, but a majority of those who lived more than nineteen minutes away said they would prefer to work in the suburbs.

- A majority of commuters thought the city's prospects were bleak. Fifty-two percent said they were pessimistic about the future of downtown Buffalo; only 23 percent were optimistic. The level of pessimism corresponded with the length of a respondent's drive to work. Just 32 percent of those who lived within nine minutes of downtown said the central city was going downhill. The ranks of pessimists rose to 50 percent among those who lived ten to nineteen minutes away and 61 percent among those whose commutes were even longer. It was clear that the ties between Buffalo and its neighbors would erode as suburbia stretched ever farther from the central city.[53]

Politicians in the Buffalo area knew exactly where the power lay. The 1995 campaign for county executive of Erie County was notable for the candidates' lack of attention to Buffalo, which contained one-third of the county's residents. Dennis Gorski, the Democratic incumbent and eventual victor, lived in suburban Cheektowaga. He struck a decidedly unusual tone for a Democrat, insisting that Buffalo deserved no special favors. "We do things for the city," he told a reporter. "Can we do more? Yes. We are going to do all we can. We will look at all the means to us that are legally permissible. *But not at the expense of any other municipality.*"[54]

Buffalo Mayor Anthony Masiello watched helplessly as Gorski and his Republican opponent battled for suburban votes, ignoring his city in their speeches and commercials. He finally ran out of patience. "It troubles me deeply," he complained. "Is Buffalo that bad that people don't want to discuss it politically? Everyone is afraid that support and help for the city translates into less voters for them in the suburbs."[55]

Masiello had just answered his own question.

6 Platform for the Twenty-First Century: The Suburban Agenda

Phyllis Schlafly didn't anticipate any surprises at the 1996 Republican convention in San Diego. There was nothing she hadn't seen during her four decades as an organizer and spokeswoman for the political right, whether it was the agony of Barry Goldwater's defeat in 1964 or the ecstasy of Ronald Reagan's triumphs in the 1980s. She remained influential at the age of seventy-two as head of two conservative lobbying groups, the Eagle Forum and the Republican National Coalition for Life. This GOP convention would be her twelfth.

Schlafly found everything in San Diego to be comfortable and familiar, just as she had expected, until the music started. Rock and roll blared from the auditorium's sound system during every break in the festivities. At a *Republican* convention. "I was really very offended by the music," she said. "The music was always horrible. Loud, so-called music." The memory, weeks later, still bothered her.[1]

But Schlafly was a professional. She ignored the din as best she could, concentrating on a job that she believed was of the utmost importance. Bob Dole, the presidential nominee-to-be, was seeking to appease pro-choice delegates by inserting a "statement of tolerance" in the Republican platform. Schlafly's mission was to prevent Dole's aides from putting such a deal together. "I kept telling them that a lot of our people really wanted to have a debate and a fight," she recalled, "and they didn't want to give an inch."[2]

The skirmish over the platform was the juiciest news coming out of an otherwise dull convention. Journalists breathlessly reported each move by Dole's team and each countermove by Schlafly's conservatives. It appeared that a bloody floor fight was in the offing.

But it did not occur. Dole recoiled from a public exhibition of Republican disharmony and opted to tuck the pro-choice statement into a platform appendix that nobody would read. His convention manager lamely heralded this "big tent approach," but reporters plainly labeled it a defeat. The platform, as a result, bore the right wing's stamp from beginning to end. It included Schlafly's plank that would ban abortions, even in cases of rape, incest, or to save the life of a mother, a stand that clearly made Dole uncomfortable. It also embraced conservative proposals to abolish four Cabinet departments, restrict immigration, end affirmative action, and ban flag burning.

There was much that Schlafly did not like about the proceedings in San Diego. She thought the convention lacked any spontaneity, she wasn't crazy about Dole being the nominee, and she had unprintable feelings about that damnable music. "Of course," she said, "you can argue we got what we wanted, so what is there to complain about?"[3]

But had she?

Dole quickly made it known that he alone would chart his campaign's course; he would not be bound to any plank adopted by the convention. Haley Barbour, chairman of the Republican National Committee, insisted that he hadn't read the ninety-four-page platform and probably never would. Even the members of the platform committee seemed to understand that their months of work had been meaningless. "It's a document with a very short shelf life," said Don Bain, a panel member from Colorado. "It's one of those things that gets done in a chaotic, unscientific way and then gets put on a shelf."[4]

Such was not always the case. Adopting the platform was one of the most important actions taken by a convention in the nineteenth and early twentieth centuries, perhaps second only to nominating the presidential ticket. But candidates in 1996 worried more about the podium than the platform; they were interested primarily in the opportunity to address the millions of television viewers who were tuned in to the convention. Positions on issues could be refined or changed in the coming weeks, depending on the results of surveys and focus groups. Dole and Bill Clinton relied on polling data more heavily than any of the presidential nominees who preceded them.

The Republican and Democratic platforms, to be blunt, were of little or no significance in 1996. The conservative coup in San Diego had less impact on Dole's campaign than did the daily report from his pollsters. Phyllis Schlafly carried less weight with the nominee than did the everyday Americans who took part in his surveys—a white female engineer in Fairfax, Virginia; a black male attorney in Lake Forest, Illinois; an Asian-American female store manager in Manhattan Beach, California. Fiery rhetoric did not fuel Dole's campaign—or Clinton's, for that matter. Numbers did.

Their polling data revealed to both candidates the wishes and hopes of the suburban electorate, the bloc that controlled 320 electoral votes and consequently held the nation's balance of power. The result was a kind of informal platform—infinitely more important than the versions produced by the two major parties—that converted the Suburban Generation's core beliefs into stands on specific issues.

This Suburban Agenda can be summarized in the following ten planks:

1. Washington must retrench. The federal government should slash its bureaucracy, balance its budget, cut its taxes, and keep its nose out of local affairs. Mother cities, in the same spirit, should abandon efforts to load their burdens upon suburban taxpayers.

2. The federal government should take all necessary steps to promote and safeguard a strong economy. It must create a healthy business climate and encourage the creation of jobs.

3. The government should help those who—in suburbia's view—have earned that help. Medicare and Social Security must be protected at all costs. Programs that assist middle-class Americans in raising their children, such as guaranteed family leave, should be encouraged. Programs that help those who aren't working, such as welfare, should be cut.

4. Essential services such as education and health care must be controlled by local governments or by individuals themselves. The federal government should not mandate the busing of suburban students to city schools, nor should it institute a system of universal health insurance.

5. Maximum mobility should be the goal. Expressways should be expanded assiduously and maintained carefully; mass transit should be assigned a low priority. The federal government must do whatever is necessary to maintain cheap sources of energy—even, as a last resort, go to war—but it also should assume a pro-environment stance whenever possible.

6. All responsible and productive people must be treated equally, regardless of their race. But programs that are perceived to give an advantage to unqualified individuals, such as affirmative action, should be scuttled. Immigration should be tightly restricted.

7. The government and the private sector must do all they can to promote social equality and economic freedom for two so-called special interest groups— women and the elderly.

8. Law and order must be maintained. Punishment should be strict; the death penalty should be meted out to the worst criminals. But these tough anti-crime measures should be accompanied by provisions for handgun control.

9. Morality should be treated as a personal matter, not a public issue. Abortion should be discussed by a woman and her doctor, not by anyone else. Religion, as a general rule, should not play a role in public policy decisions.

10. America must not aspire to be the world's policeman. Foreign nations should be treated as trading partners, not as pawns in a global chess match.

The Suburban Agenda does not fit neatly into a single ideological category. It is liberal in a few instances, conservative in others, and moderate in most. It is inspired not by the views of any political party, but by the five core beliefs of the Suburban Generation. The remainder of this chapter will examine each of the agenda's ten planks more closely. The candidate who ignores them in the future will do so at his or her peril.

1. Reinventing Government

Suburbia owes an enormous debt to big government. Federal mortgage subsidies and guarantees allowed millions of Americans to buy suburban homes after World War II. Federally funded expressways made it possible for commuters to travel easily to and from mother cities. Federal tax credits encouraged the construction of industrial plants outside of urban cores. Today's suburbs would not be as large or as prosperous without all of this government assistance.

The irony is that a majority of present-day suburbanites are opposed to big government. Exit polls in November 1996 found that 52 percent of American voters wanted the federal government to do less, while 41 percent wanted it to do more. Just one suburban state, New Jersey, bucked this national trend, and even there the results were close. Forty-nine percent of New Jersey voters were in favor of Washington doing more; 46 percent said it should do less.[5]

The issue primarily is one of cost-effectiveness. A 1997 national survey by Maritz Marketing Research learned that only four out of ten people in the highest income bracket—people who commonly live in suburbs—believed they were getting their money's worth from their federal income taxes. The level of public satisfaction actually was higher at lower income levels; a majority of those who earned less than $25,000 a year were pleased with the way their federal taxes were being used:

Share Believing They Get Their Money's Worth from Each Tax (%)		
Federal Income Taxes	State Income Taxes	Local Property Taxes
All taxpayers		
42	56	60
Annual income		
Less than $15,000		
52	62	60
$15,000–$24,999		
51	59	69
$25,000–$34,999		
38	55	53
$35,000–$44,999		
36	53	53
$45,000–$54,999		
42	61	70
$55,000–$64,999		
38	59	55
$65,000 or more		
40	55	63

Source: Tibbett Speer, "Taxing Times," *American Demographics* (April 1997): 42–44.

It came as no surprise that respondents who earned more than $45,000 felt their local property taxes gave them more value than their state or federal taxes did. This attitude is perfectly in keeping with the Suburban Generation's firm belief in decentralization. Suburbanites prefer to allocate their tax dollars to local schools, local health facilities, local parks, and other local services that they personally use and control. They are decidedly unenthusiastic about sending their hard-earned money to Washington or their state capital for faceless bureaucrats to spend.

Some critics interpret this as a knee-jerk reaction against all forms of taxation, a view seemingly confirmed by the 1997 off-year elections. Voters in the Saint Louis area rejected a sales-tax hike that would have funded a light-rail system. Their counterparts in metropolitan Denver turned down a gas-tax increase that would have supported mass transit. Plans for new stadiums were voted down in Pittsburgh and Minneapolis. New York state voters rejected a $2.4 billion school bond issue. "As soon as you call it a tax, it's dead," sighed Kevin McCarty of the U.S. Conference of Mayors.[6]

His frustration seemed, on the surface, to have merit. It is true that most suburbanites own their homes, making them especially sensitive to tax hikes. And it is equally true that the Internal Revenue Service has given them more to complain about; the total tax bite on single-income families grew from 28 percent of median income in 1955 to 36 percent in 1995. Politicians who have increased taxes (George Bush) or just talked about increasing them (Walter Mondale) have paid the electoral price for their indiscretion.

But suburbia is motivated by more than a simple dislike of taxes, as first became evident in 1978 when California voters approved Proposition 13, a landmark referendum to roll back and cap taxes. Fully 67.4 percent of suburbanites voted in favor of Proposition 13, a higher level of support than in mother cities, fringe metros, or non-metro areas. Yes votes outnumbered no votes by 1.4 million in California's suburbs, accounting for three-quarters of the referendum's statewide margin of victory. Journalists consequently characterized Proposition 13 as a pure-and-simple revolt by suburban homeowners against high taxes, and it generally is remembered that way today.[7]

Closer study shows that Proposition 13 actually was about more than tax rates. A substantial number of the referendum's supporters, according to surveys, were motivated by a desire to protest against government waste. If taxes were reduced, they told pollsters, the government would be forced to operate more efficiently. These disaffected voters were especially angered by the welfare system, which they believed was squandering millions of dollars, but they did not blindly condemn all government spending. It was an astonishing fact that backers of Proposition 13 wanted to maintain or even *increase* service levels of most government programs, with the notable exception of welfare.[8]

This attitude has continued to the present day. Word drifted through Washington in early 1998 that the federal government conceivably could run a budget surplus the following year, prompting the question of what to do with the anticipated windfall. The Gallup Poll offered 1,015 adults a range of three alternatives. Most chose not a tax cut, but a package of spending hikes for programs favored by the middle class:

Increase government spending on programs such as Social Security, Medicare, schools, the environment, and national defense 43%

Pay down the national debt 30%

Cut federal income taxes for most Americans 22%

Source: William Welch and Susan Page, "Public Isn't Banking on Budget Surpluses," *USA Today,* January 9, 1998, p. 6A.

Suburbanites say they oppose government waste, but they clearly do not oppose it across the board. Waste, in their lexicon, is defined as those programs that spend billions upon billions of dollars to help cities, minorities, and the poor. Equally expensive programs that primarily benefit the white middle class are not deemed wasteful; they are considered worthy of increased funding.

This conflict between rhetoric and reality helps to explain why suburban voters inevitably are attracted to tax cuts in theory, but are not always so enthusiastic about them once they are instituted. New Jersey is a case in point. Christine Whitman was elected governor in 1993 on a pledge to reduce state income taxes by 30 percent. She did exactly as promised, yet barely won reelection in 1997. Her opponent, Jim McGreevey, exploited the public's unhappiness with resulting reductions in state aid to municipalities. Exit polls showed New Jersey voters to be split on Whitman's tax cuts: 36 percent said they had hurt the state, 35 percent said they had helped, and 26 percent said they had made no difference.[9]

These numbers bore out a prediction that the governor had made more than a year before the election. "You do a survey in this state, and most people will tell you, 'It hasn't made any big difference to me,'" she had said. "But the biggest thing about my tax cut was that I said I was going to do it, and I did it."[10]

Suburbanites seem equally ambivalent when the federal deficit is the issue. They insist that political candidates talk about reducing the public debt, but they make this demand without fervor. Ronald Reagan, after all, expanded the deficit more than any other president, yet he remains a revered figure in suburbia. The middle class's inner conflict was best expressed by Dan Ford, a schoolteacher in suburban Dallas. "Yes, I worry about the debt," Ford told a reporter in early 1996. "But I worry more about getting my daughter into the math club at school than what some congressman is doing about the debt. The chances of my vote affecting history are so tiny when compared to teaching my children to grow up right and to give them life skills."[11]

Suburbia's thoughts on government often appear muddled and confused, sometimes even contradictory, but they have a certain coherence in their own way. These opinions can be summarized in four points:

- The federal government must retrench. It must reduce its bureaucracy. It must scale back programs that focus on people who fail to meet the suburban definition of "productive and responsible" citizens.
- Federal and state governments must commit themselves to tax cuts, though the size of the reductions is not of overriding importance. Such cuts, however, must not be made at the expense of programs that primarily serve the middle class.
- Governments also must commit themselves to deficit reduction, though the size of the reductions is not especially important. Such cuts, again, must not be made at the expense of programs that primarily serve the middle class.
- Local governments, noted for their cost-effectiveness, must take the lead in the delivery of essential services. Federal and state officials should stay out of local affairs as much as possible.

Mother cities are given exactly the same warning. They have been gazing longingly beyond their borders for half a century, dreaming of acquiring prosperous suburban tax bases. The most extreme way to accomplish this goal would be to consolidate a city and its suburbs under a single government, a step advocated by urban analyst David Rusk, a former mayor of Albuquerque. "The 'city' must be redefined to reunify city and suburb. Ideally, such reunification is achieved through metropolitan government," Rusk wrote in 1993.[12]

A few metropolitan governments *have* been established, most notably in Indianapolis, Jacksonville, and Nashville, but all three pre-date 1980. The tide has been running against urban–suburban consolidation for the past twenty years, primarily because of strong opposition from suburbanites, and there is no reason to expect this resistance to abate. Former Indianapolis Mayor William Hudnut admitted that his area's successful city-suburban merger, which was completed in 1970, would not be approved by Indiana lawmakers if it were introduced today. "It is politically desirable, but unfeasible unless a state legislature does it. And that won't happen," said Hudnut. "Over 50 percent of legislatures are dominated by suburbanites, and they don't want it."[13]

2. Dollars and Sense

No issue is more potent than the economy.

Franklin Roosevelt guided America out of the Great Depression. His plan was messy and disorganized, to be sure, and it wasn't nearly as effective in promoting recovery as the onset of World War II proved to be. But Roosevelt was perceived to be the nation's economic savior. The Democratic Party parlayed his shining image into three and a half decades of political dominance; its candidates never failed to remind voters that the Republicans had presided over the nation's economic collapse. Democrats won seven of nine presidential elections between 1932 and 1964.

Ronald Reagan redeemed the GOP's reputation. He pumped up the federal deficit to previously unimaginable dimensions, but what mattered most to voters was that he was in command during the economic boom of the 1980s. Reagan's popularity remained strong in 1988 and was a key factor in the election of George Bush.

Exit polls made it clear that voters expected Bush to maintain the pace of economic expansion. It was an assignment he could not fulfill; America slipped into a recession in 1990. "Bush promised two things," said political analyst William Schneider. "He promised to keep the recovery going and no new taxes. He broke both promises, and that was what suburban voters cared about."[14]

They took their revenge on election day in 1992, as shown by a comparison of economic trends and vote counts. States were sorted into five groups of equal size, according to the differences in their employment growth under Reagan and Bush. Voters in the first quintile—ten states whose job bases expanded much more rapidly during the Bush administration than in the Reagan years—unsurprisingly favored the incumbent. But the fifth quintile—consisting of ten states that prospered under Reagan but lost jobs during Bush's watch—gave Bill Clinton his strongest support.[15] The relationship between economic cause and political effect could not have been clearer:

| | Annual Job Growth Rates | | | 1992 Presidential Vote | | |
	Reagan Years (%)	Bush Years (%)	Change*	Bush	Clinton	Perot
Nationwide	+1.90	+0.78	−1.12	37.4	43.0	18.9
Quintiles by changes in job growth rates						
1 (biggest gains under Bush)	+0.17	+2.34	+2.17	40.2	38.6	19.9
2	+1.63	+2.53	+0.90	37.0	41.1	21.2
3	+1.30	+1.36	+0.06	38.5	42.4	18.6
4	+2.58	+0.60	−1.98	37.0	44.0	18.3
5 (biggest drops under Bush)	+2.48	−0.96	−3.44	35.9	45.0	18.5

*Change is expressed in percentage points.
Source: Author's analysis of U.S. Bureau of Labor Statistics data and official election returns.

This lesson was reinforced four years later by a battery of exit polls. Voter News Service asked each of its respondents to identify the issue that had the strongest influence on his or her decision to support Clinton, Dole, or Perot. At the top of the list was the economy, named by 21 percent as the key issue of 1996. It was the first choice in a wide range of suburban states, including California, Illinois, Massachusetts, New Jersey, Ohio, Pennsylvania, and Texas. No other issue was mentioned by more than 15 percent of respondents nationwide.[16]

There can be no doubt, then, that economic policy is of extreme importance. A smart politician is the one who keeps suburbanites happy by adhering to these three principles:

- Private enterprise must be given every opportunity to work its magic. The government's role is to assist the private sector by reducing taxes, cutting through red tape, and sponsoring programs that help entrepreneurs develop their own companies and create jobs.
- Government also must do whatever it can to ensure a wide selection of affordable housing for the middle class. "A man is not a whole and complete man unless he owns a house and the ground it stands on," wrote Walt Whitman, nicely foreshadowing one of suburbia's credos.[17] Interest rates must be kept as low as possible; the same goes for property taxes.
- Top priority, in fact, must be given to any economic policy that protects and improves the standard of living for *working* Americans, regardless of their race or economic class. Those who are employed, in suburbia's opinion, have earned the right to such assistance.

This last principle was put to the test in May 1996, when the House of Representatives debated a bill to raise the minimum wage from $4.25 to $5.15 an hour. Doctrinaire Republican conservatives insisted that a ninety-cent-an-hour wage hike would trigger layoffs, hurting the very workers it ostensibly was meant to help. "The Democratic Party is to job creation what Doctor Kevorkian is to health care: a job killer cloaked in kindness," cracked Majority Whip Tom DeLay of Texas.[18] It was this type of remark that inspired Democrats to accuse Republican leaders of heartlessly catering to business interests and ignoring the needs of low-income workers.

But the GOP's rank and file did not blindly follow its commanders. Republicans from suburban districts split evenly on the bill, fifty-three to fifty-three, even though their colleagues in fringe and nonmetro districts were steadfastly opposed. Suburban congressmen from both parties approved the bill by a margin of better than 2 to 1, clearing the way for remarkably easy passage:

	Total Vote		Republicans		Democrats	
	Yes	No	Yes	No	Yes	No
House	281	144	93	138	187	6
Components						
City districts	81	11	10	10	71	1
Suburban districts	111	53	53	53	58	0
Fringe districts	37	47	13	45	24	2
Nonmetro districts	52	33	17	30	34	3

Source: Author's analysis of congressional roll call (May 23, 1996).

Increasing the minimum wage was an especially important issue in big cities, which had a larger percentage of low-paying jobs than suburbs did. But suburban congressmen backed the legislation because it benefited workers, people whom they believed had *earned* help. Labor Secretary Robert Reich hailed suburbia's support as the key to the bill's victory. "The ideological opposition mounted by Republican House leaders," he said, "was simply no match for the pragmatism of Republican moderates."[19]

3. Helping the Deserving

Bill Clinton felt reasonably secure at the beginning of 1998. He was a year into his second term in the White House, with no future campaign to worry about. The Twenty-Second Amendment prohibited him from running again for the presidency, making him, in political parlance, a lame duck.

The time seemed right for Clinton to address one of the most controversial topics in American politics: the future of the Social Security system. He decided to convene a series of public meetings. The opening session in Kansas City was a typically flashy White House production, complete with guest speakers and a national satellite hookup.

Clinton characteristically was cautious in his opening remarks, promising to "act with care as we make needed repairs" in Social Security. He declined to offer a detailed proposal of his own. "If I advocated a specific plan right now," he said, "all the debate would be about that."[20]

One of the panelists in Kansas City was Pennsylvania Senator Rick Santorum, a conservative Republican and frequent Clinton critic. The president charitably had offered the senator a ride to the meeting on Air Force One, and the two had chatted en route. Reporters later asked Santorum if he was disappointed that the president had been so noncommittal; the senator surprised them with his understanding tone. "He doesn't want to get out ahead of the American public or Congress," he said mildly. The reporters asked why not. "He mentioned he doesn't want another Medicare catastrophe," was the reply.[21]

Santorum's measured response suddenly made sense. The mere mention of Medicare, the nation's health-care program for the elderly, revived bitter memories for most Republicans. One of their goals upon assuming control of Congress in 1995 had been to revamp Medicare dramatically; they pushed a bill through the House of Representatives to cut $270 billion from the program over seven years. The division between the parties could not have been sharper. Republicans supported the Medicare cuts, 227 to 6, while Democrats opposed them, 194 to 4.

The resulting barrage of public disapproval caught the Republicans off guard, teaching them that voters were not unhappy with *all* multibillion-dollar government programs. The GOP spent the ensuing year apologizing for its haste and pledging to keep Medicare inviolate in the future.

The same spirit that inspired suburbanites to support an increase in the minimum wage also motivated their defense of Medicare and scores of other federal programs. It was the spirit of Worker Liberalism, whose basic tenet, according to David Kusnet and Ruy Teixeira, is its insistence on "fair play for those who work, who retire after a lifetime of work, who are looking for work or preparing for work, or who are unable to work through no fault of their own."[22] This belief echoed through a 1995 Gallup Poll, which asked respondents whether specific federal programs should be scaled back in order to reduce the federal deficit. Only one-fifth of suburbanites said they could accept cuts in Medicare and Social Security, two programs that primarily benefited retired workers and their families. But two-thirds approved of reductions in funding for food stamps and welfare, programs that targeted people outside the workforce. It was notable that support for cutting food stamps and welfare was stronger in suburbia than in the rest of the country:

	Share Supporting Program Cuts to Reduce the Deficit (%)			
	Nationwide	Urban	Suburban	Rural
Medicare	19	18	19	20
Social Security	20	22	21	16
School lunches	28	27	28	27
Medicaid	29	29	31	27
More police grants	28	27	30	27
College loans	31	28	31	36
Aid to farmers	43	39	46	43
Defense spending	52	54	55	45
Food stamps	60	56	64	61
Welfare in general	65	62	70	64
Funding the arts	66	62	67	70

Source: "Deficit Reduction vs. Avoiding Serious Cuts in Key Programs," *Gallup Poll Monthly* (March 1995): 26–27.

Suburbanites are especially enthusiastic about any legislation that helps them raise their families. A 1996 national poll by Penn & Schoen Associates found that 94 percent of parents favored federal income tax credits to help pay for college and 89 percent favored a doubling of tax credits for child care and preschool.[23] Clinton's family leave bill, which guaranteed most workers twelve weeks of unpaid leave to care for a new child or sick family member, was approved in 1993 despite strong opposition from business groups. Suburban congressmen backed family leave by a vote of ninety-eight to sixty-seven.

Social legislation to help the disadvantaged, however, meets with a much colder reception. The sense among suburban voters is that the poor don't deserve more than minimal government assistance, and Congress has acted accordingly. The Center on Budget and Policy Priorities, a liberal research organization, estimated that 93 percent of the entitlement cuts by Congress in 1995 and 1996 were made in antipoverty programs.* The biggest reductions were in food stamps ($27.4 billion) and Supplemental Security Insurance for the disabled ($22.7 billion).[24]

But those cuts paled in comparison to the welfare-reform proposal that worked its way through Congress in 1996. Its sponsors promised that the package would save $54 billion through 2002 by cutting food-stamp funding, limiting welfare recipients to five years of payments, and denying a variety of federal benefits to legal immigrants. The legislation also would transfer control of welfare policy from Washington to states and localities. The House of Representatives approved the reform bill by a 3 to 1 margin, with suburban congressmen voting yes by the lopsided count of 144 to 23.[25]

Liberals warned of dire consequences. "It appears that Congress

---

*An entitlement is defined as a program that automatically provides aid to qualified beneficiaries.

has wearied of the war on poverty and decided to wage war against poor people instead," said Hugh Price, president of the National Urban League.[26] The president of the Children's Defense Fund, Marian Wright Edelman, was one of Clinton's personal friends, yet she condemned him for signing the welfare bill. "It will leave a moral blot on his presidency and on our nation," she said.[27]

Most suburbanites were untroubled. Exit polls showed that welfare reform was wildly popular even in such a progressive suburban state as Minnesota, which had a long history of supporting social legislation. Only 15 percent of Minnesota voters said in November 1996 that welfare reform went too far, compared to 43 percent who complained that it didn't cut enough. National results broke along similar lines, with just 18 percent of all American voters and 25 percent of Clinton supporters maintaining that welfare reform was too harsh:

	(%)		
	Cuts Too Much	**About Right**	**Doesn't Cut Enough**
All voters	18	37	39
Clinton voters	25	41	27
Dole voters	7	33	54
Perot voters	19	34	42

Source: Voter News Service exit poll, November 5, 1996, as posted on CNN/Time AllPolitics website (http://allpolitics.com), November 12, 1996 [henceforth referred to as VNS exit poll 1996].

Clinton had vetoed two previous welfare-reform bills, but he signed the 1996 version. "Today, we have an historic opportunity to make welfare what it was meant to be: *a second chance, not a way of life*," the president said just prior to the House vote, proving that he understood why the middle class was so enthusiastic about the bill. He called the legislation "the best chance we will have for a long, long time" to shift the emphasis from welfare to work; he insisted further that it would benefit America's children in the long run.[28]

House Speaker Newt Gingrich, himself an outspoken proponent of welfare reform, was among those listening. He scoffed that the president's true motivation for signing the bill was much simpler. "He can't avoid it and get reelected," said Gingrich. "That is the only reason."[29]

4. A Matter of Control

Maryland Governor Parris Glendening decided to extend a helping hand to Baltimore's ailing educational system in 1997. He offered the city's schools $254 million in state aid over five years, about 10 percent more than they normally would receive. All other schools in the state would get just $167 million during the same period.

Critics detected a political payback. Glendening, after all, couldn't have been elected governor without considerable help from Baltimore; the city and two of Maryland's twenty-three counties were the only places he carried on his way to a narrow victory in 1994. But the governor insisted he was motivated merely by a desire to help students who had been placed at a disadvantage by their urban environment.

The state legislature narrowly approved Glendening's plan, much to the displeasure of suburban officials. State Senator Patrick Hogan, a Republican whose district was near Washington, D.C., grew angrier after Baltimore officials said they needed even more state aid. "In my mind, it's not peanuts," he snapped. "I think it's a heck of a lot of money. There are a lot of jurisdictions around the state that could use more money." Montgomery County Executive Douglas Duncan, a Democrat like Glendening, refused to appear with him on a local tour shortly after the vote.[30]

The embattled governor went ahead with his trip. One of his stops was at an elementary school in Rockville, a Washington suburb, where he talked with students about the funding dispute. He asked them how they would have spent an extra $20 million, had it been available. "Maybe you should give it to kids who are less fortunate, to kids who don't have access to the education that we have," said a girl named Rose. Glendening beamed. "I'm going to nominate you for the Pulitzer Prize [sic]," he said.[31]

Rose's parents most likely would have approved of her altruism in theory, but not in practice. Residents of suburbia, as we have seen, are highly suspicious of central authority, both the federal and state varieties. They gladly accept funding from Washington and their state capital; Montgomery County, after all, sought as much money as it could get from Glendening. But suburbanites do not want their tax dollars routed through distant government agencies to be spent in big cities. It's their money, as far as they are concerned, and they want it kept where it can do them some good.

Suburbia's passion for control is strongest on those matters that hit closest to home, such as education and recreation. Local property taxes generate most of the funds for such services, thereby ensuring local authority over the spending of that money. If suburbanites want to build a new school or park, they simply raise taxes. "They can satisfy these demands through increased suburban and county expenditures, guaranteeing the highest possible return to themselves on their tax dollars, while continuing to maintain policies of fiscal conservatism at the federal level," wrote journalist Thomas Edsall. "Suburbanization has permitted whites to satisfy liberal ideals revolving around activist government, while keeping to a minimum the number of blacks and the poor who share in government largess."[32]

Self-sufficiency is suburbia's ideal. Its residents insist upon taking direct responsibility for essential services, and history shows they will resist fiercely any effort to usurp this authority. Suburbanites faced down the federal government when it ordered the busing of urban minority students to suburban schools in the 1970s; they eventually won in the Supreme Court. Opposition to busing was unabated in 1996, when a Gallup Poll found 65 percent of suburbanites against it, a higher negative percentage than in cities or rural areas.[33]

There is an element of consistency to this faith in self-reliance, unfair though it might seem. Suburbanites believe that mother cities should be held to the identical standard. If cities want to spend more money on their parks, they should raise it from city taxpayers, not from outsiders. If they want to achieve racial balance in their schools, they should shift students within the city's borders, not beyond them. So says suburbia.

This belief is manifested in a slightly different way when the subject is health care. Census Bureau statistics show that whites are much more likely than minorities to have health insurance. Upper- and middle-class people are more likely than poor people to be covered, and the same is true of college-educated adults in comparison to those who merely attended high school:

	Health Insurance Status in 1995 (%)	
	Covered	Not Covered
All persons	84.6	15.4
Race		
Whites	85.8	14.2
Blacks	79.0	21.0
Hispanics	66.7	33.3
Household income		
Less than $25,000	76.1	23.9
$25,000–$49,999	83.8	16.2
$50,000–$74,999	90.7	9.3
$75,000 or more	93.3	6.7
Education		
No high school diploma	75.7	24.3
High school graduate only	82.3	17.7
Some college	85.2	14.8
Associate degree	88.2	11.8
Bachelor's degree or more	91.8	8.2

Source: U.S. Census Bureau data.

Bill Clinton was shocked and disappointed when the middle class turned against his proposal for universal health insurance in 1994, in effect killing the legislation. But the chart above makes it clear that no other outcome was likely. Most of the demographic groups concentrated in suburbia—whites, the well-to-do, college graduates—had private coverage already, essentially removing their incentive to endorse a potentially costly, bureaucratic plan. Poorer, less-educated residents of big cities had more at stake in the health care debate, but they also had fewer votes. Congress, following suburban tradition, decided that they should continue to fend for themselves.

5. Getting Around

The Boston area enjoyed a population boom in the 1990s. Or, more accurately, *parts* of the Boston area enjoyed a boom. The city itself wasn't doing so well, but its suburbs were expanding with great speed, stretching farther and farther from the urban core. Suburban officials found it easy to explain this rapid growth. It was all in the numbers, they said. Not population numbers, *highway* numbers.

Kingston, a small town thirty-five miles southeast of Boston, was typical, experiencing a 15.5 percent increase in population between 1990 and 1996. "The highway upgrades with Route 44 and Route 3, the fact that we've got our own commuter rail station—all that makes us appealing to the commuter," said Olavo DeMacedo, chairman of Kingston's selectmen. It was the same story in nearby Taunton, about forty miles due south of Boston. "Jobs in general are migrating away from the central cities, and for us, the proximity to 495 and 128 is the key," said Stephen Smith, who headed Taunton's planning district.[34]

Boston was one of the most crowded cities in America, with 11,400 persons per square mile in 1992. But Bristol County, which included Taunton, and Plymouth County, which contained Kingston, offered the breathing room that urban refugees craved. Bristol's population density was 911 persons per square mile, Plymouth's was just 666.[35]

It was the expressways and four-lane highways—the 44's and 3's and 495's and 128's—that made it possible for suburbanites to spend their workdays in or near Boston, then retreat at night to their own quiet acreage far from skyscrapers and traffic jams. These commuters shuttled in and out of the urban world by car; four of every five workers residing in Bristol and Plymouth counties drove by themselves to their jobs. Just 40 percent of the workers who lived in Boston did the same; nearly as many used public transportation.[36]

Americans always have been partial to the automobile, but their attachment grew stronger as suburbia grew larger. Employers and stores, which long ago had been concentrated downtown, are widely dispersed in the Suburban Age, making it less convenient—often impossible—to reach them by mass transit. The share of American workers driving alone to their jobs consequently rose from 64 percent in 1980 to 73 percent in 1990. The number of carpoolers fell from 20 percent to 13 percent during the same period, while transit riders slipped from 6 percent to 5 percent.[37]

This trend was abetted by the nation's willingness to spend unlimited sums on road construction—the Interstate Highway Act of 1956 being the most prominent example—and its relative frugality with bus and subway systems. "The inevitable result of the bias in American transport funding, a bias that existed for a generation before the interstate highway program was initiated, is that the United States now has the world's best road system and very nearly its worst public-transit offerings," wrote historian Kenneth Jackson.[38] Seventy-five percent of the federal government's transportation-related spending in the first decades after World War II went to highways, according to some estimates, while just 1 percent was allocated for urban mass transit.

Suburbanites, quite simply, want roads. More roads, better roads, wider roads, faster roads.

They also want petroleum. America's love affair with the automobile is an expensive one, consuming ever-increasing amounts of oil. Residents of suburbia expect the federal government to take whatever steps are necessary to maintain affordable, dependable sources of petroleum. That includes military action; the 1991 Gulf War proved that the United States will fight to protect the suburban way of life.

Experts differ on the reliability of America's petroleum supplies in the coming century. Trend-watchers John Naisbitt and Patricia Aburdene wrote in *Megatrends 2000* that they saw "almost no chance" that the energy crisis of the 1970s could be repeated.[39] But a group of seventeen futurists concluded that oil will cease being the dominant source of energy within twenty to fifty years. "Most agree that this transition will not be accomplished without turbulence and possibly slowed economic growth," wrote Joseph Coates and Jennifer Jarratt, who reviewed the panel's work. "Most note that we cannot continue to use energy as we have been."[40]

If an energy crisis were to occur, would it loosen suburbia's economic grip on America? Not in the least. Suburbs grew rapidly in the 1970s, after all, even though drivers were forced to pay inflated gasoline prices and endure long lines at service stations. A future oil shortage, if anything, would hurt mother cities by discouraging suburban commuters from trekking downtown on a daily basis. Many companies headquartered in the urban core would have no choice but to open satellite offices or allow their outlying employees to work at home. The typical suburban edge city, according to Joel Garreau, would survive an energy crisis more easily because it has a better mixture of homes, offices, and stores. "It is, on average, an *improvement* in per capita fuel efficiency over the old suburbia-downtown arrangement, since it moves everything closer to the homes of the middle class," he wrote.[41]

Mass transit, commonly promoted as an ideal way to conserve energy, does not figure into the suburban vision of the twenty-first century. Los Angeles began constructing a twenty-one-mile subway system in the early 1990s at a cost of $270 million per mile, even though experts doubted a sufficient number of commuters would use it. "This is building for a lost cause," said Martin Wachs, director of UCLA's Institute of Transportation Studies. "A subway is a nineteenth-century technology, and Los Angeles is a twentieth-century city. In the struggle between centralization and decentralization, decentralization has already won."[42]

Oregon voters punctuated this point in November 1996 with their rejection of Measure 32, which would have provided $375 million in state lottery money to build a light-rail line between Portland and suburban Clackamas Town Center. City voters were enthusiastic, but Portland's suburbs and the rest of the state sent Measure 32 down to defeat:

	Yes (%)	No (%)	Margin
Statewide	46.9	53.1	No by 82,206
Components (share of state vote in percent)			
Portland (16.2)	60.8	39.2	Yes by 46,292
Portland suburbs (39.1)	48.8	51.2	No by 12,533
Fringe metros (15.1)	45.9	54.1	No by 16,354
Nonmetro areas (29.6)	37.3	62.7	No by 99,611

Source: Author's analysis of official election returns.

Bill Sizemore, who coordinated the campaign against the light-rail referendum, interpreted the results as an endorsement for more road-building. "The best answer is a better freeway system," he said. "It's not necessarily cheaper, but at least we know people will use it."[43]

Suburbia's insistence on an inefficient, polluting mode of transportation contradicts its equally strong demand for a clean environment. Exit pollsters interviewed Oregon voters in November 1996—on the very day that they were rejecting Measure 32—and asked whether they placed a higher priority on protecting the environment or creating jobs. Forty-eight percent chose the environment, while 41 percent opted for economic growth.[44] The Gallup Poll had posed the same question a year earlier to a nationwide sample of suburban respondents, yielding results that were even more dramatic. Fifty-eight percent said the environment was more important; just 36 percent picked the economy.[45] The only reasonable interpretation is that suburbanites believe they can have their cars and clean air, too. Available scientific evidence is not quite as sanguine.

6. Black and White

There are plenty of signs that race relations in the United States have improved. Polls show Americans to be more liberal on racial issues than they were three decades ago. Several cities with white majorities have elected African-American mayors. And suburbia slowly, but steadily, is being integrated. Its minority population had climbed to 19.7 million by 1990 and is projected to soar to 46.3 million by 2020.[46]

But is progress being made quickly enough? Whites typically say yes, minorities generally say no. A national survey in 1996 by Knight-Ridder News Service found that 60 percent of black respondents considered race relations to be one of the most important issues facing the nation, but just 37 percent of white participants agreed. Almost as many whites—35 percent—said that America already had overcompensated for previous racial inequities. They contended that African-Americans had gained a substantial advantage in the job market, thanks to a wide range of civil rights programs.[47]

The most controversial of these programs is affirmative action, the blanket name for several initiatives designed to increase minority participation in the workforce. Some affirmative-action regulations require private companies to establish goals and timetables for hiring or promoting minorities; other parts stipulate that government agencies must allot a portion of their contracts to minority-owned companies. Critics—and they are legion—either say that affirmative action has worked so well that it no longer is needed, or they charge that it discriminates by giving jobs to less-qualified minorities at the expense of qualified whites.[48]

The dispute over affirmative action typifies America's broader controversy over all racial issues. The Suburban Generation finds itself torn because of conflicting core beliefs. Its members generally are moderate and tolerant, but they also are opposed to central authority and to providing assistance to the urban underclass. They can assert in one survey that all races must be treated equally, yet say in another that busing should never be used to achieve school desegregation. White suburbanites, in truth, don't really believe that America ever will solve its racial problems. They support integration in theory, but only if it proceeds at a measured pace with a minimum of government assistance.

These beliefs were put to the test in 1996 in California, where voters decided the fate of Proposition 209, a state constitutional amendment to eliminate government-sponsored affirmative-action programs. Republicans quickly lined up in support of 209. "This (seeks) to undo a terrible unfairness so that opportunity is offered not just to some Californians, but to all Californians," said Republican Governor Pete Wilson.[49] Democrats were opposed; President Clinton was among those who urged Californians to vote no.

Residents of mother cities, to no one's surprise, rejected Proposition 209 overwhelmingly. Seventy-nine percent of Oakland voters pulled the "no" lever, as did 71 percent in San Francisco and 59 percent in Los Angeles. But the suburban tide was strongly pro-209, yielding a margin of more than 720,000 votes in favor of the referendum and sweeping it to victory:

	Margin
Statewide	Yes by 879,729
Components (share of state vote in percent)	
Mother cities (19.0)	No by 291,111
Suburbs (63.7)	Yes by 723,679
Fringe metros (13.4)	Yes by 340,277
Nonmetro areas (3.9)	Yes by 106,884

Source: Author's analysis of official election returns.

Enthusiasm for Proposition 209 crossed party lines, as exit polls showed. Eighty-two percent of Dole's supporters and 71 percent of Perot's backers voted yes on the referendum. Clinton had some success in rallying opposition, but even 34 percent of his voters were in favor of 209.[50]

Jesse Jackson was greatly offended by the outcome. He saw no difference between the California governor's support of 209 and George Wallace's refusal to desegregate the University of Alabama in the early 1960s. "Wilson has done essentially the same thing to Clinton," Jackson said. "If he can end affirmative action and face the president down in California, then the other forty-nine states have a green light."[51] There was some truth to what he said. Most elected officials previously had shied from taking a stand on such a controversial topic, but they gained courage after seeing the widespread suburban support for ditching affirmative action in California. "The politicians now find it hard to resist," political scientist Seymour Martin Lipset said after the drive for 209 had gotten underway.[52]

Public sentiment follows similar lines on another race-related issue —immigration. The Census Bureau has estimated that America will add 880,000 immigrants each year until 2050, including 324,000 Hispanics, 323,000 Asians, and 60,000 blacks—figures that trouble most suburbanites. Exit polls in such ethnically diverse states as California, New York, and Texas in 1996 found popular agreement that the rate of immigration should be reduced. "The United States has got to choose between its own huddled masses and the world's huddled masses," said former Colorado Governor Richard Lamm. "Immigrants are God's children; they're wonderful people. But I have a bigger bond with the unemployed autoworker in Detroit than with the person in Bangladesh."[53]

Congress responded to this public mood in 1996 with legislation to increase border controls and to ease procedures for detaining and deporting illegal immigrants. The House of Representatives approved the bill by a lopsided vote of 305 to 123. Congressmen from city districts voted no by a 2 to 1 margin, but suburbanites were heavily in favor:

	Total Vote		Republicans		Democrats	
	Yes	No	Yes	No	Yes	No
House	305	123	229	5	76	117
Components						
City districts	30	65	19	2	11	63
Suburban districts	135	33	106	3	29	30
Fringe districts	70	12	57	0	13	12
Nonmetro districts	70	13	47	0	23	12

Source: Author's analysis of congressional roll call (September 25, 1996).

A note of caution: It would be a mistake to interpret suburbia's votes on affirmative action and immigration as a complete repudiation of American diversity. The Suburban Generation opposes racial quotas and untrammeled access for refugees, to be sure, but it remains tolerant at heart. It will reject any candidate who stoops to race-baiting.

Texas Governor George Bush, son of the former president, quickly grasped this distinction. He warned his fellow politicians to be "very careful not to use divisive language" on race-related issues. He condemned affirmative action "because quotas balkanize our society," yet insisted that he wanted all races represented in his state's workforce and its university system. And legal immigrants, Bush declared, deserved to be welcomed as full Americans. "It's one thing to say we're going to protect our borders," he said, "and it's another thing to say we don't want you here."[54]

7. Other Interests

Republicans have a sly way of referring to the racial and ethnic minority groups that wield so much clout within the Democratic Party. They call them "special interests." Even fellow Democrats have been known to use the term. John Glenn and Gary Hart were frustrated by Walter Mondale's ability to line up support from so many of these groups, as well as labor unions, in advance of the 1984 primaries. They labeled him a tool of the special interests, an appellation that fatally damaged Mondale's campaign against Ronald Reagan in the fall.

But the Suburban Generation is not opposed to *all* special-interest groups. There are two that it believes are deserving of all the government assistance they can attract: women and the elderly.

These exceptions were illuminated by a Pew Research Center survey in late 1997 which asked respondents to rate the amount of attention that the federal government devoted to various groups of citizens. Poor people were identified as the bloc that was most heavily ignored by Washington; 65 percent of respondents said the poor did not get enough attention from the government. The three runners-up were groups much closer to suburbia's heart: the elderly (60 percent), the middle class (54 percent), and women (39 percent):

	(%)		
	Get Less Than They Should	About Right Amount	Get More Than They Should
Poor people	65	23	10
Elderly people	60	31	8
Middle class people	54	36	9
Women	39	46	13
Religious people	27	46	22
Black people	26	46	24
White people	17	59	19
Business leaders	9	37	50

Source: Pew Research Center for The People and The Press, *Deconstructing Distrust* (March 10, 1998), online (http://www.people-press.org/trustrpt.htm).

Suburbanites' concerns about women and the elderly are based on more than a smidgen of self-interest. The 1990 census counted 53 million females in suburbia, as well as 13 million people who were sixty-five or older. There were more members of either group in the suburbs than in mother cities, fringe metros, or nonmetro areas.

Suburban women, in fact, constituted one of the most powerful interest groups in the 1996 election, encompassing one-quarter of all American voters. And they were solidly in Bill Clinton's camp: 52 percent of suburban women supported the president, while 39 percent backed Bob Dole. Women's votes made the difference for Clinton in the suburbs, since suburban men favored Dole by a margin of 5 percentage points.[55]

The status of women, of course, has evolved dramatically in recent decades. The typical suburban woman in 1960 was a housewife; she has a full-time paying job today. Women accounted for just 10 percent of the workforce in many professions in 1970, but have risen to what John Naisbitt and Patricia Aburdene call "a critical mass ranging from 30 to 50 percent in much of the business world, including banking, accounting, and computer science."[56] This change is reflected in America's prototypical suburb. Sixty-one percent of the women in Levittown, New York, worked outside their homes in 1990, nearly two-and-a-half times the 1960 figure of 26 percent.[57]

Suburban women seek government help that is targeted to their dual roles as heads of households and breadwinners; their interests range from family-leave legislation to entrepreneurial assistance. The latter is especially important because the number of women-owned businesses is growing faster than the number of businesses overall, according to the Census Bureau, and this growth is concentrated in suburbia. The Atlanta metropolitan area contained 82,800 women-owned firms in 1992, for example, but only 10,000 were in the city of Atlanta. The other 72,800—88 percent of the regional total—were in the suburbs. Metros from coast to coast had similar ratios: 74 percent of all women-owned businesses in metropolitan Seattle were suburban, as were 78 percent in the Denver area and 91 percent in metropolitan Detroit.[58]

Suburbanites also are generally interested in programs that help the elderly, as would be expected from people who tend to be older than their urban counterparts. The median age of suburban residents in 1990 was 33.3, substantially higher than the median of 31.6 in central cities.[59]

The biggest issue for the elderly, as noted earlier in this chapter, is the continued survival of Medicare and Social Security. Not their reform, a topic more popular with younger generations, but their *survival.* Most politicians understand the necessity of protecting these time-honored systems. The few slow learners have suffered for their ignorance, as congressional Republicans did with Medicare in 1995 and Barry Goldwater did with Social Security more than three decades earlier. Goldwater casually suggested at the start of his 1964 presidential campaign that Social Security be made voluntary. One of New Hampshire's leading newspapers carried a bold headline the next morning: "Goldwater Sets Goals: End Social Security." The Republican never recovered. Lyndon Johnson made sure of that by producing a television commercial that showed two hands tearing up a Social Security card. Saint Petersburg, Florida, already a haven for senior citizens, had voted Republican for twenty years. It went Democratic in 1964.[60]

The elderly will become increasingly powerful in suburbia as the twenty-first century unfolds. Surveys by the American Association of Retired Persons have found that an overwhelming number of senior citizens do not want to move into retirement homes or migrate to Southern states. They prefer to stay right where they are—and as self-sufficient as possible.

Some suburban neighborhoods, as a result, already have high concentrations of people in their sixties, seventies, and even eighties. Planners have taken to referring to such places as naturally occurring retirement communities, or NORCs. A study in the Washington, D.C., area found several suburban NORCs in Montgomery County, Maryland, and Arlington County, Virginia, with more in the process of developing. "It's there for all to see," said Terry Lynch, director of Arlington's agency on aging. "We recognize that this is a growing issue for us."[61]

8. Law and Order

Most Americans feel reasonably safe at home.

A 1996 Knight-Ridder News Service poll asked respondents about their likelihood of being victimized by crime in their own neighborhoods. Two-thirds—66 percent—felt they were at low risk, and another 23 percent said their danger was at a moderate level. Just 11 percent said they lived in high-risk areas.[62]

But if that's the case, why do similar surveys consistently find Americans to be preoccupied with the need for law and order? Participants in a 1994 Conference Board poll, for example, identified crime as the nation's worst problem; fully 90 percent said it had reached serious dimensions. A 1995 poll by the Regional Plan Association asked people in the Atlanta, Dallas, Los Angeles, New York City, and Seattle areas to name the first ingredient needed to create a positive quality of life.* They didn't opt for good schools or a clean environment or a strong economy; they cited a low level of crime as the key factor.[63]

Television is the primary cause of this contradiction. Rocky Moun-

---

*The Conference Board is a research organization that analyzes economic trends and business policies. The Regional Plan Association is a planning group that specializes in transportation studies. Both are based in New York City.

tain Media Watch, a Denver-based TV watchdog, analyzed local news programs in fifty-five cities in 1998. It found that half of the typical TV newscast was devoted to coverage of crimes and disasters; nearly 75 percent of the lead stories dealt with such violent topics. "If it bleeds, it leads," said Paul Klite, Media Watch's executive director. "Disaster, crime, war. All these stories get an emotional reaction, and viewers have been conditioned and seduced to watch. To deliver eyeballs to advertisers, it's great. But local TV news is not an accurate mirror of real life. It gives the public a distorted view of the world."[64]

That view is particularly skewed when urban centers are the subject, since most crimes reported on television occur in cities. White suburbanites have plenty of other reasons to be alienated from the largely black city of Detroit, but TV's constant drumbeat of Detroit crime stories has added fear to the equation. A study by the *Detroit News* found that crimes and disasters consumed 43 percent of local news time on the city's TV stations. One Detroit station devoted 54 percent of its newscasts to such mayhem, while spending an average of eighteen seconds per night covering politics and government.[65]

It is no surprise, then, that suburbanites have come to fear the spread of violent crime, even though relatively few have been its victims. They consider cities to be breeding grounds for criminals, and they worry that their quieter, safer communities might one day be overrun by such brutes. The same Knight-Ridder poll that asked Americans to rate the crime risk in their own neighborhoods also had them characterize the risk in the largest cities in their states. Seventy-two percent said the danger of being victimized in a city was high; just 6 percent said it was low.[66]

This explains why public safety is the rare issue on which city dwellers and suburbanites agree. Both groups take a strong stance in favor of law and order; both enthusiastically supported President Clinton's landmark proposal to fund the hiring of 100,000 new police officers. The final version of the president's 1994 crime bill established a six-year, $30.2 billion trust fund that was designed not only to pay for the new officers, but also to create community policing programs and to build new prisons. Big cities had the most to gain; seventy-two urban congressmen voted in favor, while only twenty-two were opposed. Suburban members also backed the bill by a count of 100 to 69. Congressmen from fringe and nonmetro districts, on the other hand, were opposed by a margin of almost 2 to 1.[67]

This urban–suburban alliance is equally strong on the related subject of punishment. Residents of both types of communities advocate strict sentences for convicted criminals, favoring the death penalty for heinous cases of murder. These sentiments even prevail in Massachusetts, the most liberal of all suburban states. A 1996 exit poll asked Massachusetts voters what the maximum sentence should be for murder; they overwhelmingly chose death over two less-severe forms of punishment:

	(%)		
	Death Penalty	Life with No Parole	Long Prison Term
All Massachusetts voters	56	34	6
Clinton voters	46	41	8
Dole voters	75	19	3
Perot voters	63	30	2

Source: VNS exit poll 1996.

But suburbanites do not believe in taking the fight against crime into their own hands; they do not believe that homeowners have an unlimited right to bear arms. Suburbia's representatives in the House signaled their endorsement of gun control by backing the 1993 Brady Bill, which established a five-day waiting period before an individual could purchase a handgun. Sixty-four suburban Democrats and thirty-eight suburban Republicans joined forces to vote yes.[68]

GOP leaders, to their subsequent misfortune, paid little heed to the bipartisan nature of this support. They pushed forward a controversial bill in 1996 to repeal the ban on nineteen types of semiautomatic weapons. Conservative Republicans, prodded by the National Rifle Association, demanded a roll call, even though the legislation's chances of becoming law were nil. The Senate had little enthusiasm for repeal, and President Clinton promised a veto, if necessary. Moderate Republicans were distressed when the vote was scheduled. "The president will look like a leader, and Congress will look like we succumbed to a special interest," moaned Connecticut Republican Christopher Shays, who represented a suburban district.[69]

The House approved repeal by a surprisingly small margin, as thirty-one suburban Republicans defected to vote no. Suburbanites from both parties opposed repeal by the narrowest of margins—eighty to seventy-nine:

	Total Vote		Republicans		Democrats	
	Yes	No	Yes	No	Yes	No
House	239	173	183	42	56	130
Components						
City districts	22	64	14	6	8	58
Suburban districts	79	80	70	31	9	49
Fringe districts	64	17	53	3	11	14
Nonmetro districts	74	12	46	2	28	9

Source: Author's analysis of congressional roll call (March 22, 1996).

The Republicans ultimately paid a price for trying to lift the ban on assault weapons, exactly as Shays had predicted. Polls showed the repeal campaign to be wildly unpopular. Democratic challengers cited it as proof that the GOP had lost touch with mainstream America. "Newt Gingrich bent his knee and is kissing the ring of the NRA," charged Congressman Charles Schumer, a New York Democrat.[70] Eight suburban Republican congressmen who had supported repeal were thrown out of office in November 1996.

One Republican who didn't get the message was Al Salvi, the party's 1996 U.S. Senate nominee in Illinois. Salvi defiantly applauded the effort to lift the assault-weapons ban, and he belittled anyone who suggested that handgun sales should be restricted. That most definitely included his Democratic opponent, Richard Durbin, an ardent supporter of gun control.

Voters made their sentiments clear in November. Durbin trounced Salvi by 655,000 votes statewide, including a 62,000-vote bulge in the normally Republican suburbs of Chicago. "We set out to change the debate on guns in Illinois, and I think we did," the senator-elect said. "In the Chicagoland area, a lot of suburban legislators who thought that this was a free vote are rethinking it this morning."[71] Exit polls added fuel for thought, showing that gun owners were a relatively small minority in Illinois, constituting just 31 percent of the electorate. Those who did *not* own guns had voted overwhelmingly for Durbin.[72]

Salvi, for one, was convinced. He reversed his field a few months later, abruptly announcing his support for gun control. His conversion, he said, was the product of discussions with thousands of Illinois residents, including doctors and police officers who had seen the results of gun-related violence firsthand. "The citizens, people like the doctor and a cop who made a similar plea, changed my mind," he said.[73] The voters had spoken, and Salvi had bent. It was a situation that every politician could understand.

9. Live and Let Live

Vickie Couglin set high moral standards for herself; what others did was their own business. Couglin, a thirty-six-year-old aerospace engineer in the Los Angeles suburb of Torrance, vowed never to cheat on her husband because "all you have is your own integrity." Surely, a reporter suggested, she must be disappointed that her president didn't seem to live as pure a life. It was early 1998; Bill Clinton was awash in rumors of marital infidelities. "Nobody's perfect," Couglin shrugged, "and I don't want to judge anybody."[74]

Her attitude was typical. Clinton's popularity ratings soared even as he became mired in the Monica Lewinsky scandal, puzzling political commentators who had thought the nation was becoming more conservative. These Washington insiders greatly underestimated the tolerant spirit of the Suburban Generation. Baby boomers had been taught for thirty years to show respect for other cultures and ways of life, even those of which they privately disapproved. School had drummed this lesson into them, television had reinforced it, and the adults of the 1990s were behaving accordingly. "The unwillingness of Americans to judge one another," said Boston University sociologist Alan Wolfe, "is one of the great triumphs of the 1960s."[75]

It also is one of the reasons why suburbanites have little interest in the Religious Right's social agenda. Adults who are raising children are worried primarily about issues that hit close to home, according to a 1996 poll conducted by Penn & Schoen Associates for the National Parenting Association. Public safety topped their list of concerns, named by 30 percent of survey participants. It was followed by drug abuse (21 percent), quality of education (17 percent), and the cost of education (15 percent). "Not one single respondent mentioned gay marriages or abortion," said association president Sylvia Ann Hewlett. "It's not even on their radar screens."[76]

Abortion, in particular, is viewed by most suburbanites as a personal matter, not a public issue; as something to be settled between a woman and her doctor, not between Democrats and Republicans. A 1995 Gallup Poll found that only 15 percent of respondents believed abortion should be made illegal, while more than twice as many—33 percent—said it should be legal in all cases.[77] Suburbanites, especially those with high incomes, were more likely than other groups to support abortion rights:

	(%)		
	Legal Always	Legal in Certain Cases	Illegal Always
Nationwide	33	50	15
Type of community			
Urban	37	46	14
Suburban	34	51	11
Rural	24	53	21
Household incomes			
Less than $20,000	25	52	20
$20,000–$29,999	34	45	19
$30,000–$49,999	37	47	11
$50,000 or more	38	54	7

Source: "Legality, Morality of Abortion," *Gallup Poll Monthly* (March 1995): 30.

Gallup then instructed respondents to set aside their opinions about the legal status of abortion. It rephrased the question on a personal level, asking if they believed that having an abortion was morally wrong. Fifty-one percent of the participants agreed that it was, while 34 percent said it wasn't, a difference of 17 percentage points.[78] A plurality in each type of community maintained that abortion was wrong, but the smallest difference was found in suburbia:

	Wrong (%)	Not Wrong (%)	Mixed Feelings (%)	Difference
Nationwide	51	34	13	+17
Type of community				
Urban	49	35	12	+14
Suburban	49	37	12	+12
Rural	55	27	16	+28

Source: "Legality, Morality of Abortion," *Gallup Poll Monthly* (March 1995): 30.

Suburbanites generally do not believe in abortion, according to these poll results, but they refuse to impose their feelings on others. The Religious Right had no such concerns in 1996, cheerfully saddling Bob Dole with the tough anti-abortion plank that contributed to his defeat. Exit polls that year showed the electorate to be decidedly pro-choice: 60 percent of American voters said abortion should be legal in most or all cases, while only 12 percent thought it should be outlawed completely. Dole voters, conservative though most were, tended toward the same views: 41 percent supported legalized abortion in most or all instances, compared to just 20 percent who advocated making it illegal.[79]

The message is clear: The Suburban Generation considers moral codes and religious beliefs to be wonderful compasses to guide an individual's actions, but not to shape public policy, at least not in cases outside the realm of public safety. There is unanimous agreement that "thou shalt not kill," but only a minority of Americans insist that "thou shalt not have an abortion."

Suburbanites, however, do not have an unblemished record of tolerance. They often waver when gambling or gay rights are at issue.

Big cities are searching frantically for ways to stem the outflow of people and wealth to suburbia. Some urban leaders are convinced that legalized gambling is the panacea for their ills. Casinos, they say, will create jobs, lure suburban high-rollers, and spark an urban renaissance. Voters in 1996 approved three casinos for Detroit, perhaps the most desperate big city in America.[80]

But suburbanites aren't convinced that gambling will have a positive impact. A 1996 exit poll in Connecticut showed that 62 percent of voters opposed additional casinos in the state, with only 34 percent in favor. Partisan preferences were unimportant; majorities of Clinton, Dole, and Perot supporters all answered in the negative.[81]

Voters in Ohio, another suburban state, also turned thumbs down on legalized gambling in 1996. The pro-casino lobby spent $8 million to drum up support for Issue 1, a referendum that would have allowed riverboat gambling, while opponents could muster only $500,000. Issue 1 lost anyway, by 62 percent to 38 percent. "I hope today's resounding defeat of Issue 1 will at last convince those people who have been promoting it over the years that the people of Ohio don't want casino gambling—not yesterday, not today, not ever," said Governor George Voinovich.[82]

Suburbia seems to be more liberal on the question of gay rights. A 1997 poll by the Tarrance Group and Lake Sosin Snell & Associates found that 68 percent of Americans favored federal legislation to outlaw discrimination against homosexuals. Nine states and 165 counties and municipalities already had implemented laws forbidding biased treatment based on a person's sexual orientation, according to the Human Rights Campaign, a Washington lobbying group.[83]

But there have been exceptions. Colorado voters in 1992 approved Amendment 2, which repealed existing gay rights ordinances throughout the state.* Colorado for Family Values, the point group behind the referendum, ran TV commercials with footage from wild gay pride parades in California; it warned that similar behavior could be expected in Colorado. Sixty percent of Denver voters rejected Amendment 2, but 52.5 percent of those going to the polls in Denver's suburbs voted yes.[84]

The thought of gay weddings bothers suburbanites even more. Congress passed the Defense of Marriage Act in 1996, defining marriage as a union between a man and a woman, thereby precluding gay couples from receiving federal spousal benefits. "How does the fact that I love another man . . . threaten your marriage?" asked Massachusetts Democrat Barney Frank, who is gay.[85] His colleagues responded emphatically with a 342 to 67 vote in favor of the bill. Urban congressmen were somewhat divided, with 51 supporting the measure and 39 opposed, but suburban representatives left little doubt, casting 140 yes votes and just 21 no votes.

10. Looking Inward

Arthur Vandenberg entered national politics at the top. He was a newspaper editor in Michigan for twenty-two years before suddenly

---

*The U.S. Supreme Court in 1996 ruled Amendment 2 unconstitutional.

being appointed to the U.S. Senate in 1928. He demonstrated natural aptitude for his new profession, rising to become Republican Minority Leader by the mid-1930s. Vandenberg used his post as a sounding board for his isolationist views; he was determined that American boys would not fight in another foreign war. "We all have our sympathies and our natural emotion in behalf of the victims of national or international outrage all around the globe," he said. "But we are not, we cannot be, the world's protector or the world's policeman."[86]

Conversion came instantly upon the bombing of Pearl Harbor. "That day ended isolation for any realist," Vandenberg conceded.[87] He reversed his positions completely, becoming a leading advocate of the Marshall Plan and the United Nations. Democratic presidents counted on him to lead the bipartisan battle against the small band of enduring isolationists, a group he once led but now scorned.

Vandenberg's vision of the postwar era became reality. America, as he had predicted, did not retreat to its isolationist shell. It assumed the point position for the world's democracies as they confronted the Soviet Union in a seemingly never-ending Cold War. "Let every nation know, whether it wishes us well or ill," declared John Kennedy in 1961, "that we shall pay any price, bear any burden, meet any hardship, support any friend, oppose any foe to assure the survival and the success of liberty."[88] Wars in Korea and Vietnam and smaller crises in Berlin and Cuba became part of the natural order of life.

But the United States inevitably wearied of its role. The decade-long Vietnam War eroded America's resolve to bear any overseas burden; the sorry end to that conflict shattered the nation's confidence that it could oppose any military foe. A growing number of Americans began to echo the prewar Vandenberg; they no longer wished to be the world's policeman. It seemed an unnecessary job, anyway, once the Soviet empire collapsed in 1991.

What was striking about the 1992 and 1996 presidential campaigns —the first after the end of the Cold War—was their single-minded emphasis on domestic policy. Indiana Senator Richard Lugar, who ran briefly for the Republican presidential nomination in 1996, was the sole maverick. He tried to make international affairs an issue, but found that his opponents would not rise to the bait. "The other candidates seemed to know little, or even to care much, about foreign policy," Lugar later wrote. "They expressed little or no interest in discussing America's role in the world or the remarkable opportunities to build peace and prosperity for future generations."[89]

Lugar's opponents simply were being realistic. Most suburbanites—indeed, most Americans—have been looking inward since the mid-

1970s. They demand that domestic concerns be given priority over international matters. The result has been an ad hoc foreign policy consisting of isolated initiatives ranging from Grenada and Panama to Bosnia and Somalia. Total spending for the State Department, foreign aid, U.S. contributions to the United Nations, and all other international operations dropped from $25 billion in 1984 to $18 billion in 1996, a cut of 51 percent when adjusted for inflation. American military forces were slashed from 2.1 million service members during the waning days of the Cold War to 1.5 million in 1997—a "pretty damn big reduction," in the words of former Defense Secretary William Perry.[90]

But not too big for suburbanites. They see no one to fear on the world horizon. The Pentagon, after all, has predicted a "period of strategic pause" between now and 2010, with no new superpower expected to emerge to challenge the United States.[91] If that's the case, voters ask, why not scale back our international commitments and concentrate on our needs here at home?

Suburbia's only real interest in most foreign countries these days is an economic one. The annual value of American exports swelled tenfold from $43 billion in 1970 to $422 billion in 1991, the year Bill Clinton announced his candidacy for president.[92] Clinton pledged to fuel further expansion by lowering trade barriers; his immediate goal was to win congressional support for the North American Free Trade Agreement (NAFTA) that had been negotiated with Canada and Mexico. A sizable number of House Democrats opposed the new president, insisting that passage of NAFTA would open the door for American factories to move to Mexico at the expense of thousands of American jobs.

Clinton persevered, and the House of Representatives approved NAFTA in November 1993 by a margin of just thirty-four votes. Big-city congressmen rejected free trade, and their nonmetro colleagues were evenly divided. It therefore fell to suburbia to do Clinton's heavy lifting. Suburban congressmen supplied 40 percent of all yes votes; they and their counterparts from fringe districts pushed NAFTA to victory:

	Total Vote		Republicans		Democrats	
	Yes	No	Yes	No	Yes	No
House	234	200	132	43	102	156
Components						
City districts	41	55	9	4	32	51
Suburban districts	93	75	69	21	24	54
Fringe districts	57	27	34	9	23	18
Nonmetro districts	43	43	20	9	23	33

Source: Author's analysis of congressional roll call (November 17, 1993).

The free-trade vote, coming just ten months into his first term, gave Clinton an early indication that his centrist policies played better in suburbia than in the Democratic Party's traditional big-city base. It confirmed that his future success would depend on his ability to nudge the party toward the middle of the political road, in the opinion of Will Marshall, president of the Progressive Policy Institute, an offshoot of the Democratic Leadership Council. "NAFTA was a watershed, a turning point toward the realization that (Clinton's) administration will continually face a choice between what the country wants and what the old guard in the party wants," said Marshall. "The circle cannot always be squared; sometimes you have to choose."[93]

Clinton had chosen to side with suburbia, and he had won. It would not be the last time.

7 Brave New World: America's Political Future

Few politicians bother to ponder the long-term future. Theirs is a here-and-now business—racing to make this morning's roll call, hustling to deliver this afternoon's speech, scheming to get on this evening's TV newscast. The hectic environment in which politicians work is not conducive to contemplation, which is why elected officials rarely think ahead by even five days or five months, let alone five years.

Adding to the problem, as noted earlier, is the fact that most politicians, like most generals, stand always ready to re-fight the last war. They focus so intently on what worked in the past election that they fail to see the changed conditions of the next one, often to their own detriment. This impulse is evident in every presidential campaign, regardless if it is an unpredictable contest that redefines the political landscape, like 1992, or a dull race that ratifies the status quo, like 1984.

The latter year proved how widespread political nearsightedness can be. Eight Democrats sought the 1984 nomination to challenge the popular Republican incumbent, Ronald Reagan. Walter Mondale would take the honors, only to suffer a horrible defeat in the general election, just as most experts had predicted from the start. Columnists Jack Germond and Jules Witcover found the whole process so mind-numbingly boring that they entitled their book about the 1984 campaign *Wake Us When It's Over*.[1]

Germond, Witcover, and their political brethren apparently were too drowsy to note a crucial demographic change taking hold across America. The emerging suburban majority was beginning to flex its muscles as never before. Suburban states would give Reagan 278 electoral votes in November 1984, eight more than he needed for victory, making him the first president to owe his election *solely* to suburbia. American politics was at the dawn of a new era, but most of the Democratic contenders failed to see the approaching sunrise. They looked back into the dark past for inspiration:

- John Glenn presented himself as a mythic hero, a man whose strength and determination had met the challenges of outer space and would be equal to the demands of the Oval Office. His entire campaign seemed grounded in 1962, the year he had become the first American to orbit earth. Glenn was banking heavily on a pub-

licity boost from *The Right Stuff,* a movie about space pioneers that
would be released in 1984. It was a strategy that caused New York
Governor Mario Cuomo to dismiss him as a "celluloid candidate."[2]

- Reubin Askew and Ernest Hollings both sought to be the next
  Jimmy Carter, a dubious proposition just four years after Carter's
  landslide loss to Reagan. Askew and Hollings were playing the
  tired, sadly outdated game of regional politics, offering no dis-
  tinctive credentials other than their Southernness. Neither
  seemed to realize that Carter's improbable win in 1976 was more
  a product of Watergate than of his Georgian birth.
- Alan Cranston portrayed himself as the candidate of the future, a
  difficult role indeed for a seventy-year-old career politician. He
  had gone so far as to dye his white eyebrows orange in an effort to
  recapture his political youth. Cranston harped on the issue of a
  nuclear weapons freeze, proof that his clairvoyance was of a very
  limited variety: The Cold War would be over in five short years.[3]
- George McGovern ran as, well, George McGovern, the man who
  had carried only Massachusetts and the District of Columbia
  against Richard Nixon twelve years before.

And then there was Mondale, a stiff, overly cautious son of the liberal
Democratic establishment, a man whom some Carter staffers had
derided as "Vice President Mundane." He set out to win the nomination
by courting party leaders and special-interest groups, exactly as Franklin
Roosevelt and Harry Truman had done in their eras. Mondale, in a sense,
was one of the last of the New Dealers. He pledged to raise taxes to fund
expanded social programs—what was good enough for FDR was good
enough for him—and was stunned by the resulting political firestorm.

The Democratic field was so tired and myopic that the seventy-
three-year-old Reagan seemed, in comparison, to be a fresh, innovative candidate. "Trouble is, our opponents treat each new idea the old-
fashioned way: They spurn it," the president joked about the Democrats. "I hate to say this, but the age factor may play a part in this
election. Their ideas are just too old."[4]

There were two exceptions. Gary Hart and Jesse Jackson sensed the
tremors rumbling beneath the political landscape. Hart insisted the
Democratic Party had to move beyond the rhetoric of the New Deal and
the Great Society; it had to do more than just promise something different to every constituent group. "The election of 1984 is, at its heart,
not a choice between Democrats and Republicans, or liberals or conservatives, but a choice between the past and the future," he declared.[5]
Young professionals, most of them suburbanites, rallied to his cause.

Jackson, for his part, understood that urban blacks were in danger of losing their influence within the Democratic Party unless they broadened their base. He envisioned a Rainbow Coalition that would bring together poor and working-class people of all races—people with common interests and needs—to counter the growing power of the suburban middle class. "The Rainbow Coalition of many colors and circumstances can save this nation if we have a mind to work," he told his audiences. "Our time has come."[6]

It was no coincidence that two outsiders—Hart, a loner by temperament, and Jackson, an African-American—were the only Democratic candidates in 1984 who felt the pulse of the future. Neither came close to the nomination, but their ideas lived on in a sense that Mondale's did not. Hart, in particular, paved the way for another outsider, an obscure Arkansas governor named Bill Clinton, who reached the White House in 1992 because of his intuition that the Democratic Party's electoral future lay in suburbia.

The coming century will present new challenges. Both major parties will strive to heal—or at least paper over—internal divisions that might endanger their abilities to connect with the influential suburban electorate. Both will try to prevent the emergence of a third party that might become a pesky challenger. A few enlightened individuals will discover the correct course to political success in the Suburban Age, but it's a safe bet that most Democratic and Republican leaders—the Reubin Askews, Alan Cranstons, and Walter Mondales of the twenty-first century—will look to the past to guide them.

They won't have a chance.

The Numbers Game

The Pew Research Center for The People and The Press has the kind of pretentious name that one would expect of a national think tank. It's a name that conjures up images of serious researchers, all in white lab coats, conducting meticulous studies into the most arcane aspects of American life. And, indeed, the Pew Research Center is attracted to exactly that type of work. It was entirely in character when it decided in 1994 to take on the seemingly impossible task of identifying and categorizing the various ornery, unpredictable, and free-thinking species of American voters.*

---

*The organization actually was known in 1994 as the Times Mirror Center for The People and The Press. It was renamed the Pew Research Center shortly thereafter.

The center surveyed 4,800 people in July 1994, asking them a wide array of questions: Which candidate did they vote for in 1992? What did they like to watch on TV? What were their religious beliefs? Who were their personal heroes? Which issues did they consider to be most important? What kind of music did they like? A team of analysts sifted through the resulting piles of computer printouts, using the data to classify voters into ten distinct groups.[7]

The political climate, of course, is fluid. The ten categories that were identified so carefully in 1994 have changed a bit in the intervening years, and they will continue to evolve in the years to come. But the center's report remains valuable because it offers a snapshot of the stresses that are tearing at the American political system near the end of the twentieth century, stresses that eventually could cause political upheaval. Everyone will be affected, Republicans, Democrats, and independents alike.

Republicans

The Pew Research Center identified three groups—together constituting about 34 percent of American adults—that prefer the Republican Party. Yet they differ in substantial ways, despite their mutual attachment to the GOP:

Enterprisers: These people are Rush Limbaugh's crowd; they are pro-business and anti–social welfare. Economic issues are most important to them; nothing gets them more excited than a nice, big tax cut. Their level of social tolerance is moderate to low.

Moralists: Many of these religious and cultural conservatives are former Democrats. They are churchgoers, socially intolerant, and opposed to social welfare. They are critical of big business, believing it makes too much money, and they also dislike big government.

Libertarians: These voters have a history of supporting the GOP, yet are not completely comfortable with the party because it welcomes the Religious Right. They are pro-business and anti–social welfare, but are highly tolerant. Their views on abortion are downright liberal.

Moralists form the largest group within the modern Republican Party, accounting for 44 percent of all Republican-leaning adults. Enterprisers are the party's most loyal members, giving 78 percent of their votes to George Bush in 1992 and 88 percent to Bob Dole four years later. Libertarians, on the other hand, simply tolerated Bush and largely abandoned Dole:*

---

*Every column but one in the following chart—and the two subsequent charts—shows data collected by the Times Mirror Center in 1994 and the Pew Research Center

Group	Share of Adults (%)			1992 Presidential Vote (%)			1996 Presidential Vote (%)		
	1994	1996	GOP	Clinton	Bush	Perot	Clinton	Dole	Perot
Enterprisers	10	12	35	6	78	14	6	88	3
Moralists	18	15	44	14	66	20	20	66	7
Libertarians	4	7	21	20	52	27	39	34	12

Source: Times Mirror Center for The People and The Press, *The New Political Landscape* (Washington, D.C.: Times Mirror Co., 1994), pp. 12–14; Pew Research Center for The People and The Press, *Voter Typology* (October 25, 1996), online (http://www.people-press.org/oct96rpt.htm).

The three Republican groups dislike big government and large federal social programs, but they disagree on many key issues. Enterprisers and Libertarians are fond of the business community, for example, but Moralists distrust it. And Enterprisers and Moralists strongly oppose federally funded abortions, yet Libertarians have no objection to them.

Democrats

The Democratic Party is split four ways, according to the Pew Research Center. The party's constituent groups span the spectrum from liberal to conservative, from young to old, from upper-middle-class to poor. All four tend to vote Democratic, but sometimes that's all they have in common:

Seculars: These voters are true liberals and proud of it. They have Democratic values, though many prefer to call themselves independents. This is the most socially tolerant of all ten groups, yet its members are not at all religious. Most Seculars are white; many are highly educated and affluent.

New Democrats: These are middle-class moderates who are not strongly committed to the Democratic Party, though most call themselves Democrats. They are religious and more supportive of the business community than other Democratic groups are.

New Dealers: This group once was a key part of Franklin Roosevelt's New Deal coalition. Its members generally are older and did not go to college. A substantial number of them have connections to labor unions. They are strongly conservative on issues of race and social welfare.

---

in 1996. The author calculated each group's percentage of Republican (or Democratic or independent) adults, based on its 1996 share of all American adults, as shown in the column to the immediate left. Results from the 1992 election are based on respondents' recollections in 1994. Results from the 1996 election are based on respondents' answers in October 1996, shortly before the actual vote. The 1996 columns do not include the small number of respondents who said they did not know how they were going to vote.

Partisan Poor: These are the disadvantaged people who are the beneficiaries of Democratic social programs. More than 40 percent are
racial minorities. They are very poor, and most tend to be very religious, intolerant, and anti-business.

These four groups have divided the Democratic Party fairly evenly,
with each providing between one-fifth and one-third of the party's
total membership:

Group	Share of Adults (%)			1992 Presidential Vote (%)			1996 Presidential Vote (%)		
	1994	1996	Dem	Clinton	Bush	Perot	Clinton	Dole	Perot
Seculars	9	7	19	72	11	14	90	2	2
New Democrats	10	12	33	68	15	15	86	5	4
New Dealers	7	8	22	69	13	17	74	10	12
Partisan Poor	7	9	25	82	8	9	92	4	3

Source: Times Mirror Center, *The New Political Landscape*, pp. 18–21; Pew Research Center, *Voter Typology*, online.

"I don't belong to an organized political party," Will Rogers once
joked. "I'm a Democrat." The Pew Research Center's report makes
one wonder if *anyone* could keep the Democratic Party organized,
given the intense stresses among its four constituent groups. Seculars
and the Partisan Poor have their liberalism in common, but otherwise
are not at all alike. Most Seculars are white, well-off, and satisfied; the
Partisan Poor are multiracial, impoverished, and angry. New Democrats and New Dealers are similarly moderate, but are split by their attitudes toward government and big business. New Democrats feel more
kindly toward both than New Dealers do.

Independents

That leaves three groups to occupy what the Pew Research Center calls
the "detached center." These voters are upset with both parties; many
are so disillusioned that they refuse to vote. Their views vary widely; they
agree only in their dislike of both the Democrats and the Republicans:

New Economy Independents: This is the most important swing group
in the electorate; it gave Ross Perot strong support in 1992. Most of its
members have jobs, but their incomes are average and their middle-
class status seems precarious. They are pro–social welfare, but not
especially sympathetic to blacks.

Bystanders: These people choose not to participate in the political
process. They tend to be young, poor, and undereducated.

Embittereds: Members of this group feel financially pressured. They
have family ties to the Democratic Party, but lack faith in the party's

ability to improve their lives. They distrust government and corporations, and they are socially and religiously intolerant.

New Economy Independents dominate the ranks of the politically unaligned, accounting for nearly half of all independent adults:

Group	Share of Adults (%)			1992 Presidential Vote (%)			1996 Presidential Vote (%)		
	1994	1996	Ind	Clinton	Bush	Perot	Clinton	Dole	Perot
New Econ Inds	18	14	47	45	24	29	53	14	16
Bystanders	8	10	33	—	—	—	—	—	—
Embittereds	7	6	20	51	27	21	45	37	11

Source: Times Mirror Center, *The New Political Landscape*, pp. 15–17; Pew Research Center, *Voter Typology*, online.

The Pew Research Center's report proves that America's political system is not the smoothly functioning two-party mechanism that professors and journalists rhapsodize about. It's more like a ten-party system, with blocs of voters shifting their allegiances depending upon the issue that is prominent at any given moment. Most elected officials grow indecisive and skittish as they seek solid footing in this political quicksand. It is no surprise that they come to rely on public opinion polls, rather than personal principles, to be their guides.

Those candidates who successfully reach the White House in the coming century will be the ones who are able to corral strong support from several of these blocs, especially in suburbia. It will not be an easy task, given that the electorate is so statistically dispersed. No single group accounts for more than one-sixth of suburban voters. New Economy Independents are most numerous, claiming 15,160 of every 100,000 adults in the typical suburban region. They are followed by Moralists (14,940), Enterprisers (14,550), New Democrats (11,950), and Libertarians (10,000).[8] The ingredients of this political stew, then, are one independent group, three that lean toward the Republicans, and one that favors the Democrats. Fashioning a winning coalition from elements with such disparate inclinations will be a neat trick indeed.

But it can be done. The Pew Research Center's study offers a few important clues for the politician who seeks common ground in the suburbs. The 1994 poll asked respondents for their views on several key issues, including these six questions:

- Should the capital gains tax be reduced to encourage investment in U.S. companies?
- Should a two-year limit be placed on how long someone can receive welfare benefits?

- Should policy be changed so that illegal immigrants are not eligible for welfare, Medicaid, and other government benefits?
- Should the sale of handguns be restricted?
- Should government Medicaid benefits be used to help pay for abortions for low-income women?
- Should the United States enter into free trade agreements with other countries?

A majority of suburbanites, as we learned in the previous chapter, would answer yes to all six of these questions. This knowledge provides a way to measure how comfortable each group is with the Suburban Agenda. Eighty-three percent of Enterprisers, for example, were in favor of cutting the capital gains tax, the strongest endorsement from any bloc. At the bottom of the scale were the Partisan Poor, only 54 percent of whom backed such a cut. We can use these poll results to establish a ranking system, awarding Enterprisers a 1 in the "Tax" column in the chart below, then sorting the other groups in descending order of support until reaching the Partisan Poor at 10.*

Adding each bloc's rankings for all six questions yields a score that reflects its commitment to key elements of the Suburban Agenda. The lower its score, the more likely that a group will reflect suburbia's prevailing views. Libertarians top the list with eighteen points, followed closely by New Economy Independents, Seculars, and Enterprisers:†

	Per 100,000 Suburban Adults	Tax	Welfare	Immig	Guns	Abort	Trade	Total
Sympathetic groups								
Libertarians	10,000	2	3	1	7	2	3	18
New Econ Inds	15,160	3	5	4	2	3	5	22
Seculars	8,790	5	8	7	1	1	1	23
Enterprisers	14,550	1	1	2	10	9	1	24
Unsympathetic groups								
Moralists	14,940	4	1	3	9	10	7	34
New Democrats	11,950	7	6	9	3	5	4	34
Embittereds	4,160	5	7	6	5	8	7	38
Bystanders	8,660	9	9	8	4	4	6	40
New Dealers	5,540	8	4	4	8	7	10	41
Partisan Poor	6,240	10	10	10	6	6	9	51

Source: Author's analysis of data from Times Mirror Center, *The New Political Landscape*, pp. 83–85.

---

*There were ties in some categories. Seventy-five percent of Enterprisers and Seculars, for example, supported free trade, the highest figure in the category. Both groups received a score of 1.

†The six categories are arranged on the chart from left to right (with abbreviated headings) in the same order in which the questions were listed above.

The four sympathetic groups, to be sure, do not agree on everything. One obvious point of contention is party preference. Libertarians and Enterprisers lean toward the Republicans, Seculars are Democrats, and New Economy Independents are unaligned. Specific issues, such as gun control, also are troublesome. Seculars are America's staunchest advocates of restrictions on handgun sales; Enterprisers are the strongest opponents.

But politics, as Germany's Otto von Bismarck once said, is the art of the possible. Perhaps a crafty strategist will come along one day with a plan to unite the four sympathetic groups in a powerful coalition. Or maybe an unforeseen event will compel them to cooperate despite their differences, much as the Great Depression turned people from all walks of life into supporters of the New Deal. It doesn't matter how it happens. Either scenario will change American politics forever.

And make no mistake, the potential is there. These four blocs collectively account for almost half of all suburban adults—48,500 of every 100,000—and more than half of all suburban *voters*. Bringing them together will be a tempting challenge for any politician who fancies himself or herself a first-rate coalition-builder.

The key question, then, is not what divides the sympathetic groups, but what bonds them. A close reading of the Pew Research Center's study yields these defining characteristics:

- They generally dislike political labels. New Economy Independents, of course, shun party affiliation. Seculars lean toward the Democrats, but often prefer to distance themselves from partisan politics and call themselves independents. Libertarians are equally uncomfortable with the GOP.
- They tend to be tolerant. Seculars, Libertarians, and New Economy Independents, for instance, think more favorably of the gay rights movement than any of the other seven blocs do.[9]
- They do not look kindly on central authority in either the public or private sectors. Enterprisers, Libertarians, and New Economy Independents all worry that government is too intrusive in the lives of average Americans. Seculars, despite their Democratic lineage, are not particularly enthusiastic about the power exerted by big labor unions. Libertarians, despite their Republican heritage, express doubts about the clout wielded by the National Rifle Association.
- They put the highest priority on economic growth. Each of the four sympathetic groups strongly endorses tax cuts and free trade, with Enterprisers leading the way on both issues. This sup-

port is unsurprising, given that Libertarians, Enterprisers, and Seculars have the highest income levels of all ten blocs.

There undoubtedly would be stresses in any coalition that brought together these four groups. Enterprisers are not as tolerant as the other blocs, for example, and Seculars are not as opposed to big government. But would these disagreements differ from the antagonisms currently dividing social moderates and the Religious Right within the Republican Party or Northern liberals and Southern conservatives within the Democratic Party? Of course not.

Change is coming. Suburbanites want their government to be socially moderate, fiscally responsible, and attuned to suburban needs. Neither major party consistently fits the bill. Republicans often are too conservative, too intolerant; Democrats often are too liberal, too urban-oriented.

The party that repositions itself will be the one that is successful in the twenty-first century. A wide array of anecdotal, historical, and statistical evidence suggests that the party that turns away from its more extreme elements—Republicans from the Moralists, Democrats from the Partisan Poor and New Dealers—would attract moderates from the other party, not to mention independents looking for a political home. Such a coalition could dominate the Suburban Age.

The Republicans

Republicans are accustomed to fighting among themselves. Thomas Dewey, champion of the GOP's moderate Eastern wing, and Robert Taft, standard-bearer for Midwestern conservatism, waged a long, bitter war for party control during the 1940s and early 1950s. Dewey won the big battles, securing the Republican presidential nomination himself in 1944 and 1948, then helping Dwight Eisenhower do the same in 1952. A frustrated Taft blasted his rival as a "ruthless political dictator," while the mere mention of Taft's name would cause Dewey to break his rule against swearing in the presence of ladies.[10]

The combatants changed, but the infighting continued during the decades that followed. Conservatives finally scored a breakthrough when Barry Goldwater won the GOP's presidential nod in 1964. "Extremism in the defense of liberty is no vice. Moderation in the pursuit of justice is no virtue," the nominee crowed in his acceptance speech.[11] Party professionals were more concerned about the extreme nature of Goldwater's subsequent defeat; he carried just six states against Lyndon Johnson. The moderate wing regained control and generally held it until 1980, when a more appealing conservative named Ronald Reagan came along.

This internecine warfare claimed several high-profile casualties. Among them was Nelson Rockefeller, the usually moderate, occasionally liberal governor of New York, who ran three times for the presidency. Polls showed that his popularity among Democrats and independents stood him an excellent chance of victory in a general election. His problem was that he never was able to win the Republican nomination. He was blocked in 1960 by Richard Nixon's excellent advance work, stymied in 1964 by negative public reaction to his divorce and remarriage, and crippled in 1968 by his own indecision. But Rockefeller offered a far simpler explanation for his plight, blaming conservative Republicans for zealously blocking the rise of a new Dewey. "I think if I'd been nominated," Rockefeller once mused, "I would have been elected."[12] It was an awfully big *if.*

William Weld was aware of this history when he weighed the possibility of running for president in 1996. The Massachusetts governor passed several conservative litmus tests; he was tough on crime, welfare reform, and taxes. But he also was pro-choice and an advocate of gay rights. Weld described his political orientation as "fiscally conservative, socially libertarian, pro-environment, tolerant, inclusive," a perfect description of a believer in the Suburban Agenda.[13] The Republican right, however, considered Weld to be an ideological descendent of Dewey and Rockefeller—and thus thoroughly unacceptable. He opted to run for the Senate, not the White House, and lost a close election to Democratic incumbent John Kerry.

The philosophical barriers that discouraged Weld would be equally forbidding to Elizabeth Dole, Colin Powell, Christine Whitman, Pete Wilson, or any other Republican with moderate tendencies who might wish to run for president in 2000. The right wing has solidified its control of the Republican Party since Reagan's ascension in 1980, and the Religious Right has played an increasingly important leadership role within the GOP. The Moralists expanded from 10 percent of the adult population in 1987 to an impressive 18 percent in 1994, according to the Pew Research Center.[14] The latter figure constituted more than half of all Republican-leaning adults at the time, a share that has receded slightly since then.

Journalists cluck about the absurdity of a single party that encompasses moderates such as Weld and Whitman and doctrinaire conservatives such as Jesse Helms and Pat Robertson. But the GOP is following a time-honored tradition. American politicians have always been willing to cooperate with their philosophical opposites if such an arrangement promises a payoff at the ballot box. Northern liberals and Southern conservatives coexisted for decades in the Democratic Party for precisely that reason. John Kennedy had virtually nothing in common with James Eastland, Mississippi's race-baiting senator, yet he solicited Eastland's support whenever possible. "After all, the Senate is a body where you have to get along with people regardless of how much you disagree," Kennedy told friends. "I've always got along pretty well with old Eastland."[15]

Pragmatists within the Republican Party recognize the need to act in a similar fashion. Michigan Senator Spencer Abraham, an opponent of abortion, willingly sponsored a fundraising dinner for Weld's Senate campaign, even though Weld was pro-choice. "There are certain issues a party has to agree to disagree about," said Abraham, whose practical nature had served him well during his tenure as chairman of the Michigan GOP. What truly mattered, he contended, was that he and Weld thought alike on economic policy. "I'm sure we will disagree on everything involving the abortion issue," he said. "That's the kind of thing majority parties learn to do."[16]

Hard-core Republican conservatives, however, are not particularly interested in going along to get along. They are no more inclined to compromise with the party's moderate wing than Taft was with Dewey. The difference is that Taft was in the minority and usually lost, while his conservative heirs now call the shots. Mere agreement on economic issues does not satisfy them; they also insist that moderates endorse conservative social policies. Rick Santorum, a combative senator from Pennsylvania, embodied this spirit at the 1996 Republican convention. "I am more committed now than ever in the belief that the issue of abortion and those other social issues are, in the long term, going to be the most powerful for the Republicans," he declared.[17]

The right wing's demands for ideological purity are taken seriously by most Republican centrists, who make concessions when necessary. George Bush and Bob Dole are exhibits A and B.

Bush and Dole first sought the presidency in 1980, positioning themselves as moderate alternatives to Ronald Reagan. Neither was particularly subtle about it. Bush, in a turn of phrase he would come to regret, characterized Reagan's predilection for supply-side theories as "voodoo economics." Dole was more sarcastic, as was his bent. "Good news is, a bus full of supply-siders went over a cliff last night," he would joke. "Bad news is, there were three empty seats."[18]

Reagan left both men for dead on the primary trail that spring, then resurrected Bush as his vice president. Bush's transformation was shockingly immediate. He became such a dedicated convert to Reaganomics that he issued his famous "read my lips, no new taxes" pledge during his own presidential campaign in 1988. Dole also learned to toe the line. He ran for president in 1996 on a platform that called for a 15 percent tax cut and featured strong anti-abortion language. Peter Powell, a New Hampshire political insider, was bewildered by Dole's rightward shift in his state's presidential primary. "Look at Bob Dole," said Powell. "Here's a man who has distinguished himself by making sensible decisions in Congress and showing a good spirit of compromise to hold the middle ground. Now he's trying to be more conservative than Pat Buchanan."[19]

Yet neither Bush nor Dole could do enough to ingratiate himself with the most zealous of conservatives. The Religious Right never felt entirely comfortable with the two nominees because they lacked the passion and fire of true believers. Was it the economy that propelled Bill Clinton to victory in 1992 and 1996? Not at all, said Christian broadcaster Pat Robertson, who contended that Clinton benefited from Republican softness on abortion and other social issues. "Dole's advisers—he's got the same group, in a sense, that were advising Bush in 1992—they studiously avoided television advertising which pointed to the moral dilemma in our country, and consequently he never did mobilize his base," carped Robertson as he watched Clinton lay claim to a second term.[20]

If the Republicans fail to become the dominant political force of the early twenty-first century, this split between the party's moderate and right wings will be the most likely cause. The GOP, after all, appears ideally positioned to harness suburbia's growing power. Most of the Suburban Agenda's planks read as if they were ripped from the Republican platform—reducing the size of the federal government, cutting taxes, taking strong measures to fight crime, to name but a few. "Certainly on the question of the role of government, the tone of public opinion is with the Republicans," observed Andrew Kohut of the Pew Research Center in 1996. "On social programs, it is with the Republicans. On issues of race, it is with the Republicans."[21]

But the GOP, no matter how strong its affinity with suburban voters, has not been able to fashion anything resembling a permanent majority. Reagan won two presidential terms by stunningly large margins, but even the Great Communicator's coattails were not strong enough to drag fellow Republicans into control of the House of Representatives. Bush carried the Reagan legacy forward in 1988 because the economy was strong and his Democratic opponent was weak. But when Republicans were forced to square off with Clinton, a crafty, suburban-oriented Democrat who had the economy on *his* side, they lost badly in 1992 and 1996. Even their newly won majorities in the House and Senate could not ease the sting that Republicans felt from being locked out of the White House.

"It's a time for reflection in our party," said retiring New Hampshire Governor Steve Merrill after Dole's defeat. "The tide is moving toward Republican ideals. The best proof of that is that Democrats ran on our campaign themes. But the losses we've suffered at the presidential level should cause us to reflect that we really have not explained our vision of the future as well as we should have."[22]

Perhaps that's because the GOP's vision so often is blurry or diffuse. What follows is a five-step prescription that would bring those views into focus, transforming the Republican Party into the majority party of the Suburban Age:

1. The Republicans must concentrate on those issues that unite them.

The future, by all rights, should be a bright one for the Republican Party. The nation's demographic trends will be running in its favor. Mother cities, nearly all of them controlled by Democrats, will continue to lose jobs, wealth, and political influence. Suburban states, which supported Republican candidates in every presidential election from 1968 through 1988, will continue to gain power.

The GOP's position will be strengthened further by the fact that the party reflects the dominant suburban viewpoint in so many ways. Suburbanites are ardent individualists; the Republican Party has preached the gospel of individualism since the Civil War. Suburbanites believe in local control of essential services; so do the Republicans. Suburbanites generally are conservative on economic and public safety issues; the Republicans are, too.

Retired General Colin Powell urged delegates to the 1996 Republican convention to concentrate on the many beliefs they held in common, not the few on which they disagreed. "I became a Republican because I believe our party best represents the principles of freedom, opportunity, and limited government upon which our nation was founded, because I believe the policies of our party will lead to greater economic growth, because I truly believe the federal government has become too large and too intrusive in our lives," he said.[23]

A majority of suburban voters would agree with each of Powell's points, and they gladly would support a candidate who espoused them. But the Republicans became embroiled in peripheral controversies in 1992 and 1996, forcing Bush and Dole to jump through ideological hoops for the amusement of the Religious Right. The need for unity was forgotten. The Republicans consequently failed to carry suburbia for the first time since 1964. It was no coincidence that they lost both elections as well.

2. *The Republicans must resist any strategy based on regionalism.*

Too many politicians, as we have seen in chapter 3, still are tantalized by regional politics, a sadly outmoded concept if ever there were one.

Republicans enviously recall the lock that the Democratic Party had on the South for generations. The Solid South, even at the tail end of its existence, was a model of political efficiency. Southern states gave 625 of their 880 electoral votes between 1940 and 1960 to the Democrats, leaving only 200 for the Republicans.* Democrats won 1,250 House of Representatives seats from Southern districts during the same period, Republicans just 75.

There are those within the Republican Party who believe the GOP could establish a Solid South of its own. Ralph Reed, who, in the early and mid-1990s, was executive director of the Christian Coalition, a core component of the Religious Right dismissed Dole as a remnant of the party's Midwestern past. The future, he suggested, would be personified by the Southern wing of the party, which included House Speaker Newt Gingrich and Senate Majority Leader Trent Lott.[24]

That, of course, is nonsense. It cannot be denied that the South has grown in influence, but it nonetheless has just 163 electoral votes, only 104 of which it gave to Dole. The true path to future Republican success is suburban, not Southern. Gingrich, to his credit, understands the need for such a national strategy. "We have a challenge to rebuild our base in the Northeast, and we have to work with the (Republican governors there) to do that," he said after the 1996 election. "But we have showed we are very competitive in every other section of the country."[25]

3. *The Republicans must recognize that morality is a personal issue.*

Orange County, California, leans heavily to the right. It was a hotbed of support for Barry Goldwater in 1964 and the launching pad for Ronald Reagan's successful campaign for governor two years later. Orange County voters, over the years, enthusiastically supported referendums to reduce property taxes and scuttle affirmative action. Fully two-thirds of 600 county Republicans surveyed by the *Los Angeles Times* in 1996 described themselves as conservatives.

If any place would be receptive to the Religious Right's social agenda, surely it would be Orange County. But that is not the case. Fifty-five percent of the county Republicans polled by the *Times* maintained that any decision on abortion should be left to a woman and her doctor;

---

*The other fifty-five went to minor-party candidates or slates of unpledged electors.

only 10 percent said flatly that abortion should be illegal. The results did not differ substantially even when confined to those respondents who described themselves as religious conservatives; just 24 percent of that subset called for the illegalization of abortion in all cases.[26]

Equally surprising was the subdued manner in which Orange County Republicans discussed the topic of homosexuality. Nearly four in ten favored civil rights protections for gays. "I don't judge people, and I don't think people should be judged," said Eric Fuchser, a survey participant. "There shouldn't be discrimination for any group."[27]

The Orange County poll reinforces the point that most suburbanites, no matter what their political orientation, are tolerant individuals. If the Republican Party were to follow Rick Santorum's advice by stressing a severe social agenda that included making abortion illegal, it would surrender suburbia to the Democrats. Doubters should recall what happened after the 1996 Republican convention saddled Dole with a tough anti-abortion plank; one-third of the Republican women in California switched to Clinton. It is clear that relatively few suburban voters identify with the Religious Right; a much larger number worry about its intractability. "If the Democrats have had a racial problem in the minds of many voters for the past quarter-century," wrote analyst Albert Menendez, "the Republicans now have a religious problem."[28]

The GOP cannot forget that economic success is the key to the suburban voter's heart. Reagan and Bush didn't reach the White House because of conservative stands on social issues. They won because the economy was strong, taxes were being cut, and the nation was optimistic. If the Republicans ever nominate a right-wing social firebrand for president, he or she will lose as badly as Goldwater did. Maybe worse.

4. The Republicans must be more inclusive.

The Republican Party is stereotyped—with good reason—as a party of middle-aged and elderly white men. There are few women in its upper echelons, and even fewer minorities. The one-dimensional nature of the GOP's leadership has become a significant political weakness in a rapidly diversifying nation.

Colin Powell sounded the cry for change in his 1996 convention address, calling on the party to expand its base and its interests. "A nation as great and diverse as America deserves leadership that opens its arms not only to those who have already reaped the rewards of the American dream," he said, "but to those who strive and struggle each day, often against daunting odds, to make that dream come true."[29]

Most residents of suburbia would agree with Powell's sentiments, as long as emphasis is placed on "strive and struggle," a phrase that neatly reflects the Suburban Generation's belief that all citizens deserve to be treated equally, provided they are productive and responsible. White suburbanites plainly are not eager to help impoverished blacks and Hispanics in the inner city, but they increasingly are willing to accept middle-class minorities as neighbors. The number of Hispanics in suburbia will swell by 14 million between 1990 and 2020, with accompanying increases of 6.8 million Asian-Americans and 5.6 million African-Americans.

A majority of these newcomers will have middle- or upper-class lifestyles, making them naturally sympathetic to Republican economic principles. But relatively few will vote for the GOP unless it abandons its indifferent, occasionally hostile attitude toward minorities. "An unwritten plank in the party's platform is that it can win the offices it needs without black votes," concluded Andrew Hacker in his 1995 study of black America. "And by sending a message that it neither wants nor needs ballots cast by blacks, it feels it can attract even more votes from a much larger pool of white Americans."[30] Republicans must scrap this strategy in favor of inclusiveness, or they will pay the price as suburbia slowly diversifies. Bob Dole received just 13 percent of the suburban black vote and 22 percent of the suburban Hispanic vote in 1996. Future Republican nominees will ignore such potentially rich lodes of votes at their peril.

5. *The Republicans must be moderate.*

Elizabeth Hager, a former New Hampshire state legislator, felt compelled to vote in the Republican presidential primary in 1996. But she was unhappy with the field of candidates, each of whom seemed eager to appear more conservative than the others. None espoused her moderate beliefs, so she finally decided to turn in a blank ballot. "It's hurtful," she said, "but I am really cross." She was not alone. A February 1996 survey by pollster Gerry Chervinsky showed that fully 40 percent of Republican voters in New Hampshire considered themselves to be moderates; another 8 percent said they were liberals.[31]

Many self-described conservatives aren't all that conservative either, for that matter, as the *Los Angeles Times* found in Orange County. Six of every ten county Republicans favored such supposedly liberal proposals as stricter environmental regulations and stronger gun control laws. "I don't think our founding fathers had Uzis in mind when they were discussing the right to bear arms," said Sherry Wilson, a Huntington Beach accountant and registered Republican. "It's ridiculous. There are so many nuts out there today."[32]

Keep in mind that these are *Republicans* speaking. Democrats and independents are even more inclined toward the middle of the road. Exit polls reported that nearly half of all voters in 1996 considered themselves to be moderates, while just one-third were conservatives.[33] Bill Clinton targeted centrist voters; Bob Dole aimed his campaign to the right. The results were predictable:

	Popular Vote (%)		
	Clinton	**Dole**	**Perot**
Nationwide	49	41	8
Components (share of U.S. vote in percent)			
Moderates (47)	57	33	9
Conservatives (33)	20	71	8
Liberals (20)	78	11	7

Source: Voter News Service exit poll, November 5, 1996, as posted on CNN/*Time* AllPolitics website (http://allpolitics.com), November 12, 1996 [henceforth referred to as VNS exit poll 1996].

Moderate voters held the balance of power in 1996—favoring Clinton over Dole by a margin of 24 percentage points—and will be equally powerful in future elections. They, not conservatives, will determine the fate of the Republican Party in the coming century. The GOP's only hope of winning their support is to move not to the right on social issues, but toward the center, where it will find most suburban voters.

Such a shift could bring a substantial bonus. A tolerant, middle-of-the-road Republican Party could expect to attract Democratic and independent suburbanites who have become uncomfortable with the Democratic Party's traditional urban orientation. Most conservative voters—Enterprisers and Libertarians, to be specific—almost certainly would be part of this new Republican coalition, provided it met one simple condition. They would insist that the GOP not deviate from its current economic theories, which exalt free enterprise and advocate reductions in taxes and bureaucratic red tape. Most suburban moderates, who tend toward conservatism themselves when it comes to economic matters, would go along happily.

The Religious Right, of course, would not accept this realignment quietly. It surely would fight to the death for control of the party, in keeping with the long tradition of Republican intraparty wars. Taft gave no quarter to Dewey, after all, nor did Goldwater to Rockefeller. But it is a simple fact that hard-core conservatives are out of touch with the suburban center. The Republican Party, in the long run, would be better off if their influence were reduced or eliminated.

The Democrats

Franklin Roosevelt never much believed in efficiency. His New Deal spawned dozens of government agencies to fight the depression. Critics were appalled by the bloated bureaucracy and confused by the tangle of new acronyms: AAA, NRA, WPA, SEC. They derided the whole concoction as "alphabet soup." Then came World War II, and Roosevelt created another 156 agencies. Many were directly competitive; several were obviously useless. The president didn't care. He seemed to thrive on chaos. "The boss appoints four men to do the job of one," laughed Bronx Democratic leader Ed Flynn, "or one man to do the job of four."[34]

Roosevelt built the modern Democratic Party the same way. He cobbled together an incongruous coalition of big-city political machines and liberal reformers, labor unions and agrarian radicals, African-Americans and white segregationists. About the only thing these disparate groups had in common was their support for Roosevelt himself.

Few were particularly happy with this cumbersome alliance. Blacks, for example, felt they weren't rewarded sufficiently for the hundreds of thousands of votes they supplied in Northern cities. A. Philip Randolph, head of the Brotherhood of Sleeping Car Porters, hounded the president to desegregate the army and enact basic civil rights legislation. FDR did as little as he could, fearful of damaging the delicate political mechanism he had crafted. Other Democrats counseled patience. "The Negro knows that the Roosevelt administration has been his salvation in these days of turmoil, strife, and depression," said Missouri Senator Harry Truman. "He must not now switch from the Democratic Party, which has done so much for him and will ever continue to work in his best interests."[35]

Southern whites wondered if the party was willing to do the same for them. They gave Roosevelt all of their 146 electoral votes in each of his first three elections, yet began to worry that he was taking them for granted. North Carolina Senator Josiah Bailey snapped that Roosevelt seemed much cozier with Northern political bosses and labor unions, not to mention blacks. "The president is just as loyal to [Jersey City's] Frank Hague and the [Chicago] Kelly machine as he is to our party," Bailey charged. "He is just as loyal to the AFL and the CIO as he is to any party, and he is much more loyal to these institutions than he is to what we call Southern Democracy, which I think he despises."[36]

Roosevelt's New Deal coalition was unwieldy, to be sure. It also was boisterous, contrary, and just plain unruly. The only thing that could be said in its favor was that it worked. The coalition elected its creator to an unprecedented four terms in the White House, then propelled Truman to his upset victory in 1948. Most of its elements reunited after Dwight Eisenhower's presidency to score two more victories for John Kennedy and Lyndon Johnson. The New Deal coalition, all in all, won seven elections. Its champions received a total of 2,968 electoral votes in those contests, their opponents just 762.

But something had to give; constituent groups with so little in common could not remain united forever. Roosevelt would not have been surprised to learn that racial tensions would trigger the coalition's disintegration. African-Americans and conservative Southern whites had coexisted uneasily in the Democratic Party; the ill will between them escalated as blacks struggled toward political parity. "When the Negroes have an opportunity of voting, they will naturally vote against any of us who run," worried South Carolina Senator Burnet Maybank in 1944. "However, I hope this will be in the distant future."[37]

That day would come more quickly than the white South wished. The Civil Rights Act of 1964 and the Voting Rights Act of 1965 placed blacks on an equal footing before the law and in the voting booth, initiating a shift of power within the Democratic Party. The urban unrest of the late 1960s accelerated the process. White Southerners defected to the Republicans, as did other conservative Democrats. Crumbling big-city machines, Northern liberals, and minority groups suddenly were at the party's core.

This realignment flew in the face of demographic logic. America was growing more conservative and more suburban as the 1970s progressed, yet the Democrats tied themselves more tightly to liberal causes and cities. The party, as a result, lost five of six presidential elections between 1968 and 1988, most by lopsided margins. The sole Democratic win—Jimmy Carter's narrow victory in 1976—would not have been possible without the Watergate crisis. There were signs of slippage in Congress, as well. The Democrats lost control of the Senate between 1981 and 1987, their first stint in a congressional minority since 1955. They retained their majority in the House, but the number of Democrats holding House seats dropped from 292 at Carter's inauguration to 252 in 1985.

It was only after reaching the White House that Carter's team learned how severely the Democratic Party had deteriorated. The new president's chief of staff, Hamilton Jordan, assumed the party would be a powerful tool at his disposal. He found he was wrong. "The Democratic Party was like a phony facade on a Hollywood set," he recalled in 1982. "Thirty years ago, it was a collection of several groups of reliable voters: the big-city ethnics of the Northeast and Midwest, working people, Jews, liberals, and white Southerners. The base of the party was the big-city machines, which, corrupt or not, provided certain practical services for the people."[38]

But the machines were gone, victims of the same decay that was destroying the cities they had once governed. The epitome of the big-city boss had been Richard Daley, the long-time mayor of Chicago whose electoral legerdemain had clinched Kennedy's 1960 victory and whose endorsement had sewed up Carter's nomination sixteen years later.[39] Daley, however, died a month after the 1976 election, leaving a void in his city and his party.

Big-city mayors in the 1990s could only dream of the power their predecessors had exercised. Chicago again offered the perfect example. Daley's son became mayor, but he was merely a shadow of his father. He was low-key, generally uninspiring, and certainly no boss. It could be argued, in fact, that the only real political machines remaining in America were in suburbia, as in DuPage County, Illinois, west of Chicago. DuPage was so solidly Republican that it hadn't elected a Democrat to countywide office in fifty years. The Democrats didn't even bother to run candidates for county board chairman, treasurer, clerk, or sheriff in 1998.

It was this disintegration of the Democratic Party's old power structure that inspired Gary Hart to pronounce its epitaph in 1984. "The New Deal has run its course," he said. "The party is over."[40] Democratic leaders scoffed at Hart's pessimism; they ran Walter Mondale's campaign exactly as they would have run Kennedy's or Johnson's. The resulting landslide defeat proved Hart correct; the only question was what shape the new party would take. Democrats have been searching for an answer ever since.

Their biggest conundrum involves mother cities, which remain the most loyal sources of Democratic support anywhere in the country. The problem is that the party's close ties with urban America have tarnished its image among those suburban voters who now hold the nation's levers of power.

Cities will remain influential within the Democratic Party for two reasons. The first is the disproportionate clout they wield in primary elections. We saw in chapter 3 that New York City supplied 52.1 percent of the votes in the 1992 statewide Democratic presidential primary. Paul Tsongas appealed strongly to suburbanites; Jerry Brown did well upstate. But New York City had the final say on which candidate would win the state's convention delegates, and New York City preferred Bill Clinton. Case closed.

Other mother cities exercise similar power within the Democratic Party in heavily populated states from Pennsylvania to California— power that seems excessive in comparison to their population. New York City was home to just 40 percent of New York state's residents in 1992, and it cast less than 31 percent of the state's votes in that year's general election. But its strong concentration of Democratic voters means that New York City—and other mother cities—will continue to play a key role in selecting Democratic candidates.

The second factor allowing cities to maintain their influence within the party is their consistent ability to crank out large Democratic margins every November. Mother cities contain an ever-decreasing share of the nation's residents—down from 28.9 percent in 1940 to 17.9 percent in 1990—but their electoral clout has not diminished accordingly. The exodus of the white middle class drained most Republicans to suburbia, transforming cities that once had competitive two-party systems into strongholds for the Democratic Party. That's why New York City's share could drop from more than 50 percent of statewide general-election votes in the 1940s to about 30 percent in the 1990s, yet Bill Clinton could win the city by a larger margin than Franklin Roosevelt ever did:

	NYC Share of State Vote (%)	Margins	
		New York City	Rest of State
1940	51.2	718,459 D	494,019 R
1944	52.7	771,213 D	454,622 R
1948	51.1	488,257 D	549,216 R
1952	47.9	359,439 D	1,207,651 R
1956	44.7	61,578 D	1,659,140 R
1960	42.4	791,118 D	407,452 R
1964	41.7	1,381,712 D	1,287,831 D
1968	38.5	695,722 D	325,184 R
1972	36.4	83,123 D	1,324,817 R
1976	32.8	716,717 D	427,950 R
1980	30.9	332,900 D	498,359 R
1984	32.4	491,558 D	1,036,712 R
1988	31.2	675,388 D	409,377 R
1992	30.6	949,361 D	148,440 D
1996	31.1	1,172,711 D	649,974 D

Source: Author's analysis of U.S. Census Bureau data and official election returns.

New York, it must be remembered, is a special case. It was a city state throughout this period, one of just two left in America by the 1980s. New York City remained strong enough in 1988 to carry its state for a liberal Democrat like Michael Dukakis, giving him more than enough votes to offset George Bush's suburban and upstate strength. Mother cities in suburban states also voted Democratic by large margins, but they lacked New York City's power to deliver electoral votes. Philadelphia and Pittsburgh went strongly for Dukakis, but Bush carried Pennsylvania anyway. The same held true for Chicago and Illinois, as well as Los Angeles and California.

And that is the crux of the Democrats' problem. Liberal, urban-oriented candidates still can win Democratic primaries in many states, and they still can win large general-election margins in big cities—larger, in fact, than a generation ago. But they do not win support in moderate, suburban-oriented states, the very places that now run America. Robert Kennedy, a liberal Democrat if ever there were one, got a sneak preview of this trend way back in 1968. Kennedy rolled into Oregon after a string of primary victories in other states, but his presidential campaign suddenly fell flat. Oregon's white middle-class voters rejected his brand of urban liberalism, administering the first electoral defeat suffered by any member of the Kennedy clan. "This state," Kennedy muttered, "is like one giant suburb."[41] The same complaint could have been made about dozens of states by the 1980s, but Mondale and Dukakis did not adjust their tactics to suit this new reality.

It fell to Bill Clinton to change the party's course, steering it in a direction more acceptable to the suburban majority. The success of his helmsmanship was certified in 1996, when he became the first Democrat since Franklin Roosevelt to win successive presidential elections. But it is yet to be decided whether the party will maintain Clinton's heading after he leaves the White House. Vice President Al Gore undoubtedly will promise a continuation of Clinton's policies if he is elected president in 2000. But House Minority Leader Richard Gephardt, who represents a city district in Saint Louis, seems certain to oppose Gore and to try to push the party back toward its liberal, urban past.

This forthcoming confrontation will be a heated one. "We are really seeing the birthing pains for a new Democratic Party," Democratic pollster Alan Secrest said in 1995. "And it is not apt to be especially pretty in the early going."[42] What follows is a five-step plan that could ease the process, turning the Democratic Party into the Suburban Age's dominant political force:

1. The Democrats must make suburban voters their primary target.

Jim McGreevey tackled a thankless assignment in 1997. The relatively obscure state legislator accepted the Democratic nomination for governor of New Jersey, which matched him against Republican Christine Whitman, the telegenic incumbent who was being mentioned widely as a possible presidential candidate.

The odds against McGreevey were long, especially in a state where 89 percent of all voters lived in suburbs. His solution was to shun his party's traditional urban-oriented strategies. He focused instead on two mainstays of suburban life—cars and homes—and blasted New Jersey's high auto insurance rates and property taxes. Doug Schoen, McGreevey's pollster, said the challenger was "positioned to take advantage of the frustration of suburban voters (by addressing) the reason they moved to the suburbs: They want to be able to afford to live there and to drive to their jobs."[43] It nearly worked. The Democrat came within a single percentage point of upsetting Whitman.

McGreevey's pragmatism was reminiscent of the approach taken by a certain presidential candidate half a decade earlier. Bill Clinton was unusual among Democrats in devoting the bulk of his attention to average, rather than disadvantaged, citizens. His seven-page announcement of candidacy in October 1991 included ten references to the middle class; the highlight was Clinton's pledge to devote his administration to "restoring the hopes of the forgotten middle class."[44] Suburbanites rallied to his cause.

Future Democrats will have no alternative but to follow the lead of Clinton and McGreevey. The numbers, though stated before, bear repeating. There were twenty-three suburban states with 320 electoral votes in 1996, compared to two city states with thirty-six electoral votes. The choice could not be more obvious.

The danger, of course, is that the party's urban constituents, especially minorities, will be threatened by its shift to suburban values. Democratic candidates will need to make minor concessions to big-city voters when possible and give verbal reassurances to them more frequently, especially on economic issues. "History shows our alliance with Democrats set us up to be taken for granted. . . . The Democratic Party continues, nonetheless, to count on the proposition that blacks, while angry, have nowhere else to go," warned Lenora Fulani, an African-American woman who ran for president as an independent in 1988 and 1992.[45] The party once made the same mistake with Southern whites, with disastrous results.

2. *The Democrats must stress their ability to keep the economy strong.*

Clinton's aides were quite pleased with the catchphrase they dreamed up in 1992. "It's the economy, stupid," they would remind themselves whenever their campaign drifted off target.

Their slogan really wasn't as original as these staffers thought. It has *always* been the economy. Herbert Hoover could have told them that; the Great Depression brought his sparkling career to an abrupt end in 1932. Thomas Dewey could have seconded the point; Democratic whispers about an imminent Republican recession destroyed his chances in 1948. Jimmy Carter could have clinched the argument;

high interest rates and soaring unemployment left him vulnerable to defeat in 1980.

Exit polls confirmed that economic factors again were supreme in 1996. Most Clinton voters said their personal financial situations had improved since 1992, setting them apart from Dole and Perot supporters, who were considerably less satisfied:

	(%)		
	Clinton Voters	Dole Voters	Perot Voters
Personal financial situation in past four years			
Gotten better	49	19	21
Stayed the same	40	49	35
Gotten worse	11	32	44

Source: Ronald Brownstein, "Optimism, Moderation Power Clinton's Victory," *Los Angeles Times,* November 6, 1996, p. A1.

Clinton surprised the experts by amassing a better record of employment growth than his two predecessors. America added an average of 2.72 million jobs during each of his first three years in office, compared to 1.85 million annually under Reagan and 0.83 million each year under Bush.[46] Yet voters mysteriously remained reluctant to admit that a Democrat could manage the economy as effectively as a Republican. A 1994 poll by the Pew Research Center found that 45 percent of respondents believed the Republicans were the better choice to keep the nation prosperous; only 33 percent picked the Democrats. Pollsters repeated the question in the midst of widespread Clintonian prosperity in 1998, but the Democrats still could do no better than tie the Republicans at 40 percent each.[47]

Millions of suburban voters obviously find it difficult to shake their mental picture of the Democratic Party as a wasteful, fiscally inept organization that is more interested in the urban poor than the middle class. Future Democratic candidates can allay suburbia's concerns by stressing their commitment to creating jobs, promoting international trade, and reducing governmental red tape for businesses.

3. The Democrats must drop their belief in big government.

Nothing was more effective for Ronald Reagan than his characterization of all Democrats as "tax-and-spend" liberals. The Democratic Party was proud of the governmental infrastructure it built under Roosevelt, Truman, Kennedy, and Johnson. This massive bureaucracy had conquered the depression, fought three wars, and sent a man to the moon. But the public began to lose faith in big government when order dissolved into chaos in the late 1960s and throughout the 1970s. Reagan, who insisted that smaller was better, was the beneficiary in 1980.

Anti-government sentiment remained strong in the 1990s, inspiring Clinton to abandon his party's traditional beliefs. "The era of big government is over," he declared in his 1996 State of the Union address.[48] That year's Democratic platform expanded on the president's theme with language that shocked party veterans. "The mission of today's Democratic Party is to expand opportunity, not bureaucracy," it said. "We have worked hard over the last four years to rein in big government, slash burdensome regulations, eliminate wasteful programs, and shift problem-solving out of Washington and back to people and communities who understand their situations best."[49]

Clinton's words were applauded by suburbanites who disapproved of central authority. Exit polls showed that 52 percent of voters in November 1996 wanted the federal government to do less; every suburban state but New Jersey agreed.[50] And the president's actions fit his words. He cut federal employment by 212,000 during his first four years in office, and he persuaded Congress to approve a landmark balanced budget agreement in 1997.

Liberals were disappointed with this shift; they had hoped that Clinton would strike more boldly against America's social ills. "I don't think anybody expected in 1992 that one of the crowning achievements of the Clinton administration would be to balance the federal budget," said Robert Reich, Clinton's first labor secretary.[51] The left wing will push its pro-government beliefs again in 2000, but times have changed, and the Democratic Party has, too. The simple fact is that no Democrat could win an election in the Suburban Age by imitating Franklin Roosevelt's empire-building style.

4. *The Democrats must emphasize their beliefs in fair play and tolerance.*

Suburbanites are not arch-conservatives. They are moderate and tolerant; they believe that all productive and responsible people should be treated equally and should be allowed to live as they wish.

Democrats come closer than Republicans to this point of view, and the voters know it. It was the Democratic Party that led the political battle for civil rights and social reform during the past half-century; it is the Democratic Party, as a result, that is conceded to be more open, more inclusive, and more committed to the ideal of fair play. This image was reflected in the results of a Pew Research Center poll in March 1998. Respondents said they believed that Democrats were best able to resist pressure from big business and other powerful groups, and were more likely than Republicans to govern in an honest and ethical way.[52]

Its reputation for fairness could be one of the Democratic Party's most powerful weapons on the suburban political battleground. Residents of suburbia want a conciliatory, inclusive leader, a role that President Clinton has played well. "I think talking is better than fighting," Clinton said in launching an initiative to reduce racial tensions. "I believe when people don't talk and communicate and understand, their fears, their ignorance, and their problems are more likely to fester."[53] The contrast with the shrill rhetoric of the Republican Religious Right could not have been sharper.

But Democrats must be careful not to misinterpret suburban tolerance. It has its limits. Suburbanites still have no interest in subsidizing big cities; they still want affirmative action and other social programs scaled back. Clinton understood this, pledging a calm, reasoned effort to promote diversity without resorting to strict racial quotas. "We can get there," he said, "if we move beyond the slogans."[54]

5. The Democrats must be moderate.

The Democratic Party, in Jesse Jackson's opinion, faces a critical choice. It must decide whether to adhere wholeheartedly to its liberal traditions or to follow the lead of the centrist Democratic Leadership Council, which Jackson characterized as "Democrats who comb their hair to the left like Kennedy, while moving their minds to the right like Reagan."[55] Jackson, of course, would prefer the first option. Logic dictates the second.

Exit polls in November 1996 found most Americans near the middle of the political spectrum: 47 percent of voters identified themselves as moderates, 33 percent as conservatives, and 20 percent as liberals.[56] The results were even more interesting when broken down according to candidate preference:

	(%)		
	Clinton Voters	Dole Voters	Perot Voters
Liberal	31	5	17
Moderate	55	37	51
Conservative	14	57	32

Source: VNS exit poll 1996.

Liberals claim to be the heart of the Democratic Party, but they clearly overstate their influence. Fifty-five percent of Clinton's supporters were moderates; less than one-third were liberals. Moderates also prevailed among the independents who supported Perot in 1996, a group that conceivably could be won over by a middle-of-the-road Democratic campaign.

Nowhere is the political center more powerful than in suburbia. Moderates outnumbered liberals in every single suburban state in 1996, sometimes by a margin of better than 3 to 1. Twenty-two percent of all voters in the presidential election were classified as suburban moderates; just 7 percent were urban liberals.[57] "If you want to view the political decay of American liberalism, look at its spawning ground—the great cities," concluded Harold Meyerson, executive editor of *L.A. Weekly*. "In the late 1990s, there are simply no remaining strongholds of municipal liberalism."[58] It was true. New York City and Los Angeles were led by Republican mayors, Chicago by an uncharismatic Democrat.

Jackson's leftward course would please urban liberals, but it would ruin the Democratic Party, dooming it to repeat the ill-conceived Mondale and Dukakis campaigns of the 1980s. Prudence—not to mention demographics—favors a permanent move to the center. A Democratic Party that stressed open-mindedness on social issues and competence in fiscal matters could develop a strong suburban base, attracting independents and Republicans alienated by the strident harangues of the GOP's conservative wing. Most big-city voters would have no real alternative but to stick with this new Democratic coalition, so long as it continued to advocate civil rights and a limited form of urban aid.

Such a realigned Democratic Party would be reminiscent of the Republican Party's Eastern wing in the 1940s and 1950s. Thomas Dewey and Dwight Eisenhower had been comfortable with Democratic social reforms, yet more conservative on economic policy. Some analysts consider the parallel so strong that they have called Clinton a Democratic Eisenhower. "The good news is that we may elect a Republican president this year," laughed Republican consultant Alex Castellanos in the summer of 1996. "The bad news is that it may be Bill Clinton."[59]

Out of the Mainstream

There was a time when Sam Nunn had been considered presidential timber, but those heady days were long gone by 1996. The Georgia senator's problem was that he really didn't fit in. He was too conservative to suit most of his fellow Democrats, yet he had taken a few liberal stands that didn't sit well with the Republicans, notably his opposition to the Persian Gulf War. He was, in a sense, a man without a party.

Nor was he alone. Millions of Americans were discontented with the two-party system. Their feelings of alienation were so strong that Nunn believed a permanent third party would emerge to represent them; he said as much on NBC's *Meet the Press* in July 1996. Host Tim Russert asked if he would be willing to help get such a movement off the ground. "Well, I've always been sort of a bad Democrat, and if I joined the Republican Party, I'd be a bad Republican," Nunn mused. "So maybe there is a third party out there in my future."[60]

Nunn's vision seems to have logic on its side. It is difficult to imagine that a country so large and so diverse wouldn't have room for a third major party. Great Britain and Canada, the nations whose political traditions are closest to America's, have vigorous multi-party systems. Why couldn't the United States follow their lead? A large number of voters clearly would prefer a greater range of political options. Fifty-three percent of those surveyed in 1994 by the Times Mirror Center, the predecessor of the Pew Research Center, endorsed creation of a third party. Support was strongest in suburbia, where 58 percent gave thumbs up, though majorities in big cities and rural areas also voted yes.[61]

But history suggests it would be extremely difficult to establish the party of Nunn's dreams, regardless of popular sentiment. Just eight independent or third-party candidates were able to draw at least 1 million popular votes in the twentieth century's twenty-five presidential elections, and only four of those candidates earned any electoral votes at all:

Candidate	Party	Year	PV (%)	EV
Theodore Roosevelt	Progressive	1912	27.4	88
Ross Perot	Independent	1992	18.9	0
Robert La Follette	Progressive	1924	16.6	13
George Wallace	American Independent	1968	13.5	46
Ross Perot	Reform	1996	8.4	0
John Anderson	National Unity	1980	6.6	0
Strom Thurmond	States' Rights Democratic	1948	2.4	39
Henry Wallace	Progressive	1948	2.4	0

Source: Author's analysis of official election returns.

Theodore Roosevelt easily outperformed the century's other third-party hopefuls, receiving 27.4 percent of the popular vote and 88 electoral votes in 1912. Yet his candidacy was far from a success; it actually dramatized the impossibility of reaching the White House without a Democratic or Republican nomination. Roosevelt was a former president, a man with powerful connections, one of the most famous people in the world. He had breezed to victory as a Republican in 1904, but he was able to carry just six states as a minor-party nominee in 1912, losing to political neophyte Woodrow Wilson by more than two million popular votes.

The only other third-party candidates on the list above to receive support in the Electoral College during the twentieth century were segregationists George Wallace and Strom Thurmond, whose combined total of 85 electoral votes came entirely from the South, and Midwestern firebrand Robert La Follette, who carried only his home state of Wisconsin. Third parties, all in all, do not have an impressive record.

Their task has not been made any easier by the entrenched political powers, who have stacked federal and state election laws against the emergence of new parties. Democratic and Republican presidential nominees, for example, automatically qualify for the November ballot. Independents are required to follow different procedures in each state to achieve ballot status; they must comply with fifty different regulations and meet fifty different deadlines. Democratic and Republican candidates also receive public campaign funds as a matter of course. Third-party challengers do not; they become eligible for retroactive funding only if they win at least 5 percent of the popular vote in November—a big gamble, to be sure.[62]

The poor records of previous third parties and the unevenness of the current playing field have discouraged most independents from challenging the Democrats and Republicans. But a brave soul seems to emerge every third election or so—George Wallace in 1968, John Anderson in 1980, Ross Perot in 1992 and 1996—and there is no reason to doubt that this trend will continue. Future third-party candidates are likely to represent one of three groups: Perot's Reform Party, urban liberals, or the unaligned middle class.*

Reform Party

Ross Perot blew through the 1992 campaign like a breath of fresh air. The plain-spoken, self-made billionaire declared that he could restructure the federal government as easily as he had conquered the private sector. Washington had failed the American people, he said, and he would launch a populist crusade to right the wrongs committed by professional politicians. Perot pledged that balancing the federal budget would be his first goal as president, and he insisted it would be accomplished easily.

Perot's blunt, simple message had a special appeal at a time when the economy had stagnated and public confidence in President Bush had ebbed. His independent candidacy drew 18.9 percent of the national vote, topping every third-party standard-bearer of the twentieth century except Theodore Roosevelt. Perot did best in suburban states, where his share reached 19.8 percent. Experts agreed that he

---

*A fourth potential source might be the Religious Right, which could choose the third-party route if the Republicans suddenly—and shockingly—adopted a liberal stance on social issues.

would be a key player in the next presidential election; he could not be ignored. "The time is ripe for the kind of populist movement that coalesced around Ross Perot," wrote analyst Albert Menendez.[63]

But it was not to be. Perot plummeted to just 8.4 percent of the vote in his second try. His slippage was worst in suburban states, where he received 8 million votes fewer in 1996 than in 1992. Surveys showed that his supporters now tended to be lower-income residents of non-metro areas. "They have a more blue-collar feel, less of a suburban feel," said pollster Frank Luntz, who had worked for Perot in the previous campaign. "Some suburban voters looked at him and decided he wasn't presidential."[64]

That was part of it; most Americans indeed found it difficult to imagine someone with Perot's quirky temperament occupying the Oval Office. Even more important was America's new optimism. Perot had been a vehicle for protest votes in 1992, but the economy was stronger in 1996, inspiring a majority of Americans to view President Clinton's performance with approval. Perot's candidacy was hampered further by the fact that Clinton and Bob Dole were so eager to cut into his base that they assiduously courted his supporters. Exit polls showed that two-thirds of the 1992 Perot voters who cast ballots again in 1996 opted for a different candidate the second time, with the bulk choosing Dole:

| | Voted for in 1996 (%) | | |
Voted for in 1992	Clinton	Dole	Perot
Clinton	85	9	4
Bush	13	82	4
Perot	22	44	33

Source: VNS exit poll 1996.

Perot had run as a true independent in 1992, but his 1996 campaign was organized under the banner of the Reform Party. He persisted in the fiction that this new party was a popular movement, not his personal creation, saying early in the year that he would support anyone it nominated for president. But his benevolence vanished when former Colorado Governor Richard Lamm stepped forward to seek the Reform Party's endorsement. Perot quickly announced his own candidacy, crushed Lamm, and took the nomination himself.

The Reform Party will be eligible for limited federal funding in 2000 and has qualified for ballot status in several states, thanks to Perot's performance in 1996. But its only hope of becoming a permanent third party is to broaden its base, which means its founder must step into the background. "It became too much a cult of personality and too little a movement," said Luntz of Perot's second campaign. Lamm expressed the same sentiment more caustically. "You can't build up a party by an autocrat," he said.[65]

Perot preferred to emphasize the positive. "You created a party in all fifty states in less than a year," he told his supporters on election night. "Everybody said it couldn't be done—and you did it."[66] But creating a party and sustaining it are two different things. The Reform Party must reestablish its suburban base and find a fresh candidate, or it will die. The prognosis admittedly is not good. Perot began hinting in 1997 that he might run again in 2000. The history of presidential politics is littered with three-time losers: William Jennings Bryan, Thomas Dewey, Robert Taft, Adlai Stevenson, and Hubert Humphrey, to name a few. Ross Perot seems determined to join their ranks.

An Urban Liberal Party

Jesse Jackson and the Democratic Party appear to be synonymous. Jackson, after all, has been a source of controversy or a man of influence—often both—in every Democratic campaign since 1972. His liberal beliefs seem to be perfectly synchronized with the party's New Deal principles. He sought the Democratic presidential nomination himself in 1984 and 1988, becoming the first African-American to be a serious contender for the White House.

But Jackson never has been particularly happy with the Democrats. He organized Chicago blacks to vote against a Democratic prosecutor in 1972. "Don't worry about Democrat and Republican, you ain't neither one. You're black and you're trapped," he told his followers.[67] Jackson also worked for a Republican gubernatorial candidate in 1968 and a Republican senator in 1972. Both won their races in Illinois, but he took no real joy in the outcomes. "We are doomed to remain in the hip pocket of the Democratic Party and the rumble seat of the Republican Party," he complained in 1971. "I do not trust white Republicans or white Democrats. I want a black party."[68]

Jackson put a name to this dream. The Liberation Party would bring together blacks and white liberals in a coalition that would challenge both established parties. He never completely abandoned this vision, not even after becoming a Democratic power in his own right. Jackson carefully weighed running for president as an independent in 1992 or 1996 before backing off. But he refused to rule out a third-party candidacy in the future. "Everybody's so interested in watching the front door," he said. "Might not even be coming in that way. Might be coming around on them from another way when nobody's even watching."[69]

It was unnecessary to create an African-American third party as long as the Democrats advocated liberal policies that benefited big cities and minorities. But the situation became complicated when Clinton shifted the Democratic aim away from urban liberals and toward suburban moderates. Frustrated big-city voters stuck with Clinton in 1996, seeing no alternative. It is impossible to imagine them shifting in protest to the inhospitable Republicans, but they might well be attracted to a third party.

The chief goal of such a movement would be to frighten the Democrats back to the left. The key to Clinton's two victories, after all, was that he picked up millions of white votes in suburbia *without* losing minority votes in mother cities. Bob Dole still was favored slightly by whites in 1996—winning 46 percent of their votes to Clinton's 43 percent—but the president clinched his reelection with overwhelming support from blacks and Hispanics. Twenty-seven percent of Clinton's votes came from members of minority groups, compared to just 7 percent of Dole's and 9 percent of Perot's:

| | Share of Each Candidate's Votes (%) | | | | |
	Whites	Blacks	Hispanics	Asians	Others
Clinton	73	17	7	1	2
Dole	93	3	2	1	1
Perot	90	4	3	1	1

Source: VNS exit poll 1996.

If a minority-oriented party had siphoned off two-thirds of Clinton's black and Hispanic votes, the president would have ended up in a virtual dead heat with Dole. Both men consequently might have fallen short of a majority in the Electoral College, thereby passing the final decision to the House of Representatives, where the Republican majority gleefully would have elected Dole.

This scenario sums up the appeal and the danger of an urban third-party movement. Minority voters find the idea alluring because it would make them more powerful; it would force the Democratic Party to listen to them again. A 1994 University of Chicago study found that 50 percent of African-American respondents supported creation of a black-dominated political party.[70] But this sense of well-being is countered by the fear that such a party would open the White House door for a conservative Republican. That possibility is what stopped Jackson from running as an independent in 1996. "I did not want our wing to give aid and comfort to the Gingrich-Buchanan-Dole forces, which I see as so destructive and such a big threat," he said.[71]

A minority-oriented party never could be anything more than a protest vehicle. It would be too small to elect a president by itself. Black and Hispanic voters together accounted for just 15 percent of the electorate in 1996, and legitimate doubts exist about their ability to cooperate politically.* An urban party that also incorporated white liberals would be stronger, but it would be extremely difficult to assemble. Jackson liked to refer to supporters of his two presidential campaigns as the Rainbow Coalition, but the rainbow's white stripe had been very thin.

The likelihood remains that minority voters will feel the need to do *something* in the future. Suburbia will grow more powerful as the new century unfolds; cities will become weaker. The Democratic Party can be expected to show less and less interest in the fate of urban minorities; the Republican Party will exhibit virtually none.

Jackson remains the person best able to voice urban America's outrage at these trends. Reporters asked him in 1997 whether he might run for president in 2000. "I am eligible," he replied warily. "I am old enough, and I've done it before. It is premature to make that decision, but I am troubled by those who have shifted us away from the moral center, who leave working-class people full of anxiety and the real poor without a safety net."[72] It was easy to picture him making a third try for the White House, but not quite as easy to see him doing it as a Democrat.

A Middle Class Party

There was a time when Americans readily identified themselves as Democrats or Republicans. Their political orientation was something they were proud of; it was part of who they were. But the Vietnam War and Watergate began to erode that pride, and party ties have been weakening ever since. More than a quarter of all 1996 voters called themselves independents. Suburban independents had become especially influential, forming the fourth-largest group in the electorate, according to a breakdown by sector and party:

---

*A perfect example is the 1996 campaign for mayor of metropolitan Miami, as recounted in chapter 4.

Group	Share of U.S. Vote (%)	Group's 1996 Presidential Vote (%)		
		Clinton	Dole	Perot
Suburban Democrats	18	83	10	5
Suburban Republicans	17	13	80	6
Urban Democrats	14	87	7	4
Suburban independents	13	42	36	17
Urban Republicans	10	13	80	6
Urban independents	7	49	30	16
Rural Democrats	7	79	15	6
Rural Republicans	7	14	80	6
Rural independents	5	37	41	20

Source: VNS exit poll 1996.

The rapid growth in the ranks of independent voters has tempted more than one politician to fantasize about creating a moderate third party targeted at the middle class. Such a party conceivably would be especially popular in suburbia, offering an alternative to urban-oriented Democrats on the left and socially conservative Republicans on the right. "Most European countries have minor parties with a centrist cast, as well as 'green' (environmentalist) parties," political analyst Kevin Phillips wrote in 1982, "and it may well be that . . . American minor parties . . . will be able to stake out similar turf and roles."[73]

Ross Perot's Reform Party might have fulfilled this prophecy, but didn't. Several of its stands were too populist to suit the middle class, its political base in nonmetro areas was too limited, and the party itself was too much a personal vehicle driven by its founder's enormous bank account. A considerably better model for a new centrist coalition would be John Anderson's all-but-forgotten National Unity Party.

Anderson, once a hero of conservative Republicans, began a leftward drift in 1968 that led to his splinter presidential candidacy twelve years later. The Illinois congressman had been honored by a conservative organization in the late 1960s for "standing firm against the liberal pressures in Washington." But his vote for open-housing legislation signaled a break with the right. He later opposed the Vietnam War and was one of the first Republicans to demand Richard Nixon's resignation after Watergate.

Anderson sought the presidency in 1980, first as a Republican, then as the head of his own party after abandoning hope of the GOP nomination. He positioned himself as a middle-of-the-road alternative to Ronald Reagan and Jimmy Carter, denying that he was a spoiler. "What's to spoil?" he asked.[74]

Most third parties reach out to the disaffected, but Anderson aimed at middle- and upper-class voters. He was particularly popular in university towns and in the affluent suburbs around cities such as

Boston, Denver, and San Francisco. A substantial number of his backers were liberal Republicans who couldn't stomach Reagan and were equally averse to pulling the lever for Carter. Anderson was their halfway house; surveys would show that 70 percent of the Republicans who voted for him in 1980 supported Walter Mondale in 1984.[75]*

The National Unity ticket appeared strong in its early months, drawing better than 10 percent support in summer polls, but it plummeted to 6.6 percent by November. "This campaign must not, shall not, and will not end for me," Anderson shouted to supporters on election night. "That (losing) was a decision deferred."[76] But his brave talk vanished by 1984. Anderson declined to run again, even though he was eligible for $6 million in federal campaign funds. The National Unity Party was on the ballot only in Kentucky in 1984, then quietly disappeared.

There is no doubt that a third party similar to Anderson's would find a constituency. Seculars—those liberal, affluent Democrats identified by the Pew Research Center—might form the core of such a movement. Seculars have Democratic values, yet generally do not feel a close attachment to their party. They endorse broad sections of the Suburban Agenda, including its call for tolerance and its support of education and the environment. Sixty-two percent of Seculars who were surveyed in 1994 agreed that America needed a third party, and they clearly did not mean one with Ross Perot as its leader.[77]

But Anderson's fate inspires serious doubts about the long-term prospects for a new middle-class party. He ran for the presidency when public dissatisfaction with the Democrats and Republicans was at its zenith, yet he did not receive a single vote in the Electoral College. Millions of prospective supporters abandoned him after realizing he had no chance of victory, in turn causing his funding sources to dry up during the last weeks of the campaign. The final indignity occurred when both major parties agreed to bar Anderson from a televised debate days before the election.

Any new third party can count on similar treatment. It also can expect the Democrats and Republicans to move quickly to co-opt its base of support. Richard Nixon stole George Wallace's thunder by shifting to the right before the 1972 election, helping to bury the American Independent Party. Walter Mondale courted Anderson's supporters in 1984, writing the final chapter in the history of the National Unity Party. Bill Clinton and Bob Dole targeted Ross Perot's loyalists in 1996, cutting his 1992 vote total by more than half. This pat-

---

*Anderson was among them; he publicly endorsed Mondale.

tern suggests that a middle-class third party would struggle unless its competitors mysteriously gravitated to extreme positions at the same time, perhaps pitting the Republican second coming of Barry Gold-water against a Democratic clone of George McGovern. It seems very, very unlikely to happen.

Counting the Votes

That leaves the two major parties to vie for suburbia's heart in the coming century. The presidential election of 2000 will be their next major battle.

A political campaign, of course, is not confined to a single year. Aspirants for the Democratic and Republican nominations in 2000 had begun their planning and fundraising even before Bill Clinton appeared in front of the Old State House in Little Rock to give thanks for his reelection. Al Gore, Dick Gephardt, Trent Lott, Newt Gingrich, and dozens of other political leaders jockeyed for TV time that evening in November 1996, hoping to increase their visibility by the tiniest bit. The next presidential election, after all, was just four years away.

Demographers already have determined the lay of the land for this upcoming contest. The United States will have 274 million residents in 2000, according to Census Bureau analysts. Fully 42.4 percent of Americans will be living in suburbs, nearly doubling the population of the next-largest sector, fringe metros, which will be at 21.7 percent. Nonmetro areas will account for 19.9 percent of the nation's residents, and mother cities will bring up the rear with a paltry 16.0 percent.

The imbalance of political power will be even more pronounced. Suburbs will control twenty-four states in 2000, accounting for 353 electoral votes, eighty-three more than the minimum needed for victory. The other sectors will be insignificant in comparison: Nonmetro states will have exactly one hundred electoral votes, fringe states will have eighty-two, and the sole remaining city state (the District of Columbia) will have three.

Suburbia, to be blunt, will be more firmly in control in 2000 than ever before.

President Clinton remained sensitive to this trend as he began his second term. He continued to emphasize policies designed to appeal to the large pool of moderate suburbanites who disdained cities and disliked central authority. Such was the case in May 1997, when Clinton worked out a deal with congressional Republicans to eliminate the federal deficit by 2002. The agreement included a provision for net tax cuts of $85 billion over five years. "Take this balanced budget and write it into law," Clinton admonished Congress during a ceremony in the White House Rose Garden.[78]

The nation turned its attention to the upcoming congressional debate. Prospective presidential candidates, fully aware of the long-term importance of the budget issue, began establishing their battle lines, even though the election still was three years off. Much was at stake.

The two major Democratic contenders set themselves on opposite sides. Vice President Gore feverishly toiled behind the scenes to gain support for the agreement; House Minority Leader Gephardt passionately condemned the deal. A mixture of belief and calculation inspired each man to take the stand he did.

Gore was convinced that Clinton's vision of the Democratic Party's future was the correct one; the vice president had seen firsthand that a suburban-oriented, middle-of-the-road campaign was the key to success on a national scale. Balancing the federal budget, in his opinion, would allay the concerns of moderate Republicans and independents. It also would mesh with Gore's belief that the formula for economic prosperity required fiscal responsibility, technological innovation, and unfettered global trade. He warned Americans to ignore political doomsayers who condemned the transition to an information-based economy and who sought "to pull the nation down to protect anyone from losing."[79]

Gephardt thought the balanced budget agreement was a terrible mistake. It was something the minority leader might have expected from a Republican president, but certainly not a Democrat. It favored the wealthy with its tax cuts, as far as he was concerned, and it didn't allocate enough money for education, roads, bridges, or children's health. "This budget agreement is a budget of many deficits—a deficit of principle, a deficit of fairness, a deficit of tax justice, and, worst of all, a deficit of dollars," he charged.[80] Gephardt positioned himself as the defender of the party's traditional urban base. He worried that less-skilled and less-educated workers would be left behind by the evolution of America's economy, and that international free trade simply would make things worse.

Both of these Democratic contenders had run ineffectual campaigns for president in 1988; each knew that 2000 would be his last chance. The weakness of Gore's first presidential try was exemplified by his willingness to put his 1988 New York primary campaign in the hands of New York City's controversial mayor; he had "played country bumpkin to . . . Ed Koch's city slicker," in analyst William Schneider's words.[81] Gore drew just 10 percent of the New York vote and disappeared from the race shortly thereafter. Gephardt ran a one-note, neo-isolationist campaign in 1988, notable only for his incessant demands for "trade fairness." He won the Iowa caucuses, partly because he was from neighboring Missouri, but he foundered in larger, suburban states.

The irony was that Gephardt and Gore once had been united on most issues. They, along with Clinton, had been founding members of the Democratic Leadership Council in the mid-1980s, working together to push their party back into the moderate mainstream. Gephardt had come off as a conservative on some economic issues—even supporting Ronald Reagan's tax-cut package in 1981—but since had shifted to the left. He voted against Clinton on free trade in 1993 and again on welfare reform in 1996. Big-city congressmen sided with Gephardt on both issues. Their suburban counterparts—and Congress itself—backed the president.

Republicans enjoyed watching the Democrats squabble over the budget. The GOP was not similarly divided; most of its House members were solidly behind the agreement. John Kasich, chairman of the House Budget Committee, basked in praise for negotiating the pact with Clinton. "Cooperation between Congress and the president is resulting in smaller government," he said happily, "and it is resulting in people having more power."[82] Speaker Gingrich shared his enthusiasm and hinted at conservative victories to come. "This is just one step in a journey," he said. "Just as last year we passed welfare reform. And after this step, we'll pass other steps."[83] Kasich and Gingrich were among several Republicans who were entertaining thoughts of running for president in 2000.

The debate itself was a fiery one, putting conservative Republicans in the unusual position of defending Clinton against the attacks of liberal Democrats. Massachusetts Congressman Barney Frank, a member of the latter camp, insisted that Clinton had sold out his party and its most loyal constituents. "I sent a letter addressed to the Democratic president of the United States," said Frank. "It came back 'addressee unknown.' "[84]

The liberals may have had the best lines, but they did not have the votes. The roll call finally took place at 3 A.M. on May 21, and the agreement passed easily by a count of 333 to 99. Almost 90 percent of the Republicans voted yes. Urban Democrats opposed the balanced budget deal by a 5 to 4 margin, but their suburban Democratic colleagues voted yes by better than 2 to 1:

	Total Vote		Republicans		Democrats	
	Yes	No	Yes	No	Yes	No
House	333	99	201	26	132	72
Components						
City districts	52	42	20	2	32	40
Suburban districts	140	29	90	8	50	21
Fringe districts	73	10	46	8	27	2
Nonmetro districts	68	18	45	8	23	9

Source: Author's analysis of congressional roll call (May 21, 1997).

Most insiders agreed that Gore and the Republicans were the winners. They had rallied impressive support in favor of balancing the budget, demonstrating the widespread popularity of conservative fiscal policy. They would be able to advertise themselves in 2000 as sound, sober administrators who had the necessary vision and skills to guide America's economy into a new century.

Gephardt claimed that he also had achieved *his* objective. He had stood up against a bill that he believed was unfair to the disadvantaged members of society, and he had brought America's attention to its inequities. House Majority Leader Richard Armey, a Republican, thought that Gephardt might have accomplished something else, too. "He has positioned himself excellently to command the liberal base of the Democratic Party in the primaries," said Armey. "I think from his point of view it is a wise decision."[85]

Gephardt would draw this distinction in bolder strokes in the coming months. "We need a new progressivism for a new century," he declared in a widely publicized speech at Harvard University. "We need a Democratic Party where principles trump tactics. We need a Democratic Party that is a movement for change, and not a money machine." He spoke caustically about certain politicians "who talk about the political center, but fail to understand that if it is only defined by others, it lacks core values. And who too often market a political strategy masquerading as policy."[86] He didn't name names. He didn't need to.

It was clear that Gephardt had decided to gamble with his political future. He was betting that the Democratic Party would return to its liberal roots in 2000; that it would reject Clinton's record in favor of the legacy of Roosevelt, Truman, Kennedy, and Johnson; that it would restore control to the constituents who had supported the party so well for so long—poor people, minorities, residents of big cities.

Gephardt's strategy had merely one flaw. It ignored the critical, indisputable fact that suburbs will be calling the shots in America from now on.

APPENDICES

A America's Mother Cities

The 1940 census identified ninety-three cities with populations of more than 100,000. This book refers to those communities as mother cities.

The chart below shows the 1940, 1990, and 2020 populations of all mother cities, as well as their growth rates for the periods of 1940–1990 and 1990–2020. Figures for 1940 and 1990 are U.S. Census Bureau data. Figures for 2020 are the author's projections derived from a statistical model that he created (as are all projections found in these appendices). Please refer to the note on p. 108 for a more complete description of the derivation process.

		Population			Change (%)	
Mother City	State	1940	1990	2020	1940–1990	1990–2020
Akron	Ohio	244,791	223,019	231,692	− 8.9	+ 3.9
Albany	New York	130,577	101,082	109,866	− 22.6	+ 8.7
Atlanta	Georgia	302,288	394,017	416,232	+ 30.3	+ 5.6
Baltimore	Maryland	859,100	736,014	725,500	− 14.3	− 1.4
Birmingham	Alabama	267,583	265,968	305,493	− 0.6	+14.9
Boston	Massachusetts	770,816	574,283	606,687	− 25.5	+ 5.6
Bridgeport	Connecticut	147,121	141,686	146,076	− 3.7	+ 3.1
Buffalo	New York	575,901	328,123	303,725	− 43.0	− 7.4
Cambridge	Massachusetts	110,879	95,802	104,864	− 13.6	+ 9.5
Camden	New Jersey	117,536	87,492	89,793	− 25.6	+ 2.6
Canton	Ohio	108,401	84,161	77,367	− 22.4	− 8.1
Charlotte	North Carolina	100,899	395,934	640,073	+292.4	+61.7
Chattanooga	Tennessee	128,163	152,466	165,352	+ 19.0	+ 8.5
Chicago	Illinois	3,396,808	2,783,726	2,530,718	− 18.0	− 9.1
Cincinnati	Ohio	455,610	364,040	384,928	− 20.1	+ 5.7
Cleveland	Ohio	878,336	505,616	469,097	− 42.4	− 7.2
Columbus	Ohio	306,087	632,910	831,867	+106.8	+ 31.4
Dallas	Texas	294,734	1,006,877	1,277,479	+241.6	+26.9
Dayton	Ohio	210,718	182,044	177,082	− 13.6	− 2.7
Denver	Colorado	322,412	467,610	481,592	+ 45.0	+ 3.0
Des Moines	Iowa	159,819	193,187	235,075	+ 20.9	+21.7
Detroit	Michigan	1,623,452	1,027,974	1,005,049	− 36.7	− 2.2
Duluth	Minnesota	101,065	85,493	81,463	− 15.4	− 4.7
Elizabeth	New Jersey	109,912	110,002	109,783	+ 0.1	− 0.2
Erie	Pennsylvania	116,955	108,718	100,444	− 7.0	− 7.6
Fall River	Massachusetts	115,428	92,703	102,762	− 19.7	+10.9
Flint	Michigan	151,543	140,761	130,391	− 7.1	− 7.4
Fort Wayne	Indiana	118,410	173,072	203,618	+ 46.2	+17.6

Mother City	State	Population			Change (%)	
		1940	1990	2020	1940–1990	1990–2020
Fort Worth	Texas	177,662	447,619	615,509	+151.9	+37.5
Gary	Indiana	111,719	116,646	105,989	+ 4.4	− 9.1
Grand Rapids	Michigan	164,292	189,126	206,070	+ 15.1	+ 9.0
Hartford	Connecticut	166,267	139,739	129,481	− 16.0	− 7.3
Honolulu	Hawaii	179,326	365,272	464,515	+103.7	+27.2
Houston	Texas	384,514	1,630,553	1,709,609	+324.1	+ 4.8
Indianapolis	Indiana	386,972	731,327	908,674	+ 89.0	+24.3
Jacksonville	Florida	173,065	635,230	819,818	+267.0	+29.1
Jersey City	New Jersey	301,173	228,537	280,312	− 24.1	+22.7
Kansas City	Kansas	121,458	149,767	158,980	+ 23.3	+ 6.2
Kansas City	Missouri	399,178	435,146	469,476	+ 9.0	+ 7.9
Knoxville	Tennessee	111,580	165,121	185,931	+ 48.0	+12.6
Long Beach	California	164,271	429,433	616,742	+161.4	+43.6
Los Angeles	California	1,504,277	3,485,398	3,588,653	+131.7	+ 3.0
Louisville	Kentucky	319,077	269,063	273,833	− 15.7	+ 1.8
Lowell	Massachusetts	101,389	103,439	173,041	+ 2.0	+67.3
Memphis	Tennessee	292,942	610,337	752,613	+108.3	+23.3
Miami	Florida	172,172	358,548	378,212	+108.2	+ 5.5
Milwaukee	Wisconsin	587,472	628,088	742,842	+ 6.9	+18.3
Minneapolis	Minnesota	492,370	368,383	460,588	− 25.2	+25.0
Nashville	Tennessee	167,402	488,374	672,513	+191.7	+37.7
Newark	New Jersey	429,760	275,221	224,263	− 36.0	−18.5
New Bedford	Massachusetts	110,341	99,922	99,303	− 9.4	− 0.6
New Haven	Connecticut	160,605	130,474	139,485	− 18.8	+ 6.9
New Orleans	Louisiana	494,537	496,938	525,620	+ 0.5	+ 5.8
New York City	New York	7,454,995	7,322,564	7,522,415	− 1.8	+ 2.7
Norfolk	Virginia	144,332	261,229	269,908	+ 81.0	+ 3.3
Oakland	California	302,163	372,242	444,388	+ 23.2	+19.4
Oklahoma City	Oklahoma	204,424	444,719	609,309	+117.5	+37.0
Omaha	Nebraska	223,844	335,795	442,370	+ 50.0	+31.7
Paterson	New Jersey	139,656	140,891	129,064	+ 0.9	− 8.4
Peoria	Illinois	105,087	113,504	122,250	+ 8.0	+ 7.7
Philadelphia	Pennsylvania	1,931,334	1,585,577	1,622,436	− 17.9	+ 2.3
Pittsburgh	Pennsylvania	671,659	369,879	340,353	− 44.9	− 8.0
Portland	Oregon	305,394	437,319	753,832	+ 43.2	+72.4
Providence	Rhode Island	253,504	160,728	187,408	− 36.6	+16.6
Reading	Pennsylvania	110,568	78,380	73,643	− 29.1	− 6.0
Richmond	Virginia	193,042	203,056	204,620	+ 5.2	+ 0.8
Rochester	New York	324,975	231,636	227,986	− 28.7	− 1.6
Sacramento	California	105,958	369,365	635,350	+248.6	+72.0
Saint Louis	Missouri	816,048	396,685	386,632	− 51.4	− 2.5
Saint Paul	Minnesota	287,736	272,235	385,217	− 5.4	+41.5
Salt Lake City	Utah	149,934	159,936	200,500	+ 6.7	+25.4
San Antonio	Texas	253,854	935,933	1,147,606	+268.7	+22.6
San Diego	California	203,341	1,110,549	1,678,907	+446.2	+51.2
San Francisco	California	634,536	723,959	844,948	+ 14.1	+16.7
Scranton	Pennsylvania	140,404	81,805	76,872	−4 1.7	− 6.0
Seattle	Washington	368,302	516,259	670,310	+ 40.2	+29.8
Somerville	Massachusetts	102,177	76,210	93,193	− 25.4	+22.3
South Bend	Indiana	101,268	105,511	115,919	+ 4.2	+ 9.9
Spokane	Washington	122,001	177,196	226,952	+ 45.2	+28.1
Springfield	Massachusetts	149,554	156,983	152,930	+ 5.0	− 2.6
Syracuse	New York	205,967	163,860	172,986	− 20.4	+ 5.6
Tacoma	Washington	109,408	176,664	263,521	+ 61.5	+49.2
Tampa	Florida	108,391	280,015	293,378	+158.3	+ 4.8
Toledo	Ohio	282,349	332,943	328,743	+ 17.9	− 1.3
Trenton	New Jersey	124,697	88,675	92,969	− 28.9	+ 4.8

Mother city	State	Population 1940	Population 1990	Population 2020	Change 1940–1990	Change 1990–2020
Tulsa	Oklahoma	142,157	367,302	451,934	+158.4	+23.0
Utica	New York	100,518	68,637	67,513	– 31.7	– 1.6
Washington	D.C.	663,091	606,900	623,000	– 8.5	+ 2.7
Wichita	Kansas	114,966	304,011	383,792	+164.4	+26.2
Wilmington	Delaware	112,504	71,529	83,050	– 36.4	+16.1
Worcester	Massachusetts	193,694	169,759	194,377	– 12.4	+14.5
Yonkers	New York	142,598	188,082	178,013	+ 31.9	– 5.4
Youngstown	Ohio	167,720	95,732	82,133	– 42.9	–14.2
TOTAL		38,167,315	44,486,735	49,526,870	+ 16.6	+11.3

B Inner America's Metropolitan Areas

Inner America is the collective name for the sixty-seven metropolitan areas that contain all ninety-three mother cities and their suburbs.

The U.S. Office of Management and Budget (OMB) sets official metropolitan boundaries, using counties as its building blocks. The chart below shows the number of counties that made up each metro area under OMB's 1995 definitions. This book applies those 1995 boundaries throughout the period of 1940–2020 to allow uniform comparisons.

Most metropolitan areas are named after their mother city or cities, such as the Atlanta or Minneapolis-Saint Paul metros. But several areas include additional mother cities that are not identified in official metropolitan names. (Example: Long Beach is a mother city in the Los Angeles metro.) These cities are listed in the footnotes.

The chart below shows each metro area's total population in 1940, 1990, and 2020, as well as the share of all metropolitan residents who lived in the suburbs. (Example: The six-county Albany metro had 611,203 residents in 1940. Fully 78.6 percent of those people lived in the suburbs; the rest lived in the mother city.) Suburbs are defined as all parts of the metro area outside its mother city or cities. Figures for 1940 and 1990 are based on U.S. Census Bureau data. Figures for 2020 are the author's projections.

Metro Area	Counties	1940 Population	1940 Sub (%)	1990 Population	1990 Sub (%)	2020 Population	2020 Sub (%)
Albany	6	611,203	78.6	861,424	88.3	986,298	88.9
Atlanta	20	820,579	63.2	2,959,950	86.7	5,215,731	92.0
Birmingham	4	545,718	51.0	840,140	68.3	1,072,470	71.5
Boston[1]	10	3,940,645	61.8	5,685,998	78.7	6,515,646	78.9
Buffalo	2	958,487	39.9	1,189,288	72.4	1,184,577	74.4

Metro Area	Counties	1940 Population	Sub (%)	1990 Population	Sub (%)	2020 Population	Sub (%)
Canton	2	252,336	57.0	394,106	78.6	399,932	80.7
Charlotte	7	489,903	79.4	1,162,093	65.9	1,720,939	62.8
Chattanooga	5	248,735	48.5	424,347	64.1	505,794	67.3
Chicago[2]	13	5,078,947	30.9	8,239,820	64.8	9,446,710	72.1
Cincinnati	13	1,055,164	56.8	1,817,571	80.0	2,136,226	82.0
Cleveland[3]	8	1,886,863	40.5	2,859,644	74.5	2,951,277	76.3
Columbus	6	575,961	46.9	1,345,450	53.0	1,687,211	50.7
Dallas-Fort Worth	12	936,180	49.5	4,037,282	64.0	7,412,332	74.5
Dayton	4	479,622	56.1	951,270	80.9	1,032,537	82.8
Denver	7	512,449	37.1	1,980,140	76.4	3,036,753	84.1
Des Moines	3	238,179	32.9	392,928	50.8	501,788	53.2
Detroit[4]	10	2,927,014	39.4	5,187,171	77.5	5,472,794	79.3
Duluth	2	254,036	60.2	239,971	64.4	222,097	63.3
Erie	1	180,889	35.3	275,572	60.5	278,890	64.0
Fort Wayne	6	267,125	55.7	456,281	62.1	541,860	62.4
Grand Rapids	4	442,338	62.9	937,891	79.8	1,135,101	81.8
Hartford	3	538,054	69.1	1,123,678	87.6	1,253,021	89.7
Honolulu	1	257,696	30.4	836,231	56.3	1,175,682	60.5
Houston	8	735,553	47.7	3,731,131	56.3	5,449,311	68.6
Indianapolis	9	701,896	44.9	1,380,491	47.0	1,740,018	47.8
Jacksonville	4	247,449	30.1	906,727	29.9	1,295,018	36.7
Kansas City[5]	11	840,341	38.0	1,582,875	63.0	2,054,529	69.4
Knoxville	6	298,247	62.6	585,960	71.8	779,002	76.1
Los Angeles[6]	5	3,252,720	48.7	14,531,529	73.1	20,849,218	79.8
Louisville	7	497,784	35.9	948,829	71.6	1,090,186	74.9
Memphis	5	485,744	39.7	1,007,306	39.4	1,398,918	46.2
Miami	2	307,533	44.0	3,192,582	88.8	4,242,245	91.1
Milwaukee	5	971,091	39.5	1,607,183	60.9	1,870,335	60.3
Minneapolis-Saint Paul	13	1,110,951	29.8	2,538,834	74.8	3,501,339	75.8
Nashville	8	432,769	61.3	985,026	50.4	1,503,006	55.3
New Orleans	8	631,869	21.7	1,285,270	61.3	1,517,831	65.4
New York City[7]	29	13,361,042	32.6	19,462,450	55.7	21,492,236	59.0
Norfolk	15	432,030	66.6	1,443,244	81.9	2,053,253	86.9
Oklahoma City	6	398,043	48.6	958,839	53.6	1,352,895	55.0
Omaha	5	353,723	36.7	639,580	47.5	823,524	46.3
Peoria	3	230,860	54.5	339,172	66.5	366,148	66.6
Philadelphia[8]	14	3,674,049	41.2	5,892,937	70.4	6,818,334	73.7
Pittsburgh	6	2,371,145	71.7	2,394,811	84.6	2,270,748	85.0
Portland	8	643,817	52.6	1,793,476	75.6	2,806,810	73.1
Providence	4	666,650	62.0	916,270	82.5	1,007,523	81.4
Reading	1	241,884	54.3	336,523	76.7	373,474	80.3
Richmond	13	376,879	48.8	865,640	76.5	1,169,071	82.5
Rochester	6	657,035	50.5	1,062,470	78.2	1,177,354	80.6
Sacramento	4	238,913	55.6	1,481,102	75.1	2,770,660	77.1
Saint Louis	12	1,569,410	48.0	2,492,525	84.1	3,065,496	87.4
Salt Lake City	3	284,121	47.2	1,072,227	85.1	1,733,924	88.4
San Antonio	4	393,159	35.4	1,324,749	29.4	1,770,525	35.2
San Diego	1	289,348	29.7	2,498,016	55.5	4,173,814	59.8
San Francisco-Oakland	10	1,779,365	47.4	6,253,311	82.5	9,396,971	86.3
Scranton	4	810,876	82.7	638,466	87.2	631,721	87.8
Seattle[9]	6	863,585	44.7	2,970,328	76.7	4,943,055	81.1
South Bend	1	161,823	37.4	247,052	57.3	292,676	60.4
Spokane	1	164,652	25.9	361,364	51.0	477,214	52.4
Springfield	2	404,568	63.0	602,878	74.0	624,956	75.5
Syracuse	4	471,489	56.3	742,177	77.9	828,915	79.1
Tampa	4	291,622	62.8	2,067,959	86.5	2,963,304	90.1
Toledo	3	419,755	32.7	614,128	45.8	643,173	48.9
Tulsa	5	333,088	57.3	708,954	48.2	927,864	51.3
Utica	2	263,163	61.8	316,633	78.3	341,138	80.2

Metro Area	Counties	1940 Population	Sub (%)	1990 Population	Sub (%)	2020 Population	Sub (%)
Washington-Baltimore	33	2,482,968	38.7	6,727,050	80.0	8,967,632	85.0
Wichita	3	197,036	41.7	485,270	37.4	620,311	38.1
Youngstown	3	462,687	63.8	600,895	84.1	573,552	85.7
TOTAL	**455**	**69,300,855**	**44.9**	**146,792,485**	**69.7**	**190,634,292**	**74.0**

Additional mother cities:
1. Cambridge, Fall River, Lowell, New Bedford, Somerville, Worcester
2. Gary
3. Akron
4. Flint
5. Name is shared by two mother cities: Kansas City, Kansas, and Kansas City, Missouri
6. Long Beach
7. Bridgeport, Elizabeth, Jersey City, Newark, New Haven, Paterson, Trenton, Yonkers
8. Camden, Wilmington
9. Tacoma

C Components of Inner America's Metropolitan Areas

The list below includes the official names, mother cities, and component counties of all sixty-seven metropolitan areas in Inner America, based on 1995 boundaries set by the U.S. Office of Management and Budget. MSA means Metropolitan Statistical Area; CMSA, Consolidated Metropolitan Statistical Area; NECMA, New England County Metropolitan Statistical Area.

Albany metro area
Official name: Albany-Schenectady-Troy MSA
Mother city: Albany
Metro components: Albany, Montgomery, Rensselaer, Saratoga, Schenectady, and Schoharie counties in New York

Atlanta metro area
Official name: Atlanta MSA
Mother city: Atlanta
Metro components: Barrow, Bartow, Carroll, Cherokee, Clayton, Cobb, Coweta, DeKalb, Douglas, Fayette, Forsyth, Fulton, Gwinnett, Henry, Newton, Paulding, Pickens, Rockdale, Spalding, and Walton counties in Georgia

Birmingham metro area
Official name: Birmingham MSA
Mother city: Birmingham
Metro components: Blount, Jefferson, Saint Clair, and Shelby counties in Alabama

Boston metro area
Official name: Boston-Worcester-Lawrence-Lowell-Brockton NECMA
Mother cities: Boston, Cambridge, Fall River, Lowell, New Bedford, Somerville, and Worcester
Metro components: Bristol, Essex, Middlesex, Norfolk, Plymouth, Suffolk, and Worcester counties in Massachusetts; Hillsborough, Rockingham, and Strafford counties in New Hampshire

Buffalo metro area
Official name: Buffalo-Niagara Falls MSA
Mother city: Buffalo
Metro components: Erie and Niagara counties in New York

Canton metro area
Official name: Canton-Massillon MSA
Mother city: Canton
Metro components: Carroll and Stark counties in Ohio

Charlotte metro area
Official name: Charlotte-Gastonia-Rock Hill MSA
Mother city: Charlotte
Metro components: Cabarrus, Gaston, Lincoln, Mecklenburg, Rowan, and Union counties in North Carolina; York County in South Carolina

Chattanooga metro area
Official name: Chattanooga MSA
Mother city: Chattanooga
Metro components: Catoosa, Dade, and Walker counties in Georgia; Hamilton and Marion counties in Tennessee

Chicago metro area
Official name: Chicago-Gary-Kenosha CMSA
Mother cities: Chicago and Gary
Metro components: Cook, DeKalb, DuPage, Grundy, Kane, Kankakee, Kendall, Lake, McHenry, and Will counties in Illinois; Lake and Porter counties in Indiana; Kenosha County in Wisconsin

Cincinnati metro area
Official name: Cincinnati-Hamilton CMSA
Mother city: Cincinnati
Metro components: Dearborn and Ohio counties in Indiana; Boone, Campbell, Gallatin, Grant, Kenton, and Pendleton counties in Kentucky; Brown, Butler, Clermont, Hamilton, and Warren counties in Ohio

Cleveland metro area
Official name: Cleveland-Akron CMSA
Mother cities: Akron and Cleveland
Metro components: Ashtabula, Cuyahoga, Geauga, Lake, Lorain, Medina, Portage, and Summit counties in Ohio

Columbus metro area
Official name: Columbus MSA
Mother city: Columbus
Metro components: Delaware, Fairfield, Franklin, Licking, Madison, and Pickaway counties in Ohio

Dallas-Fort Worth metro area
Official name: Dallas-Fort Worth CMSA
Mother cities: Dallas and Fort Worth
Metro components: Collin, Dallas, Denton, Ellis, Henderson, Hood, Hunt, Johnson, Kaufman, Parker, Rockwall, and Tarrant counties in Texas

Dayton metro area
Official name: Dayton-Springfield MSA
Mother city: Dayton
Metro components: Clark, Greene, Miami, and Montgomery counties in Ohio

Denver metro area
Official name: Denver-Boulder-Greeley CMSA
Mother city: Denver
Metro components: Adams, Arapahoe, Boulder, Denver, Douglas, Jefferson, and Weld counties in Colorado

Des Moines metro area
Official name: Des Moines MSA
Mother city: Des Moines
Metro components: Dallas, Polk, and Warren counties in Iowa

Detroit metro area
Official name: Detroit-Ann Arbor-Flint CMSA
Mother cities: Detroit and Flint
Metro components: Genesee, Lapeer, Lenawee, Livingston, Macomb, Monroe, Oakland, Saint Clair, Washtenaw, and Wayne counties in Michigan

Duluth metro area
Official name: Duluth-Superior MSA
Mother city: Duluth
Metro components: Saint Louis County in Minnesota; Douglas County in Wisconsin

Erie metro area
Official name: Erie MSA
Mother city: Erie
Metro component: Erie County in Pennsylvania

Fort Wayne metro area
Official name: Fort Wayne MSA
Mother city: Fort Wayne
Metro components: Adams, Allen, DeKalb, Huntington, Wells, and Whitley counties in Indiana

Grand Rapids metro area
Official name: Grand Rapids-Muskegon-Holland MSA
Mother city: Grand Rapids
Metro components: Allegan, Kent, Muskegon, and Ottawa counties in Michigan

Hartford metro area
Official name: Hartford NECMA
Mother city: Hartford
Metro components: Hartford, Middlesex, and Tolland counties in Connecticut

Honolulu metro area
Official name: Honolulu MSA
Mother city: Honolulu
Metro component: Honolulu County in Hawaii

Houston metro area
Official name: Houston-Galveston-Brazoria CMSA
Mother city: Houston
Metro components: Brazoria, Chambers, Fort Bend, Galveston, Harris, Liberty, Montgomery, and Waller counties in Texas

Indianapolis metro area
Official name: Indianapolis MSA
Mother city: Indianapolis
Metro components: Boone, Hamilton, Hancock, Hendricks, Johnson, Madison, Marion, Morgan, and Shelby counties in Indiana

Jacksonville metro area
Official name: Jacksonville MSA
Mother city: Jacksonville
Metro components: Clay, Duval, Nassau, and Saint Johns counties in Florida

Kansas City metro area
Official name: Kansas City MSA
Mother cities: Kansas City, Kansas, and Kansas City, Missouri
Metro components: Johnson, Leavenworth, Miami, and Wyandotte counties in Kansas; Cass, Clay, Clinton, Jackson, Lafayette, Platte, and Ray counties in Missouri

Knoxville metro area
Official name: Knoxville MSA
Mother city: Knoxville
Metro components: Anderson, Blount, Knox, Loudon, Sevier, and Union counties in Tennessee

Los Angeles metro area
Official name: Los Angeles-Riverside-Orange County CMSA
Mother cities: Long Beach and Los Angeles
Metro components: Los Angeles, Orange, Riverside, San Bernardino, and Ventura counties in California

Louisville metro area
Official name: Louisville MSA
Mother city: Louisville
Metro components: Clark, Floyd, Harrison, and Scott counties in Indiana; Bullitt, Jefferson, and Oldham counties in Kentucky

Memphis metro area
Official name: Memphis MSA
Mother city: Memphis
Metro components: Crittenden County in Arkansas; DeSoto County in Mississippi; Fayette, Shelby, and Tipton counties in Tennessee

Miami metro area
Official name: Miami-Fort Lauderdale CMSA
Mother city: Miami
Metro components: Broward and Dade counties in Florida

Milwaukee metro area
Official name: Milwaukee-Racine CMSA
Mother city: Milwaukee
Metro components: Milwaukee, Ozaukee, Racine, Washington, and Waukesha counties in Wisconsin

Minneapolis-Saint Paul metro area
Official name: Minneapolis-Saint Paul MSA
Mother cities: Minneapolis and Saint Paul
Metro components: Anoka, Carver, Chisago, Dakota, Hennepin, Isanti, Ramsey, Scott, Sherburne, Washington, and Wright counties in Minnesota; Pierce and Saint Croix counties in Wisconsin

Nashville metro area
Official name: Nashville MSA
Mother city: Nashville
Metro components: Cheatham, Davidson, Dickson, Robertson, Rutherford, Sumner, Williamson, and Wilson counties in Tennessee

New Orleans metro area
Official name: New Orleans MSA
Mother city: New Orleans
Metro components: Jefferson, Orleans, Plaquemines, Saint Bernard, Saint Charles, Saint James, Saint John the Baptist, and Saint Tammany parishes in Louisiana

New York City metro area
Official name: New York-Northern New Jersey-Long Island CMSA
Mother cities: Bridgeport, Elizabeth, Jersey City, Newark, New Haven, New York City, Paterson, Trenton, and Yonkers
Metro components: Fairfield and New Haven counties in Connecticut; Bergen, Essex, Hudson, Hunterdon, Mercer, Middlesex, Monmouth, Morris, Ocean, Passaic, Somerset, Sussex, Union, and Warren counties in New Jersey; Bronx, Dutchess, Kings, Nassau, New York, Orange, Putnam, Queens, Richmond, Rockland, Suffolk, and Westchester counties in New York; Pike County in Pennsylvania

Norfolk metro area
Official name: Norfolk-Virginia Beach-Newport News MSA
Mother city: Norfolk
Metro components: Currituck County in North Carolina; Gloucester, Isle of Wight, James City, Mathews, and York counties and Chesapeake, Hampton, Newport News, Norfolk, Poquoson, Portsmouth, Suffolk, Virginia Beach, and Williamsburg independent cities in Virginia

Oklahoma City metro area
Official name: Oklahoma City MSA
Mother city: Oklahoma City
Metro components: Canadian, Cleveland, Logan, McClain, Oklahoma, and Pottawatomie counties in Oklahoma

Omaha metro area
Official name: Omaha MSA
Mother city: Omaha
Metro components: Pottawattamie County in Iowa; Cass, Douglas, Sarpy, and Washington counties in Nebraska

Peoria metro area

Official name: Peoria-Pekin MSA

Mother city: Peoria

Metro components: Peoria, Tazewell, and Woodford counties in Illinois

Philadelphia metro area

Official name: Philadelphia-Wilmington-Atlantic City CMSA

Mother cities: Camden, Philadelphia, and Wilmington

Metro components: New Castle County in Delaware; Cecil County in Maryland; Atlantic, Burlington, Camden, Cape May, Cumberland, Gloucester, and Salem counties in New Jersey; Bucks, Chester, Delaware, Montgomery, and Philadelphia counties in Pennsylvania

Pittsburgh metro area

Official name: Pittsburgh MSA

Mother city: Pittsburgh

Metro components: Allegheny, Beaver, Butler, Fayette, Washington, and Westmoreland counties in Pennsylvania

Portland metro area

Official name: Portland-Salem CMSA

Mother city: Portland

Metro components: Clackamas, Columbia, Marion, Multnomah, Polk, Washington, and Yamhill counties in Oregon; Clark County in Washington

Providence metro area

Official name: Providence-Warwick-Pawtucket NECMA

Mother city: Providence

Metro components: Bristol, Kent, Providence, and Washington counties in Rhode Island

Reading metro area

Official name: Reading MSA

Mother city: Reading

Metro component: Berks County in Pennsylvania

Richmond metro area

Official name: Richmond-Petersburg MSA

Mother city: Richmond

Metro components: Charles City, Chesterfield, Dinwiddie, Goochland, Hanover, Henrico, New Kent, Powhatan, and Prince George counties and Colonial Heights, Hopewell, Petersburg, and Richmond independent cities in Virginia

Rochester metro area

Official name: Rochester MSA

Mother city: Rochester

Metro components: Genesee, Livingston, Monroe, Ontario, Orleans, and Wayne counties in New York

Sacramento metro area

Official name: Sacramento-Yolo CMSA

Mother city: Sacramento

Metro components: El Dorado, Placer, Sacramento, and Yolo counties in California

Saint Louis metro area

Official name: Saint Louis MSA

Mother city: Saint Louis

Metro components: Clinton, Jersey, Madison, Monroe, and Saint Clair counties in Illinois; Franklin, Jefferson, Lincoln, Saint Charles, Saint Louis, and Warren counties and Saint Louis independent city in Missouri

Salt Lake City metro area

Official name: Salt Lake City-Ogden MSA

Mother city: Salt Lake City

Metro components: Davis, Salt Lake, and Weber counties in Utah

San Antonio metro area

Official name: San Antonio MSA

Mother city: San Antonio

Metro components: Bexar, Comal, Guadalupe, and Wilson counties in Texas

San Diego metro area

Official name: San Diego MSA

Mother city: San Diego

Metro component: San Diego County in California

San Francisco-Oakland metro area

Official name: San Francisco-Oakland-San Jose CMSA

Mother cities: Oakland and San Francisco

Metro components: Alameda, Contra Costa, Marin, Napa, San Francisco, San Mateo, Santa Clara, Santa Cruz, Solano, and Sonoma counties in California

Scranton metro area

Official name: Scranton–Wilkes-Barre–Hazleton MSA

Mother city: Scranton

Metro components: Columbia, Lackawanna, Luzerne, and Wyoming counties in Pennsylvania

Seattle metro area

Official name: Seattle-Tacoma-Bremerton CMSA

Mother cities: Seattle and Tacoma

Metro components: Island, King, Kitsap, Pierce, Snohomish, and Thurston counties in Washington

South Bend metro area

Official name: South Bend MSA

Mother city: South Bend

Metro component: Saint Joseph County in Indiana

Spokane metro area

Official name: Spokane MSA

Mother city: Spokane

Metro component: Spokane County in Washington

Springfield metro area
Official name: Springfield NECMA
Mother city: Springfield
Metro components: Hampden and Hampshire counties in Massachusetts

Syracuse metro area
Official name: Syracuse MSA
Mother city: Syracuse
Metro components: Cayuga, Madison, Onondaga, and Oswego counties in New York

Tampa metro area
Official name: Tampa-Saint Petersburg-Clearwater MSA
Mother city: Tampa
Metro components: Hernando, Hillsborough, Pasco, and Pinellas counties in Florida

Toledo metro area
Official name: Toledo MSA
Mother city: Toledo
Metro components: Fulton, Lucas, and Wood counties in Ohio

Tulsa metro area
Official name: Tulsa MSA
Mother city: Tulsa
Metro components: Creek, Osage, Rogers, Tulsa, and Wagoner counties in Oklahoma

Utica metro area
Official name: Utica-Rome MSA
Mother city: Utica
Metro components: Herkimer and Oneida counties in New York

Washington-Baltimore metro area
Official name: Washington-Baltimore CMSA
Mother cities: Baltimore and Washington
Metro components: District of Columbia; Anne Arundel, Baltimore, Calvert, Carroll, Charles, Frederick, Harford, Howard, Montgomery, Prince George's, Queen Anne's, and Washington counties and Baltimore independent city in Maryland; Arlington, Clarke, Culpeper, Fairfax, Fauquier, King George, Loudoun, Prince William, Spotsylvania, Stafford, and Warren counties and Alexandria, Fairfax, Falls Church, Fredericksburg, Manassas, and Manassas Park independent cities in Virginia; and Berkeley and Jefferson counties in West Virginia

Wichita metro area
Official name: Wichita MSA
Mother city: Wichita
Metro components: Butler, Harvey, and Sedgwick counties in Kansas

Youngstown metro area
Official name: Youngstown-Warren MSA
Mother city: Youngstown
Metro components: Columbiana, Mahoning, and Trumbull counties in Ohio

D Pace of Suburban Development

There is no fanfare when a state or locality reaches a population milestone. That's because nobody can identify the precise moment when a state hits the 5 million mark or a locality has exactly 100,000 residents. The Census Bureau, after all, conducts its head count just once a decade.

The chart below brings an element of specificity to this topic. It estimates the month and year when each suburban region attained or will attain several population milestones within its metropolitan area. (Example: Detroit's suburbs contained precisely 50 percent of all residents of the Detroit metro in March 1953. Those same suburbs hit 60 percent of the metro's population in March 1960 and 70 percent in August 1973.) The chart covers the period from January 1940 to April 2000.

The author based these estimates on the assumption that metros and their suburban regions grew at constant rates between each federal census. Actual growth occurred at an uneven pace, of course, but there is no accurate way to plot such year-to-year deviations.

There were a few instances when a suburban region passed a milestone, then fell back below it; the date of first passage is marked with an asterisk. A dash indicates that a suburban region has not crossed a specific population threshold; "< 1940" means that it topped the listed percentage before 1940.

Metro	Estimated Date When Suburban Region Reached Listed Share of Metro Population			
	50%	60%	70%	80%
Albany	< 1940	< 1940	< 1940	Aug. 1950
Atlanta	< 1940	< 1940	Feb. 1968	Feb. 1979
Birmingham	*< 1940	Aug. 1971	Dec. 1999	—
Boston	< 1940	< 1940	July 1959	—
Buffalo	Nov. 1952	June 1961	Jan. 1978	—
Canton	< 1940	Mar. 1947	May 1964	—
Charlotte	< 1940	< 1940	*< 1940	—
Chattanooga	Sept. 1942	*July 1958	—	—
Chicago	Aug. 1963	Apr. 1978	—	—
Cincinnati	< 1940	Nov. 1951	July 1965	Apr. 1990
Cleveland	Dec. 1952	Oct. 1961	Nov. 1975	—
Columbus	Nov. 1961	—	—	—
Dallas-Fort Worth	Apr. 1971	Nov. 1983	Aug. 1998	—
Dayton	< 1940	Oct. 1947	Nov. 1962	Oct. 1983
Denver	June 1959	Jan. 1969	Aug. 1978	Aug. 1997
Des Moines	May 1987	—	—	—
Detroit	Mar. 1953	Mar. 1960	Aug. 1973	—
Duluth	< 1940	*< 1940	—	—
Erie	Aug. 1968	Aug. 1988	—	—
Fort Wayne	< 1940	Nov. 1976	—	—
Grand Rapids	< 1940	< 1940	Jan. 1955	Aug. 1991
Hartford	< 1940	< 1940	Sept. 1942	Feb. 1959
Honolulu	July 1974	—	—	—
Houston	Sept. 1981	Jan. 1995	—	—
Indianapolis	*Apr. 1952	—	—	—
Jacksonville	*Mar. 1954	*June 1959	—	—
Kansas City	July 1959	Mar. 1984	—	—
Knoxville	< 1940	< 1940	*July 1953	—
Los Angeles	Apr. 1942	Jan. 1956	Sept. 1976	—
Louisville	Oct. 1959	Apr. 1970	Sept. 1984	—
Memphis	—	—	—	—
Miami	Nov. 1944	Oct. 1951	Oct. 1956	Nov. 1965
Milwaukee	Aug. 1963	Oct. 1983	—	—
Minneapolis-Saint Paul	Mar. 1959	June 1967	Mar. 1979	—
Nashville	*< 1940	*< 1940	*Dec. 1957	—
New Orleans	May 1972	Jan. 1987	—	—
New York City	Apr. 1967	—	—	—
Norfolk	< 1940	< 1940	Nov. 1966	Aug. 1985
Oklahoma City	Mar. 1973	—	—	—
Omaha	—	—	—	—
Peoria	< 1940	Aug. 1951	—	—
Philadelphia	June 1954	Apr. 1966	Nov. 1988	—
Pittsburgh	< 1940	< 1940	< 1940	Apr. 1968
Portland	< 1940	Oct. 1953	Apr. 1970	—
Providence	< 1940	< 1940	Sept. 1955	Sept. 1973
Reading	< 1940	Jan. 1954	July 1969	—
Richmond	Mar. 1948	Jan. 1959	Oct. 1978	—
Rochester	< 1940	Feb. 1957	Dec. 1968	June 1999

	Estimated Date When Suburban Region Reached Listed Share of Metro Population			
Metro	**50%**	**60%**	**70%**	**80%**
Sacramento	< 1940	Nov. 1945	*Apr. 1959	—
Saint Louis	Mar. 1944	Sept. 1955	Jan. 1965	May 1978
Salt Lake City	Nov. 1944	July 1955	Jan. 1965	July 1977
San Antonio	—	—	—	—
San Diego	June 1973	—	—	—
San Francisco-Oakland	Oct. 1942	Jan. 1952	Feb. 1960	July 1977
Scranton	< 1940	< 1940	< 1940	< 1940
Seattle	May 1948	Apr. 1964	Oct. 1975	—
South Bend	Apr. 1972	—	—	—
Spokane	Feb. 1981	—	—	—
Springfield	< 1940	< 1940	Mar. 1966	—
Syracuse	< 1940	Nov. 1951	June 1966	—
Tampa	< 1940	< 1940	*Aug. 1948	May 1976
Toledo	—	—	—	—
Tulsa	*< 1940	—	—	—
Utica	< 1940	< 1940	May 1961	—
Washington-Baltimore	July 1952	Feb. 1960	July 1971	Apr. 1990
Wichita	—	—	—	—
Youngstown	< 1940	< 1940	Jan. 1955	Dec. 1974
INNER AMERICA TOTAL	**Sept. 1951**	**Oct. 1965**	**Apr. 1991**	—

E Racial Divisions in Inner America

The chart below shows the racial compositions of mother cities and their suburban regions in 1990. W means white; B, black; N, Native American; A, Asian-American; H, Hispanic. (Example: 74.1 percent of the people in the city of Albany in 1990 were white, while 94.9 percent of all residents of Albany's suburbs were white.)

Rows might not add to 100 percent because of rounding and the omission of other racial groups. All figures are the author's analysis of 1990 U.S. Census Bureau data.

	Mother Cities (%)					Suburbs (%)				
Metro Area	**W**	**B**	**N**	**A**	**H**	**W**	**B**	**N**	**A**	**H**
Albany	74.1	20.2	0.3	2.3	3.2	94.9	2.3	0.2	1.1	1.5
Atlanta	30.3	66.8	0.1	0.9	1.9	77.3	18.7	0.2	1.9	2.0
Birmingham	35.8	63.2	0.1	0.5	0.4	86.2	12.7	0.2	0.4	0.5
Boston	72.1	13.8	0.2	4.8	9.0	93.5	1.6	0.1	1.8	3.0
Buffalo	63.1	30.3	0.7	1.0	4.9	95.1	2.4	0.6	0.9	1.0
Canton	80.0	18.1	0.5	0.3	1.1	95.6	3.2	0.2	0.4	0.6
Charlotte	64.8	31.7	0.3	1.8	1.4	84.7	13.8	0.3	0.5	0.7
Chattanooga	64.6	33.6	0.2	0.9	0.6	96.2	2.5	0.2	0.5	0.6
Chicago	37.0	40.3	0.2	3.4	19.1	83.5	7.0	0.1	2.8	6.5
Cincinnati	60.2	37.9	0.2	1.1	0.7	94.2	4.5	0.1	0.7	0.5
Cleveland	55.7	39.6	0.3	1.0	3.4	90.3	7.2	0.1	1.0	1.4
Columbus	73.9	22.5	0.2	2.3	1.1	95.5	2.9	0.2	0.8	0.6
Dallas-Fort Worth	50.5	26.7	0.4	2.0	20.5	81.7	6.5	0.5	2.5	8.8

Metro Area	Mother Cities (%)					Suburbs (%)				
	W	**B**	**N**	**A**	**H**	**W**	**B**	**N**	**A**	**H**
Dayton	58.1	40.4	0.2	0.6	0.7	91.2	6.8	0.2	1.0	0.8
Denver	61.6	12.4	0.8	2.2	23.0	85.3	2.4	0.5	2.1	9.7
Des Moines	87.9	7.0	0.3	2.3	2.4	97.5	0.6	0.1	0.8	1.0
Detroit	24.0	72.1	0.4	0.7	2.8	90.9	5.3	0.4	1.6	1.8
Duluth	95.6	0.9	2.1	0.9	0.6	97.2	0.3	1.7	0.4	0.4
Erie	85.1	11.8	0.2	0.5	2.4	98.2	0.7	0.1	0.5	0.5
Fort Wayne	79.4	16.6	0.3	1.0	2.7	97.8	0.5	0.2	0.4	1.0
Grand Rapids	75.0	18.2	0.7	1.1	5.0	92.2	3.9	0.5	0.9	2.6
Hartford	30.6	36.1	0.2	1.3	31.7	91.0	4.1	0.1	1.5	3.3
Honolulu	25.5	1.2	0.3	68.4	4.6	33.3	4.3	0.4	53.4	8.6
Houston	40.7	27.5	0.2	3.9	27.7	71.6	9.8	0.3	3.0	15.4
Indianapolis	75.3	22.6	0.2	0.9	1.1	96.1	2.5	0.2	0.6	0.7
Jacksonville	70.3	25.0	0.3	1.8	2.6	88.8	7.6	0.3	1.1	2.2
Kansas City	64.3	29.4	0.5	1.2	4.7	94.0	2.8	0.4	1.0	1.8
Knoxville	82.4	15.7	0.2	1.0	0.7	96.3	2.3	0.2	0.7	0.5
Los Angeles	38.7	13.1	0.3	9.6	38.2	54.0	6.1	0.4	8.5	31.0
Louisville	68.9	29.5	0.2	0.7	0.7	92.5	6.2	0.2	0.5	0.6
Memphis	43.7	54.7	0.2	0.8	0.7	79.1	19.0	0.2	0.8	0.9
Miami	12.2	24.7	0.1	0.5	62.5	52.4	16.5	0.1	1.4	29.6
Milwaukee	60.9	30.2	0.8	1.8	6.3	94.5	2.3	0.3	0.8	2.1
Minneapolis-Saint Paul	78.8	10.4	2.4	5.3	3.0	95.9	1.1	0.4	1.6	1.0
Nashville	73.3	24.2	0.2	1.4	0.9	91.8	6.8	0.2	0.6	0.6
New Orleans	33.1	61.4	0.1	1.8	3.5	75.9	17.5	0.4	1.5	4.7
New York City	42.5	26.5	0.2	6.2	24.5	82.1	7.8	0.1	3.1	6.9
Norfolk	55.6	38.7	0.4	2.4	2.9	69.6	25.7	0.3	2.3	2.1
Oklahoma City	73.0	15.8	4.0	2.3	5.0	85.4	5.8	5.1	1.4	2.4
Omaha	82.3	13.0	0.6	1.0	3.1	94.3	2.4	0.3	1.0	2.1
Peoria	75.8	20.8	0.2	1.7	1.6	98.0	0.6	0.2	0.4	0.8
Philadelphia	49.8	40.5	0.2	2.5	7.0	87.0	8.6	0.2	1.7	2.5
Pittsburgh	71.7	25.6	0.2	1.6	0.9	94.8	4.1	0.1	0.5	0.5
Portland	83.0	7.5	1.1	5.2	3.2	91.7	0.7	0.9	2.4	4.3
Providence	65.1	12.7	0.8	5.7	15.7	94.7	1.4	0.3	1.0	2.5
Reading	71.6	8.8	0.1	0.9	18.5	97.4	0.9	0.1	0.6	1.0
Richmond	43.0	55.0	0.2	0.9	0.9	76.0	21.1	0.3	1.5	1.1
Rochester	58.4	30.8	0.4	1.7	8.7	94.6	2.5	0.3	1.2	1.4
Sacramento	53.5	14.8	0.9	14.4	16.3	79.9	4.0	0.9	5.1	10.1
Saint Louis	50.2	47.4	0.2	0.9	1.3	86.6	11.2	0.2	0.9	1.0
Salt Lake City	82.7	1.6	1.4	4.6	9.7	91.6	0.8	0.6	1.9	5.1
San Antonio	36.3	6.8	0.2	1.0	55.7	64.9	5.7	0.3	1.3	27.8
San Diego	58.8	8.9	0.5	11.1	20.7	70.8	3.7	0.7	4.5	20.3
San Francisco-Oakland	40.4	21.6	0.4	23.7	13.9	65.8	5.5	0.5	12.3	15.9
Scranton	96.8	1.6	0.1	0.9	0.7	98.2	0.8	0.1	0.4	0.5
Seattle	74.5	10.2	1.4	10.3	3.6	88.9	2.6	1.1	4.6	2.8
South Bend	74.7	20.7	0.3	0.9	3.4	95.9	1.5	0.3	1.1	1.2
Spokane	92.1	1.9	1.9	2.0	2.1	94.8	0.9	1.0	1.5	1.8
Springfield	63.7	18.2	0.2	1.0	16.9	91.8	1.4	0.1	1.5	5.2
Syracuse	73.8	19.9	1.2	2.1	2.9	96.5	1.4	0.4	0.8	0.9
Tampa	59.1	24.4	0.2	1.3	15.0	87.0	6.3	0.2	1.0	5.4
Toledo	75.2	19.6	0.2	1.0	4.0	94.9	1.4	0.2	0.9	2.6
Tulsa	78.1	13.5	4.5	1.4	2.6	86.7	2.4	9.0	0.4	1.5
Utica	85.0	10.3	0.2	1.1	3.4	95.4	2.3	0.2	0.6	1.5
Washington-Baltimore	33.6	61.8	0.3	1.4	3.0	75.8	15.8	0.2	4.2	4.1
Wichita	80.3	11.1	1.1	2.5	5.0	94.5	1.5	0.9	0.7	2.5
Youngstown	57.8	37.7	0.2	0.3	4.0	94.8	3.9	0.1	0.4	0.8
TOTAL	**50.9**	**27.6**	**0.4**	**5.1**	**16.0**	**80.7**	**7.1**	**0.4**	**3.5**	**8.4**

F Income Gaps between Cities and Suburbs

The chart below shows the 1989 per capita incomes for mother cities and suburban regions within each metro area in Inner America. Per capita income is determined by totaling the money received annually by all residents of a particular community (including children) and dividing the sum by the community's population.

The gap between urban and suburban per capita incomes is expressed from the city's perspective. (Example: The mother city of Albany had a per capita income of $13,742, which was 10.4 percent below the corresponding average of $15,339 for Albany's suburbs.) All figures are the author's analysis of statistics from the U.S. Census Bureau, which collects such detailed local income data once every decade.

| | **Per Capita Incomes** | | |
Metro Area	**Mother Cities**	**Suburbs**	**Gap (%)**
Albany	$13,742	$15,339	−10.4
Atlanta	$15,279	$16,884	− 9.5
Birmingham	$10,127	$14,802	−31.6
Boston	$14,606	$18,467	−20.9
Buffalo	$10,445	$14,529	−28.1
Canton	$10,133	$13,585	−25.4
Charlotte	$16,793	$13,484	+24.5
Chattanooga	$12,332	$12,684	− 2.8
Chicago	$12,742	$18,263	−30.2
Cincinnati	$12,547	$14,775	−15.1
Cleveland	$10,102	$15,953	−36.7
Columbus	$13,151	$15,768	−16.6
Dallas-Fort Worth	$15,334	$15,993	− 4.1
Dayton	$ 9,946	$15,067	−34.0
Denver	$15,590	$16,502	− 5.5
Des Moines	$13,710	$16,193	−15.3
Detroit	$ 9,560	$17,282	−44.7
Duluth	$12,484	$11,178	+11.7
Erie	$10,715	$13,361	−19.8
Fort Wayne	$12,726	$14,589	−12.8
Grand Rapids	$12,070	$14,082	−14.3
Hartford	$11,081	$20,055	−44.7
Honolulu	$18,554	$14,474	+28.2
Houston	$14,261	$15,445	− 7.7
Indianapolis	$14,478	$15,452	− 6.3
Jacksonville	$13,661	$15,263	−10.5
Kansas City	$12,949	$16,249	−20.3
Knoxville	$12,108	$13,630	−11.2
Los Angeles	$16,128	$16,561	− 2.6
Louisville	$11,527	$14,321	−19.5
Memphis	$11,682	$14,648	−20.2
Miami	$ 9,799	$15,594	−37.2
Milwaukee	$11,106	$17,009	−34.7
Minneapolis-Saint Paul	$14,361	$17,518	−18.0

Metro Area	Per Capita Incomes		Gap (%)
	Mother Cities	Suburbs	
Nashville	$14,490	$14,643	− 1.0
New Orleans	$11,372	$12,404	− 8.3
New York City	$15,700	$21,382	−26.6
Norfolk	$11,643	$13,870	−16.1
Oklahoma City	$13,528	$13,044	+ 3.7
Omaha	$13,957	$13,870	+ 0.6
Peoria	$14,039	$13,674	+ 2.7
Philadelphia	$11,938	$18,129	−34.1
Pittsburgh	$12,580	$14,005	−10.2
Portland	$14,478	$14,630	− 1.0
Providence	$11,838	$15,438	−23.3
Reading	$11,041	$15,686	−29.6
Richmond	$13,993	$16,417	−14.8
Rochester	$11,704	$16,181	−27.7
Sacramento	$14,087	$15,846	−11.1
Saint Louis	$10,798	$15,613	−30.8
Salt Lake City	$13,482	$11,774	+14.5
San Antonio	$10,884	$14,101	−22.8
San Diego	$16,401	$16,075	+ 2.0
San Francisco-Oakland	$17,991	$19,977	− 9.9
Scranton	$11,108	$12,136	− 8.5
Seattle	$16,769	$16,428	+ 2.1
South Bend	$11,949	$14,267	−16.2
Spokane	$12,375	$13,217	− 6.4
Springfield	$11,584	$15,016	−22.9
Syracuse	$11,351	$14,325	−20.8
Tampa	$13,277	$14,546	− 8.7
Toledo	$11,894	$15,860	−25.0
Tulsa	$15,434	$12,008	+28.5
Utica	$10,726	$12,196	−12.1
Washington-Baltimore	$15,106	$20,290	−25.5
Wichita	$14,516	$13,946	+ 4.1
Youngstown	$ 8,544	$12,579	−32.1
INNER AMERICA TOTAL	$14,069	$17,051	−17.5

G Inner America versus Outer America

Inner America comprises all ninety-three mother cities (places that had at least 100,000 residents in 1940) and their suburbs. Outer America consists of everything else—specifically, fringe metros and nonmetro areas.

Fringe metros are metropolitan areas that lack mother cities. A few fringe metros—Las Vegas and Phoenix, for example—were sparsely settled in 1940, but subsequently blossomed into sizable urban centers. Most remain relatively small today, such as Altoona, Pennsylvania, and Lincoln, Nebraska.

Nonmetro areas are all counties that are outside the official metropolitan boundaries set by the U.S. Office of Management and

Budget (OMB). This book applies OMB's 1995 boundaries throughout the period of 1940–2020 to allow uniform comparisons.

The chart below shows the populations of the two components of Inner America (mother cities and suburbs) and the two of Outer America (fringe metros and nonmetro areas). It also shows each component's share of the total U.S. population. Figures for 1940–1990 are the author's analysis of U.S. Census Bureau data. Figures for 2000–2020 are the author's projections.

| | Inner America | | | Outer America | | | |
| | Mother Cities | | Suburbs | | Fringe Metros | | Nonmetro Areas | |
Year	Population	Share (%)	Population	Share (%)	Population	Share (%)	Population	Share (%)
1940	38,167,315	28.9	31,133,540	23.6	20,128,851	15.2	42,734,863	32.3
1950	42,910,650	28.4	40,890,639	27.0	24,832,645	16.4	42,691,864	28.2
1960	45,157,927	25.2	60,082,442	33.5	31,362,899	17.5	42,719,907	23.8
1970	46,494,108	22.9	76,697,744	37.7	36,583,622	18.0	43,436,452	21.4
1980	43,642,039	19.3	89,156,019	39.4	44,462,365	19.6	49,285,382	21.8
1990	44,486,735	17.9	102,305,750	41.1	51,313,129	20.6	50,604,259	20.3
2000	44,007,004	16.0	116,492,027	42.4	59,565,150	21.7	54,556,819	19.9
2010	46,064,741	15.5	128,335,185	43.1	66,151,429	22.2	57,153,644	19.2
2020	49,526,870	15.3	141,107,422	43.7	72,322,180	22.4	59,762,528	18.5

H State-by-State Census Data, 1940–2020

The following pages contain data from every federal census from 1940 through 1990, as well as projections for 2000, 2010, and 2020. The charts show each state's population, as well as the share of its residents living in mother cities, suburbs, fringe metros, and nonmetro areas. Percentages might not add precisely to 100 due to rounding.

Figures for 1940–1990 are the author's analysis of U.S. Census Bureau data. Figures for 2000–2020 are a combination of Census Bureau projections of statewide populations and the author's projections of population distribution within the four classifications of communities.

1940 Census

State	Population	Mother Cities (%)	Suburbs (%)	Fringe Metros (%)	Nonmetro Areas (%)
Alabama	2,832,961	9.4	9.8	32.4	48.3
Alaska	72,524	0.0	0.0	0.0	100.0
Arizona	499,261	0.0	0.0	67.0	33.0
Arkansas	1,949,387	0.0	2.2	25.2	72.6
California	6,907,387	42.2	38.3	14.3	5.3
Colorado	1,123,296	28.7	16.9	17.1	37.3

State	Population	Mother Cities (%)	Suburbs (%)	Fringe Metros (%)	Nonmetro Areas (%)
Connecticut	1,709,242	27.7	56.6	7.3	8.4
Delaware	266,505	42.2	25.2	12.9	19.7
District of Columbia	663,091	100.0	0.0	0.0	0.0
Florida	1,897,414	23.9	20.7	37.6	17.8
Georgia	3,123,723	9.7	18.2	17.5	54.7
Hawaii	422,770	42.4	18.5	0.0	39.0
Idaho	524,873	0.0	0.0	17.4	82.6
Illinois	7,897,241	44.3	22.7	8.6	24.4
Indiana	3,427,796	21.0	24.9	18.7	35.4
Iowa	2,538,268	6.3	5.7	17.9	70.1
Kansas	1,801,028	13.1	11.1	6.5	69.3
Kentucky	2,845,627	11.2	10.1	13.8	64.9
Louisiana	2,363,880	20.9	5.8	34.2	39.1
Maine	847,226	0.0	0.0	37.7	62.3
Maryland	1,821,244	47.2	37.6	4.8	10.5
Massachusetts	4,316,721	38.3	56.6	3.7	1.4
Michigan	5,256,106	36.9	27.2	15.9	20.0
Minnesota	2,792,300	31.6	14.0	7.3	47.2
Mississippi	2,183,796	0.0	1.2	13.8	84.9
Missouri	3,784,664	32.1	15.6	9.8	42.5
Montana	559,456	0.0	0.0	14.9	85.1
Nebraska	1,315,834	17.0	4.8	8.4	69.8
Nevada	110,247	0.0	0.0	47.6	52.4
New Hampshire	491,524	0.0	50.2	0.0	49.8
New Jersey	4,160,165	29.4	70.6	0.0	0.0
New Mexico	531,818	0.0	0.0	31.0	69.0
New York	13,479,142	66.3	22.3	3.5	7.9
North Carolina	3,571,623	2.8	9.4	41.0	46.8
North Dakota	641,935	0.0	0.0	20.3	79.7
Ohio	6,907,612	38.4	32.6	7.2	21.8
Oklahoma	2,336,434	14.8	16.5	4.6	64.1
Oregon	1,089,684	28.0	26.5	9.7	35.8
Pennsylvania	9,900,180	30.0	34.5	18.5	17.0
Rhode Island	713,346	35.5	57.9	0.0	6.5
South Carolina	1,899,804	0.0	3.1	51.3	45.6
South Dakota	642,961	0.0	0.0	14.7	85.3
Tennessee	2,915,841	24.0	22.2	9.8	44.0
Texas	6,414,824	17.3	14.9	26.9	40.9
Utah	550,310	27.2	24.4	10.9	37.5
Vermont	359,231	0.0	0.0	23.8	76.2
Virginia	2,677,773	12.6	27.0	17.7	42.7
Washington	1,736,191	34.5	27.6	10.2	27.7
West Virginia	1,901,974	0.0	2.4	31.7	65.9
Wisconsin	3,137,587	18.7	17.2	24.3	39.8
Wyoming	250,742	0.0	0.0	22.9	77.1
TOTAL	132,164,569	28.9	23.6	15.2	32.3

1950 Census

State	Population	Mother Cities (%)	Suburbs (%)	Fringe Metros (%)	Nonmetro Areas (%)
Alabama	3,061,743	10.6	10.4	36.5	42.4
Alaska	128,643	0.0	0.0	0.0	100.0
Arizona	749,587	0.0	0.0	76.9	23.1
Arkansas	1,909,511	0.0	2.5	29.2	68.4
California	10,586,223	36.4	45.0	14.4	4.3
Colorado	1,325,089	31.4	20.2	18.7	29.8

State	Population	Mother Cities (%)	Suburbs (%)	Fringe Metros (%)	Nonmetro Areas (%)
Connecticut	2,007,280	24.9	59.8	7.2	8.0
Delaware	318,085	34.7	34.1	11.9	19.3
District of Columbia	802,178	100.0	0.0	0.0	0.0
Florida	2,771,305	20.9	28.6	37.5	13.0
Georgia	3,444,578	9.6	21.1	20.5	48.8
Hawaii	499,794	49.6	21.0	0.0	29.4
Idaho	588,637	0.0	0.0	21.1	78.9
Illinois	8,712,176	42.8	26.4	9.2	21.5
Indiana	3,934,224	20.6	27.6	19.1	32.7
Iowa	2,621,073	6.8	6.1	20.1	67.1
Kansas	1,905,299	15.6	14.0	7.3	63.0
Kentucky	2,944,806	12.5	12.0	14.8	60.6
Louisiana	2,683,516	21.3	7.4	37.8	33.5
Maine	913,774	0.0	0.0	39.5	60.5
Maryland	2,343,001	40.5	46.6	3.8	9.1
Massachusetts	4,690,514	36.4	58.4	3.8	1.3
Michigan	6,371,766	34.4	32.3	16.2	17.1
Minnesota	2,982,483	31.4	17.3	7.2	44.0
Mississippi	2,178,914	0.0	1.1	17.9	80.9
Missouri	3,954,653	33.2	18.9	10.0	37.8
Montana	591,024	0.0	0.0	18.4	81.6
Nebraska	1,325,510	18.9	5.5	9.8	65.7
Nevada	160,083	0.0	0.0	63.5	36.5
New Hampshire	533,242	0.0	52.2	0.0	47.8
New Jersey	4,835,329	25.7	74.3	0.0	0.0
New Mexico	681,187	0.0	0.0	39.5	60.5
New York	14,830,192	63.5	25.3	3.5	7.7
North Carolina	4,061,929	3.3	9.6	43.0	44.1
North Dakota	619,636	0.0	0.0	23.1	76.9
Ohio	7,946,627	36.5	37.0	6.6	19.8
Oklahoma	2,233,351	19.1	18.4	5.7	56.8
Oregon	1,521,341	24.6	28.3	12.1	35.1
Pennsylvania	10,498,012	29.7	35.6	18.9	15.9
Rhode Island	791,896	31.4	60.8	0.0	7.8
South Carolina	2,117,027	0.0	3.4	54.6	42.0
South Dakota	652,740	0.0	0.0	18.0	82.0
Tennessee	3,291,718	25.1	25.4	10.6	38.9
Texas	7,711,194	22.3	15.2	30.6	31.9
Utah	688,862	26.4	30.0	12.2	31.3
Vermont	377,747	0.0	0.0	25.4	74.6
Virginia	3,318,680	13.4	34.6	15.7	36.2
Washington	2,378,963	32.5	33.0	11.2	23.2
West Virginia	2,005,552	0.0	2.4	33.2	64.4
Wisconsin	3,434,575	18.6	19.1	25.6	36.8
Wyoming	290,529	0.0	0.0	27.2	72.8
TOTAL	151,325,798	28.4	27.0	16.4	28.2

1960 Census

State	Population	Mother Cities (%)	Suburbs (%)	Fringe Metros (%)	Nonmetro Areas (%)
Alabama	3,266,740	10.4	11.5	41.6	36.4
Alaska	226,167	0.0	0.0	36.6	63.4
Arizona	1,302,161	0.0	0.0	83.5	16.5
Arkansas	1,786,272	0.0	2.7	34.4	63.0
California	15,717,204	29.9	53.9	12.9	3.4
Colorado	1,753,947	28.2	29.2	20.9	21.7

State	Population	Mother Cities (%)	Suburbs (%)	Fringe Metros (%)	Nonmetro Areas (%)
Connecticut	2,535,234	18.6	66.7	7.3	7.4
Delaware	446,292	21.5	47.4	14.7	16.4
District of Columbia	763,956	100.0	0.0	0.0	0.0
Florida	4,951,560	15.5	37.2	38.7	8.5
Georgia	3,943,116	12.4	22.8	22.9	41.9
Hawaii	632,772	46.5	32.6	0.0	20.9
Idaho	667,191	0.0	0.0	22.7	77.3
Illinois	10,081,158	36.2	35.8	9.5	18.5
Indiana	4,662,498	20.3	31.6	18.0	30.0
Iowa	2,757,537	7.6	6.7	22.5	63.2
Kansas	2,178,611	17.3	19.7	8.5	54.5
Kentucky	3,038,156	12.9	16.5	16.7	53.9
Louisiana	3,257,022	19.3	11.1	41.2	28.5
Maine	969,265	0.0	0.0	40.8	59.2
Maryland	3,100,689	30.3	59.3	2.7	7.7
Massachusetts	5,148,578	30.2	64.4	4.1	1.2
Michigan	7,823,194	26.1	42.2	16.5	15.2
Minnesota	3,413,864	26.5	27.1	7.5	39.0
Mississippi	2,178,141	0.0	1.1	23.4	75.5
Missouri	4,319,813	28.4	28.5	9.7	33.4
Montana	674,767	0.0	0.0	22.6	77.4
Nebraska	1,411,330	21.4	7.3	11.9	59.5
Nevada	285,278	0.0	0.0	75.8	24.2
New Hampshire	606,921	0.0	55.5	0.0	44.5
New Jersey	6,066,782	19.2	80.8	0.0	0.0
New Mexico	951,023	0.0	0.0	45.6	54.4
New York	16,782,304	55.2	33.9	3.5	7.4
North Carolina	4,556,155	4.4	9.4	46.0	40.2
North Dakota	632,446	0.0	0.0	27.0	73.0
Ohio	9,706,397	30.9	44.9	6.1	18.1
Oklahoma	2,328,284	25.2	19.5	6.9	48.4
Oregon	1,768,687	21.1	31.5	13.4	34.0
Pennsylvania	11,319,366	26.1	39.9	19.4	14.6
Rhode Island	859,488	24.1	66.3	0.0	9.5
South Carolina	2,382,594	0.0	3.3	59.2	37.5
South Dakota	680,514	0.0	0.0	23.1	76.9
Tennessee	3,567,089	25.5	29.4	10.7	34.3
Texas	9,579,677	26.7	16.2	32.2	24.9
Utah	890,627	21.3	41.4	12.3	25.0
Vermont	389,881	0.0	0.0	27.4	72.6
Virginia	3,966,949	13.2	42.2	14.5	30.1
Washington	2,853,214	31.1	37.6	10.5	20.8
West Virginia	1,860,421	0.0	2.8	37.6	59.6
Wisconsin	3,951,777	18.8	22.2	26.4	32.6
Wyoming	330,066	0.0	0.0	33.3	66.7
TOTAL	**179,323,175**	**25.2**	**33.5**	**17.5**	**23.8**

1970 Census

State	Population	Mother Cities (%)	Suburbs (%)	Fringe Metros (%)	Nonmetro Areas (%)
Alabama	3,444,165	8.7	12.7	44.2	34.4
Alaska	300,382	0.0	0.0	41.5	58.5
Arizona	1,770,900	0.0	0.0	86.0	14.0
Arkansas	1,923,295	0.0	2.5	38.1	59.4
California	19,953,134	26.1	58.8	12.3	2.9
Colorado	2,207,259	23.3	36.7	22.6	17.4

State	Population	Mother Cities (%)	Suburbs (%)	Fringe Metros (%)	Nonmetro Areas (%)
Connecticut	3,031,709	14.9	69.9	7.6	7.5
Delaware	548,104	14.7	55.7	14.9	14.7
District of Columbia	756,510	100.0	0.0	0.0	0.0
Florida	6,789,443	16.4	36.7	39.7	7.2
Georgia	4,589,575	10.8	29.6	22.6	37.0
Hawaii	768,561	42.3	39.6	0.0	18.1
Idaho	712,567	0.0	0.0	24.4	75.6
Illinois	11,113,976	31.5	41.8	9.9	16.8
Indiana	5,193,669	23.4	29.5	18.4	28.7
Iowa	2,824,376	7.4	7.7	24.9	59.9
Kansas	2,246,578	19.8	20.0	9.5	50.7
Kentucky	3,218,706	11.2	20.2	18.2	50.4
Louisiana	3,641,306	16.3	15.1	41.4	27.1
Maine	992,048	0.0	0.0	41.2	58.8
Maryland	3,922,399	23.1	68.3	2.1	6.5
Massachusetts	5,689,170	25.7	68.7	4.3	1.2
Michigan	8,875,083	21.5	47.0	16.7	14.8
Minnesota	3,804,971	22.2	35.3	7.9	34.7
Mississippi	2,216,912	0.0	1.6	27.1	71.2
Missouri	4,676,501	24.2	34.9	10.2	30.8
Montana	694,409	0.0	0.0	24.4	75.6
Nebraska	1,483,493	23.4	9.3	12.2	55.1
Nevada	488,738	0.0	0.0	81.8	18.2
New Hampshire	737,681	0.0	58.7	0.0	41.3
New Jersey	7,168,164	15.4	84.6	0.0	0.0
New Mexico	1,016,000	0.0	0.0	50.4	49.6
New York	18,236,967	50.8	38.6	3.4	7.2
North Carolina	5,082,059	4.8	10.2	48.3	36.7
North Dakota	617,761	0.0	0.0	31.7	68.3
Ohio	10,652,017	27.2	49.8	5.8	17.2
Oklahoma	2,559,229	27.3	21.4	7.3	44.0
Oregon	2,091,385	18.2	36.2	14.7	30.9
Pennsylvania	11,793,909	23.7	42.2	20.0	14.1
Rhode Island	946,725	18.9	71.1	0.0	10.0
South Carolina	2,590,516	0.0	3.3	62.5	34.2
South Dakota	665,507	0.0	0.0	25.0	75.0
Tennessee	3,923,687	34.3	22.0	10.7	33.0
Texas	11,196,730	27.9	21.3	30.1	20.6
Utah	1,059,273	16.6	48.0	13.2	22.2
Vermont	444,330	0.0	0.0	30.2	69.8
Virginia	4,648,494	12.0	48.5	13.6	25.9
Washington	3,409,169	25.1	46.9	9.4	18.6
West Virginia	1,744,237	0.0	3.3	39.1	57.5
Wisconsin	4,417,731	16.2	24.5	28.2	31.1
Wyoming	332,416	0.0	0.0	32.4	67.6
TOTAL	203,211,926	22.9	37.7	18.0	21.4

1980 Census

State	Population	Mother Cities (%)	Suburbs (%)	Fringe Metros (%)	Nonmetro Areas (%)
Alabama	3,893,888	7.3	13.6	44.8	34.3
Alaska	401,851	0.0	0.0	43.4	56.6
Arizona	2,718,215	0.0	0.0	86.6	13.4
Arkansas	2,286,435	0.0	2.2	40.0	57.9
California	23,667,902	23.2	60.5	13.0	3.2
Colorado	2,889,964	17.0	43.2	23.0	16.7

State	Population	Mother Cities (%)	Suburbs (%)	Fringe Metros (%)	Nonmetro Areas (%)
Connecticut	3,107,576	13.0	71.3	7.7	8.0
Delaware	594,338	11.8	55.2	16.5	16.5
District of Columbia	638,333	100.0	0.0	0.0	0.0
Florida	9,746,324	11.9	39.2	41.6	7.3
Georgia	5,463,105	7.8	35.0	21.4	35.8
Hawaii	964,691	37.8	41.2	0.0	21.0
Idaho	943,935	0.0	0.0	27.2	72.8
Illinois	11,426,518	27.4	45.3	10.1	17.2
Indiana	5,490,224	20.7	31.6	18.4	29.2
Iowa	2,913,808	6.6	9.0	25.5	58.9
Kansas	2,363,679	18.7	22.0	9.4	49.9
Kentucky	3,660,777	8.2	20.6	18.7	52.6
Louisiana	4,205,900	13.3	17.7	43.3	25.7
Maine	1,124,660	0.0	0.0	40.2	59.8
Maryland	4,216,975	18.7	72.4	1.9	7.0
Massachusetts	5,737,037	23.2	70.3	5.1	1.4
Michigan	9,262,078	16.7	49.5	17.1	16.7
Minnesota	4,075,970	18.0	39.5	8.0	34.4
Mississippi	2,520,638	0.0	2.1	29.8	68.0
Missouri	4,916,686	18.3	37.7	11.3	32.6
Montana	786,690	0.0	0.0	24.0	76.0
Nebraska	1,569,825	20.0	13.1	13.3	53.6
Nevada	800,493	0.0	0.0	83.2	16.8
New Hampshire	920,610	0.0	60.0	0.0	40.0
New Jersey	7,364,823	13.2	86.8	0.0	0.0
New Mexico	1,302,894	0.0	0.0	54.1	45.9
New York	17,558,072	46.8	41.6	3.5	8.1
North Carolina	5,881,766	5.4	9.5	48.9	36.2
North Dakota	652,717	0.0	0.0	35.9	64.1
Ohio	10,797,630	23.3	52.2	5.9	18.6
Oklahoma	3,025,290	25.3	24.9	6.8	43.0
Oregon	2,633,105	14.0	38.9	15.5	31.7
Pennsylvania	11,863,895	20.2	43.2	21.4	15.2
Rhode Island	947,154	16.6	74.9	0.0	8.6
South Carolina	3,121,820	0.0	3.4	64.3	32.3
South Dakota	690,768	0.0	0.0	28.0	72.0
Tennessee	4,591,120	31.5	23.9	10.9	33.7
Texas	14,229,191	25.8	25.2	30.1	18.9
Utah	1,461,037	11.2	51.1	15.2	22.5
Vermont	511,456	0.0	0.0	30.3	69.7
Virginia	5,346,818	9.1	51.6	13.4	25.8
Washington	4,132,156	19.9	51.3	10.3	18.5
West Virginia	1,949,644	0.0	4.0	36.8	59.2
Wisconsin	4,705,767	13.5	25.0	29.0	32.5
Wyoming	469,557	0.0	0.0	29.9	70.1
TOTAL	**226,545,805**	**19.3**	**39.4**	**19.6**	**21.8**

1990 Census

State	Population	Mother Cities (%)	Suburbs (%)	Fringe Metros (%)	Nonmetro Areas (%)
Alabama	4,040,587	6.6	14.2	46.3	32.9
Alaska	550,043	0.0	0.0	41.1	58.9
Arizona	3,665,228	0.0	0.0	87.4	12.6
Arkansas	2,350,725	0.0	2.1	42.1	55.8
California	29,760,021	21.8	61.4	13.6	3.2
Colorado	3,294,394	14.2	45.9	24.3	15.6

State	Population	Mother Cities (%)	Suburbs (%)	Fringe Metros (%)	Nonmetro Areas (%)
Connecticut	3,287,116	12.5	71.3	7.8	8.4
Delaware	666,168	10.7	55.6	16.7	17.0
District of Columbia	606,900	100.0	0.0	0.0	0.0
Florida	12,937,926	9.8	37.8	45.3	7.1
Georgia	6,478,216	6.1	41.4	19.7	32.8
Hawaii	1,108,229	33.0	42.5	0.0	24.5
Idaho	1,006,749	0.0	0.0	29.4	70.6
Illinois	11,430,602	25.3	48.4	10.0	16.2
Indiana	5,544,159	20.3	32.6	18.5	28.5
Iowa	2,776,755	7.0	10.2	26.1	56.8
Kansas	2,477,574	18.3	25.7	9.8	46.2
Kentucky	3,685,296	7.3	21.5	19.5	51.7
Louisiana	4,219,973	11.8	18.7	44.4	25.1
Maine	1,227,928	0.0	0.0	40.3	59.7
Maryland	4,781,468	15.4	75.9	1.6	7.2
Massachusetts	6,016,425	22.8	70.4	5.4	1.5
Michigan	9,295,297	14.6	51.3	16.9	17.2
Minnesota	4,375,099	16.6	44.1	8.2	31.2
Mississippi	2,573,216	0.0	2.6	31.3	66.0
Missouri	5,117,073	16.3	40.1	11.9	31.8
Montana	799,065	0.0	0.0	23.9	76.1
Nebraska	1,578,385	21.3	14.0	14.6	50.1
Nevada	1,201,833	0.0	0.0	84.4	15.6
New Hampshire	1,109,252	0.0	61.9	0.0	38.1
New Jersey	7,730,188	12.0	88.0	0.0	0.0
New Mexico	1,515,069	0.0	0.0	55.6	44.4
New York	17,990,455	46.7	41.6	3.4	8.2
North Carolina	6,628,637	6.0	9.8	50.3	34.0
North Dakota	638,800	0.0	0.0	40.3	59.7
Ohio	10,847,115	22.3	53.5	5.6	18.6
Oklahoma	3,145,585	25.8	27.2	6.4	40.6
Oregon	2,842,321	15.4	39.3	15.1	30.2
Pennsylvania	11,881,643	18.7	43.6	22.6	15.1
Rhode Island	1,003,464	16.0	75.3	0.0	8.7
South Carolina	3,486,703	0.0	3.8	65.7	30.5
South Dakota	696,004	0.0	0.0	31.7	68.3
Tennessee	4,877,185	29.0	27.8	10.8	32.4
Texas	16,986,510	23.7	29.9	29.9	16.6
Utah	1,722,850	9.3	53.0	15.6	22.2
Vermont	562,758	0.0	0.0	31.5	68.5
Virginia	6,187,358	7.5	57.6	12.1	22.9
Washington	4,866,692	17.9	55.5	9.6	17.1
West Virginia	1,793,477	0.0	5.3	36.4	58.3
Wisconsin	4,891,769	12.8	25.2	30.1	31.9
Wyoming	453,588	0.0	0.0	29.6	70.4
TOTAL	248,709,873	17.9	41.1	20.6	20.3

2000 Projections

State	Population	Mother Cities (%)	Suburbs (%)	Fringe Metros (%)	Nonmetro Areas (%)
Alabama	4,451,000	6.3	14.7	47.2	31.8
Alaska	654,000	0.0	0.0	40.3	59.7
Arizona	4,798,000	0.0	0.0	87.9	12.1
Arkansas	2,629,000	0.0	2.1	43.9	54.0
California	32,523,000	18.9	63.8	13.8	3.6
Colorado	4,168,000	11.3	48.9	25.0	14.8

State	Population	Mother Cities (%)	Suburbs (%)	Fringe Metros (%)	Nonmetro Areas (%)
Connecticut	3,285,000	10.9	72.3	7.9	8.9
Delaware	767,000	9.9	55.9	16.8	17.4
District of Columbia	520,000	100.0	0.0	0.0	0.0
Florida	15,232,000	8.6	36.5	48.0	6.8
Georgia	7,874,000	5.1	46.9	18.4	29.7
Hawaii	1,256,000	30.2	42.3	0.0	27.5
Idaho	1,346,000	0.0	0.0	31.1	68.9
Illinois	12,050,000	21.6	51.8	10.3	16.3
Indiana	6,044,000	20.3	33.0	18.7	28.0
Iowa	2,900,000	7.3	11.0	26.5	55.1
Kansas	2,669,000	17.9	29.0	10.1	43.0
Kentucky	3,993,000	6.8	22.2	20.1	51.0
Louisiana	4,425,000	11.0	19.3	45.1	24.5
Maine	1,258,000	0.0	0.0	40.3	59.7
Maryland	5,274,000	13.6	78.0	1.3	7.1
Massachusetts	6,200,000	22.0	70.7	5.8	1.5
Michigan	9,680,000	13.7	52.2	16.6	17.5
Minnesota	4,830,000	16.3	47.0	8.1	28.5
Mississippi	2,813,000	0.0	3.1	32.7	64.2
Missouri	5,540,000	14.9	42.0	12.3	30.9
Montana	950,000	0.0	0.0	23.9	76.1
Nebraska	1,706,000	22.1	14.8	15.6	47.5
Nevada	1,873,000	0.0	0.0	85.2	14.8
New Hampshire	1,224,000	0.0	63.1	0.0	36.9
New Jersey	8,176,000	10.2	89.8	0.0	0.0
New Mexico	1,861,000	0.0	0.0	58.9	41.1
New York	18,147,000	43.7	43.9	3.6	8.8
North Carolina	7,779,000	6.5	9.9	51.3	32.3
North Dakota	660,000	0.0	0.0	43.7	56.3
Ohio	11,317,000	21.8	54.3	5.3	18.5
Oklahoma	3,373,000	26.2	29.4	6.1	38.4
Oregon	3,399,000	16.8	39.4	14.9	28.9
Pennsylvania	12,201,000	17.6	44.1	23.2	15.1
Rhode Island	997,000	15.3	75.8	0.0	8.9
South Carolina	3,857,000	0.0	4.0	66.7	29.2
South Dakota	776,000	0.0	0.0	34.6	65.4
Tennessee	5,656,000	27.8	30.3	10.7	31.3
Texas	20,120,000	20.1	35.1	29.8	14.9
Utah	2,208,000	8.1	54.1	15.9	21.9
Vermont	616,000	0.0	0.0	32.3	67.7
Virginia	6,997,000	6.6	61.8	11.1	20.6
Washington	5,857,000	16.7	59.5	8.1	15.7
West Virginia	1,840,000	0.0	6.6	36.1	57.4
Wisconsin	5,328,000	12.3	25.1	31.2	31.4
Wyoming	524,000	0.0	0.0	29.5	70.5
TOTAL	274,621,000	16.0	42.4	21.7	19.9

2010 Projections

State	Population	Mother Cities (%)	Suburbs (%)	Fringe Metros (%)	Nonmetro Areas (%)
Alabama	4,800,000	6.1	14.9	47.9	31.1
Alaska	744,000	0.0	0.0	41.0	59.0
Arizona	5,522,000	0.0	0.0	88.3	11.7
Arkansas	2,839,000	0.0	2.1	45.0	53.0
California	37,644,000	17.8	64.5	14.1	3.6
Colorado	4,660,000	10.2	50.2	25.3	14.2

State	Population	Mother Cities (%)	Suburbs (%)	Fringe Metros (%)	Nonmetro Areas (%)
Connecticut	3,400,000	11.1	72.0	7.9	9.0
Delaware	816,000	9.7	55.9	16.8	17.5
District of Columbia	559,000	100.0	0.0	0.0	0.0
Florida	17,363,000	7.9	35.9	49.4	6.7
Georgia	8,822,000	4.6	50.0	17.6	27.8
Hawaii	1,440,000	28.4	42.3	0.0	29.2
Idaho	1,558,000	0.0	0.0	32.1	67.9
Illinois	12,513,000	20.6	53.3	10.2	15.8
Indiana	6,317,000	20.4	33.3	18.8	27.5
Iowa	2,971,000	7.6	11.5	26.9	53.9
Kansas	2,847,000	17.8	30.8	10.3	41.1
Kentucky	4,172,000	6.5	22.6	20.5	50.4
Louisiana	4,684,000	10.6	19.7	45.5	24.1
Maine	1,322,000	0.0	0.0	40.4	59.6
Maryland	5,657,000	12.5	79.5	1.2	6.9
Massachusetts	6,433,000	22.2	70.3	5.9	1.6
Michigan	9,835,000	13.3	52.6	16.5	17.5
Minnesota	5,148,000	16.6	48.4	8.1	26.8
Mississippi	2,972,000	0.0	3.4	33.6	63.0
Missouri	5,865,000	14.2	43.1	12.5	30.2
Montana	1,039,000	0.0	0.0	23.9	76.1
Nebraska	1,807,000	22.9	15.3	16.2	45.7
Nevada	2,131,000	0.0	0.0	85.8	14.2
New Hampshire	1,326,000	0.0	63.9	0.0	36.1
New Jersey	8,638,000	10.0	90.0	0.0	0.0
New Mexico	2,156,000	0.0	0.0	60.8	39.2
New York	18,530,000	43.9	43.8	3.5	8.8
North Carolina	8,553,000	6.8	10.0	52.0	31.2
North Dakota	690,000	0.0	0.0	45.5	54.5
Ohio	11,504,000	21.8	54.7	5.2	18.3
Oklahoma	3,638,000	26.6	30.5	6.0	36.9
Oregon	3,802,000	17.6	39.6	14.8	28.1
Pennsylvania	12,352,000	17.4	44.1	23.6	14.9
Rhode Island	1,039,000	16.1	75.1	0.0	8.8
South Carolina	4,204,000	0.0	4.2	67.4	28.4
South Dakota	824,000	0.0	0.0	36.3	63.7
Tennessee	6,179,000	27.2	31.7	10.6	30.5
Texas	22,857,000	19.0	37.3	29.9	13.8
Utah	2,551,000	7.5	54.8	16.0	21.7
Vermont	652,000	0.0	0.0	32.9	67.1
Virginia	7,627,000	6.0	64.6	10.4	19.0
Washington	6,657,000	15.9	61.5	7.6	15.0
West Virginia	1,849,000	0.0	7.4	35.9	56.8
Wisconsin	5,590,000	12.4	24.9	31.9	30.8
Wyoming	607,000	0.0	0.0	29.4	70.6
TOTAL	297,705,000	15.5	43.1	22.2	19.2

2020 Projections

State	Population	Mother Cities (%)	Suburbs (%)	Fringe Metros (%)	Nonmetro Areas (%)
Alabama	5,098,000	6.0	15.0	48.2	30.8
Alaska	839,000	0.0	0.0	42.1	57.9
Arizona	6,109,000	0.0	0.0	88.6	11.4
Arkansas	2,996,000	0.0	2.0	45.6	52.4
California	45,278,000	17.2	64.9	14.3	3.6
Colorado	5,012,000	9.6	51.0	25.5	13.9

State	Population	Mother Cities (%)	Suburbs (%)	Fringe Metros (%)	Nonmetro Areas (%)
Connecticut	3,620,000	11.5	71.8	7.8	9.0
Delaware	847,000	9.8	55.9	16.8	17.5
District of Columbia	623,000	100.0	0.0	0.0	0.0
Florida	19,633,000	7.6	35.7	50.1	6.6
Georgia	9,551,000	4.4	51.6	17.3	26.7
Hawaii	1,679,000	27.7	42.4	0.0	30.0
Idaho	1,681,000	0.0	0.0	32.7	67.3
Illinois	13,121,000	20.2	54.0	10.2	15.6
Indiana	6,479,000	20.6	33.4	18.8	27.2
Iowa	3,019,000	7.8	11.8	27.2	53.3
Kansas	3,027,000	17.9	31.7	10.3	40.1
Kentucky	4,281,000	6.4	22.8	20.7	50.1
Louisiana	4,990,000	10.5	19.9	45.7	23.9
Maine	1,395,000	0.0	0.0	40.4	59.6
Maryland	6,070,000	12.0	80.2	1.1	6.7
Massachusetts	6,733,000	22.7	69.9	5.9	1.6
Michigan	10,000,000	13.4	52.7	16.5	17.5
Minnesota	5,407,000	17.1	49.0	8.0	25.8
Mississippi	3,090,000	0.0	3.5	34.1	62.4
Missouri	6,138,000	13.9	43.6	12.6	29.8
Montana	1,094,000	0.0	0.0	23.9	76.1
Nebraska	1,892,000	23.4	15.5	16.5	44.6
Nevada	2,242,000	0.0	0.0	86.2	13.8
New Hampshire	1,410,000	0.0	64.4	0.0	35.6
New Jersey	9,239,000	10.0	90.0	0.0	0.0
New Mexico	2,455,000	0.0	0.0	61.6	38.4
New York	19,358,000	44.3	43.5	3.5	8.7
North Carolina	9,110,000	7.0	10.0	52.4	30.6
North Dakota	715,000	0.0	0.0	46.3	53.7
Ohio	11,672,000	22.1	54.7	5.0	18.2
Oklahoma	3,930,000	27.0	31.0	5.9	36.1
Oregon	4,177,000	18.0	39.7	14.7	27.6
Pennsylvania	12,566,000	17.6	44.0	23.7	14.7
Rhode Island	1,104,000	17.0	74.3	0.0	8.7
South Carolina	4,516,000	0.0	4.3	67.8	28.0
South Dakota	854,000	0.0	0.0	37.2	62.8
Tennessee	6,529,000	27.2	32.4	10.5	29.9
Texas	25,731,000	18.5	38.4	29.9	13.2
Utah	2,780,000	7.2	55.2	16.0	21.6
Vermont	673,000	0.0	0.0	33.2	66.8
Virginia	8,203,000	5.8	66.0	10.0	18.1
Washington	7,446,000	15.6	62.5	7.4	14.5
West Virginia	1,850,000	0.0	7.8	35.8	56.4
Wisconsin	5,789,000	12.8	24.6	32.2	30.3
Wyoming	668,000	0.0	0.0	29.2	70.8
TOTAL	322,719,000	15.3	43.7	22.4	18.5

Electoral College

The Electoral College determines who wins a presidential election. Each state's electoral votes are awarded to the nominee who receives the most popular votes in that state. The top candidate is not required to draw a majority of popular votes; a plurality (one or more votes in excess of the next leading candidate) is all that's needed to earn the state's support in the Electoral College.

This book uses the same principle to measure the political balance of power. It puts states in four categories according to their population patterns: A city state is one in which mother cities have the most residents. A suburban state is one where the suburbs have the population edge. A fringe state is dominated by fringe metros, a nonmetro state by nonmetro areas.

Each state's classification is determined solely by the type of community that holds a plurality of population. A majority is not required. (Example: Missouri's 1996 estimated population was divided this way: 14.8 percent in mother cities, 40.6 percent in suburbs, 12.5 percent in fringe metros, and 32.1 percent in nonmetro areas. Missouri therefore was a suburban state in 1996.)

States are classified in all elections listed according to the metropolitan boundaries established by the U.S. Office of Management and Budget in 1995. The result is a slight overemphasis of suburban power in the early years of the study period. New Hampshire, for example, is classified as a suburban state long before it actually became suburbanized. But the overriding benefit of this system is that it allows direct comparisons of suburban growth over several decades in standardized geographic areas.

The chart below shows the number of states and electoral votes in each category.

Figures for 1940–1996 are the author's analysis of U.S. Census Bureau data. Figures for 2000–2024 are the author's projections. "EV" means electoral votes.

	City States		Suburban States		Fringe States		Nonmetro States	
Year	States	EV	States	EV	States	EV	States	EV
1940	8	162	6	85	3	18	31	266
1944	7	138	7	108	4	23	30	262
1948	7	136	8	116	5	33	28	246
1952	3	78	14	194	7	73	24	186
1956	3	78	14	194	8	84	23	175
1960[1]	2	48	17	240	8	84	23	165
1964[2]	3	50	18	252	8	88	22	148
1968	3	50	19	264	8	88	21	136
1972	4	58	20	277	9	96	18	107
1976	2	44	21	281	9	96	19	117
1980	2	44	21	281	9	96	19	117
1984	2	39	22	288	9	106	18	105
1988	2	39	22	288	9	106	18	105
1992	2	36	23	320	8	82	18	100
1996	2	36	23	320	8	82	18	100
2000	1	3	24	353	8	82	18	100

Year	City States		Suburban States		Fringe States		Nonmetro States	
	States	EV	States	EV	States	EV	States	EV
2004	1	3	25	362	9	96	16	77
2008	2	34	24	331	9	96	16	77
2012	2	32	24	332	9	98	16	76
2016	2	32	24	332	9	98	16	76
2020	2	32	24	332	9	98	16	76
2024	2	31	24	333	9	99	16	75

1. Alaska and Hawaii cast their first electoral votes in 1960.
2. The District of Columbia cast its first electoral votes in 1964.

J Presidential Election Summaries, 1940–1996

The chart below summarizes the results of every presidential election between 1940 and 1996, including breakdowns for city states, suburban states, fringe states, and nonmetro states.

Left-hand columns show each category's popular vote total, as well as its share of all votes nationwide. (Example: 20,784,474 people voted in city states in 1940, accounting for 41.7 percent of the U.S. total.)

Right-hand columns show each major candidate's percentage of the popular votes cast within each category, along with his number of electoral votes. (Example: Franklin Roosevelt received 52.8 percent of the popular votes cast in city states in 1940, good for 143 electoral votes.)

All votes in a particular state were allocated to its designated category, reflecting the power wielded by the state's dominant type of community. That's why all 1996 votes in New York—whether cast in cities, suburbs, or rural areas—were included in the city states total, while all California votes were lumped in with suburban states. Figures are the author's analysis of official election returns and U.S. Census Bureau data.

1940

Category	U.S. Total		Franklin Roosevelt (D)		Wendell Willkie (R)	
	Votes	Share (%)	PV (%)	EV	PV (%)	EV
City states	20,784,474	41.7	52.8	143	46.7	19
Suburban states	9,416,332	18.9	53.0	85	46.6	0
Fringe states	735,509	1.5	74.8	18	25.1	0
Nonmetro states	18,964,103	38.0	57.0	203	42.6	63
TOTAL	49,900,418		54.7	449	44.8	82

1944

Category	U.S. Total		Franklin Roosevelt (D)		Thomas Dewey (R)	
	Votes	Share (%)	PV (%)	EV	PV (%)	EV
City states	17,301,258	36.1	51.6	113	48.0	25
Suburban states	12,600,985	26.3	53.0	108	46.5	0
Fringe states	778,053	1.6	69.5	23	29.4	0
Nonmetro states	17,296,374	36.1	54.7	188	44.1	74
TOTAL	**47,976,670**		**53.4**	**432**	**45.9**	**99**

1948

Category	U.S. Total		Harry Truman (D)		Thomas Dewey (R)		Other*	
	Votes	Share (%)	PV (%)	EV	PV (%)	EV	PV (%)	EV
City states	16,766,431	34.4	48.0	67	47.6	69	4.4	0
Suburban states	13,852,995	28.4	48.5	45	48.2	71	3.3	0
Fringe states	1,375,732	2.8	42.1	15	27.6	0	30.3	18
Nonmetro states	16,798,668	34.4	52.6	176	41.4	49	6.0	21
TOTAL	**48,793,826**		**49.6**	**303**	**45.1**	**189**	**5.4**	**39**

*Includes Strom Thurmond (SR), Henry Wallace (P), and all minor candidates. Thurmond received 2.4 percent of the national popular vote and 39 electoral votes. Wallace received 2.4 percent of the national popular vote and 0 electoral votes.

1952

Category	U.S. Total		Dwight Eisenhower (R)		Adlai Stevenson (D)	
	Votes	Share (%)	PV (%)	EV	PV (%)	EV
City states	12,239,400	19.9	55.5	78	43.8	0
Suburban states	25,936,529	42.1	55.3	194	44.1	0
Fringe states	5,611,992	9.1	51.4	41	48.6	32
Nonmetro states	17,762,997	28.9	55.8	129	43.8	57
TOTAL	**61,550,918**		**55.1**	**442**	**44.4**	**89**

1956

Category	U.S. Total*		Dwight Eisenhower (R)		Adlai Stevenson (D)	
	Votes	Share (%)	PV (%)	EV	PV (%)	EV
City states	12,160,452	19.6	60.6	78	39.3	0
Suburban states	26,723,810	43.1	58.3	194	41.2	0
Fringe states	6,048,372	9.8	51.8	51	45.4	32
Nonmetro states	17,094,274	27.6	55.6	134	43.7	41
TOTAL	**62,026,908**		**57.4**	**457**	**42.0**	**73**

*Walter Jones (I) received 1 electoral vote.

1960

Category	U.S. Total*		John Kennedy (D)		Richard Nixon (R)	
	Votes	Share (%)	PV (%)	EV	PV (%)	EV
City states	7,475,784	10.9	52.5	48	47.3	0
Suburban states	37,428,612	54.4	50.2	135	49.5	105
Fringe states	7,494,378	10.9	50.6	64	46.7	14
Nonmetro states	16,439,445	23.9	47.0	56	52.0	100
TOTAL	**68,838,219**		**49.7**	**303**	**49.5**	**219**

*Harry Byrd (I) received 15 electoral votes.

1964

Category	U.S. Total		Lyndon Johnson (D)		Barry Goldwater (R)	
	Votes	Share (%)	PV (%)	EV	PV (%)	EV
City states	7,572,143	10.7	69.3	50	30.6	0
Suburban states	38,519,366	54.5	63.0	252	36.8	0
Fringe states	8,633,368	12.2	50.2	55	47.3	33
Nonmetro states	15,919,633	22.5	58.3	129	41.6	19
TOTAL	**70,644,510**		**61.1**	**486**	**38.5**	**52**

1968

Category	U.S. Total		Richard Nixon (R)		Hubert Humphrey (D)		George Wallace (AI)	
	Votes	Share (%)	PV (%)	EV	PV (%)	EV	PV (%)	EV
City states	7,198,484	9.8	43.5	0	50.8	50	5.0	0
Suburban states	41,132,555	56.2	45.1	169	45.5	95	9.0	0
Fringe states	10,310,018	14.1	36.3	42	32.4	25	31.1	21
Nonmetro states	14,570,818	19.9	43.7	90	38.2	21	17.9	25
TOTAL	**73,211,875**		**43.4**	**301**	**42.7**	**191**	**13.5**	**46**

1972

Category	U.S. Total*		Richard Nixon (R)		George McGovern (D)	
	Votes	Share (%)	PV (%)	EV	PV (%)	EV
City states	8,800,796	11.3	59.2	55	40.2	3
Suburban states	45,458,327	58.5	58.0	262	40.0	14
Fringe states	11,495,671	14.8	68.4	96	30.1	0
Nonmetro states	11,963,760	15.4	64.6	107	33.5	0
TOTAL	**77,718,554**		**60.7**	**520**	**37.5**	**17**

*John Hospers (L) received 1 electoral vote.

1976

Category	U.S. Total* Votes	Share (%)	Jimmy Carter (D) PV (%)	EV	Gerald Ford (R) PV (%)	EV
City states	6,703,000	8.2	52.6	44	46.7	0
Suburban states	46,662,965	57.2	48.7	109	49.0	171
Fringe states	13,528,305	16.6	51.8	83	46.8	13
Nonmetro states	14,661,619	18.0	51.6	61	46.6	56
TOTAL	**81,555,889**		**50.1**	**297**	**48.0**	**240**

*Ronald Reagan (R) received 1 electoral vote.

1980

Category	U.S. Total Votes	Share (%)	Ronald Reagan (R) PV (%)	EV	Jimmy Carter (D) PV (%)	EV	Other* PV (%)	EV
City states	6,377,196	7.4	45.7	41	44.8	3	9.4	0
Suburban states	48,850,041	56.5	50.3	253	39.9	28	9.8	0
Fringe states	15,447,791	17.9	53.7	96	41.6	0	4.6	0
Nonmetro states	15,840,193	18.3	51.3	99	42.1	18	6.6	0
TOTAL	**86,515,221**		**50.7**	**489**	**41.0**	**49**	**8.2**	**0**

*Includes John Anderson (NU) and all minor candidates. Anderson received 6.6 percent of the national popular vote.

1984

Category	U.S. Total Votes	Share (%)	Ronald Reagan (R) PV (%)	EV	Walter Mondale (D) PV (%)	EV
City states	7,018,098	7.6	52.6	36	47.0	3
Suburban states	53,227,284	57.4	57.6	278	41.7	10
Fringe states	17,696,981	19.1	63.4	106	36.2	0
Nonmetro states	14,710,479	15.9	60.6	105	38.6	0
TOTAL	**92,652,842**		**58.8**	**525**	**40.6**	**13**

1988

Category	U.S. Total* Votes	Share (%)	George Bush (R) PV (%)	EV	Michael Dukakis (D) PV (%)	EV
City states	6,678,560	7.3	46.6	0	52.5	39
Suburban states	52,842,208	57.7	52.5	240	46.5	48
Fringe states	17,900,007	19.5	58.0	106	41.2	0
Nonmetro states	14,174,034	15.5	54.1	80	44.9	24
TOTAL	**91,594,809**		**53.4**	**426**	**45.6**	**111**

*Lloyd Bentsen (D) received 1 electoral vote.

1992

Category	U.S. Total Votes	Share (%)	Bill Clinton (D) PV (%)	EV	George Bush (R) PV (%)	EV	Ross Perot (I) PV (%)	EV
City states	7,154,497	6.9	50.8	36	33.1	0	15.4	0
Suburban states	65,872,241	63.1	43.3	258	36.3	62	19.8	0
Fringe states	15,170,125	14.5	40.6	18	42.1	64	16.6	0
Nonmetro states	16,228,151	15.5	40.7	58	39.7	42	19.0	0
TOTAL	**104,425,014**		**43.0**	**370**	**37.4**	**168**	**18.9**	**0**

1996

Category	U.S. Total Votes	Share (%)	Bill Clinton (D) PV (%)	EV	Robert Dole (R) PV (%)	EV	Ross Perot (RE) PV (%)	EV
City states	6,501,855	6.8	60.2	36	30.0	0	7.8	0
Suburban states	60,167,764	62.5	49.6	237	40.1	83	8.4	0
Fringe states	14,712,129	15.3	46.8	51	44.7	31	7.6	0
Nonmetro states	14,892,816	15.5	45.2	55	44.0	45	9.4	0
TOTAL	**96,274,564**		**49.2**	**379**	**40.7**	**159**	**8.4**	**0**

Party abbreviations: AI—American Independent, D—Democratic, I—Independent, L—Libertarian, NU—National Unity, P—Progressive, R—Republican, RE—Reform, SR—States' Rights Democratic.

Notes

Listed below are the sources of information for *The United States of Suburbia*. Complete citations are included for all sources except the U.S. Census Bureau, other federal agencies, and state and local boards of elections. A single chart in this book often is based on data from several Census Bureau reports or statistics from dozens of state elections boards; these agencies are cited in a general way in order to keep these footnotes concise. A reference to "author's analysis" means that the author has used raw data from the listed source to generate original statistics.

Preface

1. Michael Lewis, *Trail Fever* (New York: Alfred A. Knopf, 1997), p. 289.
2. Cited in Kenneth Jackson, *Crabgrass Frontier* (New York: Oxford University Press, 1985), p. 28.
3. Cited in G. Scott Thomas, *The Pursuit of the White House* (New York: Greenwood Press, 1987), p. vii.

1. Blue Tide: Election Night 1996

1. NBC, November 5, 1996, 7 P.M. (EST).
2. Bill Nichols, "Native Son Is Toasted in Little Rock," *USA Today*, November 6, 1996, p. 4A.
3. Thomas Edsall and Dan Balz, "Straightaway till November, Then a Fork," *Washington Post*, August 26, 1996, p. A15.
4. Bob Woodward, *The Choice* (New York: Simon & Schuster, 1996), p. 420.
5. Jeffrey Roberts, "Parties Tuning in to Suburbs' Hopes," *Denver Post*, August 25, 1996, p. A1.
6. Author's analysis of U.S. Census Bureau data.
7. Chris Kelley, "'Infomercial for Suburbs': Presidential Campaign Seems Devoid of Attention to Problems of Cities," *Chicago Tribune*, November 2, 1996, p. 6.
8. "But Why Didn't They Mention Cities?" *Buffalo News*, October 8, 1996, p. B2.
9. Author's analysis of Clinton–Dole debate transcript, October 6, 1996.
10. Howard Wilkinson, "Dole Needed Bigger Slice of Hamilton County Pie," *Cincinnati Enquirer*, November 7, 1996, p. A5.
11. Voter News Service exit poll, November 5, 1996, as posted on CNN/*Time* AllPolitics website (http://allpolitics.com), November 12, 1996 [henceforth referred to as VNS exit poll 1996].
12. NBC, November 5, 1996, 7:40 P.M. (EST).

13. CBS, November 5, 1996, 7:50 P.M. (EST).

14. ABC, November 5, 1996, 8:10 P.M. (EST).

15. Author's analysis of U.S. Census Bureau data; VNS exit poll 1996.

16. Andrew Miga and Joe Battenfeld, "Kerry Gets the Nod from Massachusetts Voters," *Boston Herald*, November 6, 1996, p. 3.

17. Susan Kuczka and Lisa Black, "Lake County Democrats Overwhelm a Stunned GOP," *Chicago Tribune*, November 7, 1996, p. 9.

18. Ken Armstrong, "In Defeat, Salvi Maintains Hope Bid for Senate, House May Be in His Future," *Chicago Tribune*, November 7, 1996, p. 2; Elizabeth Schwinn, "Targets of Gun Control Advocates Lose in 10 Contests," *Portland Oregonian*, November 7, 1996, p. A19; author's analysis of official election returns.

19. CBS, November 5, 1996, 8:30 P.M. (EST).

20. Lois Romano, "The Win Blows in Little Rock," *Washington Post*, November 6, 1996, p. F2.

21. ABC, November 5, 1996, 9:10 P.M. (EST).

22. VNS exit poll 1996.

23. Patricia Lopez Baden, "Wellstone's Strategy Pays Dividends," *Minneapolis Star-Tribune*, November 6, 1996, p. 17A.

24. Richard Wolf, "Voters' Message Seems to Be: End Partisanship," *USA Today*, November 6, 1996, p. 1A.

25. NBC, November 5, 1996, 10:15 P.M. (EST).

26. VNS exit poll 1996.

27. Royal Ford, "Shaheen Victory Shows Power of the Middle," *Boston Globe*, November 7, 1996, p. B18.

28. CNN, November 5, 1996, 6:25 P.M. (EST).

29. "A Pitched Battle for the House," *USA Today*, November 6, 1996, p. 11A; VNS exit poll 1996.

30. ABC, November 5, 1996, 10:40 P.M. (EST).

31. Mimi Hall, "Perot Party's Legacy Could Be Its Effort," *USA Today*, November 5, 1996, p. 8A.

32. CBS, November 5, 1996, 10:42 P.M. (EST).

33. VNS exit poll 1996.

34. David Postman, Jim Simon, Lynne Varner, and Jack Broom, "Locke Wins Decisively," *Seattle Times*, November 6, 1996, p. B1.

35. Deeann Glamser, "A True 'American Dream' for Asian-American Locke," *USA Today*, November 7, 1996, p. 16A.

36. VNS exit poll 1996.

37. Gebe Martinez, "Sanchez Holds Slim Lead over Dornan in 46th District Race," *Los Angeles Times*, November 6, 1996, p. 1; Faye Fiore and Janet Hook, "Absentee Ballots Key to Dornan Cliffhanger," *Los Angeles Times*, November 7, 1996, p. 3.

38. Walter Shapiro, "Dole Marathon Gives Measure of the Man," *USA Today*, November 4, 1996, p. 2A; Judy Keen, "'Last Crusade' Over, He Looks Ahead," *USA Today*, November 6, 1996, p. 4A.

39. CNN, November 5, 1996, 11:23 P.M. (EST).

40. David Broder, "Is Clinton Reinventing Democratic Party?" *Buffalo News*, August 18, 1997, p. B3.

41. CBS, November 6, 1996, 12:05 A.M. (EST).

42. Ibid., 12:15 A.M. (EST).

2. Inevitable as Sunrise: 1939–1990

1. Alice Goldfarb Marquis, *Hopes and Ashes* (New York: Free Press, 1986), pp. 202–204, 205–209.

2. Kenneth Jackson, *Crabgrass Frontier* (New York: Oxford University Press, 1985), p. 13; author's analysis of U.S. Census Bureau data.

3. Ross Gregory, *America 1941* (New York: Free Press, 1989), p. 89.

4. Jon Teaford, *The Rough Road to Renaissance* (Baltimore: Johns Hopkins University Press, 1990), pp. 10–18.

5. Marquis, *Hopes and Ashes*, pp. 205–209.

6. Jon Teaford, *The Twentieth-Century American City* (Baltimore: Johns Hopkins University Press, 1986), p. 74.

7. Jackson, *Crabgrass Frontier*, pp. 232–33; Teaford, *Twentieth-Century*, p. 100.

8. Jackson, *Crabgrass Frontier*, pp. 234–37.

9. Kevin Phillips, *Boiling Point* (New York: Random House, 1993), pp. 15–18.

10. James Howard Kunstler, *The Geography of Nowhere* (New York: Simon & Schuster, 1993), pp. 102–104.

11. Teaford, *Twentieth-Century*, p. 110.

12. Robert Fishman, *Bourgeois Utopias* (New York: Basic Books, 1987), p. 166.

13. Teaford, *Renaissance*, pp. 93–95.

14. Jackson, *Crabgrass Frontier*, pp. 249–50.

15. Teaford, *Twentieth-Century*, pp. 99, 110.

16. Frank Lloyd Wright, *The Living City* (New York: Horizon Press, 1958), pp. 50, 67.

17. Theodore White, *The Making of the President 1960* (New York: Atheneum, 1961), p. 250.

18. Gregory, *America 1941*, p. 93; White, *The Making of the President 1960*, p. 265.

19. Teaford, *Twentieth-Century*, p. 103; Jackson, *Crabgrass Frontier*, p. 241.

20. Cited in Irwin Ross, *The Loneliest Campaign* (New York: Signet, 1968), p. 248.

21. Ibid.

22. William Manchester, *The Glory and the Dream* (Boston: Little, Brown & Co., 1973), p. 226.

23. Ibid., p. 365.

24. Allen Yarnell, *Democrats and Progressives* (Berkeley: University of California Press, 1974), pp. 34–35.

25. Ross, *The Loneliest Campaign*, p. 21.

26. Ibid., p. 172.

27. Author's analysis of official election returns.

28. White, *The Making of the President 1960*, p. 267.

29. Author's analysis of official election returns.

30. Ibid.

31. Ibid.

32. Teaford, *Renaissance*, pp. 62–63; author's analysis of official election returns.

33. Jackson, *Crabgrass Frontier*, pp. 257–59; William Whyte, *City* (New York: Doubleday, 1988), p. 284.

34. White, *The Making of the President 1960*, pp. 196–97.

35. Author's analysis of official election returns.

36. Ibid.

37. Teaford, *Twentieth-Century*, pp. 136–37.

38. "Black-White Relations: Always a Problem?" *Gallup Poll Monthly* (October 1995): 9.

39. Thomas Byrne Edsall and Mary Edsall, *Chain Reaction* (New York: W. W. Norton & Co., 1991), p. 48.

40. Ibid., pp. 21, 88.

41. Manchester, *The Glory and the Dream*, p. 1285.

42. Edsall and Edsall, *Chain Reaction*, pp. 181–82.

43. Teaford, *Renaissance*, pp. 210–11.

44. Jackson, *Crabgrass Frontier*, p. 266.

45. Joel Garreau, "Edge Cities in Profile," *American Demographics* (February 1994): 26.

46. Author's analysis of U.S. Census Bureau data and official election returns.

47. Author's analysis of U.S. Census Bureau data.

48. Ibid.

49. Teaford, *Renaissance*, p. 217.

50. Ibid., p. 231.

51. Cited in Whyte, *City*, p. 284.

52. Teaford, *Twentieth-Century*, pp. 140–41.

53. Author's analysis of U.S. Bureau of Labor Statistics data.

54. Fred Branfman, "Moving toward the Abyss," *Salon* (June 3, 1996): online; *Current Biography Yearbook 1975* (New York: H. W. Wilson Co., 1976), p. 50.

55. Kevin Phillips, *The Politics of Rich and Poor* (New York: Random House, 1990), pp. 48–49 (emphasis added); Teaford, *Renaissance*, p. 261.

56. Kevin Phillips, *Post-Conservative America* (New York: Random House, 1982), pp. 125–27; author's analysis of official election returns.

57. Jimmy Carter, *Keeping Faith* (New York: Bantam, 1982), p. 552.

58. Hamilton Jordan, *Crisis* (New York: G. P. Putnam's Sons, 1982), p. 357.

59. *Inaugural Addresses of the Presidents of the United States* (Washington, D.C.: U.S. Government Printing Office, 1989), p. 333.

60. Teaford, *Renaissance*, p. 261.

61. Whyte, *City*, p. 328.

62. Phillips, *Boiling Point*, p. 50.

63. Cited in ibid., pp. 103–104.

64. Cited in Phillips, *The Politics of Rich and Poor*, p. 87.

65. Tom Watson, "Liberal, Pragmatic Mondale Follows Careful Path to Power," *Congressional Quarterly Weekly Report* (October 8, 1983): 2079.

66. "Campaign '84: The Inside Story," *Newsweek* (November/December 1984 special issue): 86.

67. "Reagan Accepts Presidential Nomination," *Congressional Quarterly Weekly Report* (August 25, 1984): 2124.

68. Tom Watson, "Hart Pushes 'Third Options' in Long-Shot Presidential Bid," *Congressional Quarterly Weekly Report* (December 3, 1983): 2535–39.

69. "Campaign '84," *Newsweek*, p. 45.

70. Harrison Donnelly, "Democrats Launch the Mondale-Ferraro Team," *Congressional Quarterly Weekly Report* (July 21, 1984): 1737; "A 'Retreat of Civil Rights,'" *USA Today*, May 21, 1997, p. 13A; Marshall Frady, *Jesse* (New York: Random House, 1996), p. 357.

71. Peter Canellos, "A Look Back at Career," *Boston Globe*, January 4, 1989, p. 22; "We Want to Say Thank You," *Boston Globe*, December 21, 1990, p. 35.

72. Christine Chinlund, "Bush Stumps to Cement His Illinois Lead," *Boston Globe,* October 30, 1988, p. 26.

73. John Aloysius Farrell, "New Jersey: A Key State Turns Sour on Dukakis," *Boston Globe,* October 3, 1988, p. 8.

74. George Will, "There They Go Again, Those Democrats," *Washington Post,* November 13, 1988, p. C7.

3. No Longer Sub to the Urb: 1991–1996

1. Sara Fritz and William Eaton, "Congress Authorizes Gulf War," *Los Angeles Times,* January 13, 1991, p. 1.

2. Timothy McNulty, "Roots of Crisis Lie in Policy, Personalities of Leaders," *Chicago Tribune,* January 13, 1991, p. 5.

3. George Will, "Bush's Iraqi Alibi," *Washington Post,* August 10, 1990, p. A15.

4. Ibid.

5. Tom Kenworthy and Helen Dewar, "U.N. Chief, Europeans Discuss Peace Plan," *Washington Post,* January 12, 1991, p. A1.

6. Dan Balz and Molly Moore, "Bush Asks Nation to Back 'Defensive' Mission as U.S. Forces Begin Arriving in Saudi Arabia," *Washington Post,* August 9, 1990, p. A1.

7. McNulty, "Roots of Crisis," p. 5.

8. E. J. Dionne Jr., "For Bush, a Risky Commitment," *Washington Post,* August 9, 1990, p. A1.

9. Will, "Bush's Iraqi Alibi," p. A15.

10. Dianne Dumanoski, "Poll Says 50 Percent of Americans Believe Troops in Gulf to Protect Oil," *Boston Globe,* January 13, 1991, p. 1.

11. Richard Meyer, "War Mood: A Nation Divided," *Los Angeles Times,* January 13, 1991, p. 1.

12. David Lightman, "Democratic Forum to Provide Stage for Lieberman's Ascending Star," *Hartford Courant,* May 6, 1991, p. A1.

13. G. Scott Thomas, *The Rating Guide to Life in America's Fifty States* (Amherst, N.Y.: Prometheus Books, 1994), pp. 71–72.

14. Miranda Spivack, "Portrait of Christy," *Hartford Courant,* June 23, 1991, p. A12; Tom Baxter and A. L. May, "Democratic Factions Battling for Soul of Party," *Atlanta Journal & Constitution,* May 5, 1991, p. A8.

15. Lightman, "Democratic Forum," p. A1.

16. A. L. May, "Nunn's 'Tough Vote' against War Brings Tough Times," *Atlanta Journal & Constitution,* March 10, 1991, p. A2.

17. Joseph Serwach and David Martin, "Wofford: An 'A' Student," *Harrisburg Patriot-News,* November 7, 1991, p. A1; Mary McGrory, "The Lessons of Pennsylvania," *Washington Post,* November 7, 1991, p. A2.

18. Joseph Serwach, Joe Koscinski, and William Yingling Jr., "Vote 'Sends Signal' for '92," *Harrisburg Patriot-News,* November 6, 1991, p. A1.

19. Author's analysis of U.S. Bureau of Labor Statistics data.

20. "Wofford Mandate: Middle Class Demands Recognition," *Harrisburg Patriot-News,* November 7, 1991, p. A18.

21. William Yingling Jr., "Wofford's Health-Care Theme Turned on Voters," *Harrisburg Patriot-News,* November 7, 1991, p. A14 (emphasis added).

22. Richard Scammon and Ben Wattenberg, *The Real Majority* (New York: Berkley Medallion, 1971), pp. 70–72.

23. Richard Tapscott, "The Suburbs No Shoo-In for Clinton," *Washington Post*, July 13, 1992, p. D1.

24. Kevin Phillips, *Boiling Point* (New York: Random House, 1993), p. xvii.

25. E. J. Dionne Jr., *They Only Look Dead* (New York: Simon & Schuster, 1996), pp. 68–69, 111.

26. Richard Tapscott, "Black, Suburban Voters Courted in Maryland," *Washington Post*, March 2, 1992, p. A8.

27. Ibid.

28. Dionne, *They Only Look Dead*, pp. 68–69.

29. David Broder, "Disillusioned Public Puts Social Issues at Top of Fall Campaigns," *Washington Post*, October 2, 1994, p. A1.

30. Author's analysis of U.S. Bureau of Labor Statistics data.

31. Andrew Hacker, *Two Nations* (New York: Ballantine, 1995), p. 211.

32. Lynne Duke, "Rights Leaders Expect Race Relations to Test Clinton," *Washington Post*, November 11, 1992, p. A14.

33. Ibid.

34. Thomas Edsall and E. J. Dionne Jr., "White, Younger, Lower-Income Voters Turn against GOP," *Washington Post*, November 4, 1992, p. A21.

35. Bob Woodward, *The Choice* (New York: Simon & Schuster, 1996), pp. 126, 195.

36. William Eaton and Karen Tumulty, "Clinton Deficit Plan Squeaks through House," *Los Angeles Times*, August 6, 1993, p. 1; Doyle McManus, "Key Challenges Await Clinton," *Los Angeles Times*, January 20, 1993, p. 6.

37. Edwin Chen and Robert Rosenblatt, "Clinton Promises Sweeping Coverage in Health Care Plan," *Los Angeles Times*, September 11, 1993, p. 1.

38. Yingling, "Wofford's Health-Care Theme," p. A14.

39. Dionne, *They Only Look Dead*, p. 197.

40. Kenneth Cooper, "Gingrich: 'Cooperation, Yes. Compromise, No,' " *Washington Post*, November 12, 1994, p. A1.

41. Author's analysis of official election returns.

42. Richard Morin, "Derailed Democrats Search for the Road to Recovery," *Washington Post*, November 13, 1994, p. A1.

43. Ibid.

44. Cited in Adam Pertman, "Bill Clinton: Mediator Who Loves Politics," *Boston Globe*, January 10, 1992, p. 1.

45. Ibid.

46. Dick Polman, "Clinton Swerves Adroitly on Issues," *Philadelphia Inquirer*, May 26, 1996, p. E1.

47. Jill Lawrence, "Clinton Back in Step with 'New Democrats,' " *USA Today*, August 26, 1996, p. 8A.

48. "Jackson: Convention Is All about Theater," *USA Today*, August 29, 1996, p. 10A (emphasis added).

49. Cooper, "Gingrich," p. A1; Woodward, *The Choice*, p. 327.

50. Dan Balz, "Republicans Sound Conciliatory Tone," *Washington Post*, November 7, 1996, p. A1.

51. Jeffrey Roberts, "Parties Tuning in to Suburbs' Hopes," *Denver Post*, August 25, 1996, p. A1.

52. Joel Garreau, "Edge Cities in Profile," *American Demographics* (February 1994): 33.

53. Cited in Sam Roberts, *Who We Are* (New York: Times Books, 1994), p. 134.

54. Dale Russakoff, "Another Kind of Help," *Washington Post*, March 20, 1994, p. A1.

55. William O'Hare, "America's Minorities—The Demographics of Diversity," *Population Bulletin* (December 1992): 23–25.

56. Hacker, *Two Nations*, p. 245.

57. Ibid., pp. 74, 86–87; Roberts, *Who We Are*, p. 42.

58. Author's analysis of U.S. Census Bureau data.

59. Dennis Kelly, "In Schools: To Have and Have Not," *USA Today*, September 10, 1996, p. 8D.

60. *The State of Learning: A Report to the Governor and the Legislature on the Educational Status of the State's Schools* (Albany: New York Education Department, 1996), pp. 72–77.

61. "Poorer Schools Getting Left Behind on Internet," *Chicago Tribune*, February 18, 1996, p. 19.

62. Author's analysis of Federal Bureau of Investigation data; Morton Winsberg, "Crime in the Suburbs: Fact and Fiction," *American Demographics* (April 1994): 11–12.

63. Adrienne Knox, "Murder Rate Drops in Newark, Elizabeth," *Newark Star-Ledger*, December 30, 1997, p. 1; Haya El Nasser, "Cause of Crime Drop Difficult to Pinpoint," *USA Today*, April 14, 1997, p. 4A.

64. Author's analysis of data from *Fortune* (May 1975 and May 15, 1995).

65. David Young, "Big Firms Seem to Like Each Other's Company," *Chicago Tribune*, May 11, 1997, p. 31.

66. Richard Forstall, "Going to Town," *American Demographics* (May 1993): 44.

67. Fred Williams and Thomas Hall, "D.C. Tax Base Plunges," *Washington Business Journal* (September 6–12, 1996): 1.

68. Jon Teaford, *The Twentieth-Century American City* (Baltimore: Johns Hopkins University Press, 1986), p. 112.

69. Author's analysis of U.S. Census Bureau data.

70. Larry Ledebur and William Barnes, "Metropolitan Disparities and Economic Growth," *National League of Cities Research Report* (September 1992): 1–2; author's analysis of U.S. Census Bureau data.

71. Author's analysis of U.S. Census Bureau data; David Lynch, "Widening Income Gap Divides USA," *USA Today*, September 23, 1996, p. 1B.

72. "Census Bureau Reports on Income Inequality in America," *U.S. Census Bureau Press Release CB96–96* (June 20, 1996); David Lynch, "Dying Dreams, Dead-End Streets," *USA Today*, September 20, 1996, pp. 1B–2B.

73. Kevin Phillips, *The Politics of Rich and Poor* (New York: Random House, 1990), pp. 24–25.

74. Larry King, *The Best of Larry King Live* (Atlanta: Turner Publishing, 1995), p. 215.

4. Two Americas: Into the Twenty-First Century

1. "Tom Peters, Performance Artist," *The Economist* (September 24, 1994): 73; John Huey, "The Leadership Industry," *Fortune* (February 21, 1994): 54.

2. George Gilder, "Civilization Can't Afford to Forget," *Forbes* (December 2, 1996): 274.

3. "City vs. Country: Tom Peters and George Gilder Debate the Impact of Technology on Location," *Forbes ASAP* (February 27, 1995), pp. 56–57.

4. Ibid., p. 56.

5. Ibid., p. 57.

6. Ibid., p. 58.

7. Ibid., p. 61.

8. Lewis Mumford, *The City in History* (New York: Harcourt Brace Jovanovich, 1961), pp. 534–35.

9. Robert Fishman, *Bourgeois Utopias* (New York: Basic Books, 1987), p. 20 (emphasis added).

10. Kevin Maney, "Will Technology Supplant Offices?" *USA Today*, April 21, 1995, p. 6B.

11. John Naisbitt and Patricia Aburdene, *Megatrends 2000* (New York: William Morrow & Co., 1990), pp. 304–306.

12. Marvin Cetron and Owen Davies, *American Renaissance* (New York: St. Martin's Press, 1989), p. 307; Marcia Mogelonsky, "Myths of Telecommuting," *American Demographics* (June 1995): 16; Maney, "Will Technology Supplant Offices?" p. 6B.

13. Joel Garreau, *Edge City* (New York: Doubleday, 1991), p. 134; *Washington Business Journal Book of Lists 1997–98* (Arlington, Va.: American City Business Journals, Inc., 1997), p. 86.

14. Alvin Toffler, *Powershift* (New York: Bantam Books, 1990), pp. 66–67.

15. Edward Cornish, "The Cyber Future," *The Futurist* (January–February 1996 supp.): 15.

16. T. J. Becker, "All Over the Map," *Chicago Tribune*, January 21, 1996), p. 5P.

17. Jerry Adler, "Bye-Bye, Suburban Dream," *Newsweek* (May 15, 1995): 45.

18. Christopher Leinberger and Charles Lockwood, "How Business Is Reshaping America," *Atlantic Monthly* (October 1986): 45; Mark Baldassare, *Trouble in Paradise* (New York: Columbia University Press, 1986), pp. 76, 91–93.

19. Author's projections of population trends.

20. Author's analysis of U.S. Bureau of Labor Statistics data.

21. Margaret Webb Pressler, "Bethesda Comes into Its Own Downtown," *Washington Post*, June 10, 1996, p. F12.

22. Cited in Kenneth Jackson, *Crabgrass Frontier* (New York: Oxford University Press, 1985), p. 68; Sam Roberts, *Who We Are* (New York: Times Books, 1994), pp. 218–19.

23. George Gallup, *The Gallup Poll: Public Opinion 1935–1971* (New York: Random House, 1972), p. 825.

24. William Schneider, "The Suburban Century Begins," *Atlantic Monthly* (July 1992): 33; Jon Teaford, *The Rough Road to Renaissance* (Baltimore: Johns Hopkins University Press, 1990), p. 287.

25. Teaford, *Renaissance*, pp. 254–57, 300.

26. Author's analysis of U.S. Census Bureau data; David Lynch, "Widening Income Gap Divides USA," *USA Today*, September 23, 1996, p. 2B.

27. Jon Pepper, "Detroit Has Taken Giant Steps in Its Comeback, but Barriers Remain on the Road to the Renaissance," *Detroit News*, May 4, 1997, p. B11.

28. G. Scott Thomas, "What Downtown Workers Think about Downtown," *Business First* (July 29, 1996): 29.

29. John Herbers, *The New Heartland* (New York: Times Books, 1986), pp. 209–10.

30. Author's projections of population trends.

31. Fishman, *Bourgeois Utopias*, p. 120.

32. Carol Jouzaitis, "Older Suburbs Are Facing Survival Squeeze," *USA Today*, December 22, 1997, p. 6A.

33. Baldassare, *Trouble in Paradise*, p. 12.

34. Author's analysis of U.S. Census Bureau data; Roberts, *Who We Are*, p. 133.

35. Author's analysis of U.S. Census Bureau data.

36. Jouzaitis, "Older Suburbs," p. 6A.

37. William O'Hare, "America's Minorities—The Demographics of Diversity," *Population Bulletin* (December 1992): 2.

38. Author's projections of population trends.

39. Ibid.

40. Andrew Hacker, *Two Nations* (New York: Ballantine, 1995), pp. 215–16.

41. DeWayne Wickham, "Mayor's Task: Bridge Cuban-Black Gap," *USA Today*, October 7, 1996, p. 17A.

42. Andrea Stone, "In Northeast, Barriers as Old as Tradition," *USA Today*, June 10, 1996, p. 9A.

43. Author's analysis of U.S. Census Bureau data; Roberts, *Who We Are*, p. 86; author's projections of population trends.

44. Teaford, *Renaissance*, p. 306 (emphasis added).

45. Michael Dawson, "Alone in the Crowd: The Political Isolation of Poverty," *Chicago Tribune*, August 16, 1993, p. 13.

46. Carl Rowan, *The Coming Race War in America* (Boston: Little, Brown & Co., 1996), p. 282.

47. Richard Morin, "A Distorted Image of Minorities," *Washington Post*, October 8, 1995, p. 1.

48. Author's projections of population trends.

49. "Black-White Relations: Always a Problem?" *Gallup Poll Monthly* (October 1995): 9.

50. Author's analysis of U.S. Census Bureau data; author's projections of population trends.

51. Fred Bayles, "Charities See Donations Shifting Away from Urban Poor," *USA Today*, February 12, 1998, p. 4A.

52. Author's projections of population trends.

53. Alex Marshall, "The Quiet Integration of Suburbia," *American Demographics* (August 1994): 9–10.

54. Joel Garreau, "Edge Cities in Profile," *American Demographics* (February 1994): 32.

55. Jonathan Kaufman, "Migration Patterns," *Chicago Tribune*, September 8, 1996, p. 7N.

56. Herbers, *New Heartland*, p. 183; Garreau, *Edge City*, p. 153; Voter News Service exit poll, November 5, 1996, as posted on CNN/*Time* AllPolitics website (http://allpolitics.com), November 12, 1996.

57. Glenn O'Neal, "College Poll Finds Optimism about Race," *USA Today*, February 5, 1998, p. 4D.

58. Jim Simon, "Locke Making Heritage Pay Off in Race for Governor," *Seattle Times*, October 2, 1996, p. A1 (emphasis added).

59. Ibid. (emphasis added).

60. "A 'Retreat of Civil Rights,' " *USA Today*, May 21, 1997, p. 13A.

61. Robert McCarthy, "Conservative Democrats Are Successful Ones," *Buffalo News*, September 1, 1996, p. F12.

62. Richard Wolf, "Cities Report More Hunger, Homelessness," *USA Today*, December 15, 1997, p. 1A.

63. Judy Rakowsky, "Ranks of Homeless, Hungry on Rise," *Boston Globe,* December 16, 1997, p. B6.

64. O'Hare, "America's Minorities," p. 29.

65. Maria Puente and Sandra Sanchez, "Experts Call Educational Gap National Threat," *USA Today,* September 6, 1995, p. 1A.

66. Kim Willis, "Mixed Report Card," *USA Today,* November 30, 1995, p. 1D.

67. Cheryl Russell, "True Crime," *American Demographics* (August 1995): 24.

68. William Whyte, *City* (New York: Doubleday, 1988), p. 287.

69. U.S. Census Bureau data.

70. Ellen Neuborne, "Welfare Bill May Deplete Job Supply," *USA Today,* July 29, 1996, p. 1B.

71. Cetron and Davies, *American Renaissance,* p. 247.

72. Leinberger and Lockwood, "How Business," p. 43.

73. David Lynch, "Dying Dreams, Dead-End Streets," *USA Today,* September 20, 1996, p. 2B.

74. David Rusk, *Cities Without Suburbs* (Washington, D.C.: Woodrow Wilson Center Press, 1993), p. 128.

75. Dan Balz, "Looming Choices Will Shape Candidacies," *Washington Post,* July 29, 1996, p. A13; Chris Kelley, " 'Infomercial for Suburbs': Presidential Campaign Seems Devoid of Attention to Problems of Cities," *Chicago Tribune,* November 2, 1996, p. 6.

76. John Harris and John Yang, "Clinton to Sign Bill Overhauling Welfare," *Washington Post,* August 1, 1996, p. A1.

77. Daniel Patrick Moynihan, *Miles to Go* (Cambridge, Mass.: Harvard University Press, 1996), p. 229 (emphasis added).

78. Harris and Yang, "Clinton to Sign," p. A1.

79. Ibid.

80. Guy Gugliotta and Ruth Marcus, "Election-Year Politics Help Democrats Deal with Differences on Welfare," *Washington Post,* August 2, 1996, p. A8.

81. Moynihan, *Miles to Go,* p. 57.

5. Levittown's Children: The Suburban Viewpoint

1. Ted Anthony, "Making a House a Home in Famous Suburb," *Denver Rocky Mountain News,* January 19, 1997, p. 43A.

2. William Manchester, *The Glory and the Dream* (Boston: Little, Brown & Co., 1973), pp. 431–32.

3. Kenneth Jackson, *Crabgrass Frontier* (New York: Oxford University Press, 1985), p. 237.

4. Anthony, "Making a House," p. 43A; Cara Trager, "Levittown Still an Opportunity for First-Time Homebuyers," *Newsday,* January 24, 1997, p. D2.

5. Author's analysis of U.S. Census Bureau data; Trager, "Levittown," p. D2.

6. Frank Lloyd Wright, *The Living City* (New York: Horizon Press, 1958), p. 31.

7. Author's analysis of U.S. Census Bureau data.

8. Wright, *The Living City,* p. 68 (emphasis added).

9. Author's analysis of U.S. Census Bureau data.

10. Ibid.

11. Ibid.

12. Joel Garreau, *Edge City* (New York: Doubleday, 1991), p. 122.

13. Cheryl Russell, "The Master Trend," *American Demographics* (October 1993): 30.

14. Joel Garreau, "Edge Cities in Profile," *American Demographics* (February 1994): 26–29.

15. Ibid.

16. "Comparing Polls on Clinton's Approval Rating," *USA Today*, January 27, 1998, p. 4A.

17. Richard Scammon and Ben Wattenberg, *The Real Majority* (New York: Berkley Medallion, 1971), p. 19.

18. Ibid., p. 170.

19. Les Blumenthal, "GOP Operative Reconsiders Suburban Strategy after Oregon Vote," *Tacoma News Tribune*, February 4, 1996, p. E5; William Claiborne, "Democrats Hail Oregon Win as Rejection of GOP Agenda," *Washington Post*, February 1, 1996, p. A13.

20. Dan Balz, "Erosion of GOP's Suburban Strength Threatens Dole's Prospects," *Washington Post*, May 14, 1996, p. A1.

21. Richard Morin and Mario Brossard, "Who to Watch in '96," *Washington Post*, July 14, 1996, p. C1.

22. Author's analysis of Voter News Service exit poll, November 5, 1996, as posted on CNN/*Time* AllPolitics website (http://allpolitics.com), November 12, 1996 [henceforth referred to as VNS exit poll 1996].

23. Balz, "Erosion," p. A1.

24. Haya El Nasser and Paul Overberg, "Suburban Communities Spurt to Big-City Status," *USA Today*, November 19, 1997, p. 4A (emphasis added).

25. Robert Fishman, *Bourgeois Utopias* (New York: Basic Books, 1987), p. 4.

26. Karlyn Bowman, "Not All Useful Surveys Are Just about Politics," *Roll Call* (January 9, 1997), online (http://www.rollcall.com).

27. David Broder, "Next Generation of GOP Leaders Test-Driving Models of Governance," *Washington Post*, August 14, 1996, p. A23 (emphasis added).

28. VNS exit poll 1996.

29. Author's analysis of U.S. Census Bureau data.

30. Ibid.

31. Ibid.

32. Matt Lait, "Majority Are Less Uniform in Views Than GOP Leaders," *Los Angeles Times*, July 8, 1996, p. A1.

33. U.S. Census Bureau data.

34. Lait, "Majority Are Less Uniform," p. A1.

35. Manchester and Whyte both cited in Harry Ashmore, *Hearts and Minds* (New York: McGraw-Hill, 1982), p. 141.

36. Bowman, "Not All Useful Surveys."

37. Ellen Graham and Cynthia Crossen, "God, Motherhood, and Apple Pie," *Wall Street Journal*, December 13, 1996, p. R4.

38. Cited in ibid.

39. David Kusnet and Ruy Teixeira, "Tuesday's Secret Result: A Winning Brand of Liberalism," *Washington Post*, November 10, 1996, p. C4.

40. Ibid.

41. Pew Research Center for The People and The Press, *Deconstructing Distrust: How Americans View Government* (March 10, 1998), online (http://www.people-press.org/trustrpt.htm).

42. Lait, "Majority Are Less Uniform," p. A1.

43. Kusnet and Teixeira, "Tuesday's Secret Result," p. C4.

44. Cited in John Herbers, *The New Heartland* (New York: Times Books, 1986), p. 193.

45. Cited in Jon Teaford, *The Rough Road to Renaissance* (Baltimore: Johns Hopkins University Press, 1990), p. 202.

46. Cited in James Tyson, "Fur Flies over Control of a Tiny Chicago Airport," *Christian Science Monitor,* December 17, 1996, p. 4.

47. Peter Manso, "Playboy Interview: Ed Koch," *Playboy* (April 1982): 70.

48. Cited in Thomas Byrne Edsall and Mary Edsall, *Chain Reaction* (New York: W. W. Norton & Co., 1991), p. 175.

49. Cited in David Lynch, "Dying Dreams, Dead-End Streets," *USA Today,* September 20, 1996, p. 2B.

50. Jon Teaford, *The Twentieth-Century American City* (Baltimore: Johns Hopkins University Press, 1986), pp. 154, 156.

51. Author's analysis of U.S. Census Bureau data.

52. G. Scott Thomas, "The Changing Face of Downtown Buffalo," *Business First* (July 29, 1996): 1.

53. Ibid.

54. Susan Schulman, "City's Problems Rarely Addressed by Gorski, Greco," *Buffalo News,* October 16, 1995, p. A1 (emphasis added).

55. Ibid.

6. Platform for the Twenty-First Century: The Suburban Agenda

1. Rich Lowry, "Scenes from Convention Life, Part 8," *National Review* (September 16, 1996): 36.

2. Ibid.

3. Ibid.

4. William Claiborne, "Little Dissent as Delegates Ratify Strongly Conservative Platform," *Washington Post,* August 13, 1996, p. A13.

5. Voter News Service exit poll, November 5, 1996, as posted on CNN/*Time* AllPolitics website (www://allpolitics.com), November 12, 1996 [henceforth referred to as VNS exit poll 1996].

6. Richard Wolf, "Taxes Take the Biggest Hit at Polls," *USA Today,* November 6, 1997, p. 1A.

7. Author's analysis of official election returns.

8. Mark Baldassare, *Trouble in Paradise* (New York: Columbia University Press, 1986), p. 128.

9. Rich Hampson, "New Jersey's Whitman Wrestles with Dual Reputations," *USA Today,* August 14, 1997, p. 6A; Voter News Service exit poll, November 4, 1997, as posted on CNN/*Time* AllPolitics website (http://allpolitics.com), November 6, 1997 [henceforth referred to as VNS exit poll 1997].

10. David Broder, "Next Generation of GOP Leaders Test-Driving Models of Governance," *Washington Post,* August 14, 1996, p. A23.

11. Larry Copeland, "Real People Really Worried," *Tacoma News Tribune,* January 14, 1996, p. H1.

12. David Rusk, *Cities Without Suburbs* (Washington, D.C.: Woodrow Wilson Center Press, 1993), p. 85.

13. Cited in Susan Schulman, "Giambra Softens Position on Government Consolidation," *Buffalo News*, June 3, 1997, p. A4.

14. Jeffrey Roberts, "Parties Tuning in to Suburbs' Hopes," *Denver Post*, August 25, 1996, p. A1.

15. Author's analysis of U.S. Bureau of Labor Statistics data and official election returns.

16. VNS exit poll 1996.

17. Cited in Kenneth Jackson, *Crabgrass Frontier* (New York: Oxford University Press, 1985), p. 50.

18. Jonathan Weisman, "Republican Defectors Help Propel Minimum Wage Bill to Passage," *Congressional Quarterly Weekly Report* (May 25, 1996): 1461, 1463.

19. Ibid., p. 1461.

20. Ceci Connolly, "President, Advisers Stage First Road Show on Social Security Issues," *Washington Post*, April 8, 1998, p. A6; Robert Shogan, "Clinton Open to Wider Reform of Social Security," *Los Angeles Times*, April 8, 1998, p. A1.

21. Connolly, "President, Advisers," p. A6.

22. David Kusnet and Ruy Teixeira, "Tuesday's Secret Result: A Winning Brand of Liberalism," *Washington Post*, November 10, 1996, p. C4.

23. Lisa Hamm, "Survey Says Parents Aren't Concerned with Conservative Agenda," *Buffalo News*, October 12, 1996, p. A2.

24. Robert Kuttner, "The Either/Or Budget Fallacy," *Washington Post*, January 8, 1997, p. A25.

25. Jeffrey Katz, "After 60 Years, Most Control Is Passing to States," *Congressional Quarterly Weekly Report* (August 3, 1996): 2190; author's analysis of congressional roll call (July 31, 1996).

26. Katz, "After 60 Years," p. 2195.

27. Ibid.

28. Ibid., pp. 2190–95 (emphasis added).

29. Ibid.

30. Charles Babington, "Glendening Finds Montgomery Chilly," *Washington Post*, April 11, 1997, p. D1; Terry Neal, "Baltimore Fears Pact with State Will Bedevil It," *Washington Post*, March 23, 1997, p. B1.

31. Babington, "Glendening Finds," p. D1.

32. Thomas Byrne Edsall and Mary Edsall, *Chain Reaction* (New York: W. W. Norton & Co., 1991), p. 228.

33. "Gallup Referendum: Selected Issues," *Gallup Poll Monthly* (May 1996): 6.

34. Jeff McLaughlin, "With Population Boom, New Challenges," *Boston Globe*, November 30, 1997, p. 1.

35. U.S. Census Bureau data.

36. Ibid.

37. Sam Roberts, *Who We Are* (New York: Times Books, 1994), p. 167.

38. Jackson, *Crabgrass Frontier*, p. 250.

39. John Naisbitt and Patricia Aburdene, *Megatrends 2000* (New York: William Morrow & Co., 1990), pp. 24–25.

40. Joseph Coates and Jennifer Jarratt, "What Futurists Believe: Agreements and Disagreements," *The Futurist* (November–December 1990): 23.

41. Joel Garreau, *Edge City* (New York: Doubleday, 1991), p. 8 (emphasis in original).

42. Karen Brandon, "L.A. Subway Digging a Well of Trouble," *Chicago Tribune,* July 23, 1995, p. 4.

43. Gordon Oliver, "Tri-Met Mum about Future of Light Rail," *Portland Oregonian,* November 17, 1996, p. C1.

44. VNS exit poll 1996.

45. "Top Priority: Environment or Economy?" *Gallup Poll Monthly* (April 1995): 19.

46. Author's analysis of U.S. Census Bureau data; author's projections of population trends.

47. Angie Cannon, "Election in Black and White," *San Jose Mercury News,* February 4, 1996, p. 14A.

48. Holly Idelson, "Pressure Builds for Retreat on Affirmative Action," *Congressional Quarterly Weekly Report* (June 3, 1995): 1578, 1580.

49. Bill Stall and Dan Morain, "Prop. 209 Wins, Bars Affirmative Action," *Los Angeles Times,* November 6, 1996, p. A1.

50. VNS exit poll 1996.

51. "A 'Retreat of Civil Rights,' " *USA Today,* May 21, 1997, p. 13A.

52. Idelson, "Pressure Builds," p. 1582.

53. William O'Hare, "America's Minorities—The Demographics of Diversity," *Population Bulletin* (December 1992): 15; VNS exit poll 1996; Mimi Hall, "Ex-Colo. Gov Expected to Make Third-Party Run," *USA Today,* July 8, 1996, p. 4A.

54. Broder, "Next Generation," p. A23.

55. VNS exit poll 1996.

56. Naisbitt and Aburdene, *Megatrends 2000,* p. 217.

57. Paul Taylor, "Fading American Dream Haunts WWII Generation," *Washington Post,* February 1, 1996, p. A1.

58. D'Vera Cohn and Kirstin Downey Grimsley, "Women-Owned Firms' Surge Mirrored Here," *Washington Post,* March 6, 1996, p. D1; author's analysis of U.S. Census Bureau data.

59. U.S. Census Bureau data.

60. Theodore White, *The Making of the President 1964* (New York: Atheneum, 1965), pp. 103–104, 301–303, 323, 384.

61. Susan Levine, "As Tenants Age, High-Rises Become Retirement Havens," *Washington Post,* July 4, 1996, p. A1.

62. Lori Montgomery, "Crime Is Lurking in the Corners of Worried Voters' Minds," *San Jose Mercury News,* February 4, 1996, p. 15A.

63. Cheryl Russell, "True Crime," *American Demographics* (August 1995): 22; Stephen Wagner, "Cities That Satisfy," *American Demographics* (September 1995): 19.

64. Jillian Lloyd, "Film at 10: Whose News Judgment?" *Christian Science Monitor,* April 3, 1998, p. 1.

65. Tim Kiska, "Local TV News Shows Hooked on Violence," *Detroit News,* February 16, 1997, p. A1.

66. Montgomery, "Crime Is Lurking," p. 15A.

67. Author's analysis of congressional roll call (August 21, 1994).

68. Author's analysis of congressional roll call (November 10, 1993).

69. Alan Greenblatt, "Repeal of Assault Weapons Ban Unlikely to Go Beyond House," *Congressional Quarterly Weekly Report* (March 23, 1996): 803.

70. Ibid., p. 803.

71. Author's analysis of official election returns; Flynn McRoberts, "Durbin Comes Out from the Friendly Shadow of Simon," *Chicago Tribune,* November 7, 1996, p. 1.

72. VNS exit poll 1996.

73. "Salvi: No 'Weasel' on Gun Control," *Chicago Tribune,* August 24, 1997, p. 18.

74. G. Pascal Zachary, "Straight-Laced Public Yawns at Scandal," *Wall Street Journal,* February 9, 1998, p. B1.

75. Ibid.

76. Hamm, "Survey Says," p. A2.

77. "Legality, Morality of Abortion," *Gallup Poll Monthly* (March 1995): 30.

78. Ibid.

79. VNS exit poll 1996.

80. Jon Pepper, "Detroit Has Taken Giant Steps in Its Comeback, but Barriers Remain on the Road to the Renaissance," *Detroit News,* May 4, 1997, p. B11.

81. VNS exit poll 1996.

82. James Bradshaw, "Riverboat Casinos Vote Comes up Snake Eyes," *Columbus Dispatch,* November 6, 1996, p. 1A.

83. Steven Chapman, "Uh, Jerry, They Like Ellen Better," *Chicago Tribune,* May 4, 1997, p. 23.

84. Michael Booth, "Gay-Rights Ban Narrowly Winning," *Denver Post,* November 4, 1992, p. 14A; author's analysis of official election returns.

85. Holly Idelson, "House Weighs in against Same-Sex Marriages," *Congressional Quarterly Weekly Report* (July 13, 1996): 1976.

86. C. David Tompkins, *Senator Arthur H. Vandenberg: The Evolution of a Modern Republican* (East Lansing: Michigan State University Press, 1970), p. 161.

87. Ibid., p. 171.

88. *Public Papers of John F. Kennedy 1961* (Washington, D.C.: U.S. Government Printing Office, 1962), p. 1.

89. Richard Lugar, "Why I Ran for President," *Washington Post,* July 10, 1996, p. A17.

90. David Broder, "Lugar's Advice," *Washington Post,* November 24, 1996, p. C7; Bradley Graham, "Military Forces Are Near 'Breaking Point,' GOP Report Charges," *Washington Post,* April 9, 1997, p. A14; Bradley Graham, "Perry Resists Cuts in Military Force As His Tour Ends," *Washington Post,* January 16, 1997, p. A12.

91. Bradley Graham, "Pentagon Assesses Future Demands on a Smaller Military Force," *Washington Post,* April 2, 1997, p. A6.

92. U.S. Census Bureau data.

93. Thomas Edsall, " 'New' Image of Democrats Emerges under Clinton," *Washington Post,* January 27, 1994, p. A6.

7. Brave New World: America's Political Future

1. Jack Germond and Jules Witcover, *Wake Us When It's Over* (New York: Macmillan, 1985).

2. Ibid., p. 105.

3. Ibid., pp. 126–27.

4. Ibid., p. 464.

5. Peter Goldman and Tony Fuller, *The Quest for the Presidency 1984* (New York: Bantam Books, 1985), p. 400.

6. Ibid., pp. 105–108.

7. Times Mirror Center for The People and The Press, *The New Political Landscape* (Washington, D.C.: Times Mirror Co., 1994).

8. Author's analysis of data from Times Mirror Center, *The New Political Landscape*, pp. 12–21, 72, and Pew Research Center for The People and The Press, *Voter Typology* (October 25, 1996), online (http://www.people-press.org/oct96rpt.htm).

9. Times Mirror Center, *The New Political Landscape*, p. 107.

10. Richard Norton Smith, *Thomas E. Dewey and His Times* (New York: Simon & Schuster, 1982), pp. 34, 588.

11. Theodore White, *The Making of the President 1964* (New York: Atheneum, 1965), p. 217.

12. Richard Scammon and Ben Wattenberg, *The Real Majority* (New York: Berkley Medallion, 1971), pp. 157–61; G. Scott Thomas, *The Pursuit of the White House* (New York: Greenwood Press, 1987), pp. 269–70.

13. Bob Woodward, *The Choice* (New York: Simon & Schuster, 1996), pp. 114–15.

14. Times Mirror Center, *The New Political Landscape*, p. 66.

15. Arthur Schlesinger Jr., *A Thousand Days* (Boston: Houghton Mifflin, 1965), p. 31.

16. David Broder, "Next Generation of GOP Leaders Test-Driving Models of Governance," *Washington Post*, August 14, 1996, p. A23.

17. Ibid.

18. Richard Ben Cramer, *What It Takes* (New York: Vintage Books, 1993), p. 66.

19. David Broder, "Ignored and Indignant: Moderates Feel Slighted in New Hampshire," *Washington Post*, February 19, 1996, p. A1.

20. CBS, November 5, 1996, 7:50 P.M. (EST).

21. Thomas Edsall and Dan Balz, "Straightaway till November, Then a Fork," *Washington Post*, August 26, 1996, p. A15.

22. David Broder, " 'Five Republican Parties' Seek Leader," *Washington Post*, November 7, 1996, p. A23.

23. Kevin Merida, "Powell Makes Plea for Diverse Party," *Washington Post*, August 13, 1996, p. A1.

24. Broder, "Five Republican Parties," p. A23.

25. Ibid.

26. Matt Lait, "Majority Are Less Uniform in Views Than GOP Leaders," *Los Angeles Times*, July 8, 1996, p. A1.

27. Ibid.

28. Albert Menendez, *The Perot Voters* (Amherst, N.Y.: Prometheus Books, 1996), p. 200.

29. Merida, "Powell Makes Plea," p. A1.

30. Andrew Hacker, *Two Nations* (New York: Ballantine, 1995), p. 209.

31. Broder, "Ignored and Indignant," p. A1.

32. Lait, "Majority Are Less Uniform," p. A1.

33. Voter News Service exit poll, November 5, 1996, as posted on CNN/*Time* AllPolitics website (http://allpolitics.com), November 12, 1996 [henceforth referred to as VNS exit poll 1996].

34. Smith, *Thomas E. Dewey*, p. 399.

35. William Manchester, *The Glory and the Dream* (Boston: Little, Brown & Co., 1973), pp. 244–45; Harry Truman, *Freedom and Equality* (Columbia: University of Missouri Press, 1969), p. 7.

36. Robert Garson, *The Democratic Party and the Politics of Sectionalism, 1941–1948* (Baton Rouge: Louisiana State University Press, 1974), p. 93.

37. Ibid., p. 177.

38. Hamilton Jordan, *Crisis* (New York: G. P. Putnam's Sons, 1982), p. 328.

39. Jules Witcover, *Marathon* (New York: Viking, 1977), p. 350.

40. Tom Watson, "Hart Pushes 'Third Options' in Long-Shot Presidential Bid," *Congressional Quarterly Weekly Report* (December 3, 1983): 2535–39.

41. Jules Witcover, *Eighty-Five Days* (New York: Ace, 1969), p. 202.

42. Michael Tackett, "Democratic Party Searching for Redefinition," *Chicago Tribune*, October 1, 1995, p. 18.

43. Author's analysis of U.S. Census Bureau data; Thomas Edsall, "Dissident Wing of GOP Hopes to Derail Whitman," *Washington Post*, October 31, 1997, p. A1.

44. Bob Woodward, *The Agenda* (New York: Simon & Schuster, 1994), pp. 20, 28.

45. Lenora Fulani, "Blacks Need to Leave Dems, GOP Behind," *USA Today*, September 6, 1996, p. 11A.

46. Author's analysis of U.S. Bureau of Labor Statistics data.

47. Pew Research Center for The People and The Press, *March 1998 News Interest Index* (April 3, 1998), online (http://www.people-press.org/mar98que.htm).

48. Ann Devroy, "Clinton Embraces GOP Themes in Setting Agenda," *Washington Post*, January 24, 1996, p. A1.

49. "Platforms Diverge on Modernizing Government," *Washington Post*, August 28, 1996, p. A23.·

50. VNS exit poll 1996.

51. Susan Page, "Budget Deal Lauded; More Work to Come," *USA Today*, May 5, 1997, p. 2A.

52. Pew Research Center, *March 1998*, online.

53. Elizabeth Shogren, "Clinton Defends Efforts to Spur Racial Dialogue," *Los Angeles Times*, December 17, 1997, p. A1.

54. Ibid.

55. Marshall Frady, *Jesse* (New York: Random House, 1996), p. 478.

56. VNS exit poll 1996.

57. Ibid.

58. E. J. Dionne Jr., "Urban Politics in the 1990s," *Washington Post*, February 17, 1998, p. A15.

59. E. J. Dionne Jr., "Clinton Swipes the GOP's Lyrics," *Washington Post*, July 21, 1996, p. C1.

60. David Broder, "GOP, Democrats Wearing Out?" *Buffalo News*, August 18, 1996, p. 10.

61. Times Mirror Center, *The New Political Landscape*, p. 56.

62. Paul Abramson, John Aldrich, and David Rohde, *Change and Continuity in the 1988 Elections* (Washington, D.C.: Congressional Quarterly Press, 1991), p. 298.

63. Menendez, *The Perot Voters*, p. 218.

64. Linda Feldmann, "Perot's Back, but Support Has Shifted since '92 Run," *Christian Science Monitor*, July 15, 1996, p. 3.

65. Mimi Hall, "Perot Party's Legacy Could Be Its Effort," *USA Today*, November 5, 1996, p. 8A.

66. CBS, November 5, 1996, 10:42 P.M. (EST).

67. Frady, *Jesse*, pp. 282–85.

68. Ibid.

69. Ibid., pp. 285, 480.

70. Michael Dawson, "Can the Democrats Count on the Black Vote?" *Chicago Tribune*, August 28, 1996, p. 21.

71. Susan Page, "For Liberals, Clinton Only Choice," *USA Today*, March 26, 1996, p. 4A.

72. "A 'Retreat of Civil Rights,' " *USA Today,* May 21, 1997, p. 13A.

73. Kevin Phillips, *Post-Conservative America* (New York: Random House, 1982), p. 225.

74. Thomas, *Pursuit of the White House,* pp. 195, 369.

75. Phillips, *Post-Conservative America,* pp. 98, 228–31; Menendez, *The Perot Voters,* p. 41.

76. Warren Weaver Jr., "Anderson Says Goals of Campaign 'Must Not and Will Not End for Me,' " *New York Times,* November 5, 1980, p. 21.

77. Times Mirror Center, *The New Political Landscape,* pp. 18, 67.

78. James Toedtman, "A Step toward Balanced Budget," *Newsday* (May 17, 1997, p. A13.

79. Dan Balz, "Gore, Gephardt Argue Politics of New Economy," *Milwaukee Journal Sentinel,* June 2, 1997, p. 12.

80. Eric Pianin and John Yang, "Gephardt Denounces Balanced Budget Plan," *Washington Post,* May 21, 1997, p. A1.

81. William Schneider, "Can Gore Replicate Bush's Jump?" *Los Angeles Times,* May 18, 1997, p. M1.

82. Toedtman, "A Step," p. A13.

83. Ibid.

84. Schneider, "Can Gore Replicate?" p. M1.

85. Pianin and Yang, "Gephardt Denounces," p. A1.

86. John Yang, "Looking Back to Theodore Roosevelt, Gephardt Calls for 'New Progressivism,' " *Washington Post,* December 3, 1997, p. A16; "Mr. Gephardt's Manifesto," *Washington Post,* December 5, 1997, p. A26.

Selected Bibliography

1. Statistics from Government Agencies

Boards of elections (various states)
Federal Bureau of Investigation
Federal Election Commission
U.S. Bureau of Economic Analysis
U.S. Bureau of Labor Statistics
U.S. Census Bureau

2. Books, Reports, Articles, and Websites

Abramson, Paul, John Aldrich, and David Rohde, *Change and Continuity in the 1988 Elections.* Washington, D.C.: Congressional Quarterly Press, 1991.

Adler, Jerry. "Bye-Bye, Suburban Dream," *Newsweek* (May 15, 1995).

Anthony, Ted. "Making a House a Home in Famous Suburb," *Denver Rocky Mountain News,* January 19, 1997.

Ashmore, Harry. *Hearts and Minds* New York: McGraw-Hill, 1982.

Baldassare, Mark. *Trouble in Paradise.* New York: Columbia University Press, 1986.

Balz, Dan. "Erosion of GOP's Suburban Strength Threatens Dole's Prospects," *Washington Post,* May 14, 1996.

Baxter, Tom, and A. L. May. "Democratic Factions Battling for Soul of Party," *Atlanta Journal & Constitution,* May 5, 1991.

Blumenthal, Les. "GOP Operative Reconsiders Suburban Strategy after Oregon Vote," *Tacoma News Tribune,* February 4, 1996.

Broder, David. "Disillusioned Public Puts Social Issues at Top of Fall Campaigns," *Washington Post,* October 2, 1994.

———. " 'Five Republican Parties' Seek Leader," *Washington Post,* November 7, 1996.

———. "Is Clinton Reinventing Democratic Party?" *Buffalo News,* August 18, 1997.

"Campaign '84: The Inside Story," *Newsweek* (November/December 1984 special issue).

Cannon, Angie. "Election in Black and White," *San Jose Mercury News,* February 4, 1996.

Carter, Jimmy. *Keeping Faith.* New York: Bantam, 1982.

Cetron, Marvin, and Owen Davies, *American Renaissance.* New York: St. Martin's Press, 1989.

"City vs. Country: Tom Peters and George Gilder Debate the Impact of Technology on Location," *Forbes ASAP* (February 27, 1995).

Congressional Directory. Washington, D.C.: U.S. Government Printing Office, 1965, 1975, 1985, 1995.

Cramer, Richard Ben. *What It Takes.* New York: Vintage Books, 1993.

Current Biography Yearbook 1975. New York: H. W. Wilson Co., 1976.

Dawson, Michael. "Can the Democrats Count on the Black Vote?" *Chicago Tribune,* August 28, 1996.

DeGregorio, William. *The Complete Book of U.S. Presidents.* New York: Dembner Books, 1984.

Devroy, Ann. "Clinton Embraces GOP Themes in Setting Agenda," *Washington Post,* January 24, 1996.

Dionne, E. J., Jr., *They Only Look Dead.* New York: Simon & Schuster, 1996.

Edsall, Thomas, and E. J. Dionne Jr. "White, Younger, Lower-Income Voters Turn against GOP," *Washington Post,* November 4, 1992.

Edsall, Thomas Byrne, and Mary Edsall, *Chain Reaction.* New York: W. W. Norton & Co., 1991.

El Nasser, Haya, and Paul Overberg. "Suburban Communities Spurt to Big-City Status," *USA Today,* November 19, 1997.

Feldman, Linda. "Perot's Back, but Support Has Shifted since '92 Run," *Christian Science Monitor,* 15 July 1996.

Fishman, Robert. *Bourgeois Utopias.* New York: Basic Books, 1987.

Frady, Marshall. *Jesse.* New York: Random House, 1996.

Fulani, Lenora. "Blacks Need to Leave Dems, GOP Behind," *USA Today,* September 6, 1996.

Gallup, George. *The Gallup Poll: Public Opinion 1935–1971.* New York: Random House, 1972.

Garreau, Joel. "Edge Cities in Profile," *American Demographics* (February 1994).

———. *Edge City.* New York: Doubleday, 1991.

Garson, Robert. *The Democratic Party and the Politics of Sectionalism, 1941–1948.* Baton Rouge: Louisiana State University Press, 1974.

Germond, Jack, and Jules Witcover. *Wake Us When It's Over.* New York: Macmillan, 1985.

Goldman, Peter, and Tony Fuller. *The Quest for the Presidency 1984.* New York: Bantam Books, 1985.

Graham, Ellen, and Cynthia Crossen. "God, Motherhood, and Apple Pie," *Wall Street Journal,* December 13, 1996.

Gregory, Ross. *America 1941.* New York: Free Press, 1989.

Gunther, John. *Inside U.S.A.* New York: Harper & Brothers, 1946.

Hacker, Andrew. *Two Nations.* New York: Ballantine, 1995.

Hall, Mimi. "Perot Party's Legacy Could Be Its Effort," *USA Today,* November 5, 1996.

Hamm, Lisa. "Survey Says Parents Aren't Concerned with Conservative Agenda," *Buffalo News,* October 12, 1996.

Herbers, John. *The New Heartland.* New York: Times Books, 1986.

Inaugural Addresses of the Presidents of the United States. Washington, D.C.: U.S. Government Printing Office, 1989.

Jackson, Kenneth. *Crabgrass Frontier.* New York: Oxford University Press, 1985.

Jordan, Hamilton. *Crisis.* New York: G. P. Putnam's Sons, 1982.

Jouzaitis, Carol. "Older Suburbs Are Facing Survival Squeeze," *USA Today,* December 22, 1997.

Kaufman, Jonathan. "Migration Patterns," *Chicago Tribune,* September 8, 1996.

Katz, Jeffrey. "After 60 Years, Most Control Is Passing to States," *Congressional Quarterly Weekly Report* (August 3, 1996).

Kelley, Chris. " 'Infomercial for Suburbs': Presidential Campaign Seems Devoid of Attention to Problems of Cities," *Chicago Tribune,* November 2, 1996.

King, Larry. *The Best of Larry King Live.* Atlanta: Turner Publishing, 1995.

Kunstler, James Howard. *The Geography of Nowhere.* New York: Simon & Schuster, 1993.

Kusnet, David, and Ruy Teixeira. "Tuesday's Secret Result: A Winning Brand of Liberalism," *Washington Post,* November 10, 1996.

Kuttner, Robert. "The Either/Or Budget Fallacy," *Washington Post,* January 8, 1997.

Lait, Matt. "Majority Are Less Uniform in Views Than GOP Leaders," *Los Angeles Times,* July 8, 1996.

Lawrence, Jill. "Clinton Back in Step with 'New Democrats,'" *USA Today,* August 26, 1996.

Ledebur, Larry, and William Barnes. "Metropolitan Disparities and Economic Growth," *National League of Cities Research Report* (September 1992).

Leinberger, Christopher, and Charles Lockwood. "How Business Is Reshaping America," *Atlantic Monthly* (October 1986).

Levine, Susan. "As Tenants Age, High-Rises Become Retirement Havens," *Washington Post,* July 4, 1996.

Lewis, Michael. *Trail Fever.* New York: Alfred A. Knopf, 1997.

Lichtman, Allan, and Ken DeCell. *The Thirteen Keys to the Presidency.* Lanham, Md.: Madison Books, 1990.

Lynch, David. "Dying Dreams, Dead-End Streets," *USA Today,* September 20, 1996.

———. "Widening Income Gap Divides USA," *USA Today,* September 23, 1996.

Manchester, William. *The Glory and the Dream.* Boston: Little, Brown & Co., 1973.

Marquis, Alice Goldfarb. *Hopes and Ashes.* New York: Free Press, 1986.

Marshall, Alex. "The Quiet Integration of Suburbia," *American Demographics* (August 1994).

McLaughlin, Jeff. "With Population Boom, New Challenges," *Boston Globe,* November 30, 1997.

Menendez, Albert. *The Perot Voters.* Amherst, N.Y.: Prometheus Books, 1996.

Montgomery, Lori. "Crime Is Lurking in the Corners of Worried Voters' Minds," *San Jose Mercury News,* February 4, 1996.

Morin, Richard. "Derailed Democrats Search for the Road to Recovery," *Washington Post,* November 13, 1994.

Moynihan, Daniel Patrick. *Miles to Go.* Cambridge, Mass.: Harvard University Press, 1996.

Mumford, Lewis. *The City in History.* New York: Harcourt Brace Jovanovich, 1961.

Naisbitt, John, and Patricia Aburdene, *Megatrends 2000.* New York: William Morrow & Co., 1990.

Neal, Terry. "Baltimore Fears Pact with State Will Bedevil It," *Washington Post,* March 23, 1997.

O'Hare, William. "America's Minorities—The Demographics of Diversity," *Population Bulletin* (December 1992).

O'Neill, William. *Coming Apart.* New York: Times Books, 1971.

Peirce, Neal, and Jerry Hagstrom. *The Book of America.* New York: W. W. Norton & Co., 1983.

Pertman, Adam. "Bill Clinton: Mediator Who Loves Politics," *Boston Globe,* January 10, 1992.

Petersen, Svend. *A Statistical History of the American Presidential Elections.* New York: Frederick Ungar Publishing Co., 1963.

Pew Research Center for The People and The Press. *Deconstructing Distrust: How Americans View Government.* March 10, 1998. http://www.people-press.org/trustrpt.htm.

———. *March 1998 News Interest Index.* April 3, 1998. http://www.people-press.org/mar98que.htm.

Pew Research Center for The People and The Press. *Voter Typology*. October 25, 1996. http://www.people-press.org/oct96rpt.htm.

Phillips, Kevin. *Boiling Point*. New York: Random House, 1993.

———. *The Politics of Rich and Poor*. New York: Random House, 1990.

———. *Post-Conservative America*. New York: Random House, 1982.

"Platforms Diverge on Modernizing Government," *Washington Post*, August 28, 1996.

Public Papers of John F. Kennedy 1961. Washington, D.C.: U.S. Government Printing Office, 1962.

Roberts, Jeffrey. "Parties Tuning in to Suburbs' Hopes," *Denver Post*, August 25, 1996.

Roberts, Sam. *Who We Are*. New York: Times Books, 1994.

Ross, Irwin. *The Loneliest Campaign*. New York: Signet, 1968.

Rowan, Carl. *The Coming Race War in America*. Boston: Little, Brown & Co., 1996.

Runyon, John, Jennefer Verdini, and Sally Runyon. *Source Book of American Presidential Campaign and Election Statistics, 1948–1968*. New York: Frederick Ungar Publishing Co., 1971.

Rusk, David. *Cities Without Suburbs*. Washington, D.C.: Woodrow Wilson Center Press, 1993.

Russell, Cheryl. "The Master Trend," *American Demographics* (October 1993).

Scammon, Richard. *America at the Polls: A Handbook of American Presidential Election Statistics, 1920–1964*. Pittsburgh: University of Pittsburgh Press, 1965.

Scammon, Richard, and Alice McGillivray. *America Votes*, 21 vols. Washington, D.C.: Congressional Quarterly Press, 1956–1995.

Scammon, Richard, and Ben Wattenberg. *The Real Majority*. New York: Berkley Medallion, 1971.

Schlesinger, Arthur, Jr., *A Thousand Days*. Boston: Houghton Mifflin, 1965.

Schneider, William. "The Suburban Century Begins," *Atlantic Monthly* (July 1992).

Smith, Richard Norton. *Thomas E. Dewey and His Times*. New York: Simon & Schuster, 1982.

The State of Learning: A Report to the Governor and the Legislature on the Educational Status of the State's Schools. Albany: New York Education Department, 1996.

Tackett, Michael. "Democratic Party Searching for Redefinition," *Chicago Tribune*, October 1, 1995.

Tapscott, Richard. "Black, Suburban Voters Courted in Maryland," *Washington Post*, March 2, 1992.

———. "The Suburbs No Shoo-In for Clinton," *Washington Post*, July 13, 1992.

Taylor, Paul. "Fading American Dream Haunts WWII Generation," *Washington Post*, February 1, 1996.

Teaford, Jon. *The Rough Road to Renaissance*. Baltimore: Johns Hopkins University Press, 1990.

———. *The Twentieth-Century American City*. Baltimore: Johns Hopkins University Press, 1986.

Thomas, G. Scott. *The Pursuit of the White House*. New York: Greenwood Press, 1987.

———. *The Rating Guide to Life in America's Fifty States*. Amherst, N.Y.: Prometheus Books, 1994.

Thompson, Margaret. *Presidential Elections Since 1789*. Washington, D.C.: Congressional Quarterly Press, 1993.

Times Mirror Center for The People and The Press. *The New Political Landscape*. Washington, D.C.: Times Mirror Co., 1994.

Toffler, Alvin. *Powershift*. New York: Bantam Books, 1990.

Tompkins, C. David. *Senator Arthur H. Vandenberg: The Evolution of a Modern Republican.* East Lansing: Michigan State University Press, 1970.

Trager, Cara. "Levittown Still an Opportunity for First-Time Homebuyers," *Newsday,* January 24, 1997.

Truman, Harry. *Freedom and Equality.* Columbia: University of Missouri Press, 1969.

Weisman, Jonathan. "Republican Defectors Help Propel Minimum Wage Bill to Passage," *Congressional Quarterly Weekly Report* (May 25, 1996).

White, Theodore. *The Making of the President 1960.* New York: Atheneum, 1961.

———. *The Making of the President 1964.* New York: Atheneum, 1965.

Whyte, William. *City.* New York: Doubleday, 1988.

Will, George. "There They Go Again, Those Democrats," *Washington Post,* November 13, 1988.

Winsberg, Morton. "Crime in the Suburbs: Fact and Fiction," *American Demographics* (April 1994).

Witcover, Jules. *Eighty-Five Days.* New York: Ace, 1969.

———. *Marathon.* New York: Viking, 1977.

Wolf, Richard. "Voters' Message Seems to Be: End Partisanship," *USA Today,* November 6, 1996.

Woodward, Bob. *The Agenda.* New York: Simon & Schuster, 1994.

———. *The Choice.* New York: Simon & Schuster, 1996.

Wright, Frank Lloyd. *The Living City.* New York: Horizon Press, 1958.

Yarnell, Allen. *Democrats and Progressives.* Berkeley: University of California Press, 1974.

Index